ESSAYS IN HONOR OF
ANDRE GUNDER FRANK

The
Underdevelopment
of Development

EDITORS:
Sing C. Chew
Robert A. Denemark

The
Underdevelopment
of Development

To all our families and
In memory of Marta Fuentes
(1937-1993)

ESSAYS IN HONOR OF
ANDRE GUNDER FRANK

The

Underdevelopment

of Development

EDITORS:

Sing C. Chew
Robert A. Denemark

SAGE Publications
International Educational and Professional Publisher
Thousand Oaks   London   New Delhi

For information address:

SAGE Publications, Inc.
2455 Teller Road
Thousand Oaks, California 91320
E-mail: order@sagepub.com

SAGE Publications Ltd.
6 Bonhill Street
London EC2A 4PU
United Kingdom

SAGE Publications India Pvt. Ltd.
M-32 Market
Greater Kailash I
New Delhi 110 048 India

Printed in the United States of America

Library of Congress Cataloging-in-Publication Data

Main entry under title:

The underdevelopment of development: Essays in honor of Andre Gunder
  Frank / editors, Sing C. Chew and Robert A. Denemark.
      p.   cm.
      Contents: On development and underdevelopment / Sing C. Chew and Robert Denemark—
The underdevelopment of development / Andre Gunder Frank—On development: for Gunder
Frank / Samir Amin—Pathways toward a global anthropology / Eric R. Wolf—Underdevelopment:
culture and geography / Philip Wagner—The debt crisis revisited / Otto Kreye—Developmentalism:
a Eurocentric hoax, delusion, and chicanery / Herb Addo—Latin American underdevelopment: past,
present, and future / Theotonio Dos Santos—Asia in the world-system / Geroge Aseniero—
On the origins of economic catastrophe in Africa / Samir Amin—How to think about world history /
William H. McNeill—The "continuity thesis" in world development / Barry K. Gills—World-systems:
similarities and differences / Christopher Chase-Dunn—The art of hegemony / Albert Bergesen—
Social movements in the underdevelopment of development dialectic: a view from below /
Gerrit Huizer—Frank justice rather than Frankenstein injustice: homogenous development
as deviance in the diverse world / Pat Lauderdale—Women's interests and emancipatory
processes/ Virginia Vargas—Underdevelopment and its remedies / Immanuel Wallerstein.
      Includes bibliographical references and index.
      ISBN 0-8039-7260-1 (cloth: alk. paper)   —   ISBN 0-8039-7261-X (pb.: alk. paper)
      1. Developing countries—Dependency on foreign countries.
2. Developing countries—Economic conditions.   3. Frank, Andre
Gunder, 1929-   . I. Frank, Andre Gunder, 1929-   . II. Chew,
Sing C.   III. Denemark, Robert Allen.
HC59.7.U464   1996
338.9—dc20   95-32534

96 97 98 99 10 9 8 7 6 5 4 3 2 1

Sage Production Editor: Diana E. Axelsen

Contents

Preface   xi

1. On Development and Underdevelopment   1
   Sing C. Chew and Robert A. Denemark

2. The Underdevelopment of Development   17
   Andre Gunder Frank

**PART I: ON DEVELOPMENT
AND UNDERDEVELOPMENT**

3. On Development: For Gunder Frank   57
   Samir Amin

4. Pathways Toward a Global Anthropology   87
   Eric R. Wolf

5. Underdevelopment: Culture and Geography   101
   Philip L. Wagner

6. The Debt Crisis Revisited   115
   Otto Kreye

7. Developmentalism: A Eurocentric Hoax,
   Delusion, and Chicanery   126
   Herb Addo

PART II: ON PERIPHERAL REGIONS

8. Latin American Underdevelopment: Past, Present, and Future
   A Homage to Andre Gunder Frank   149
   Theotonio Dos Santos

9. Asia in the World-System   171
   George Aseniero

10. On the Origins of the Economic Catastrophe in Africa   200
    Samir Amin

PART III: ON THE WORLD HISTORICAL SYSTEM AND CYCLES

11. How to Think About World History   219
    William H. McNeill

12. The Continuity Thesis in World Development   226
    Barry K. Gills

13. World-Systems: Similarities and Differences   246
    Christopher Chase-Dunn

14. The Art of Hegemony   259
    Albert Bergesen

PART IV: ON SOCIAL MOVEMENTS AND SOCIAL JUSTICE

15. Social Movements in the Underdevelopment
    of Development Dialectic: A View From Below   281
    Gerrit Huizer

16. Frank Justice Rather Than Frankenstein Injustice:
    Homogenous Development as Deviance in the Diverse World   314
    Pat Lauderdale

17. Women's Interests and Emancipatory Processes   344
    Virginia Vargas

18. Underdevelopment and Its Remedies   355
    Immanuel Wallerstein

Appendix: Andre Gunder Frank
    Bibliography of Publications, 1955-1995   363

Index   405

About the Editors   423

About the Contributors   425

Andre Gunder Frank

Preface

A few years ago, the editors of this volume thought a book on development paying homage to Gunder Frank and his many years of struggle to offer an alternative conception of development to mainstream efforts would be an important exercise. Gunder was retiring from the University of Amsterdam. We wished to acknowledge his very distinguished and productive lifetime of scholarship. Gunder Frank coined the phrase "the underdevelopment of development," which became the slogan of resistance to so many people throughout the world. We also believed that such a book, undertaken collectively by Gunder's friends and colleagues, could take stock of world development and world history and provide a useful assessment and "reply" to what had taken place globally during the 1980s and early 1990s.

With this in mind, we discussed the development thematics for the book, along with Gunder's contributions. Identifying these thematics was not difficult; most readers who know of Gunder's work recognize its breadth and depth. In fact, keeping the chapters to a publishable length became more of a concern. By this time, Gunder himself was brought into our discussions, and he graciously provided his valuable input. The productive discussion occurred over two continents via E-mail, with meetings in Kingston (Canada), Washington, (DC), Arcata, (California), Irvine (California), Chicago (Illinois), and

Lund (Sweden). During this time, Marta Fuentes (Gunder's wife and intellectual companion) died, following a long illness; Gunder had major surgery; and he moved to Canada.

THE MAN AND HIS WORK

Gunder's contribution to this volume provides the reader just a glimpse of his life and his work. The title of his chapter, which we also adopted for the book, reveals that despite what has happened over the last four decades, Gunder has not given up the vision of development that spurred his work and that all of us were stimulated to follow. Acutely sensitive to the injustices of his times, the impulse that led him more than three decades ago to define the existing global developmental process as "the development of underdevelopment" continues to this day. With three decades of hindsight, Gunder is even more explicit in his insistence that we understand real development, not as a stage or a state, but as a process encompassing economic, social, and technological changes by which human welfare is improved (we hope, not at the expense of nature) and embellished with its political, cultural, and perhaps spiritual dimensions. For Gunder, unlike many others, actual development is instead a cyclical global dynamic by which some regions/peoples temporarily assume leading "developed" positions while others are underdeveloped as a result.

His recent work on world system history continues to explore the issues of development in their broadest context. As with his past forays, he is again critically questioning basic premises and frameworks—just as he did to modernization theory in the 1960s. He now queries the basic premises of world systems analysis, however, in terms of the origin, emergence, and continuity of the system's trends and dynamics. In this context, he has challenged the emergence of a capitalist world system five hundred years ago in Europe, propounded by Immanuel Wallerstein and his followers. Even capitalism as a concept and as a mode of production has been questioned! Where Wallerstein sees qualitative changes and shifts, Gunder sees continuity across world history. For Gunder, world development is a consequence of the rise and fall of regions played out through ceaseless accumulation underlined by long cycles of expansion and contraction over some five thousand years of human history. Western supremacy in the world system is thus only a temporary condition, perhaps little more than one hundred years old. The history of the system started much earlier than what we are led to believe and had its origins in Asia. These insights undermine Eurocentrism and call forth an (eco)humanocentric approach toward understanding and explaining global transformations. We believe that when the dust settles, this spearhead by Gunder will again be evaluated as (another) major epistemological and ontological contribution to our understanding of the human enterprise.

The contributions of Gunder to the study of development and the world economy have been impactful not only qualitatively but also quantitatively. By 1995, he had published 36 books, contributed 134 book chapters in various languages, and published about 600 versions of over 350 periodical articles (see Appendix). His works have appeared in twenty-five languages. It is estimated that if these publications were arranged together, they would reach about seventeen linear feet! Melvin Eggers, former chancellor of Syracuse University, in his evaluation of Gunder's work a decade ago, said:

> Frank was trained as an economist, thus it warrants looking at his record along-side other economists of stature. According to the *Social Science Citation Index* (which excludes references contained in monographs and collections of essays), Frank measures up admirably to the Nobel Laureates in economics of 1981 and 1982, James Tobin and George J. Stigler, respectively, and surpasses the 1983 Nobel Laureate, Gerard Debreu, in number of citations to his work. . . . Thus, while not a Nobel Laureate, Andre Gunder Frank has received more such exposure than the 1983 winner. . . . Thus, Andre Gunder Frank's influence as to *quantity* of journal citations is marked. (1984 memorandum from Melvin Eggers to New York State Board of Regents)

Besides his publications on development and the world system, Gunder Frank has also written extensively on geopolitical issues that underline the dynamics of the world system. His various publications, such as *Crisis: In the World Economy* and *Crisis: In the Third World,* reveal insightful analyses of contemporary political and economic issues. In fact, he pinpointed and alerted us to the systemic nature of the global economic crisis that started in the early 1970s, two years before others had pronounced its emergence. Along with his late wife, Marta Fuentes, Gunder impressed on us the need to fully consider the new social movements of change in an era of tumultuous shifts in terms of anti-systemic activities and that some of these defined "new" social movements are not that new!

THE MAN AND HIS LIFE

Gunder Frank was born in Berlin in 1929. His father, a famous German novelist, brought him to America, where he attended Ann Arbor High School and then Swarthmore College. Partly on his father's advice, he studied economics and received a Ph.D. from the University of Chicago in 1957. In 1962, to understand development and find out for himself from the "inside," he resigned from his faculty appointment at Michigan State University and went to live in Latin America, where he met and married Marta. Devoted to each other, they shared a common concern for social justice and collaborated well, publishing one book and several articles. Under Marta's influence, Gunder was made more aware of women's conditions, often including the feminist point of view in his work. Together, they had two sons, Paulo and Miguel. Paulo is a doctoral candidate at Harvard, and Miguel works as a translator for the European Parliament.

With his family, Gunder spent a total of ten years (with the exception of a few years in Canada) in several Latin American countries. There, he learned firsthand what underdevelopment meant, and his work has been enriched by this experience. His critical attitude, which could be seen in his doctoral dissertation on Soviet agriculture, was put into full use in a series of analyses of the respective conditions of the countries in which he lived and in debates with local Latin American intellectuals. His departure from Latin America came in 1973, with the violent ultra-right coup by Pinochet in Chile.

From Latin America, Gunder returned to then West Germany, where he was a visiting research fellow at the Max Planck Institute, Starnberg. At Starnberg, he revised and finalized his two-volume work *World Accumulation 1492-1789* and *Dependent Accumulation and Underdevelopment,* which had been completed earlier in Chile. This phase of his life, from the early 1970s onward, was spent mostly in Europe with teaching appointments at the Free University of Berlin, the University of Paris, the University of East Anglia, and finally at the University of Amsterdam. During this period in Europe, he launched into an intensive study of world systemic crisis and world system history and collaborated with Marta on the study of social movements. With Marta's death in 1993, and with his retirement from the University of Amsterdam, Gunder moved to Canada, completing a full circle not far from where he started his high school education many years ago.

To his friends and colleagues, Gunder has always personified what an intellectual should be: systematic, critical, energetic, and forever helpful to friends, colleagues, and students. We wish him many more years of productive scholarship.

We would like to thank Linda Hall-Martin for the logistical support necessary for the preparation of this book and for her assistance in finalizing Gunder's bibliography. Our editors, Diana Axelsen and Carrie Mullen at Sage, have been most supportive of this project. Paul Blank, Harold Denemark, Daniel Green, and April Veness provided helpful comments on various chapters, and it was a pleasure to work with our translators—W. H. Locke Anderson, Paulo Frank, and Cristian Harris. Miguel Frank kindly provided the photograph of his father for the book. We regret that we were unable to include sections on all the regions of interest and relevance. Time constraints, page limits, and political upheaval conspired against us. Likewise, our list of contributors is not as representative as we might have liked. A number of busy and talented female colleagues were unable to accept our requested deadlines in good faith. My thanks and love to Jan Tye-Chew for her comments and constant support of my work and to Ben and Siang for their patience in waiting for me on several occasions when I was busy with this book. Cindy Denemark endured various hardships with unwavering support. She has my love and thanks. Amanda and Eric have simply suggested that although books may be good things, they will be happy to have Daddy home more evenings.

Sing C. Chew
Robert A. Denemark

1

On Development and Underdevelopment

SING C. CHEW
ROBERT A. DENEMARK

THEORIES OF DEVELOPMENT
AND UNDERDEVELOPMENT

For the majority of us, development seems immanent and inevitable. Ever since the European Enlightenment, socioeconomic "development" has been deemed positive and progressive. This Western modernist position on socioeconomic knowledge, organization, and practice came to dominate the world system with the triumphant march of European powers over the globe.[1] As Western philosophy followed the flag, development came to be universally defined as natural, beneficial, and inevitable.

With this *weltanschauung,* it is the *lack* of development in any given area that appears to require explanation. At the onset of the cold war, when simplistic racial or climatic explanations of "backwardness" would no longer suffice, various perspectives on development were created that remained nonetheless consistent with this overall orientation. So evolved the "modernization" school. Lack of development is a consequence of the absence of necessary factors. To discover what those missing factors were, modernization

1

theorists would create an archetypal developmental experience derived from a review of an ideal-type Western industrial state. When a particular country experienced difficulties in achieving socioeconomic progress as defined by the West, the explanation would invariably revolve around the lack of the requisite factors. For Rostow (1960), these necessary factors included levels of financial investment required for "takeoff" and the necessary transformation in the sociopolitical sphere consistent with a Western market-oriented democratic society as derived from a reading of English history. For Parsons (1964) and McClelland (1967), the transformation of values and socio-psychological conceptions must be sufficiently advanced. For Pye (1962), Almond and Powell (1966), and especially Huntington (1968), the lack of political institutionalization leads to serious hindrances to the developmental process.

Although the focal points of various modernization theorists would differ, they all viewed the problems and obstacles to development as being temporary in nature and internally rooted. This worldview has been and continues to be the sine qua non for social, economic, and political practice in the world system today. This is the *problématique* of the study of modernity as we know it.

The modernization perspective engendered significant output. Yet, it could not explain the distribution of underdevelopment, the lack of autocentric development in the Third World, or the persistent impoverishment of vast regions of the globe. Many of its proponents continued to treat the social, political, and economic realms as essentially autonomous. Explanations of problems in one area derived from evaluations of another were considered a form of "trespassing" (Hirschman, 1981).

These shortcomings, according to Latin American *dependentistas* in the 1960s, were primarily the consequence of assumptions of linearity; inevitability; the autonomy of social, political, and economic phenomena; and most especially the exclusive concentration on conditions "internal" to a particular country (Cardoso, 1972, 1973, 1977; Dos Santos, 1970; Frank, 1967, 1968; Furtado, 1971; Sunkel, 1973). Dependency scholars would offer no less than five major challenges to this *weltanschauung*. First, social, political, and economic phenomena were intimately related. Their separation at the hands of students of political or social or economic development was illegitimate and doomed corresponding studies to ultimate failure. Second, underdevelopment must be viewed in global perspective. The modernization school ignored even the pervasive effects of colonialism in both the immediate past and the all-too-relevant present of most areas that were "underdeveloped." Third, this global context had an important historical dynamic. For modernization theorists, Europe had a developmental past, but the underdeveloped regions lacked all but a rudimentary history typified by the same underdeveloped conditions that existed in the underdeveloped present. This assumption underpinned the static and simplistic comparisons of "developed" with "underdeveloped" and was a major impediment to understanding. Fourth, the system was exploitative. The strong would tie the weak to advanced centers/zones of the world system and thus subject them to the totalizing and destructuring effects of the processes of capital accumulation on a world scale. Fifth, a direct relationship would evolve between the "externally" generated exploitation and the social, political, and economic structures within the weaker areas themselves. We would witness, in Gunder Frank's terms, the "development of underdevelopment." As a counterposition, various concepts were introduced by the *dependentistas* to account for ongoing social change. Concepts such as core-periphery, dependent development, uneven development, and metropole-satellite were created to describe the dependent state of economic transformation of specific nation-states in the periphery.

Because of its point of orientation (to promote independent self-sustaining development) and its linkage to the radical political economy of Karl Marx, dependency theory came under scrutiny from both the right and the left. From the right, the critics railed at the "ideological" nature of the dependency critique. Typical of dominant ideologies throughout the ages, the spate of value-laden assumptions inherent in the modernization school were viewed as ideologically neutral. Proponents of the ongoing behavioral revolution condemned dependency theory's fuzzy and contextually sensitive definitions. Some used that fuzziness to produce "straw" tests of dependency, with unsurprising results (e.g., Jackman, 1982). Students of developmental policy lamented the lack of alternatives short of revolution that dependency theory appeared to leave. Neoclassical economists saw nothing but failure inherent in dependency theory's lack of reverence for the market.

On the left, the denunciations were even more ferocious and were focused on the perceived lack of adherence to Marx's concepts.[2] Exchange, and not production, was alleged to rest at the heart of dependency analysis. Class analysis played a less crucial role than certain global processes (Resnick, Sinisi, & Wolff, 1985). The ensuing debates proved to be of value to all three schools, as a review of modernization literature in political science and "Marxist/neo-Marxist" literature in sociology will quickly illustrate.

The modernization literature in political science did not take particularly long to adapt to the unity of political and economic processes (e.g., Apter, 1987). Use of the term *political economy* came to be accepted, and literature from a variety of orientations was integrated with greater sophistication into the study of development. Global processes such as the politicalization of aid, the agendas of global developmental agencies, and the effects of international finance are standard topics (Haggard, Lee, & Maxfield, 1993). "External" variables are identified as some of the most critical determinants of politics in underdeveloped areas (Stallings, 1992), even in works that continue to adopt the position that one can essentially remove states from their contexts and compare them as independent units (e.g., Haggard, 1990). The potential for exploitation is well understood in the growing literature on multinational corporations (Biersteker, 1987; Encarnation, 1989). Ties between internal and external relations are viewed as central in the significant literature on the state and adjustment (Waterbury, 1992) and in the application of microeconomic and rational actor concepts to politics in underdeveloped areas (Bates, 1981). The current focus/fad of most of the literature in political science—democratization—takes as its starting point the need to find novel ways to adjust to global neoliberalism in the quest for viable democratic structures (see recent issues of *Journal of Democracy*).

For Marxists, the ensuing debate led to a further clarification of the dynamics of capitalism à la Marx. Critiques reinforced the view that capitalism is fundamentally defined by the existence of wage labor and that other forms of labor relations must be relegated to other forms. This critical discourse, known as the *modes of production debate,* further underscored the parameters of the Marxist conception of capitalism (Brenner, 1977; Foster-Carter, 1978; Taylor, 1979; Wolpe, 1980). By the 1980s, however, practitioners such as Booth (1985) and Evans and Stephens (1988) suggested that the Marxist-inspired study of development had reached an impasse. According to Booth, this impasse was the result of the Marxist intellectual framework wherein one must demonstrate that what happens in Third World societies is not only explainable but also necessary because of the logic of capitalist accumulation. This framework unnecessarily leads to an analysis that is "myopic and one-dimensional" and fails to capture the different dynamics or trajectories actually underway.

Subsequent contributions by Vandergeest and Buttel (1988), Sklair (1988), and Mouzelis (1988) have attempted to overcome this difficulty. These contributions have tended either to adopt Weberian and neo-Marxist concepts (e.g., Mouzelis, Vandergeest, and Buttel) or to clarify further the relationships among meta-theory, theory, and empirical investigation (e.g., Sklair) in an attempt to overcome the theoretical impasse. These different contributions, though approaching the problem from different theoretical perspectives (neo-Weberian and neo-Marxian), arrive at a somewhat similar position (comparative-historical) taken by Evans and Stephens (1988). In a nutshell, their work (the new comparative political economy) can be described as an effort to merge neo-Marxian discourse on state and politics with neo-Weberian ideas of classes, power, and socio-organizational structures. This new comparative political economy includes within it "some of the hypotheses of the modernization approach in altered form" and the writings of the *dependentistas* and world systems theorists (Evans & Stephens, 1988, p. 713). The comparative-historical works of Gerschenkron (1962), Polanyi (1944), and Moore (1966) are identified as keys to open the developmental lock. Such a melange of theoretical positions results in an approach that views developmental paths, not as necessary outcomes—thus avoiding teleology—but as historically contingent.

Such advances were clearly the result of intellectual cross-fertilization even though most participants will admit so only grudgingly. Throughout the 1970s, however, the concepts of dependency theory were also extended from their Latin American context to the study of social change along world systemic lines. The later works of Gunder Frank in *World Accumulation 1492-1789* (1978b), *Dependent Accumulation and Underdevelopment* (1978a), *Crisis: In the World Economy* (1980), and *Crisis: In the Third World* (1981a); Samir Amin's *Accumulation on a World Scale* (1974); Eric Wolf's *Europe and the People Without History* (1982); and Immanuel Wallerstein's *The Modern World-System* (1974) signaled that the study of development and of the Third World would have to proceed within the framework of a far better articulated study of the world system as a whole, complete with its various cycles and trends.

Methodologically, Wallerstein (1974, 1976, 1979) adduces us to rethink the conceptual schemes and categories of the social sciences. To understand and interpret social change, the false sectorializing tendency of the social sciences has to be abandoned. What was before five separately recognized social sciences (anthropology, economics, geography, political science, and sociology), with their separate meaningful units of analysis, should be seen as a single subject matter. Analysis of social change and economic transformation in the making of the modern world should consider the totality of social action and thus triangulate information from the "separate" social sciences. Notwithstanding this, the mediation of history in the understanding of social occurrences is considered necessary.

This call for a unidisciplinary social science is to be coupled with a macro-level, holistic approach that awards primacy to a historical social system having an effective global division of labor with multiple state structures. This proposal underscores the relationship between regions of the world and nation-states. In other words, it questions the orthodox assumption that an understanding of social change within a given nation-state or geographical space in the world system can be reached by analyzing and interpreting the dynamics and changes occurring within these boundaries alone.[3] The push toward a holistic, macrolevel analysis of a historical world system encourages one to view social change and economic transformation in the making of the modern world as processes that occur transnationally and transhistorically.

CRISIS OF DEVELOPMENT AND
GLOBAL IDEOLOGICAL TRANSFORMATIONS

While many of the theoretical interventions discussed above were being deliberated, other transformations were occurring that affected world developmental trajectories. For the 1980s, the crisis of the world economy continued (Frank, 1980, 1981a, 1981b). One of the most visible impacts of this crisis in the Third World was the debt issue and the subsequent adjustment programs introduced by the International Monetary Fund (IMF) and the World Bank. Including that of Eastern Europe, this debt amounted to around U.S.$1.3 trillion by the end of the 1980s. According to World Bank (1984) estimates, interest payments on this debt continue to hover between U.S.$90 and $95 billion per year. The breadth of this debt crisis not only affected capitalist-oriented Third World nations but also extended to nations in the South that were attempting populist or socialist-type socioeconomic transformation. The magnitude of this crisis challenged Third World planners and continued to sap funds from the South via debt rescheduling.

From the developmental point of view, the size of the debt was daunting, but the outcomes (including food riots) that followed in response to various "structural adjustment programs" undertaken by respective Third World governments were both alarming and disastrous (Walton & Ragin, 1990). These programs included local governmental expenditure cutbacks, monetary devaluation, reductions in subsidies for basic staples, removal of import quotas, tariff reductions, interest rate policy reforms, revision of agricultural prices, reductions in the powers of state marketing boards, and privatization of state-owned enterprises. Naturally, these conditionalities generated significant human shocks. The United Nations Children's Fund, for example, commented on the ill effects of structural adjustment on the health and well-being of Third World children of this generation (Cornia, 1987; UNICEF, 1986).

In short, most of the South experienced depressive socioeconomic conditions. Sub-Saharan Africa, a region affected severely by the debt crisis, suffered negative growth as measured by standard indicators (Amin, 1990). Per capita incomes fell throughout the 1980s and were about a quarter lower than in the mid-1970s. The value of total imports shrank by almost 40% from 1981 to 1985 (Humphreys & Jaeger, 1989, p. 6). In Latin America, the gross domestic product fell by an annual average of 0.9% between 1980 and 1988 (Kennedy, 1993, p. 302). Any increase in export performance was used to service the debt. Asia was less fully affected. It has been suggested that more funds flowed out of the South to service the debt than capital funds flowed in for investments.

Notwithstanding the issue of the questionable effectiveness of structural adjustment loans, the slant toward supply-side economics of Bank and IMF policies was particularly destabilizing. The "market bias" eschewed the role of the state and brought policies into sharp conflict with those historically in practice.[4] A serious debate on the relationship between such policies and the rise of authoritarian states was engendered. No doubt caught in the midst of severe economic duress, country after country in the South succumbed to the policy directives prescribed. The disciplining of the South was carried out by "suprastatal" institutions on behalf of the nation-states and private banks located in the core.

While most parts of the South were mired in debt, the four "tigers" or "dragons" of Asia (Singapore, Hong Kong, Taiwan, and South Korea) enjoyed export-led growth.[5] Such successes encouraged other countries (Thailand, Malaysia, and Indonesia) to follow suit. The "flying geese" formation (look East policy) depicts the Asian developmental trajectory, with Japan as the lead bird. It is ironic that while the Bank and the IMF were encouraging the debt-affected South "to let the market determine," Japan, the tigers, and those in the region that hoped to follow promulgated policies that directly reflected the importance of the state's role in these success stories. Together with this glaring contradiction in developmental strategy, the successes of this region have further differentiated the "Third World" and thus call into question the utility or even the possibility of a single, unilinear, global approach to development (Schuurman, 1993; Toye, 1987).

The role of suprastatal multilateral donor institutions such as the Bank and the IMF in setting developmental policies and, to some extent, national fiscal and economic policies for debt-depressed nations in Africa and Latin America has now shifted to Eastern Europe and to countries belonging to the former Soviet Union. With the demise of the bulk of "real and existing" socialism in the late 1980s and the collapse of the Soviet Union, the role of these institutions has become increasingly crucial in the managing and containment of financial crises. No doubt, this push for a "market-oriented" liberal approach that underlines Bank and IMF policies has reinforced the way business (capital accumulation) should be conducted. In the early 1990s, the same prescriptions that were applied in Africa, parts of western Asia, Latin America, and the Caribbean in the 1980s were being replicated in Eastern Europe and the former Soviet Union. East Germany was spared this specific fate by its unification with the former Federal Republic, although the unification process has led to its own *anschluss.*

Increasingly, what developmental choices might have been available have been narrowed.[6] Gone are the days of the Tanzanian *ujamaa* experiment or the Maoist path; these and similar potential alternatives have been precluded. Those who have engaged in the simultaneous translation of the success of the four tigers along a neoliberal story line have also given rise to the TINA syndrome: "There Is No Alternative" to capitalism. The retreat of "progressive" alternatives as theoretical strategies and praxis further adds to this state of flux whereby progressive social change seems more and more remote. Fukuyama's (1992) declaration of the triumph of Western liberalism following the collapse of the former Soviet Union and Warsaw Pact countries further signals the ongoing trend to underscore the "magic of the marketplace" and the shift away from interference in the market. From the developmentalist point of view, such a position has also been propounded by neoliberal development theory to address the stagnant (or negative growth) conditions in parts of the South, especially sub-Saharan Africa (Balassa, 1982; Bauer, 1981, 1984). This resurgence of neoliberalism in development theory has been described, in no way unfairly, as a counterrevolution (Toye, 1987).

Neoliberal voices are not the only ones that have been raised. We need also consider the postmodernist movement's negative reaction to the Enlightenment narrative of the emancipation of humankind (e.g., Lyotard, 1984) and the post-Marxist project of a heterogeneous discourse cum radical democracy (Laclau, 1990; Laclau & Mouffe, 1985). In a certain sense, these latter metatheoretical and theoretical projects reject the emancipatory grand narrative that underpins all developmental theories from the 1950s through to the world system perspective. How do we reconcile these differences? Can we? Besides the nihilistic tendencies so evident in postmodernism, Schuurman's (1993) response to the postmodern movement is to argue on empirical grounds that "the Third World does not consist of postmodern societies" (p. 27) and that therefore the struggle in the South is not on the postmodern conditions, but rather on access to modernity. Booth (1993), however, celebrates this diversity of theoretical influences (e.g., postmodernity, post-Marxism, neo-Weberianism, rational choice) and sees this rethinking as offering a source of strength from which to reconstitute developmental studies. It remains to be seen whether the rediscovery of diversity in developmental thinking will add further to the struggle for justice and freedom in the South or whether postmodernism and post-Marxism are simply Eurocentric discourses that do not relate well to the social, political, or spatial dimensions of development.

DEVELOPMENT: WHITHER NOW?

In an era when the entire concept of development is being questioned, how do we continue to address the issues of freedom and justice that underline progressive theories of development? This volume speaks to development and to choices. It is organized around the work of our friend and colleague Andre Gunder Frank.

No doubt, scholars will continue to do modernization theory. Given the "end of history" and the "triumph" of neoliberal economic and political ideas, these are likely to be dominant themes. Of course, the problems associated with this path are nonetheless manifest. To find successes in the progressive march toward "modernization" will be difficult. Quite simply, no classical political or economically liberal nation-states are among the crop of current successes (e.g., the tigers). Those that are trying to follow simultaneously in the path of the tigers and the Bank and the IMF are running headlong into important contradictions. O'Donnell (1994) warns of the sham of "delegative democracy"; Haggard and Kaufman (1992) outline a long, hard, and uncertain economic road. What, then, are the modernizers left with in terms of explanation, other than imagery? Very simply put, the answers are limited, short of reverting to TINA, worn-out arguments about culture and climate, or recourse to the growing bias against bureaucracy and the state.

Rather than succumb to the triumph of neoliberalism, we can seek to reconceptualize development in a broader historical context. The concepts of modernization were derived from the experience of the West from the 16th to the 19th centuries. On this historical era, the modernization and dependency debates were framed. Yet, world history did not begin in the 16th century. Earlier experiences in different cultural and geographical contexts might offer insights into development, and a longer historical time frame might provide the foundation for a superior understanding of the relevant processes involved. A comprehensive review of the history of world accumulation could facilitate further understanding and perhaps underscore the futility of attempting to overcome global injustice on a country-by-country basis. This long-term endeavor might have its costs in terms of lack of immediate relevance for addressing current developmental issues. Failure to successfully cope with such issues, however, may be a signal that we simply do not yet possess an adequate understanding of the dynamic linkages between regions of the world, bounded within a system characterized by cycles and trends (Frank, 1993; Frank & Gills, 1992a, 1992b).

In terms of historical reconceptualization, we should also recognize our integral relationship with Nature. For we are also Nature as such. To date, most theories of development have treated Nature as a benign substrate existing to satisfy the modernization project. Such a position is not the preserve of modernization theory. Even Marxian theories of social change assume Nature to play the role of resource substrate, although in parts of Marx's own work we can also find passages of sensitivity to the destruction of Nature by capitalism, as in capitalist agriculture (Benton, 1989, 1992).[7] The continued environmental catastrophes occurring globally and throughout history as a consequence of the global accumulation process need to be addressed in future work. History shows that severe environmental degradation has led to conditions that restrict the reproductive capacities of empires and civilizations (Perlin, 1989; Ponting, 1991).

Every age identifies its "modern" and distinguishes it from a variety of premodern, a cacophony of antimodern, and perhaps even a picture of postmodern times. Such scholarship hinges on the identification of discontinuity and perhaps quite naturally then focuses on the set of topics that have undergone or are said to be undergoing the hypothesized change. Gunder Frank has dared to ask how much has actually changed relative to that which has stayed the same. His recent work on world history continues to be provocative and non-Eurocentric. For him, the contemporary world system has had a history of at least five thousand years. By applying the methodology of world systems much farther back in time and space, he and Barry Gills have argued that the process of the accumulation of capital and associated cycles existed long before (prior to 1500) the emergence of the "capitalist modern world system." This means that capital accumulation has occurred continuously within a world system over at least the last five thousand years and that the apparent transformation from one social mode of production and organization to another (e.g., the transition from feudalism to capitalism) might rather be the continuation of cyclical changes of the world system. This view rejects the traditional conception of the genesis of capitalism and challenges orthodox Marxist understanding of the emergence of capitalism and capital accumulation and even the positions of Samir Amin (1991) and Immanuel Wallerstein (1991). The call is to abandon the concept of capitalism as a distinct mode of production (as well, the relevancy of mode of production as a heuristic concept) and of transition between modes because these constructs are viewed as obstacles to understanding the essential unity of a world system that has existed for at least five thousand years (Frank, 1991). For Frank (1991, p. 171), "the rise of Europe represented a hegemonic shift from East to West within a pre-existing system. If there was any transition then, it was this hegemonic shift within the system rather than the formation of a new system." In this regard, he states, "we are again in one of the alternating periods of hegemony and rivalry in the world system, which portends a renewed westward shift of hegemony across the Pacific." The impact of Frank's recent writings on development and its possibilities needs to be seriously considered. How many of capitalism's critics or proponents might be depended on to ask such a fundamental question? Note, as well, the investment that Gunder Frank has made in the concept of capitalism. Although most scholars would react with shock and disdain to attempts to upset the fundamental underpinning of much of their work, Gunder Frank is instead quick to offer self-criticism. In true Frank fashion, once again, he is suggesting an alternative way of examining development—much as he did when he coined the phrase "the development of underdevelopment" to describe the economic transformations of the Third World in the 1960s.

This "continuity hypothesis" has challenged many long-cherished concepts and topic areas. In the end, we discover that we do ourselves a great intellectual disservice by failing to recognize that, regardless of how we decide to divide social reality for the sake of expedience, our studies will be necessarily incomplete unless we eventually return to the fact that there has been and is but one world system.

The world system is exploitative. It is certainly not, nor has it ever been, a fair, just, or idyllic place. There are few, if any, indignities that people are above inflicting on their fellows, on Nature, or ultimately on themselves. Many people think this condition leads in and of itself to some conclusion. Some would argue that recognition of the exploitative nature of the world system means we ought to join in the orgy. Others would suggest that we drop out. Gunder Frank has refused to do either, seeking instead to both understand the system and to affect it.

We might also abandon the search for a broader, encompassing theoretical framework and look to the study of social movements for more immediate impact and relevance. We might follow the dictum "think globally and act locally" as a way of trying to reduce the suffering in small ways and places in the hope that our actions might cumulate and resonate with our desire to solve the broader problem. Such an approach might be functionally useful because it would bring locally ameliorative effects and much-needed relevance to developmental studies. In the global era, however, focusing on the local without addressing a broader framework might actually constrain our understanding of the underpinnings of the issues at hand while making it easy for pernicious international forces to undermine good works. Nonetheless, the study of social movements could be important to facilitate the progressive march of freedom and justice.

Our individual ability to affect the exploitative nature of the world system is severely limited. Structural analysis is often criticized as placing the ability of precipitating productive change outside the purview of individuals. The result is a "rational" response of resignation. Because such a response is both unfortunate and debilitating, some poststructural scholars seek instead to focus scholarship once again on the individual as the motor force of history. Such logic is illegitimate. Faced with difficulties, one does not simply redefine the problem; one needs to be both acutely aware of the limits of individual action and cognizant of the need to seek areas where such action may nonetheless be helpful. We believe that responses to this problem have to be both academic and practical.

In an era of theoretical uncertainty, increasing demise of revolutionary self-confidence, and "no logic of history," we need to reconceptualize development within the streams of world history, to take stock of what has occurred, and to recognize the world-embracing aspects of the system and its long historical development. We hope our reflections will continue the telos of the human project rooted in sustainable justice and freedom.

NOTES

1. For an interesting view of this, see Blaut (1992, 1993).

2. See, for example, Banaji (1979), Booth (1985), Brenner (1977), Laclau (1971), Leys (1977), Lipietz (1987), and Warren (1980).

3. Unfortunately, this way of analyzing social change (nation-state as unit of analysis) is practiced by Marxists, liberals, and conservatives. Besides Marx, Rosa Luxemburg, and a few others, most Marxists tend to use the nation-state as their basic unit of analysis and to consider the internal changes within it as primary factors—for example, see Lipietz (1987).

4. See, for example, the World Bank's (1989) *Sub-Saharan Africa: From Crisis to Sustainable Development.*

5. A series of factors have been identified for economic success—for example, education, high level of national savings, commitment to exports, Confucian culture, and strong political framework (e.g., see Vogel, 1991).

6. The question that needs to be asked is also whether there was any opportunity at all.

7. This 'distantiation' from Nature as a dimension of our understanding of the system of capitalism has not been the case historically in a strain of Marxism: critical theory (e.g., see Adorno & Horkheimer, 1979; Marcuse, 1956, 1964, 1992).

REFERENCES

Adorno, T., & Horkheimer, M. (1979). *Critical theory.* New York: Seabury.

Almond, G., & Powell, G. (1966). *Comparative politics: A developmental approach.* Boston: Little, Brown.

Amin, S. (1974). *Accumulation on a world scale.* New York: Monthly Review Press.

Amin, S. (1990). *Delinking.* London: Zed.

Amin, S. (1991). The ancient world-systems versus the modern capitalist world-system. *Review, 14*(3), 349-386.

Apter, D. (1987). *Rethinking development.* Newbury Park, CA: Sage.

Balassa, B. (1982). *Development strategies in semi-industrial countries.* Baltimore, MD: Johns Hopkins University Press.

Banaji, J. (1979). Gunder Frank in retreat? *Journal of Contemporary Asia, 9*(4), 479-491.

Bates, R. (1981). *Markets and states in tropical Africa: The political basis of agricultural politics.* Berkeley: University of California Press.

Bauer, P. (1981). *Equality: The Third World and economic delusion.* New York: Methuen.

Bauer, P. (1984). *Reality and rhetoric: Studies in the economics of development.* London: Weidenfeld & Nicholson.

Benton, T. (1989). Marxism and natural limits: An ecological critique and reconstruction. *New Left Review, 178,* 51-86.

Benton, T. (1992, July-August). Ecology, socialism, and the mastery of nature: A reply to Reiner Grundmann. *New Left Review, 194,* 55-75.

Biersteker, T. (1987). *Multinationals, the state, and control of the Nigerian economy.* Princeton, NJ: Princeton University Press.

Blaut, J. (1992). *1492: The debate on colonialism, Eurocentrism, and history.* Trenton, NJ: Africa World Press.

Blaut, J. (1993). *The colonizer's model of the world.* New York: Guilford.

Booth, D. (1985). Marxism and development sociology: Interpreting the impasse. *World Development, 13*(7), 761-787.

Booth, D. (1993). Development research: From impasse to a new agenda. In F. Schuurman (Ed.), *Beyond the impasse* (pp. 49-76). London: Zed.

Brenner, R. (1977). The origins of capitalist development: A critique of neo-Smithian Marxism. *New Left Review, 104,* 25-72.

Cardoso, F. (1972). Dependency and development. *New Left Review, 74,* 83-95.

Cardoso, F. (1973). Industrialization, dependency, and power in Latin America. *Berkeley Journal of Sociology, 17,* 79-95.

Cardoso, F. (1977). The consumption of dependency theory in the United States. *Latin American Research Review, 12*(3), 7-24.

Cornia, G. (1987). *Adjustment with a human face.* Oxford, UK: Clarendon.

Dos Santos, T. (1970). The structure of dependence. *American Economic Review, 40,* 231-236.

Encarnation, D. (1989). *Dislodging multinationals: India's strategy in comparative perspective.* Ithaca, NY: Cornell University Press.

Evans, P., & Stephens, J. (1988). Studying development since the sixties: The emergence of a new comparative political economy. *Theory and Society, 17*(5), 713-745.

Foster-Carter, A. (1978). The modes of production controversy. *New Left Review, 107,* 47-77.

Frank, A. G. (1967). *Capitalism and underdevelopment in Latin America: Historical studies of Chile and Brazil.* New York: Monthly Review Press.

Frank, A. G. (1968). *Latin America: Underdevelopment or revolution.* New York: Monthly Review Press.

Frank, A. G. (1978a). *Dependent accumulation and underdevelopment.* New York: Macmillan.

Frank, A. G. (1978b). *World accumulation, 1492-1789.* New York: Monthly Review Press.

Frank, A. G. (1980). *Crisis: In the world economy.* New York: Holmes & Meier.

Frank, A. G. (1981a). *Crisis: In the Third World.* New York: Holmes & Meier.

Frank, A. G. (1981b). *Reflections on the world economic crisis.* New York: Monthly Review Press.

Frank, A. G. (1991). Transitional ideological modes: feudalism, capitalism, socialism. *Critique of Anthropology, 11*(2), 171-188.

Frank, A. G. (1993). Bronze age world system cycles. *Current Anthropology, 34*(4), 383-429.

Frank, A. G., & Gills, B. K. (1992a). The five thousand year old system: An interdisciplinary introduction. *Humboldt Journal of Social Relations, 18,* 1.

Frank, A. G., & Gills, B. K. (1992b). World system cycles, crises, and hegemonical shifts. *Review, 15*(4), 621-688.

Fukuyama, F. (1992). *The end of history and the last man.* New York: Free Press.

Furtado, C. (1971). *Development and underdevelopment.* Berkeley: University of California Press.

Gerschenkron, A. (1962). *Economic backwardness in historical perspective.* Cambridge, MA: Harvard University Press.

Haggard, S. (1990). *Pathways from the periphery: The politics of growth in the newly industrializing countries.* Ithaca, NY: Cornell University Press.

Haggard, S., & Kaufman, R. (Eds.). (1992). *The politics of economic adjustment.* Princeton, NJ: Princeton University Press.

Haggard, S., Lee, C., & Maxfield, S. (Eds.). (1993). *The politics of finance in developing countries.* Ithaca, NY: Cornell University Press.

Hirschman, A. (1981). *Essays in trespassing: Economics to politics and beyond.* New York: Cambridge University Press.

Humphreys, C., & Jaeger, W. (1989). Africa's adjustment and growth. *Finance and Development, 26*(2), 6-8.

Huntington, S. (1968). *Political order in changing societies.* New Haven, CT: Yale University Press.

Jackman, R. (1982). Dependence on foreign investment and economic growth in the Third World. *World Politics, 34,* 175-196.

Kennedy, P. (1993). *Preparing for the 21st century.* New York: Vintage.

Laclau, E. (1971). Feudalism and capitalism in Latin America. *New Left Review, 67,* 19-38.

Laclau, E. (1990). *New reflections on revolution of our time.* London: Verso.

Laclau, E., & Mouffe, C. (1985). *Hegemony and socialist strategy: Toward a radical democratic politics.* London: Verso.

Leys, C. (1977). Underdevelopment and dependency: Critical notes. *Journal of Contemporary Asia, 7*(1), 92-107.

Lipietz, A. (1987). *Mirages or miracles.* London: Verso.

Lyotard, J. (1984). *The postmodern condition.* Minneapolis: University of Minnesota Press.

Marcuse, H. (1956). *Eros and civilization.* Boston: Beacon.

Marcuse, H. (1964). *One dimensional man.* Boston: Beacon.

Marcuse, H. (1992). Ecology and the critique of modern society. *Capitalism, Nature, Socialism, 3*(3), 29-38.

McClelland, D. (1967). *The achieving society.* New York: Free Press.

Moore, B. (1966). *Social origins of dictatorship and democracy.* Boston: Beacon.

Mouzelis, N. (1988). Sociology of development: Reflections on the present crisis. *Sociology, 22*(1), 23-44.

O'Donnell, G. (1994). Delegative democracy. *Journal of Democracy, 1,* 55-69.

Parsons, T. (1964, June). Evolutionary universals in society. *American Sociological Review,* pp. 339-357.

Perlin, J. (1989). *A forest journey.* Cambridge, MA: Harvard University Press.

Polanyi, K. (1944). *The great transformation.* Boston: Beacon.

Ponting, C. (1991). *A green history of the world.* New York: Penguin.

Pye, L. (1962). *Personality, politics, and nation building.* New Haven, CT: Yale University Press.

Resnick, R., Sinisi, J., & Wolff, R. (1985). Class analysis of international relations. In W. Hollist & F. Tullis (Eds.), *An international political economy* (pp. 87-123). Boulder, CO: Westview.

Rostow, W. (1960). *The stages of economic growth: A non-communist manifesto.* Cambridge, UK: Cambridge University Press.

Schuurman, F. J. (Ed.). (1993). *Beyond the impasse: New directions in development theory.* London: Zed.

Sklair, L. (1988). Transcending the impasse: Metatheory, theory, and empirical research in the sociology of development and underdevelopment. *World Development, 16*(6), 677-709.

Stallings, B. (1992). International influence on economic policy: Debt stabilization and structural reform. In S. Haggard & R. Kaufman (Eds.), *The politics of economic adjustment* (pp. 41-88). Princeton, NJ: Princeton University Press.

Sunkel, O. (1973). Transnational capitalism and national disintegration in Latin America. *Social and Economic Studies, 22,* 133-177.

Taylor, J. (1979). *From modernization to modes of production.* New York: Macmillan.

Toye, J. (1987). *Dilemmas of development: Reflections on the counterrevolution in development theory and policy.* Cambridge, MA: Blackwell.

United Nations International Children's Emergency Fund (UNICEF). (1986). *The state of the world's children.* New York: Author.

Vandergeest, P., & Buttel, F. (1988). Marx, Weber, and development sociology: Beyond the impasse. *World Development, 16*(6), 683-695.

Vogel, E. (1991). *The four little dragons.* Cambridge, MA: Harvard University Press.

Wallerstein, I. (1974). *The modern world-system 1.* San Diego: Academic Press.

Wallerstein, I. (1976). A world-systems perspective on the social sciences. *British Journal of Sociology, 27*(2), 342-352.

Wallerstein, I. (1979). *The capitalist world-economy.* New York: Cambridge University Press.

Wallerstein, I. (1991). The West, capitalism, and the modern world-system. *Review, 15*(4), 561-620.

Walton, J., & Ragin, C. (1990). Global and national sources of political protest: Third World responses to the debt crisis. *American Sociological Review, 55,* 876-890.

Warren, B. (1980). *Imperialism: Pioneer of capitalism.* London: Verso.

Waterbury, J. (1992). The heart of the matter? Public enterprise and the adjustment process. In S. Haggard & R. Kaufman (Eds.), *The politics of economic adjustment* (pp. 182-217). Princeton, NJ: Princeton University Press.

Wolf, E. (1982). *Europe and the people without history.* Berkeley: University of California Press.

Wolpe, H. (Ed.). (1980). *The modes of production debate.* London: Routledge & Kegan Paul.

World Bank. (1984). *Toward sustained development in sub-Saharan Africa.* Washington, DC: IBRD.

World Bank. (1989). *Sub-Saharan Africa: From crisis to sustainable development.* Washington, DC: IBRD.

2

The Underdevelopment of Development

ANDRE GUNDER FRANK

This autobiographical historical essay has a history of its own, which merits a brief summary. The title is an inversion of my 1966 essay "The Development of Underdevelopment." The original manuscript title, however, already concluded with "and Underdevelopment of Development" before these words were deleted to shorten the title for publication. So for me, this idea is not new. The writing of this essay itself began in 1989, before the Berlin Wall came down, as my contribution to another Festschrift—for my friend Ben Higgins. Therefore, this essay retains some of his "equity and efficiency" *problématique* and terminology. Moreover, the editors of this volume also follow his lead (Savoie, 1992) in including a wide-ranging essay by the "guest of honor." I

AUTHOR'S NOTE: Robert Denemark generously and efficiently undertook the task of cutting the essay down to size (by about two thirds), improving its sequence and style of presentation, indeed virtually rewriting it. He graciously also accepted and incorporated my comments for "correction" and further revision. The remaining demerits are mine, and much of the merit is his. Therefore, Bob merits the reader's thanks as much as mine. I am also grateful to the other editor, Sing Chew, first for initiating this project when he did not yet know what he was letting himself in for, and then in cooperation with Bob for persevering in arranging the preparation, timely (and sometimes not so timely) receipt, editing, and publication of so many excellent, topically thoughtful, and at the same time personally heartwarming contributions by my friends and colleagues, all of whom I take this opportunity to thank as well.

revised this essay for separate publication (Frank, 1991). For the present purposes but under the cloud of the illness and death of my wife, Marta Fuentes, I extended it in the years since 1989. Hence, this essay incorporates passages written over five eventful years and sometimes uses the present tense or makes future predictions to refer to events and times now long since past. It also cites some articles to more accessible later published books.

I intend to undertake a political sociology of knowledge of the study of development based on my own experience and perspective. I review the three varieties of development economics—neoclassical (right), Keynesian (center), and Marxist (left)—and autobiographically my own participation in all of them. Perhaps I can also clarify how, on further reflection, my choice for the study of development is now none of the above. I would not wish to find myself in any of these camps when H. W. Arndt (1987, pp. 162-163) can write,

> Are we then to conclude that Adam Smith, Karl Marx, Gunnar Myrdal and Peter Bauer, all proponents of material progress, must be regarded as "Right" and A. G. Frank, Dudley Seers, the Ayatollah Khomeini, and the Pope as "Left"? Or is it the other way around? Clearly there is something wrong, certainly in relation to economic development as a policy objective, with these labels.

I offer this essay as my own "contribution" to the agonizing reappraisal of development in general and to the discourse on development undertaken in this book.

FROM THE CRISIS OF DEVELOPMENT
TOWARD A CONCEPTUAL INTRODUCTION

The 1988 Congress of the International Society for Development in New Delhi, 1,000 strong, was dominated by the theme of crisis. There was a sensation of total bankruptcy in development policy, thinking, theory, and ideology. Little wonder. In Latin America, per capita income and/or product had fallen by 10% to 15%, equivalent to the level of more than a decade before. In Africa, per capita national income had fallen more than 25% to a level below that at the time of independence. These averages also hide the worsening distribution of resources, as "the poor pay more" of this decline.

The socialist countries first seemed to do well, but then they were also caught in the vise of crisis. Socialist national product and income had also fallen 25% in a four-year period in Poland. Economic and political crisis went from bad to worse in Stalinist Romania (lights out), worker-management Yugoslavia (threat of army intervention), not to mention liberated Vietnam (chaos and reprivatization). Twenty-five percent of Hungarians lived in poverty. The Brezhnev period in the U.S.S.R. was rebaptized as one of "stagnation." Many economic sectors and social indices deteriorated. The revolution of 1989 was the result.

In the short run, not development but rather crisis management has become the order of the day in much of the South and the East (with significant partial exceptions in India, China, and the East Asian Newly Industrialized Countries [NICs]). Neither advocates of neoclassical capitalist stabilization and adjustment nor neostructuralist advocates of reformist structural change or even of *perestroika* and *glasnost* promised a credible solution to the crisis, much less for development. Even so, many prefer to masquerade their own ideological, theoretical, and policy bankruptcy behind the newly fashionable neoliberal phrases of promoting economic growth (= development?) by letting "the magic of the market" "get the prices right."

For the longer run, the environmental costs of past and present developmental styles have become increasingly ominous. The need for ecologically *Sustainable Development* (Redclift, 1987) has become more urgent than when the Club of Rome referred to *The Limits of Growth* (1972). Similarly, there is greater consciousness of how, in the long run, economic "development is bad for women" and largely at their expense.

Capitalist and socialist development orthodoxies turn out to share more in common on all of these and other scores than the differences their advocates have so long fought about. Further, each of these alternatives is represented or promoted by one or more social movements. Some are reactionary against, and others progressive beyond, the postwar development orthodoxies. Islamic and various indigenous revivalists and other ethnic groups combat Western (including Marxist socialist) modernization and promote a variety of cultures instead. Environmentalists try to reverse or at least suggest ways to avoid further ecological degradation. Countless community and small-is-beautiful groups seek to protect their members' livelihoods and identities. Feminists and other women fight to change the gender structure of society. Thereby, they also improve the de facto conception and de jure definition of development. Their conceptions of equity, efficiency, and economy in development are altogether different from those measuring development by growth rates of GNP.

FROM DEVELOPMENT OF DEVELOPMENT
THINKING TO ITS UNDERDEVELOPMENT

Development was the foremost concern of all classical political economists from Petty and Hume, via Smith and Ricardo, to Mill and Marx. These same economists were also concerned with equity distribution and efficiency allocation in development. Indeed, this concern with equity and efficiency in development long dominated economics. Then, the neoclassical marginalist (counter)revolution of the 1870s subtracted both distributional equity and economic development to leave only allocational efficiency in economics. This happened just as the world economy was going into a long Kondratieff B phase crisis and its British hegemonic center was beginning its decline. One result was the growth of more monopoly capitalism (while marginalists focused on the efficiency of competition). Another result was renewed colonialism and the drain of resources and capital from South to North (while marginalists deleted development from their menu). Before this "marginal" counterrevolution, the above-cited distinctions among varieties of (development) economics would have been hard to make.

It took another Kondratieff B phase crisis in the world economy and the Keynesian response to put economists back on track. Even then, they only did so for particular Western countries. There they put macroeconomic problems, some considerations of macroequity, and development by another name (stagnation à la Hansen) back on the agenda. Development elsewhere was only of interest insofar as it might pose a competitive threat to the West. Thus, Folke Hilgerdt studied *Industrialization and Foreign Trade* (1945) in *The Network of World Trade* (1942) for the League of Nations. The Keynesians (though perhaps not Keynes) continued to accept the neoclassical tenets of (non)equity through perfect competition at the microlevel and to exclude world and Third World development from the agenda.

Another Kondratieff B phase crisis has led to the total bankruptcy of all neoclassical microtheory and (post)Keynesian macrotheory and policies. This new crisis has put on the economists' agenda the remarrying of macro- and microeconomics in a new union of world political economic development. Economists' by now congenital shortsightedness, however, prevents most from seeing either the crisis or how to resolve it. Demand-side macroeconomics must divest itself from the unrealistic assumption of a supply curve that is infinitely elastic until it becomes totally inelastic at a mythical full employment level. Supply-side microeconomics must divest itself from the unreal assumption of perfect competition and foresight.

Macro- and microeconomics must form a union that takes account of the macroeconomic effects of individual (firm) microeconomic decisions—and vice versa, the macroeconomic influences on these same microeconomic decisions. Both must devote special attention to supply-side decisions and policies of technological change and to the demand-side conditions under which they are made. Moreover, perhaps following Pasinetti (1981), we must reinsert the classical political economists' considerations of distributional equity, sectoral imbalance, and dynamic development into this new demand-and-supply-side union. Finally, all of these must be united in the face of a single world economy whose political economic development is the final arbiter of this economic theory and policy—although it is itself hardly subject to either.

If anthropology was the child of imperialism and colonialism (Asad, 1975; Gough, 1968), then new development thinking was the child of neo-imperialism and neocolonialism. It developed as an instrument of the new postwar American hegemony. American ambitions extended over the ex-colonial world in the South and against both the real old Western colonialism and the perceived threat of new Eastern colonialism and imperialism. At the end of World World II, the "newly emerging" "young nations"—like millenarian China and India!—came of post- (semi) colonial age. Simultaneously and not independently, the United States ascended to neo-imperial hegemony. That is when development studies came into their own and the new development ideology swept the world. The Chinese Communist peasant victory among one quarter of the world's population in 1949 put the fear of God into many minds. They feared its extension or indigenous repetition in newly independent India, self-liberated Korea, and elsewhere. A decade later, the Cuban Revolution would revive this same fear. Developing a more harmless alternative became a matter of the greatest urgency for the newly hegemonic United States.

Of course, the new American development of development theory also partook of American pragmatism and empiricism. "Science is Measurement" was engraved on the cornerstone of the University of Chicago building where I studied economics. Development became increasingly equated with economic development, and that became equated de facto, if not de jure, with economic growth. It, in turn, was measured by the growth of GNP per capita. The remaining "social" aspects of growth = development were called "modernization."

Development meant following step by step in our (American idealized) footsteps from tradition to modernity. The measure of it all was how fast the modern sector replaced the traditional one in each dual economy and society—that is, as long as there were no far-reaching structural reforms, let alone political revolutions. Of course, American-instigated and -supported counterrevolution and even invasion in Guatemala in 1954, Lebanon in 1958, and so on were OK. That is where I demurred.

FROM AUTOBIOGRAPHICAL
BACKGROUND TO CHICAGO ECONOMICS

My pacifist novelist father had taken me out of Nazi Germany in 1933, when I was four years old. I went to Ann Arbor High School and then to Swarthmore College. There, in part under my father's influence, I studied economics and became a Keynesian. In 1950, I started a Ph.D. in economics at the University of Chicago. I took Milton Friedman's economic theory course and passed my Ph.D. exams in economic theory and public finance with flying colors. Despite that, I received a letter from the Chicago Department of Economics advising me to leave because of my unsuitability or our incompatibility.

I went on to the University of Michigan and studied with Kenneth Boulding and Richard Musgrave. I wrote a paper on welfare economics, which proved that it is impossible to separate efficiency in resource allocation from equity in income distribution. (Ian Little would become famous for doing the same thing.) I took the paper, for which Boulding had given me an A+, back to Chicago to get at least an M.A. out of those folks. First, they made me cut out the heart of the argument, and then they gave me a C for it. Then I dropped out altogether. I became a member of the beat generation at the Vesuvius Cafe in San Francisco's North Beach before Jack Kerouac arrived there *On the Road*.

I was introduced to "development" and reentered Chicago through the back door via the availability of a research assistantship in Bert Hoselitz's Research Center in Economic Development and Cultural Change. During Bert's leave, acting director Harvey Perloff hired me, only to tell me later and to his dismay that I was "the most philosophical person" he ever met. He put me to work evaluating the early World Bank reports. I gave their reports on Ceylon, Nicaragua, and Turkey barely passing marks (1955a, 1955b).

For reasons of financial circumstance, I spent an interval at Chicago working on the Soviet economy (in a research project whose final client was the

U.S. Army Psychological Warfare Division!). As a result, I subsequently wrote my Chicago economics Ph.D. dissertation on a comparison of productivity growth between agriculture and industry in the Soviet Ukraine (summarized in 1958). In this thesis, I independently worked out the concepts and measures of general productivity, which later came to be known as *total productivity.* I stressed its role in measuring the contribution of "Human Capital and Economic Growth" in a journal edited and published at the University of Chicago (1960). According to Arndt (1987, p. 62), the idea of human capital was "almost single-handedly introduced into economics" by the then chair of the Chicago Department of Economics, T. W. Schultz, who subsequently was awarded the Nobel Prize.

At the University of Chicago, I spent more and more of my time studying anthropology and associating with anthropologists. This helped me come to the same conclusion as my friend Bert Hoselitz (but, I thought, independently of him) that the determinant factors in economic development were really social. Social change, therefore, seemed the key to both social and economic development. I wrote about social conflict and favorably reviewed Albert Hirschman's *Strategy of Economic Development* (1958). I conferred with him and Bob Lindblom about our convergent conflict studies. Hirschman would later recall this (Meier & Seers, 1984).

In 1958, I spent three months as visiting researcher at MIT's Center for International Studies (CENIS) and met Ben Higgins, W. W. Rostow, and the others. Rostow wrote his *Process of Development* (1952) and *Stages of Growth: A Non-Communist Manifesto* (1962). Although Rostow and company dealt with Keynesian-type macroeconomic and even social problems, they did so to pursue explicitly the neoclassical counterrevolutionary, and even counter-reformist, cold war ends. The quintessential modernization book, David Lerner's (1958) *Passing of Traditional Society,* appeared while I was there. At the same time, Everett Hagen wrote his *On the Theory of Social Change* (1962), David McClelland his *Achieving Society* (1961), and Ithiel de Sola Pool his right libertarian/authoritarian political works.

In 1959, at the American Anthropological Association meetings in Mexico, I gave a paper on social change and reform through social conflict. I cochaired the anthropological theory sessions with Margaret Mead. At a subsequent anthropology conference, she especially congratulated me on my delivery of a paper later published as "Administrative Role Definition and Social Change" (1963-1964). Both papers were based on my earlier analysis in "Goal

Ambiguity and Conflicting Standards: An Approach to the Study of Organization" (1958-1959).

From this idea about social change, it was but a short step for me to conclude that the really important factors in development are political. Because political change seemed difficult, if not impossible, to achieve through reform, the obvious answer seemed to be the need to start change through political revolution. It became increasingly clear to me that all development studies and thinking of U.S. origin, including my own, were not at all part of the solution to development problems. Instead, they were themselves really part of the problem because they sought to deny and obscure both the real problem and the real solution, which lay in politics.

To find out more about that, I went to Cuba in 1960, looked at political change in Kwame Nkrumah's Ghana (where I was disappointed to find little), and then in Sékou Touré's Guinea (where I mistakenly thought I had found more). Then, I decided to be consequential: I quit my assistant professorship at Michigan State University and went to find out for myself from the "inside" in the "underdeveloped" "Third" World. Because I decided I could never become an African, I went to Latin America, where acculturation seemed less daunting.

In 1962, in Mexico, I wrote about the "Janus faces" of Mexican inequality (reprinted, 1969). I saw internal colonialism there instead of separate sectors in a "dual" economy or society. In Peru, Anibal Quijano arranged for me to meet Marta Fuentes in Chile. We shared our concern for social justice, which would guide our concern for development with equity before efficiency. We married and had two children with whom, as with each other, we spoke Spanish. Together, but without consulting our children and at their cost, we embarked on the long journey "to change the world."

To begin with, I wrote a critique of an article on land reform by Jacques Chonchol. He counseled, and later practiced, slow land reform. I argued for the necessity of fast agrarian and other revolution to forestall counterreform. This was probably my first explicit critique of reformism from a more radical perspective. I also foretold that any economic integration of Latin America would help foreign investors more than local ones (reprinted, 1969). I increasingly saw the reformist house as no more than a remodeled capitalist one. I thought it was necessary to replace this one by a socialist house instead. Just how much tearing down and rebuilding this change might involve was less than clear.

I still welcomed any proposed reforms but considered them insufficient, if not altogether unworkable, and put my confidence instead in the Cuban way. Of course, Cuba was developing socially and visibly improving education and health, reducing race and gender discrimination, and so forth. It was not yet clear that this was the main forte of the Cuban way. No one yet knew that this social development was not being matched by or grounded on a concomitant development of its economic base. The inadequate or incorrect Cuban development of this economic base would ultimately make the continued social development dependent on the aid of massive foreign subsidy. This Cuban experience seems to disconfirm the Schultzian thesis (and then also mine) about the necessity and sufficiency of investment in "Human Capital and Economic Growth" (Frank, 1960).

After the 1962-1963 Sino-Soviet split and their lengthy document debates, I also accepted the Chinese line because it appeared more revolutionary. The line and praxis of the Soviet and Soviet-aligned Latin American Communist Parties were too reformist. Indeed, in praxis they were hardly distinguishable from "national bourgeois" and Comisión Económica para America Latina/ UN Economic Commission for Latin America (CEPAL/ECLA) reformism. The only big difference was that the former did, and the latter did not, refer to American imperialism as an obstacle to development in Latin America and elsewhere in the Third World.

I wrote the article "Aid or Exploitation?" (reprinted, 1969). It countered the claim of Lincoln Gordon, the American ambassador to Brazil (later implicated in the 1964 military coup), that foreign aid helped Brazil much. The article also rebutted the more reformist reply that aid only helped a little, as Roberto Campos, the Brazilian ambassador to the United States, had replied. My article contained the then radical proposition and figures to show that Brazil and Latin America were, in fact, net capital exporters to the United States, which far from aiding them, thereby exploited them. The leading Rio daily *Jornal do Brasil* gave my article a whole page and that created a political storm that led to my invitation to the Brazilian Congress by Leonel Brizola.

We had moved to Brasilia for jobs in the new University of Brasilia there. In Brazil, I wrote an article on foreign investment "Mechanisms of Imperialism" (reprinted, 1971) to counter the gospel according to which the Third World needed foreign investment and capital. Received theory was that the principal obstacle to development was the shortage of capital. I countered this universally accepted supply-side theory with the essentially Keynesian demand-side argument that the real economic obstacle was insufficient market demand for productive national investment. The same kind of Keynesian and structuralist argument also underlay the policies of Brazilian and other nationalists, like Celso Furtado. However, I criticized Furtado, the founder of SUDENE, who was then Minister of Planning before the military replaced him with Campos. I argued that his and others' policies of structural reform were insufficient to expand the internal market and generate development.

At the University of Brasilia, Ruy Mauro Marini, Theotonio Dos Santos, and his wife, Vania Bambirra, were my students; and Marta was Vania's. None of us had yet thought of what would become our dependency theory. Of course, neither could we then know how Latin American and our political developments would later entangle our personal, intellectual, and political paths.

FROM DUALISM TO DEPENDENCE

I wrote my first three theoretical works in Brasilia and later in Rio, where our first son was born in 1963. They were directed at once against development theory and policy derived from neoclassical and monetarist development theory; against Keynesian and structuralist explanations; and against CEPAL/ ECLA, Alliance for Progress, and orthodox Marxist and Communist Party theory, policy, and praxis. I put them all in the same sack. The reason was that, whatever their differences, they all shared the view that underdevelopment was original or traditional. They all posited that development would result from gradual reforms in dual economies/societies, in which the modern sector would expand and eliminate the traditional one. Like Foster-Carter (1976), Hunt (1989) regards my critique as "an archetypal example of a paradigm shift" (p. 172). She wonders whether I had read or even heard of Kuhn's book. I had not.

I quarreled with these orthodoxies more about their vision of underdevelopment than with their idea of development itself. I did not then find it remarkable that all also shared an essentially similar vision of capital accumulation through industrial growth = development. So did I! One of the subsequent critiques of my dependence paradigm change "from Rostow to Gunder Frank" (Foster-Carter, 1976) was that I only turned orthodoxy on its head. Doing so evaded and rendered impossible any fundamental other sideways critique and reformulation, which I now regard as necessary.

The first of the three works argued against dualism. It went into battle especially against the then left-right-and-center dominant version according to which Brazilian and Latin American (traditional) agriculture is feudal and that therefore capitalist reform was the order of the day.

The second work in 1963 was a much farther ranging critique of received theories. After a dozen rejections, it was finally published in 1967 under the title "Sociology of Development and Underdevelopment of Sociology" (1967b). I rejected the notion of "original" underdevelopment, "traditional" society, and subsequent "stages of growth" and the analysis of development through neo-Parsonian social pattern variables and neo-Weberian cultural and psychological categories.

The third work in 1963 sought to develop an alternative reading, interpretation, and theory of the development of underdevelopment. I saw it as the result of dependence and as the opposite side of development within a single world capitalist system. All of these ideas and terms were in the original 1963 manuscript, which was not published until 1975 as *On Capitalist Underdevelopment*. It was quite a task to pose these questions, then to rethink the answers, and finally to persuade others to rethink both.

In 1963, I also wrote a letter to Rodolfo Stavenhagen in which I criticized his work and set out the alternative dependency analyses I wanted to develop. Stavenhagen made a place for me (without pay) at the UNESCO-sponsored Research Center in Social Sciences in Rio, of which he was then a director. There I wrote my 1963 manuscript.

At this Institute in Rio also, my name became André Gunder Frank. A librarian there asked me whether the bibliographic references she had to publications by Andrew and to Andres were to the same person. I decided to avoid such problems in the future by dropping the last letters. The "Gunder" I had already acquired as a (slow) track runner in high school. My teammates so nicknamed me by cruel comparison with Gundar Haag, the Swede who then held five world records. Unfortunately, I did not know how the name was spelled.

In 1963, at a Brazilian Anthropological Society meeting in São Paulo, I criticized views (especially those of other participants including Fernando Henrique Cardoso) on dual society and development and argued for an analysis of the relations *among* these socioeconomic sectors and of their dependence on the outside. On July 1, 1964, back in Chile, I wrote an also still-available twelve-page mimeographed letter to a dozen friends in the

United States recounting my political change of heart and my theoretical change of mind up to that time. I also set out a program of research and writing for the future, some but not all of which came to pass. This private letter, along with the published article on mechanisms of imperialism, were subsequently cited in a letter to me by the U.S. government as the ideological reasons and supposedly legal grounds for which I was then barred from United States for fifteen years.

The upshot of all these theoretical and political reflections—and maybe of the unpleasant experiences in and with reformist institutions—was that continued participation in the same world capitalist system could only mean continued development of underdevelopment. The political conclusions, therefore, were to delink from the system externally and to adopt self-reliant socialism (or some undefined international socialist cooperation) internally in order to make independent or nondependent economic development possible. I hardly considered and left for crossing-that-bridge-when-we-come-to-it how such postrevolutionary economic and social development would then be promoted and organized, not to mention guaranteed. I also gave short shrift to how the necessarily not so democratic (pre)revolutionary means might or might not promote or even preclude the desirable postrevolutionary end.

These early general ideas on dependent underdevelopment in the world as a whole were my guides to more specific analyses. "The Development of Underdevelopment in Chile" was written in 1964 for the Socialist Party magazine *Aurauco.* The issue was instead devoted to a collection of Salvador Allende's speeches. My essay remained unpublished for several more years.

In 1964, I submitted an article to *La Ultima Hora,* predicting an imminent military coup in Brazil, but instead it published one by its own editor-owner, Clodomiro Almeyda (later to become Allende's foreign minister), saying that all was well in Brazil. The coup came three weeks later. On a more personal note, I went to the Santiago airport to receive Fernando Henrique Cardoso on his arrival in exile after the coup. Since then, he has thanked me for this gesture on several occasions, including in a recent public address, now as President of Brazil. After Allende's defeat in the 1964 election, we went to Mexico, and in 1965 I wrote "The Development of Underdevelopment in Brazil." In 1966, I wrote the more general "The Development of Underdevelopment," whose original title continued ". . . and the Underdevelopment of Development." The essays on Chile and Brazil, along with some others, became my first book, *Capitalism and Underdevelopment in Latin America* (1967a).

FROM GENERALIZATION TO
CRITIQUE AND APPLICATION

In Mexico, I initiated three new departures. I was the first professor at the National School of Economics of the National Autonomous University of Mexico to teach a course on economic (under)development of Latin America. I was the first person to publish an accounting of Latin America's external payments and receipts that distinguished between services and goods. With this new accounting, I clearly demonstrated that the Latin American current account deficit was caused by a large deficit on service account, especially from financial service payments. These exceeded Latin America's surplus on commercial account of excess exports over imports of goods. My "unorthodox" novelty subsequently proved to be particularly useful in the now standard calculations of the ratio of debt service to export earnings. My third initiative was to organize prominent progressive Latin American economists to sign a statement on "The Need for New Teaching and Research of Economics in Latin America."

In Mexico, I engaged in a number of debates about theoretical and political issues of development. I criticized Pablo Gonzalez Casanova's recently published book, *La Democracia en Mexico,* for being scientifically and politically unacceptable. I also debated about capitalism or feudalism (my title was "With What Mode of Production Does the Hen Lay Its Golden Eggs?") in the Sunday supplement of a national newspaper with my colleague Rodolfo Puiggros. My main message was that "if we are to understand the Latin American problematique we must begin with the world system that creates it and go outside the self-imposed optical and mental illusion of the Ibero-American or national frame" (1965, translated in 1969, p. 231). Then, along the same lines, I began to work on a "History of Mexican Agriculture From Conquest to Revolution." However, I wrote up only the first century. My then still very controversial thesis was that since the Conquest, Mexican agricultural (under)development was commercially driven and affected by transatlantic economic cycles (1979).

In Mexico also our second son was born. I met Jim Cockcroft, and with our mutual friend, Dale Johnson, we wrote the triple-barreled *Dependence and Underdevelopment: Latin America's Political Economy.*

My friends were then also writing their own dependence books. Cardoso and Faletto (1979) wrote their *Dependence and Development in Latin America.* Later, some "historians" and commentators outside Latin America would jump to the unwarranted conclusion that my writings were inspired by them, and others concluded that their book was written in answer to mine. Neither was true, although Enzo Faletto had read my chapter on Chile in 1964. Dos Santos wrote various articles on dependence. However, Theotonio always maintained rather reformist leanings. Nonetheless, others called his writings and mine, and later also those of my other Brasilia friend, Ruy Mauro Marini, "new" dependence writings. Supposedly, they led to more "revolutionary" conclusions than Cardoso and Faletto's version of dependence. They and Quijano were working in departments of CEPAL/ECLA and Instituto Latino Americano de Planificación Economíca y Social (ILPES), whose inward-looking Latin American industrialization program was running out of steam. Therefore, Prebisch himself now recommended more radical reforms, and his younger coworkers all the more so.

In 1968, via "May 1968" in Paris, where I first met Samir Amin, I returned to live in Chile and work on an International Labour Organization (ILO) project. On arrival at the airport, I was detained and taken into town to see the head of the political police and his almost foot-high file about the supposedly subversive threats I posed. He told me that "sociologia" and "socialismo" were all the same to him and sent me back out to the airport to be put on the next plane out. None left, however, before Pedro Vuscovic, from CEPAL/ECLA (and later the controversial Economics Minister of Allende), brought the latter out to the airport to bring me back in under his authority as president of the senate and therefore second in command in the country. After repeated additional interventions by Allende, I received permission to remain in Chile.

FROM THE PRODUCTION
OF DEPENDENCE TO ITS CONSUMPTION

Dependency "theory" prospered despite early and continued rejection, resistance, and attacks. This "alternative" approach found little favor with the orthodox right, some of the structuralist reformist left, the Soviet-aligned Communists, Trotskyists, and soon also the Maoists. Nonetheless, dependence was "consumed" in Latin America and elsewhere (Cardoso, 1977).

In Latin America, dependence (and I) were enshrined at the Latin American Congress of Sociology in Mexico in 1969 under the presidency of Pablo Gonzalez Casanova. At the Congress of Latin American Economists in Maracaibo, Venezuela, resistance was much fiercer. Indeed, I was run out of town.

Dependency theory and writing, including mine, also made a notable impact on and through the "theology of liberation," which was and still is spread through Catholic Church groups in Latin America. Although we have never met, the Peruvian "founder" of liberation theology, Gonzalo Gutierrez, acknowledged my influence in writing.

Back in Chile in 1968-1969, I sat down to write the theoretical introduction to the ill-fated "Reader on Underdevelopment" (Introduction and Contents in 1984). It addressed various critiques of dependence. Then, I recast the whole question in terms of the historical development of the world system as a whole. Because the Reader was unpublishable, I decided to convert its theoretical "introduction" into a separate book. I rewrote it several times until the military coup in Chile put an end to my endeavors. Until 1978, no one was willing to publish this world system manuscript either. It was finally divided into two parts, published separately as *World Accumulation 1492-1789* and *Dependent Accumulation and Underdevelopment* (1978a, 1978b). The first title traced the development of the capitalist world system from the discovery of America to the French Revolution. In doing so, it laid great stress on the role of long world economic cycles and crises of capital accumulation in shaping world development and underdevelopment. The second title concentrated on the role of the dependent Third World in world system capital accumulation over the past five hundred years. Almost nobody except Eric Wolf (1982) and Albert Bergesen (1982) took notice.

As I completed my writing in Chile, I received a draft of the first volume of Wallerstein's (1974) *Modern World-System.* The publisher asked me to write a blurb for its dust jacket. I did and said the book would become an instant classic. It did. Dos Santos also said we (in the Third World) have to study the whole system ourselves and proceeded to write on contemporary American imperialism also, and we did. Samir Amin (1974) published his *Accumulation on a World Scale,* of which he had written a draft for his Ph.D. fifteen years before. These studies on accumulation in the world system reflected the ongoing changes in world development.

FROM SOME LESSONS OF
THE CHILEAN EXPERIMENT VERSUS DEPENDENCE

In Chile, in the meantime, Allende's attempt to introduce socialist reform and reformist socialism came and went. It had my active but altogether un-

distinguished small-time participation. It was time to express political senti-
ments and to put dependency theory to practice. Our house in Chile became
a place of refuge and of discussion for *compañeros* from near and far.

The Allende government drew substantially on dependency thinking and
tried to introduce antidependency measures. Allende also sought, but failed
to receive, support from the Soviet Union. To achieve equity and efficiency
was more difficult in praxis than in theory. To begin with, as President Allende
never tired of pointing out, he was in government but not in power. That is
why I thought the peaceful reformist way would not do. Even to capture and
redirect the "potential surplus" was not so easy. Also, it turned out that improving
equity by redistributing income was not so easy. The resulting change in the
structure of consumer demand did not translate into a new structure of production. Thus, efficiency did not increase, except through lower unemployment.
Equity and social development, however, took leaps and bounds as the people
gained dignity and popular education. Political participation and democracy
mushroomed like never before.

At Centro de Estudios Sociales (CESO), my institute at the University of
Chile, Dos Santos, Marini, Pio Garcia, Marta Harnecker, and many others
debated the ins and outs of the transition to the transition to socialism. I made
myself unpopular by warning that we should instead worry about the coming
reaction and the possible transition to fascism.

In 1972, at the UNCTAD III meetings in Santiago, I heard "development
of underdevelopment" sloganized by establishment Third World delegates
from afar. So, I decided it was time to move on. In the same "UNCTAD"
building a few months later, I gave a paper at the Latin American Congress
of Sociology. It was entitled "Dependence Is Dead, Long Live Dependence
and the Class Struggle" (reprinted, 1984). The message was that dependence
itself was alive and kicking but that the usefulness of dependency theory for
political action had come and gone. That was true at least in Latin America.
More and better class struggle was supposed to be on the agenda. Of course,
more class struggle certainly would come. But it hardly became better; it came
in the form of military coups and repression.

A few months later, still in 1972, I went to Rome via Dakar. I stopped off
in Dakar for a conference at which Samir Amin wanted to introduce dependency theory to Africans. Then, in Rome in 1972, I announced that the world
had entered a new Kondratieff B phase crisis. Giovanni Arrighi had put me
on that track. I said that the socialist countries were starting to reintegrate in
the capitalist world economy. I also repeated that not dependency theory, but

rather the analysis of the world crisis of capital accumulation, was then on the analytical and theoretical agenda (reprinted, 1981b). I would spend the next twenty years full-time on this agenda, writing several crisis books (1980, 1981a, 1981b, 1982, 1983-1984, 1988) and countless articles. All seemed to no avail.

REACTION AND THE
CHICAGO BOYS IN CHILE

The Chilean experimental laboratory has also been exemplary in more recent times. Chile was again important in development theory, praxis, my own experience and thinking, and the connection among all of these. Dependency theory and policy were dead indeed. General Pinochet decapitated them with his sword on September 11, 1973. Then, he instituted an ultra-right counter-revolution and counterreform. Still confined at home by the twenty-four-hour postcoup curfew before we left for Germany, I made several predictions: (a) Politically, it would be very bloody. However, the reality of 30,000 dead and countless disappeared and tortured to this day exceeded even my worst expectations; (b) economically, Chilean agriculture would become another California—if that is efficiency. Since then, I have seen Chilean fruit in super markets in Amsterdam, Tokyo, Hawaii, and in California itself. In terms of development theory and praxis, Chile became a major example of export-led growth (albeit not much in manufactured goods, except for cluster bombs for sale to Iraq in its war with Iran).

The midwife for this transformation was Milton Friedman's monetarism carried to Chile by Arnold Harberger, the Chicago Boys and himself. The new policies were imposed by General Pinochet as equilibrium on the point of a bayonet. That was the subtitle of my *Economic Genocide in Chile* (1976). Pinochet gave the Chicago Boys free reign over economic policy. Free-to-Choose Friedman argued that the magic of the market (efficiency?) comes first and freedom (equity?) later. He was awarded the Nobel Prize for economics, not for peace. The World Bank still gives Chile pride of place for its model. For us, it has cost the assassination of literally countless personal friends, some very recently.

Monetarist and neoclassical supply-side reactionary theory and the magic of the market policy swept around the world. They were enshrined in Reaganomics, which was actually started by Jimmy Carter in 1977, and Thatcherism, which was actually started by James Callaghan in 1976 (see Frank, 1980).

These same theories and policies spread elsewhere. The four tigers in East Asia became the export-led growth model. The economic and political importance of the state in South Korea and its political repression, however, went largely unmentioned until they made world headlines when Seoul hosted the 1988 Olympics. If export-led growth has been efficient there and in Taiwan, it is also thanks to the prior increase in the equity of the distribution of income and the domestic market. These improvements occurred because of the land reforms forcibly imposed by the United States after the war. Unlike the World Bank and others, I took account of these exceptional political and strategic factors. They make these NICs more of an uncommon experience than a model that can be copied. I was also unable to recommend their hardly equitable political repression. However, I perhaps underestimated their capacity for technological upgrading and new participation in the international division of labor (1981a).

In 1974 (reprinted in 1981b), I wrote that the Third World response to the new world economic crisis would be exports to the world market. I also predicted how and why this (economically efficient?) model would be ushered in and supported by military coups, martial law, emergency rule, and so forth. These are the other (inequitable) political side of the coin of this economic model. In many cases, the political repression worked, but the export-led growth led to a depression worse than in the 1930s and to the Third World debt crisis (see 1981a, chaps. 4, 6, 7).

FROM THE CHICAGO BOYS TO DEBT CRISIS

Unlike many of my friends, I had never regarded the multinational corporations and their foreign investment as the bugaboo. Many had hoped that the replacement of the multinationals' direct foreign investment by foreign loans and bank debt would reduce, if not eliminate, dependence. The new debt crisis certainly proved them wrong. It vastly increased foreign dependence, even of "sovereign" national states. Their trade, monetary, fiscal, and social or "development" policies are even more constrained now by foreign debt than they were before by foreign investment.

The debt is an instrument of neocolonization and a drain of "surplus" from part of the South. By my calculation, this loss of capital from South to North has been on the order of U.S. $100 billion per year. The flow was more than $500 billion from 1983 through 1986; $200 billion was through debt service, more than $100 billion through capital flight, $100 billion through the 40% decline in the South's terms of trade, and $100 billion through normal remission of profits and royalty payments. Through 1989, this South to North capital flow has been another $400 billion or so. Thus, the Third World countries—and the East European "socialist" ones too—made de facto payments of more than the total of the debt owed. Yet, in the meantime, this total nearly doubled once again de jure. Hungary paid the amount of its debt three times over, and in the meantime the amount still owed doubled! Under "bourgeois" law in any "normal" capitalist country, of course, bankruptcy proceedings or Chapter 11 debt relief would have been instituted long ago for "the common good." This benefit of the "First" World's civilization, however, is not extended to the "Second" and "Third" Worlds.

Through much of the 1980s, the annual Third World debt service has been about 6.5% of its GNP. Even German war reparations in the 1920s averaged only 2% and rose to 3.5% in 1929-31, before they contributed to the rise of Hitler, who abrogated them. In my reading of history, this drain is not new but has always increased somewhere in the South during each (Kondratieff B phase) economic crisis in the North (for some evidence, see 1978a, 1978b).

The result is not development, but the development of underdevelopment. This time it is with *dis*investment in productive infrastructure and human capital and with the loss of competitiveness on the world market. As already observed above, therefore, another result is that economic "development" has practically disappeared from all but the most academic discussions. In the real world, the order of the day has become only economic or debt crisis management.

FROM DEBT CRISIS TO WORLD
ECONOMIC CRISIS, WEST, EAST, AND SOUTH

In September 1973, I arrived back in my birthplace, Berlin, as an exile from Pinochet's Chile exactly forty years after I had left it as an exile from Hitler's Germany. From 1974 to 1978, I worked in Germany. I was never able to get a professorship in Germany. The minister of culture, a former police chief who now exercised his political judgment as arbiter of all appointments, told one university president who wished to hire me that "this Frank will never get a professorship here." So I left Germany in 1978.

By contrast, in England, Rhys Jenkins and Chris Edwards, who published several serious critiques of my writings, urged me to compete for and then welcomed me as professor of social change in the School of Development Studies at the University of East Anglia. By this time, my more or less fifteen-year-old sons had cut to the heart of many issues with which I had for so long been concerned. One day, out of the blue, Paulo made his own discourse on imperialism and underdevelopment. He concluded with, "If Latin America was a colony, it could not have been feudal"! It took me years to figure this out, and I never arrived at so clear and convincing a statement of it. About the same time in 1979, soon after we had arrived in England from Germany, my younger son, Miguel, observed, "England is an underdeveloping country." I ran to my class to tell my British students, who were incredulous. After several years of British deindustrialization under the Thatcher government, I repeated Miguel's earlier observation to a later generation of students, who then reacted, "Of course."

I wrote two books on the dynamics of the global crisis during this period: *Crisis: In the Third World* (1981a) is the extension of its companion volume *Crisis: In the World Economy* (1980). Other related occasional articles of mine were collected together in *Reflections on the Economic Crisis* (1981b). A reviewer would comment:

> Andre Gunder Frank's trilogy does no less than attempt to historically trace and analyze this global crisis in the context of a long-term structural crisis of capital accumulation. Frank was a lone Marxist voice, anticipating the dangers and potentialities of the deep-rooted crisis which now, 10 years later, engulfs the capitalist, socialist and Third World regions of the world. In this trilogy, Frank expands his original insight into a comprehensive, complex, scientific, and passionate treatise. (Shank, 1982, p. 147)

The recession that began in 1989 in the United States was the longest lasting and, in many respects, the most serious of the current world economic crises. After 1967, each subsequent recession in 1969-1970, 1973-1974, and 1979-1982 had, in turn, been worse than the one before. I argued that this was because the underlying structural crisis problems had not been resolved but that inappropriate policies had instead aggravated them and paved the way for the next recession.

In 1986, I wrote that the recovery begun in 1983 generated many new problems, especially the replacement of real production, investment, and pro-ductivity growth by growing financial speculation and debt, as well as the exacerbation of imbalances among the United States, Japan, Western Europe, Eastern Europe, and the Third World, and within these regions.

Recourse to stimulatory monetary, fiscal, and exchange rate policies during the cyclical recovery of the mid-1980s did, as predicted, render continued reliance on these policies unserviceable in combatting the next recession, which began in 1989 and continues in 1995 in Japan as well as the former Soviet Union and Eastern Europe. Examples in domestic monetary policy are the accommodation of monetary policy and lower interest rates by the Federal Reserve. Examples in domestic fiscal policy are increased public (defense) expenditures, reduced taxes, and a bigger budget deficit. Examples in international economic policy are exchange rate intervention and trade policy. Therefore, easy recourse to these and similar economic policies to ensure a soft landing in, let alone provide for a sustained recovery from, the recession are likely to be, and have since 1989 indeed been, less available, effective, and adequate. In particular, the recourse to reflation, which is so dear to some economists' and policymakers' hearts, was not likely to be an adequate policy remedy in recession. All of these economic possibilities and policy options would sharpen already existing economic and political conflicts of interest (and of economic and monetary policy as other paragraphs explained) among the United States and its Japanese and European allies, as well as with Third World countries. The United States, Japan, and Western Europe could turn increasingly toward neomercantilism and/or the formation of regional blocs. These blocs would be centered on the United States in the Americas, Japan in Asia, and Germany in Western Europe and perhaps Eastern Europe. These could also promote the creation or extension of a European bloc in Western Europe or in all of Europe, including Eastern Europe. This policy to extend detente into a pan-European entente was also proposed in my *The European Challenge: From Atlantic Alliance to Pan-European Entente for Peace and Jobs* (1983-1984).

My study of the world economy in crisis increasingly included the socialist countries. I had already seen the beginnings of the reincorporation of the socialist countries in the capitalist world economy in 1972 (reprinted in 1981a). I analyzed the rapid progress of this process in detail in 1976 under the title "Long Live Transideological Enterprise! The Socialist Economies in the Capitalist International Division of Labor and West-East-South Political Economic Relations." I argued that the "Socialist Second World" occupied an intermediate position in this division of labor between the industrialized First World and the underdeveloped Third World. Until the mid-1980s, however, I still did not see clearly enough that the import-led growth in the East European socialist NICs was essentially the same as export-led growth in the capitalist NICs—the former export to import, and the latter import to export. Almost all amassed foreign and domestic debts. The difference has been that NIC growth in Eastern Europe has been less successful than in East Asia. The latter outcompetes the East Europeans.

In 1990, I wrote that economic crisis, stagnation, recession, and even depression also visited some socialist countries of Eastern Europe (1990a). In part, they were homegrown problems of transiting from extensive to intensive growth. In part, they reflected a conjuncture in the built-in political investment cycle. In part, they were the result of the importation of economic crisis, inflation, and debt from the West through the import-led growth of the 1970s. All of these strands became entangled in the early 1980s. They demonstrated that these socialist economies were not or no longer immune to the vagaries of the world capitalist economy. The revolutions of 1989 were the effect.

The economic crisis in Eastern Europe and the Soviet Union was almost certain to deepen in the short run. I argued that both deepening crisis and the marketization response would result in even greater shortages, new unemployment, rampant inflation, and the disruption of the welfare state. All of these, and particularly the latter, will be at the special cost of women and their children, whose already disproportionate burden will thereby increase still further.

Also in Eastern Europe, economic restructuring was bound to involve transitional economic dislocation in different degrees and forms. I predicted it would be absolutely the most severe in Poland, as well as in the South and East in Yugoslavia and the former Soviet Union, which have the weakest and recently most weakened economies. Romania was also weakened, especially by Ceauçescu's policy of exporting all to pay off the debt. Ceasing to export so much food can offer temporary relief, some resurrection of agriculture but not of industry. I suggested that East Germany faced, and it has indeed become the victim of, immediate *Ausverkauf* sellout to West Germans (who "carpetbagged" the entire East German economy and society by closing down its industries that were quite productive and competitive, precisely because they were so! [1994b]). The integration of East Germany into the West German state left the East Germans with scarce political economic bargaining power in Germany, the European Community (EC), and Europe. Czech and Hungarian state power may offer more competitive bargaining power and benefits to (parts of) their populations. Everywhere, the first steps toward productive integration were the sale of East European productive assets to West European firms and others, for hardly anyone in Eastern Europe itself has the means to bid successfully for "privatized" assets. Only some small ones could be run as "cooperatives," which are, in reality, firms that must compete in the market as well.

Marketization and privatization engender another, more automatic economic and social polarization of income and position, also between the genders, and among class and ethnic groups and regions. A minority will float to the surface of a perhaps first ebbing and then rising tide, and the majority will be sunk even farther below the surface. This polarization is likely to progress ethnically, nationally, and internationally. Therefore, it will further exacerbate ethnic and national tensions, conflicts, and movements within and among states. The now—and already for centuries!—more competitively privileged regions like Bohemia and their peoples are likely to improve their positions further, perhaps even by closer economic and political relations or even integration with neighbors to the West and North. Underprivileged minorities in these, and underprivileged majorities elsewhere, are likely to become increasingly marginalized. The dream of joining Western Europe may thus be realized for the few. At best, some parts of the East may become another Southern Europe, albeit at the cost to both of competing with each other, which has already raised fears in the South of Europe. The many in Eastern Europe and perhaps in the southeastern parts of the former Soviet Union, however, face the real threat instead of Latinamericanization, which has already befallen Poland. East European countries faced domestic inflation and foreign devaluation and then currency reform by shock treatment. The social costs are certain, but the economic successes thereof are not, as repeated failures in Argentina and Brazil have recently demonstrated. In some cases, particularly in the former Soviet Union, even economic Africanization and political Lebanonization—now Bosnianization—are a serious threat. In the short run, any breakup of the Second World may permit some of its members to join the (capitalist) First World, but most will be relegated to the (also capitalist) Third World (1994b).

Alongside the much-heralded failure of "really existing socialism" in the East, nobody seems to see the same failure of "really existing capitalism" in the South. All things considered, the East European model was still politically less repressive and inequitable (except partially in Romania) than in the successful East Asian and the unsuccessful South American capitalist NIC areas. In 1989, Jeanne Kirkpatrick turned out to be wrong: The "totalitarian" countries in the East changed more than the "authoritarian" ones in the South. Looking ahead, proposals to resolve the debt crisis in both regions abound. However, hardly anyone ever asks how to make the South American and East European NICs competitive against the East Asian ones and others. The debt service has made the former lose out in technological and other competition on the world market. Ironically, in Marxist terms, socialism had promoted superstructural political liberation in the Third World without ever offering any infrastructural economic alternative. All this was the case and was documented before the revolutions of 1989. These and other recent reflections on the world economic crisis and its political implications were collected together in Spanish (1988). No one was interested in the English version.

FROM NATIONAL OR CAPITALIST/SOCIALIST DEVELOPMENT TO ONE WORLD DEVELOPMENT

The idea of one world development received an unexpected helping hand from Soviet leader Mikhail Gorbachev at the United Nations on December 7, 1988:

> The existence of any "closed" societies is hardly possible today. That is why we need a radical revision of views on the sum total of the problems of international cooperation as the most essential component of universal security. The world economy is becoming a single organism, outside which no state can develop normally, regardless of the social system it might belong to or the economic level it has reached. (Gorbachev, 1988, p. 3351)

Although we may wish to regard some of these as high-sounding words, we cannot deny or evade the verity and importance of the central thrust of what Gorbachev said. Moreover, it has direct relevance to our present concern with development, if we use this word where he speaks of "progress" and "security."

I would argue that this verity is nothing new. World development—sorry, evolution—has been a fact of life for a long time. For a while, I thought it started with the birth of the world capitalist system five centuries ago. I now believe, however, in applying the rule of the American historian of China, John King Fairbank (1969), to study historical problems by pursuing them backward. Therefore, I now find the same continuing world system, including its center-periphery structure, hegemony-rivalry competition, and cyclical ups and downs, has been evolving (developing?) for five thousand years at least (1990b, 1991a; Frank & Gills, 1993; Gills & Frank, 1991). In this context, the mixtures and variations of different "modes" of production or of social systems are much less important than the constancy and continuity of the world system and its essential structure (1991b). Gorbachev dismissed the relevance of these variations among supposedly different "systems" to this real world system development. In this world system, sectors, regions, and people temporarily and cyclically assume leading and hegemonic central (core) positions of social and technological "development." They then have to cede their pride of place to new ones who replace them. Usually, this happens after a long interregnum of crisis. During this time, there is intense competition for leadership and hegemony. The core has moved around the globe in a pre-dominantly westerly direction. With some zigzags, the core has passed through Asia, East (China), Central (Mongolia), South (India), and West (Iran, Meso-potamia, Egypt, and Turkey; the latter is now called the "Middle East" in Eurocentric terminology). Then, the core passed on to Southern and Western Europe and Britain via the Atlantic to North America and now across it and the Pacific toward Japan. Who knows—perhaps one day it will pass back all the way around the world to China.

In the social evolution of this world system in recent centuries, there has also been a development of the capitalist and patriarchic system in the world. At the subsystem levels of countries, regions, or sectors, "development" has occurred through and thanks to their (temporarily) more privileged position in the inter"national" division of labor and power. We therefore need a more rounded, dynamic, and all-encompassing supply- and demand-side economics to analyze, if not to guide, world economic and technological development.

My historical work (some also in collaboration with Barry Gills) is on five thousand years of world system history in Eurasia/Africa (Afroasia/Europe) and the incorporation of the "new world" since 1492. A major purpose is to offer an alternative to Eurocentrism, which is not Afro-, Sino-, or Islamo-centered, but humanocentric instead. My principal "theoretical handle" is to extend the study of the WORLD SYSTEM (1978b; Abu-Lughod, 1989; Kohl, 1989; Wallerstein, 1974) back as far as it will go. So far, that is five thousand years, but I do not exclude going farther back, following Fairbank's admoni-tion that historical work should begin at the end and work backward as far as it will take us.

I rely on five theoretical pillars in this work. The first is the world system itself. In my current view and *per contra* Wallerstein (1974), the existence and development of the world system in which we live stretch back at least five thousand years (1990b, 1991a; Frank & Gills, 1993; Gills & Frank, 1991, 1992).

The second pillar is the process of capital accumulation as the motor force of (world system) history. Wallerstein and others regard continuous capital accumulation as the *differentia specifica* of the "modern world-system." I argue that, in this regard, the "modern" world system is not so different and that this same process of capital accumulation has played a central, if not the central, role in the world system for several millennia (see especially 1991b and Gills & Frank, 1991, as well as replies by Amin, 1991, and by Wallerstein, 1991, the latter also on the difference a hyphen [-] makes, which are also included in Frank & Gills, 1993).

The third pillar is the center-periphery structure in and of the world (system). This structure is familiar to analysts of dependence in the modern world system and especially in Latin America since 1492. I now find that this analytical category is also applicable to the world system long before that.

The fourth pillar is the alternation between hegemony and rivalry or the regional hegemonies and rivalries to succeed the previous hegemony. The world system and international relations literature has recently produced many good analyses of alternation between hegemonic leadership and rivalry for hegemony in the world system since 1492—for instance, by Wallerstein (1979), or since 1494, by Modelski (1987), and by Modelski and Thompson (1988). Hegemony and rivalry for the same, however, also mark world (system) history long before that (Gills & Frank, 1992). We have also discovered that hegemony has been both very rare and quite temporary.

The fifth pillar is the long (and short) economic cycles of alternating ascending (sometimes denominated "A") phases and descending (sometimes denominated "B") phases. In the real-world historical process and in its analysis by students of the modern world system, these long cycles are also associated with each of the previous categories; that is, an important characteristic of the modern world system is that the process of capital accumulation, changes in center-periphery position within it, and world system hegemony and rivalry are all cyclical and occur in tandem with each other. I analyzed the same for the modern world system under the titles *World Accumulation 1492-1789* and *Dependent Accumulation and Underdevelopment* (1978a, 1978b). I now find, however, that the world system cycle and many of its features also extend back long before 1492 to at least the third millennium

B.C. These long cycles are identified and dated particularly in the papers entitled "World System Cycles, Crises, and Hegemonical Shifts 1700 B.C. to A.D. 1700" (Gills & Frank, 1992; also in Frank & Gills, 1993) and "Bronze Age World System Cycles" (1993). Two other authors' independent empirically based tests offer substantial confirmation, and that of a third one is equivocal, of the existence of these cycles and their datings (cited in Frank, 1993). Economic and political crisis, or at least my analysis of it, has a central role in these ancient, as well as modern (post-1500) and contemporary cycles.

It is important to add a brief word about some implications that this "five thousand year world system" approach does and does not have. It does imply a strong counter to the still all too common Eurocentrism that exists both in general and with regard to the study of modern world history. Eurocentrism has also come under attack in other ways—for example, academically by Bernal's *Black Athena* (1987), Amin's *Eurocentrism* (1989), and more popularly by Afro-, Islamo-, and other "centrisms" and "multiculturality." These otherwise welcome critiques, however, mostly seek to replace one centrism by another and do so on a largely cultural/ideological level. Seeking the origin of the world system five thousand years ago in Asia instead of five hundred years ago in Europe adds further dimension to the critique of Eurocentrism by providing a longer real-world, historically based, "humanocentric" alternative and a real base for denying three further widely held and related presumptions: (a) that the world system began in Europe, (b) that the "rise of the West" was based on European "exceptionalism," and (c) that Europeans "incorporated" the rest of the world into their own "capitalist modern world system" after 1500. I argue instead that the rise of the West followed (from) the "decline of the East" through a shift in the center of gravity from east to west, in which the West took advantage of the existing riches of the East (and specifically bought into the flourishing Eastern market by using gold and silver that Europe pillaged from the Americas). Even with this competitive advantage, Europe did not succeed in the 16th, 17th, or even most of the 18th centuries, but not until 1775-1800 (1994, 1995a; 1995b). Western dominance has only been very recent (and led to the Eurocentric rewriting of history as part of 19th-century colonialism) and is likely to be short-lived, what with the continued westward shift of the world center of economic gravity back toward parts of Asia. This longer and wider historical perspective also places (the underdevelopment of) "development" in a different light.

At least two implications have been wrongly attributed to the idea of the five-thousand-year world system, which I think it does not merit. The first is that capitalism is five thousand years old, and that that proposition is absurd. Immanuel Wallerstein (1991) and Samir Amin (1991) argue that, after 1500, the need for ceaseless capital accumulation and the functioning of the "law of value" make for a sharp break in the nature of social processes. "Capitalism" had taken hold. My position is that capital accumulation neither began nor became "ceaseless" after 1500, but rather has been the motor force of history throughout. There was no sharp break around 1500.

Gills and I (Frank & Gills, 1993) argue that the rules of the game are not altered so much as the positions of the players. The techniques of competition change, but competitive capital accumulation remains, as it had always been, the ultimate determining process. Much of the debate centers on the definition of the term *system*. We contend that a hierarchy of core-periphery complexes in which surplus is being transferred implies the existence of a global division of labor. From this perspective, Wallerstein and Amin appear to follow Polanyi and Finley in underestimating the importance of capital accumulation via trade and the market prior to 1500. They then mistakenly seek the post-1500 "incorporation" of societies into a system of which we contend they have long since been a part. Their search for mechanisms by which societies might escape is therefore likewise misspecified.

Far from arguing that capitalism is five thousand years old, I suggest that we should dare to abandon our belief in capitalism as a distinct mode of production and separate system. Why? Because too many big patterns in world history appear to transcend or persist despite all apparent alterations in the mode of production. It therefore cannot be the mode of production that determines overall development patterns. Our search for any supposed "transitions" between "modes" further obscures both the essential continuity of the system and the nature of change. World history since 1500 may be less adequately defined by capitalism than by shifts in trade routes, centers of accumulation, and the existence/nonexistence and location of hegemonic power. I therefore conclude that the very terms and concepts of "Feudalism, Capitalism, Socialism . . . [are] Transitional Ideological Modes" (1991b) and are best abandoned for their lack of real or "scientific" basis. They obscure more of the fundamental continuity of the underlying world system than they supposedly clarify.

Another wrong conclusion is that nothing ever changes and that there is nothing to be done about it. This is not so. We do live in the same world system that began to "develop" more than five thousand years ago, but the system is not the same, or not everything is the same in the system. Many changes have occurred. Some of the "structural" features of the world system (e.g., inequality, cycles) themselves seem endogenously to generate processual and evolutionary changes in the system itself. Moreover, although the structure of the system imposes limits on "voluntaristic" action and policy to transform the system itself (e.g., from-to the supposed feudalism-capitalism-socialism-communism), alternatives are possible and many popular struggles are necessary. World system history is quite clear, however, about what will not work.

Real world system evolution has never been guided by or responsive to any global and also not too much local "development" thinking or policy. Each temporarily leading people probably considered itself the "developed" civilization and regarded others as "barbarians." Global evolution has never been uniform and has always centered in one or a few places. These places and peoples temporarily enjoyed privileged cultural, social, economic, technological, military, and political positions relative to other "dependent" ones; that is, general and especially uniform global development was and remains impossible. Lower-order national/regional/sectorial/group/individual development policy can only marginally affect but not transform the stage of global evolution. Moreover, it can only take place within the possibilities and constraints of that global evolutionary process, which it only helps to shape.

Therefore, any development "policy" for a particular country, region, sector, group, or individual must identify and promote some selected "comparative" advantage within the world economy. The policy is to find one or more niches in which to carve out a temporary position of comparative monopoly advantage in the international division of labor. Then, it may be possible to derive some temporary monopoly rent from the same. Some specialization is necessary because advantageous and even loss-avoiding presence on all industrial and technological fronts is impossible today. Of course, it is advantageous to do so in a newly leading industry or sector, which is itself able to command temporary monopoly rents. However, each such sector, and even more so each such region or group operating within it, must count on soon losing this advantage again. For soon they will be displaced by competition from others on the world market. This fact of life contradicts all postwar development thinking and policy. Moreover, Gorbachev also pointed out that a "development" policy of delinking is now unrealistic. I now also believe that such delinking is impossible. That is contrary to my own previous view.

TOWARD MARGINALIZING DUALISM?

What is a realistic prospect, however, is the growing threat to countries, regions, and peoples to be marginalized; that is, they may be involuntarily delinked from the world process of evolution or development. They are then delinked, however, on terms that are not of their own choosing. The most obvious case in point is much of sub-Saharan Africa. There is a decreasing world market in the international division of labor for Africa's natural and human resources. Having been squeezed dry like a lemon in the course of world capitalist "development," much of Africa may now be abandoned to its fate. The same fate, however, increasingly also threatens other regions and peoples elsewhere.

In other words, a dual economy and society may now indeed be in the process of formation at this stage of social evolution in the world system. This new dualism is different from the old dualism I rejected. The similarity between the two dualisms is only apparent. According to the old dualism, sectors or regions were supposedly separate; that is, they supposedly existed without past or present exploitation between them before "modernization" would join them happily ever after. Moreover, this separate dual existence was seen within countries. I correctly denied all of these propositions. In the new dualism, the separation comes after the contact and often after exploitation. The lemon is discarded after squeezing it dry. Thus, this new dualism is the result of the process of social and technological evolution, which others call "development." I myself seem to have come full circle from prioritizing determinant economic, to social, to political, back to the determinant economic factors in development. However, now I see them in world economic development.

TOWARD ALTERNATIVE SELF-DEVELOPMENT

By now it is sadly clear that none of the now available "models" of development are adequate for the present, let alone for the future. This inadequacy is true of all of these models, however they may (seem to) differ among each other. This inadequacy characterizes the magic of the world and domestic market, Western top-down political democracy, Eastern top-down economic democracy, and recent attempts at self-reliant national state delinking. Hopes are illusory, however, for a capitalist new international economic order or for the nonexistent and ever less available alternative socialist division of labor/international economic order. Nor does anything else on the horizon offer most of the population in much of this Third World any chance or hope for equity or efficiency in economic development. This is true at least as long as we, and especially they, define development in any of the orthodox more-of-the-same ways. However, it is unfortunately equally true also of the heterodox more-or-less-the-same ways so far reviewed above. As a result, by the 1980s, for instance, the grand old men Gunnar Myrdal and Raul Prebisch significantly radicalized their views and public statements shortly before they died.

So armed, we can pursue some other development alternatives, or Another Development, as the Dag Hammarskjöld Foundation called it. First, like these disadvantaged peoples themselves, we can do battle with antidevelopment or underdevelopment of development as it affects all sorts of "minority" peoples. On further inspection, however, these disadvantaged minorities turn out to be in the majority. Minorities would not demand and merit their own and others' special attention qua minorities if they did not suffer from discrimination and worse at the hands of "the majority." Ethnic, national, linguistic, racial, social, sectoral, age, vocational, and other minorities are all subject to the inequity and inefficiency of economic development. Adding them all up, they surely constitute a numerical majority both globally and nationally. The biggest "minority" (which admittedly overlaps with these others) is women. They assuredly constitute a statistical majority of the world's and probably all countries' population. Moreover, it has belatedly been statistically confirmed that women do most of the work in the world. They do all of the unpaid and much of the low-paid reproductive work. They also do much of the productive work. Women do most of the agricultural work in Africa and in many other parts of the world, including the now formerly socialist countries. Women also do much low-paid industrial and service work everywhere. Adding in these other minorities, probably almost all of the work, and especially the hard part of it, is done by "minorities."

Other costs of antidevelopment and underdevelopment of development subtract further from the welfare of this vast majority of minorities. Ever-developing threats to peace and the environment are cases in point. The Scandinavian-headed Palme Commission and Brundtland Report and the United Nations Special Session on Development and Disarmament have drawn worldwide attention to and sought to mobilize action on these problems and their connections. Although strong peace movements are more visible in the North, the problem of hot war is particularly important in and for the South. During the past four decades of accelerated Third World "development," every war in the world has taken place in the South, and every year several wars have gone on there simultaneously. Any breakout of peace, as in Ethiopia and Angola, is therefore a real (contribution to) development (1989).

Similarly, although environmental degradation may be more (locally) visible in the North (including the East), the world's most serious environmental antidevelopment is now probably taking place in the South. Important instances are the deforestation of Amazonia, Indonesia, the Himalayan slopes, and elsewhere, and the desertification in Africa and Asia. Minority regional, local, peasant, native, tribal, and other environmental movements are mobilizing to protect their own sources of livelihood. Thereby, however, they are also protecting ecological survival for all of us through another and a sustainable eco-development (Redclift, 1987).

Then, what is the "majority," and what does it do? It is the elite who have and use power—also to define and promote (their own) "development." The majority of these "minority" people do not benefit from (equity and efficiency in) economic development. Because "development" is largely the result of work by and for (the welfare of) the majority, it should see this benefit. Because the real majority do not, there must be something wrong, both in the real world and in our "majority"—but really minority—thinking about it!

The praxis of this struggle increasingly occurs in and through social movements. In the "ten theses on social movements" (Fuentes & Frank, 1989) that conclude the original essay by Marta and me in our contribution to *Transforming the Revolution: Social Movements and the World-System* (Amin, Arrighi, Frank, & Wallerstein, 1990), we had placed our bets on old "new" social movements as the most hopeful instruments and harbingers of progressive change.

RECENT DEVELOPMENTS IN SOCIAL,
NATIONALIST, AND ETHNIC MOVEMENTS

In 1992, Marta and I wrote that, of late in the West, peace and women's movements had certainly abated and that the labor movement had been notably weakened (Frank & Fuentes, 1994). Now, the peace movements mostly shine by their absence regarding the fighting in the former Yugoslavia and Soviet Union—not to mention Somalia and other parts of the Third World—

as they also mostly did during the 1990-1991 crisis and war in the Persian Gulf. The war itself set progressive social movements back West, East, and South and sharpened rabid racism instead. Women's and feminist movements, if anything, have become rather defensive against the above-mentioned anti-feminist backlashes. The labor movement seems altogether defenseless. Environmental movements still survive, although they seem not to mobilize people very much. In the Third World South, defensive movements of protest and for survival have also continued unabated, and in rural areas they also take the form of ecological/environmental defense movement. The participation and leadership of women in these defensive movements continues or still increases. At the same time, defensive and even offensive movements have grown markedly among indigenous minorities. Similar movements also grew on previous occasions at the same time as, or even in relation to, earlier peasant movements.

Apart from these "sectoral" movements, however, the previously progressive political content or direction of social movements seems to be turning rightward. In Latin America, right-wing evangelical fundamentalism is replacing more progressive community organization around the theology of liberation and other popular currents in the Catholic Church. In South Asia, right-wing Hindu and Buddhist communalism and populism are increasingly capturing popular allegiance. In the Muslim world, right-wing fundamentalism is on the rise. At the same time, the economic crisis continues and worsens and the liberal democratic and other regimes prove powerless and/or incompetent even at minimal crisis management. Thus, in several regions and many countries around the Third World—and now in the "thirdworldized" former Second World as well—civil wars and military takeovers threaten, soon to replace democratic regimes and thereby also to alter the "political opportunity structure" for social protest movements again (Frank & Fuentes, 1994).

Moreover, the course and (mis)management of the economic crisis generated shifts in positions of dominance or privilege and dependency or exploitation among countries, sectors, and different social, including gender, and ethnic groups. All of these economic changes and pressures generate social discontent, demands, and mobilization, which express themselves through enlivened social (and ethnic/nationalist) movements—with a variety of similarities and differences among them. It is well-known that economically based resentment is fed by the loss of "accustomed" absolute standards of living as a whole or in particular items *and* by related relative shifts in economic welfare among population groups. Most economic crises are polarizing, further enriching—relatively, if not also absolutely—the better off, and further impoverishing both relatively and absolutely those who were already worse off, including especially women.

This change may also generate resentments and mobilization in both groups. The less privileged mobilize to defend their livelihood and its ravage by "the system" and by those who benefit from it through corruption or otherwise. The more privileged also develop resentments against the "system"; this resentment obliges the richer to "carry" or "subsidize" at their own "expense" their "good-for-nothing," "lazy," poorer neighbors. This contributed to the breakup of Yugoslavia.

The population at large, beyond its particular(ist) ethnic, national, and other groups, also mobilizes, or at least is more readily mobilizable, in support of demands that arise out of increasing economically based resentments. These demands, however, easily become politicized to extend to and be expressed by the participatory exercise of economic, political, and civil democracy, not to mention (again) the ethnic and nationalist demands into which they can also be easily reformulated. These recently augmented economic(ally based) resentments throughout Eastern Europe and the former Soviet Union are indisputably a major factor in generating (and accounting for) the widespread popular mobilization through social (and ethnic/nationalist) movements here and now (1990b, 1994).

Thus, the very social movements that first served as vehicles of liberation could then threaten the same political democratic processes they themselves launched. Indeed, in the throes of economic and political crisis, derivative or other social movements could become vehicles of ethnic, nationalist, and class strife and rivalries—with unforeseeable consequences that could include dictatorial populist backlashes against the newly won democracy.

I hope the systematic analysis of the relations I see and suggest are at least implicit among the three concerns of international political economy, world system history, and social movements exemplified above. To give only one short explicit statement of these relations, however, in 1992 I commented on an article in *The Atlantic* about "Jihad vs. McWorld" by Bernard Barber (1992). Barber missed the essential point: The centripetal "McWorld" globalism and the centrifugal "Jihad" tribalism are not two distinct and opposed tendencies. The future and the past, as well as East and West Asia, Eastern Europe, and Northern Ireland, are all inexorably connected, if not united, in the present McWorld economic and therefore political crisis. The centrifugal national, ethnic, religious, and other outbursts are the direct result of globalizing centripetal pressures and the resultant simultaneous crisis in this process. The centrifugal manifestations are, in the words of Robert Reich, the "counter-reaction" to the painful centripetal exigencies.

Jihad is the response to the fact that, as Barber points out, "all national economies are now vulnerable to the inroads of larger, transnational markets" (1992, p. 54). The market, resource, ecological, and information-technological imperatives of globalization themselves generate the fragmentation and Lebanonization—now Bosnianization—of the world. The reason is that, although "each of the four imperatives just cited is transnational, transideo-logical, and transcultural," they do not apply "impartially" and McWorld does not "deliver peace, prosperity and relative unity" as Barber suggests (1992, pp. 59, 62). On the contrary, globalization itself generates economic polariza-tion into haves and have-nots, both on a global scale and within particular societies. Thereby, globalization also generates demands for particularist cultural identity in both. Moreover, during recurrent world economic crises like the current one, the have-nots are economically immiserated by absolute as well as relative loss of income. As the Bible correctly observes, "To those that hath shall be given; from those that hath not, shall be taken (what little they hath)." Therefore, McWorld is not in competition with, but itself gener-ates the forces of global breakdown, national dissolution, and centrifugal corruption—in short, Jihad Lebanonization (or now Bosnianization and "eth-nic cleansing"). Therefore, Barber's second option of bottom-up, grassroots, "strong" democracy in civil society—or "civil democracy," as Marta Fuentes and I have termed it—offers many alternative ways of participatory organiza-tion and mobilization simultaneously to pursue economic and identity ends. Unfortunately, in today's world, economic, political, social, cultural, and ideological crisis, grassroots social movements and their populist leaders also opt for less than civil democratic appeals, positions, and actions and Jihads and also growing rightist, racist, and "ethnic cleansing" expressions around the world. The sociopolitical manifestations also include the threat to the Maastricht process of West European unification, which was posed by the present world economic recession before its resultant political institutional manifestations in the Danish NO vote and other second thoughts elsewhere. That is not to mention the other balkanization process in Europe, which includes the Lebanonization already of Yugoslavia and the Caucasus as pre-views of what may spread to other parts of Europe, Africa, and Asia, as well as to other regions in our single but polarizing and fragmentizing McWorld.

Barber's "guess is that globalization will eventually vanquish retribaliza-tion" (1992, p. 54). It has already and repeatedly failed to do so, however, during the previous fifty years of the "American century" or the last five hundred years since Columbus "globalized" us all. Moreover, Gorbachev recently observed that the market is far older than capitalism. This market unifies but does not homogenize and instead simultaneously polarizes and thereby fragmentizes. Therefore, this McWorld market has failed to vanquish retribalization also during the last five thousand years since "national eco-nomies" in Egypt, Levant, Anatolia, the Transcaucasus, Mesopotamia, Persia, India, and Central Asia all became "vulnerable to the inroads of larger, transnational markets," which joined them all in a single world system. Today, we all still live and struggle in this same system, and as per the lemma of the peoples of the former Portuguese colonies: "A luta continua!"—the struggle continues.

REFERENCES

Abu-Lughod, J. (1989). *Before European hegemony: The world system* A.D. 1250-1350. New York: Oxford University Press.
Amin, S. (1974). *Accumulation on a world scale.* New York: Monthly Review Press.
Amin, S. (1989). *Eurocentrism.* New York: Monthly Review Press.
Amin, S. (1991). The ancient world systems versus the modern capitalist system. *Review, 14*(3), 349-386.
Amin, S., Arrighi, G., Frank, A. G., & Wallerstein, I. (1990). *Transforming the revolution: Social movements and the world-system.* New York: Monthly Review Press.
Arndt, H. W. (1987). *Economic development: The history of an idea.* Chicago: University of Chicago Press.
Asad, T. (1975). *Anthropology and the colonial encounter.* London: Ithaca.
Barber, B. (1992). Jihad vs. McWorld. *Atlantic, 269,* 53-63.
Bernal, M. (1987). *Black Athena.* New Brunswick, NJ: Rutgers University Press.
Bergesen, A. (1982). The emerging science of the world-system. *International Social Science Journal, 34,* 23-36.
Cardoso, H., & Faletto, E. (1979). *Dependence and development in Latin America.* Berkeley: University of California Press.
Club of Rome. (1972). *The limits to growth: A report for the Club of Rome's Project on the Predicament of Mankind.* New York: Universe Books.
Fairbank, J. (1969). *Trade and diplomacy on the China coast.* Stanford, CA: Stanford University Press.
Foster-Carter, A. (1976). From Rostow to Gunder Frank: Conflicting paradigms in the analysis of underdevelopment. *World Development, 3,* 167-180.
Frank, A. G. (1955a). Comments on problems of economic development. *Canadian Journal of Economics and Political Science, 21*(2), 237-241.

Frank, A. G. (1955b). The economic development of Nicaragua. *Inter American Economic Affairs, 8*(4), 559-568.

Frank, A. G. (1958). General productivity in Soviet agriculture and industry: The Ukraine 1928-1955. *Journal of Political Economy, 46,* 498-515.

Frank, A. G. (1958-59, Winter). Goal ambiguity and conflicting standards: An approach to the study of organization. *Human Organization, 17*(1), 8-13.

Frank, A. G. (1960). Human capital and economic growth. *Economic Development and Cultural Change, 8*(2), 170-173.

Frank, A. G. (1962). Mexico: The Janus faces of twentieth-century bourgeois revolution. *Monthly Review, 14*(7).

Frank, A. G. (1963, March 17). Brazil: Aid or exploitation? *Jornal do Brasil,* p. 12.

Frank, A. G. (1963-64, Winter). Administrative role definition and social change. *Human Organization, 22*(4), 238-242.

Frank, A. G. (1966). The underdevelopment of development. *Monthly Review, 18*(4).

Frank, A. G. (1967a). *Capitalism and underdevelopment in Latin America.* New York: Monthly Review Press.

Frank, A. G. (1967b, June). Sociology of development and underdevelopment of sociology. *Catalyst, 3,* 20-73.

Frank, A. G. (1969). *Latin America: Underdevelopment or revolution.* New York: Monthly Review Press.

Frank, A. G. (1971). On the mechanisms of imperialism: The case of Brazil. In K. T. Fann & D. C. Hodges (Eds.), *Readings in U.S. imperialism* (pp. 237-248). Boston: Porter Sargent.

Frank, A. G. (1975). *On capitalist underdevelopment.* Oxford, UK: Oxford University Press.

Frank, A. G. (1976). *Economic genocide in Chile.* Nottingham, UK: Spokesman Books.

Frank, A. G. (1978a). *Dependent accumulation and underdevelopment.* New York: Monthly Review Press.

Frank, A. G. (1978b). *World accumulation 1492-1789.* New York: Monthly Review Press.

Frank, A. G. (1979). *Mexican agriculture 1521-1630: Transformation of the mode of production.* Cambridge, UK: Cambridge University Press.

Frank, A. G. (1980). *Crisis: In the world economy.* New York: Holmes & Meier.

Frank, A. G. (1981a). *Crisis: In the Third World.* New York: Holmes & Meier.

Frank, A. G. (1981b). *Reflections on the economic crisis.* New York. Monthly Review Press.

Frank, A. G. (1982). *Dynamics of global crisis.* New York: Monthly Review Press.

Frank, A. G. (1983/1994). *The European challenge.* Nottingham, UK: Spokesman Press.

Frank, A. G. (1988). *El desafio de la crisis.* Madrid, Spain: IEPALA Editorial.

Frank, A. G. (1990a). East European revolution of 1989: Lessons for democratic social movements (and Socialists?). In W. K. Tabb, (Ed.), *The future of socialism: Perspectives from the left* (pp. 87-105). New York: Monthly Review Press.

Frank, A. G. (1990b). A theoretical introduction to 5000 years of world system history. *Review, 13,* 155-248.

Frank, A. G. (1991a). A plea for world system history. *Journal of World History, 2*(1), 1-28.

Frank, A. G. (1991b). Transitional ideological modes: Feudalism, capitalism, socialism. *Critique of Anthropology, 11,* 171-188.

Frank, A. G. (1993). Bronze Age world system cycles. *Current Anthropology, 34,* 383-429.

Frank, A. G. (1994a). The world economic system in Asia before European hegemony. *The Historian, 56*(4), 260-276.

Frank, A. G. (1994b). The 'Thirdworldization' of Russia and Eastern Europe. In *Russian and the Third World in the post-Soviet era.* M. Mesbahi (Ed.) (pp. 45-72). Gainesville: University Press of Florida. Also in J. Hersch & J. Schmidt (Eds.), *The aftermath of "Real Existing*

Socialism"—East Europe between Western Europe and East Asia, London: Macmillan, 1995; and under the title "Soviet and East European 'Socialism': A world economic interpretation of what went wrong, B. Gills and S. Qadir (Eds.), pp. 87-114. London: Zed.

Frank, A. G. (1995a). The modern world system revisited: Re-reading Braudel and Wallerstein. In S. K. Sanderson (Ed.), *Civilizations and world systems: Studying world-historical change.* (pp. 163-1941). Walnut Creek, CA: Altamira Press.

Frank, A. G. (1995b). The Asian-based world economy, 1400-1800: A horizontally integrative macrohistory. In preparation.

Frank, A. G., & Fuentes, M. (1994). On studying the cycles in social movements. In L. Kriesberg, M. Dobkowski, & I. Wallimann (Eds.), *Research in social movements, conflict, and change* (Vol. 17, pp. 173-196). Greenwich, CT: JAI.

Frank, A. G., & Gills, B. K. (Eds.). (1993). *The world system: From five hundred years to five thousand.* London: Routledge.

Frank, A. G., & Gills, B. K. (1995, March). *The five thousand year world system in theory and praxis.* Paper presented at the Conference on World System History: The Social Science of Long-Term Change, Lund, Sweden.

Fuentes, M., & Frank, A. G. (1989). Ten theses on social movements. *World Development, 17,* 179-197.

Gills, B. K., & Frank, A. G. (1991). The cumulation of accumulation: Theses and research agenda for 5000 years of world system history. In C. Chase-Dunn & T. Hall (Eds.), *Core/periphery relations in precapitalist worlds* (pp. 67-166). Boulder, CO: Westview.

Gills, B. K., & Frank, A. G. (1992). World system cycles, crises, and hegemonical shifts, 1700 B.C. to A.D. 1700. *Review, 15,* 621-687.

Gorbachev, M. (1988). Speech by Mikhail Gorbachev at the UN General Assembly. *Moscow News* [Suppl. to No. 51], p. 3351.

Gough, K. (1968). New proposals for anthropologists. *Current Anthropology, 5*(2), 403-435.

Hagen, E. (1962). *On the theory of social change: Economic growth begins.* Burr Ridge, IL: Irwin.

Hilgerdt, F. (1942). *The network of world trade.* Geneva: League of Nations.

Hilgerdt, F. (1945). *Industrialisation and foreign trade.* Geneva: League of Nations.

Hirschman, A. (1958). *The strategy of economic development.* New Haven, CT: Yale University Press.

Hunt, D. (1989). *Economic theories of development: An analysis of competing paradigms.* Hemel Hempstead: Harvester Wheatsheaf.

Kohl, P. (1989). The use and abuse of world systems theory: The case of the "pristine" West Asian state. In C. Lamberg-Karlovsky (Ed.), *Archaeological thought in America* (pp. 218-240). Cambridge, UK: Cambridge University Press.

Lerner, D. (1958). *Passing of traditional society: Modernizing the Middle East.* New York: Free Press.

McClelland, D. (1961). *The achieving society.* New York: Van Nostrand Reinhold.

Meier, G., & Seers, D. (Eds.). (1984). *Pioneers in development.* Oxford, UK: Oxford University Press.

Modelski, G. (1987). *Long cycles in world politics.* Seattle: University of Washington Press.

Modelski, G., & Thompson, W. (1988). *Seapower in global politics, 1494-1993.* New York: Macmillan.

Pasinetti, L. (1981). *Structural change and economic growth.* Cambridge, UK: Cambridge University Press.

Redclift, M. (1987). *Sustainable development: Exploring the contradictions.* New York: Methuen.

Rostow, W. (1952). *The process of development.* New York: Norton.

Rostow, W. (1962). *The stages of growth: A non-Communist manifesto.* Cambridge, UK: Cambridge University Press.

Savoie, D. J. (Ed.). (1992). *Equity and efficiency in economic development: Essays in honor of Benjamin Higgins.* Montreal: McGill Queens University Press.

Shank, G. (1982). The world economy in crisis according to Andre Gunder Frank. *Contemporary Marxism* (San Francisco), *5,* 147-153.

Wallerstein, I. (1974). *The modern world-system.* New York: Academic Press.

Wallerstein, I. (1979). *The capitalist world-economy: Essays.* Cambridge, UK: Cambridge University Press.

Wallerstein, I. (1991). World system versus world-systems: A critique. *Critique of Anthropology, 2,* 189-194.

Wolf, E. (1982). *Europe and the people without history.* Berkeley: University of California Press.

PART I

On Development
and Underdevelopment

3

⊞

On Development: For Gunder Frank

SAMIR AMIN

W. H. Locke Anderson, Translator

Andre Gunder Frank and the late Marta Fuentes have been among the friends closest to my heart and my thoughts since I first met them a quarter century ago. I was already aware of Frank's earlier writings, and since that time I have remained in constant dialogue with him. I have no doubt that he is the pioneer of what is known as "the dependency school" (the autobiographical sketch presented in Chapter 2 is proof of this). By this fact, Frank merits the greatest consideration among progressive thinkers of our epoch, whatever positions they have taken or take today on the theses he has developed in the past and his subsequent self-criticisms, whatever the reading they make today of the evolution of progressive thought during the half century since the end of the war. In addition, my consideration of him is fraternal, that of a comrade in arms, propelled by the same objectives for the liberation of the people.

I have, like Frank, written a great deal, and I propose similarly a rereading—my own—of what the half century just completed has been and how it has been perceived by myself and other comrades engaged in the same struggle. I look back at my *Re-Reading the Postwar Period: An Intellectual*

Itinerary (1994) and my two articles "The Ancient World Systems Versus the Modern Capitalist System" (1991) and "Capitalism and the World System" (1992). I should like to seize the occasion to call attention—in the first part—to these convergences and divergences such as I see them, but also to enlarge the debate in the second part and to extend it in the context of the contemporary critical and self-critical movement of the theory and ideology of development in the half century since the war.

I

1. Frank formulated the "dependency" thesis for the first time in Mexico in 1962 in *The Janus Face of Inequality* and then deepened and systematically developed it in subsequent years. It is good to know that the militant and the academic Frank, when he was a brilliant student, was a precocious critic of the theory-ideology of development offered by the American establishment, as much economic in its formulations as anthropological. Frank has always remained preoccupied with the refutation of this dominant discourse. It is similarly good that Frank deploys himself on the terrain of Latin America, both as thinker and militant. Others, like myself, have taken different paths, ways taken directly from the Marxist formulation and operating in the political framework, historical and cultural, in Asia and Africa, themselves passably different.

The dependency thesis, like all great (and good) theories, can be summarized in a single phrase: Modern "underdevelopment" is not "historical backwardness," the result of late and insufficient capitalist development; it is the product of capitalist development, which is polarizing by nature. To me, this phrase, which remains fundamentally correct, has seemed self-evident ever since I wrote my doctoral dissertation in 1957. For this reason, I am not genuinely at the center of the tiresome critique of bourgeois ideology—of development economics or cultural anthropology—but I have focused my efforts on the mechanisms that have engendered this polarization in the global development of capitalism. In the large body of work growing out of the "dependency" approach or the "global economy" approach, I have found important clarifications. Progress in my own effort to analyze the polarization of world capitalism owes much to these approaches.

I am certainly not the only one who has ever thought that capitalism is polarizing by the very nature of its worldwide expansion. The Marxist formulations of the conditions of struggle for the liberation of Asia and Africa have naturally led a great number of comrades to this conclusion. That does not mean, evidently, that all theses proposed in the name of Marxism claim to have adopted this point of view. Far from it. That, nonetheless, Marxism has produced the conceptual tools permitting one to arrive at this position seems to be true beyond doubt. I regret that Frank has his own position on this matter, too often incorporating Soviet Marxism and dogma.

The fact that the dependency approach had been developed in Latin America implied its own peculiarities and limits. In contrast to Asia and Africa, which were still subject to colonial status in 1945, Latin America comprised independent states, nearly as "old" (or as "new") as the United States itself. European in culture, their elites were naturally disposed to see in Europe (relayed to them by the United States) the model they wanted for their own nations, and by this fact they were open to bourgeois ideas that attributed their troubles to Iberian feudalism. In Latin America, therefore, the claim that underdevelopment was the product of capitalist expansion was a new departure. But this was not the case in Asia or Africa, which were not culturally European and were colonies. Here, on the contrary, the natural tendency on the left was to attribute all social evils, including underdevelopment, to colonization. The latter was associated strictly with capitalism by the left, whereas the right demanded independence and longed to recover the real or imagined glories of the past. All subscribed to the dependency thesis whether they knew it or not.

The real debate at the heart of Marxism was situated elsewhere. The Third International had adopted the Leninist thesis that held imperialism responsible for underdevelopment. But imperialism itself, according to this thesis, constituted a late stage of capitalist development. This thesis therefore said nothing concerning the eventual constitution of colonial peripheries in prior stages. In other respects, the accent in the analysis of imperialism had been placed on the changes affecting the centers of the system. Questions relative to the nature of the social formations of the modern periphery remained open. Were they essentially "precapitalist"? And how, then, did their submission to capitalism work in the imperialist stage? Had they been sufficiently transformed to qualify as "capitalist"? The responses to these questions depended on the strategic choices of the Communist Parties.

Should national liberation adopt the sole strategy of making a bourgeois, antifeudal revolution, affirming thereby that the national bourgeoisie had a historical role to fulfill and that a capitalist phase free from "vestiges of feudalism" must intervene before the conditions for socialist revolution would ripen? This response had been eliminated in Asia and Africa well before the theory of dependency was developed. The strategy of the "revolution uninterrupted by stages," popularized by the works of Mao, implied that, in the formation of peripheral capitalism, the bourgeoisie, subaltern as it was, could not make the bourgeois revolution. The popular classes directed by the Communist Party would have to make it in their place, immediately proceeding along the road to socialism. Around 1950, this strategic vision was dominant in the Marxism of Asia and Africa even though there were some confusions of interpretation and the tactical positions taken by Moscow would not be able to straighten these out. The strategic turnaround came later when, subsequent to the Bandung Conference (1955), it appeared, whether rightly or wrongly, that the bourgeoisie still had a historic role to fulfill. I have proposed in my *Re-Reading the Postwar Period* an interpretation of this, which I have called "the deployment and erosion of the Bandung Project (1955-1975)," based on this central question. I had called attention to the fact that the rallying of the national bourgeoisie to the project had never really been accepted here despite the support of the Soviet Union, from which it benefited. Maoism, not the theory of dependency, is at the heart of these debates. In fact, whereas the theory of dependency acquired a certain popularity in Asia and Africa beginning in 1975, as Frank notes, the Bandung Project had already run out of steam and the advocates of dependency theory joined the nationalist establishment in trying to explain its failure solely in terms of external intervention.

Be that as it may, in formulating the theory of dependency, given the conditions of Latin America, Frank raised a major question relating to the nature of peripheral capitalist formations. He pointed out that Latin America had been capitalist from the beginning because the mercantilism of 1500-1800 itself constituted the first period in the history of capitalism. He rejected the popular theses calling the system feudal, and in doing so he affirmed that the order of the day was a socialist (anticapitalist) revolution and not a bourgeois (antifeudal) revolution. Situated in the middle of the 1960s with the Moscow-aligned Communist Parties supporting the national bourgeoisie, and accepting de facto the bourgeois theories of economic development, the conclusion of the dependency school rejoined what had always been the position of Maoism in Asia and Africa.

This decisive, political position did not imply in any sense that the debate on the peripheral formations of capitalism had been closed. On this point,

opinions continued to diverge. But to understand it without sinking into fanaticism, it is necessary to admit that the real history of the worldwide expansion
of capitalism has itself taken various forms. In America, mercantilism had
destroyed the social organization of the indigenous people and had restructured colonial society in accordance with its logic. But capitalist expansion
had not operated in the same manner in China, India, the Ottoman Empire, or
later in Africa. The subalternization of the precapitalist formations that had
survived was real here. The expression "half-capitalist, half-feudalist," even
though it can be criticized as an oversimplification, is not ridiculous.

In Asia and Africa, one posed in these terms the transformation-subaltern-
ization of the precapitalist formations, integral to world capitalism and progressively peripheralized by that fact. This was even the focus of my doctoral
dissertation in 1957.

In other respects, the question of the historical status of mercantilism—the
first phase of capitalism? the transition to capitalism?—was far from agreed
on. Frank had adopted here the position that would be that of Wallerstein and
of the world-economy school, placing the beginning of capitalism at around
1500. I have developed elsewhere the arguments that put me in the camp of
those who treat mercantilism as a transition to capitalism, which only appeared
in its final form with the Industrial Revolution and the French Revolution.

2. Maoists and those of the dependency school draw many of the same
conclusions: (a) that polarization (seen from the periphery, it manifests itself
as dependency) is a fact (no one denies this); (b) that polarization is inherent
in capitalism (this viewpoint is not that of the bourgeois ideologists), although
the analysis of the mechanism of polarization opens the field to fertile debates;
(c) that the polarization inherent in capitalism gained momentum during the
mercantilist epoch, deployed itself with the industrial revolution, took its
present form with imperialism in the sense of Lenin, and perhaps has embarked on a new stage of intensification (my argument); (d) that consequently
the peoples of the periphery can only liberate themselves from its disastrous
effects by breaking with the world capitalist system (by delinking) and in
doing so breaking with the social logic of capitalism *tout court* by building
socialism; and (e) that delinking and building socialism constitute projects
that develop in revolutionary states.

These points do not exclude nuances or divergences. I have already said
that my principal emphasis has been placed on point (b). I have here related
polarization to the *global* law of value to distinguish it from the law of value
itself. On point (c), dependency and world systems theorists sometimes adopt

an extreme position (polarization was already a fact by 1500). I accent the differences that separate America from Asia and Africa and on the successive stages of polarization. The last two points (d and e) constitute a preoccupation only for those who want, beyond explanation, to change the world. In the world-economy school, those who take purely academic positions content themselves with remarking that the spread of capitalism is polarizing. Frank himself has gone further than this by extending the phenomenon of polarization to all phases of history—for five thousand years—and has erased in this the specificity of capitalism. I have expressed elsewhere the reasons why this extrapolation seems to me to be fundamentally erroneous and sterile.

It is true, on the contrary, that the countries called socialist (e.g., the U.S.S.R., China, Cuba), like the countries of the Third World which I call national-bourgeois radical (often also self-proclaimed socialist), have pretended to nullify the effects of polarization in the political framework of the national state. These countries (the countries of the East) have simultaneously delinked, in the sense in which I use the concept, and pretended to put in place socialist social relations. The others (the Third World countries in question) have proclaimed rhetorically the same objectives but have never really delinked or destroyed the social relations of capitalism.

One or the other group has run aground, in the sense that the more ambitious have put in place social relations that have not proved viable and that both have reintegrated themselves with world capitalism or are on the way to doing this. But to recognize the defeat is not to explain it. For this, it is necessary to analyze closely the experiences in question. But Frank (see the bibliography of his works in the Appendix to this book) has never interested himself in the fine points of Soviet reality.

This is why what he has written on this subject is very often idiosyncratic, superficial, and even erroneous. It claims, for example, (a) that socialist societies have not been immune to the effects of fluctuations in the world economy, (b) that by this fact, socialism and delinking have been called in question, and (c) that planning was not democratic. He accepts, banally, the designation as socialist that these regimes have given themselves, just as the dominant media repeat over and over. If these countries have failed, it follows that socialism is impossible. He replies on this level in brief, one-sided assertions that are debatable, to say the least. Take, for example, the claim that Chinese agriculture stagnated during the twenty years of Maoism; Hinton, who has a better grasp of the situation, reaches an entirely different judgment. Or the claim that socialism reproduced most of the inequalities of capitalism; it did no such thing. He takes as genuine coin the Soviet system's account of itself; the fact that Gorbachev had observed (correctly, according to Frank) that national development was impossible does not prove this is so. For my part, I say that a national bourgeois development (and this was the reality of the Soviet project) is quite out of the question. Frank regarded *perestroika* as a "radical" socialist attempt. To me, this was not at all the case. It carried on the critique of Stalinism from the right. The critique from the left, proposed by the Maoists, is not perceived by Frank, who claims to have been favorable to the Chinese line because it "appeared" to be more revolutionary. To me, this was the case. The manifestations of nationalism that were expressed in the war among China, Vietnam, and Cambodia in 1979 are therefore sad facts that call for a reevaluation of socialism. Socialism? Or the social realities of the systems in question?

Certain judgments that Frank makes on the experiences of radical nationalism in the Third World are also superficial, in my opinion—for example, that delinking in Egypt, Ghana, and other countries led to an impasse. In my opinion, the countries he cites had never been delinked.

The weakness of Frank's arguments originates in what he fails to analyze with respect to the societies in question, what was really at stake for the social forces in conflict. I have proposed, by contrast, to read this history as that of a conflict between the bourgeois project of the ruling classes (despite the socialist rhetoric behind which they hid themselves) and the aspirations of the popular classes, whose struggles had allowed the rulers to come to power. This conflict explains why the statist planning could not be democratic because it was necessary to mask its true objectives; why nationalism had been mobilized to rescue the project; but also why, for a long time, the ruling classes had been constrained to make concessions to their people and, by this fact, constrained to delink; why the capitalist aspirations of the ruling classes had led to the shattering revision of the last years, which I do not analyze in the language of democratic revolution (which Frank accepts, along with the dominant media), or as antisocialist counterrevolution (as the dogmatic Stalinists say), but as an acceleration of the natural evolution of the bourgeois project (as Mao had foreseen more than thirty years earlier).

Frank draws from these public statements, whose real sources he does not seriously analyze, the preconceived conclusion he wishes to reach: not only that polarization is inevitable in the logic of capitalism (which is always true, in my opinion) but that it is a "law of history," transcending the nature of the systems, whether capitalist or socialist. Frank has even come to the conclusion that polarization has characterized the entire history of humanity for five thousand years. He therefore constructs his self-critique by drawing from the established fact of failure in the East and South the conclusion that a project of development that is different, humane, and non-polarizing is impossible in the framework of national strategies and that it is necessary to elevate the struggle to the world level, as he proposes, to attain this level, the outlines of a strategy based on "social movements."

I shall build on this autocritique and the propositions that Frank deduces from it the three rapid observations that follow, to which I shall return:

(i) Although Frank considers that the experiments that "failed" signify the failure of the socialism that inspired them, I see in their "failure" the inadequacy of the national bourgeois project—which had assigned itself the task of overcoming the effects of polarization without abandoning the bourgeois point of view. Their impasse is real and even graver than the ruling classes imagine because their reintegration into the capitalist world system will not let them avoid a head-on collision with the effects of polarization, against which they have conceived their project. From national bourgeois in character, the project will become that of the bourgeois who accept a comprador position. This reversal will vindicate our thesis, which Frank has defended and which I myself maintain: that capitalism is polarizing by nature.

(ii) A serious analysis of the forces that led the socialist project into an impasse and caused the drift toward capitalism effectively poses the problem. The question Frank raises—Is development (admittedly in a direction that conflicts with the logic of polarization) possible within the framework of states delinked from the dominant capitalist world system?—is a real question. But it is not new and runs throughout the history of Marxism. Did Trotsky not say in his day that "socialism in one country" was a utopia and propose instead an alternative vision of world revolution? Mao, in his turn, proposed a strategy of transition "in one country" different from that put forward by Stalin and his successors. This strategy having failed, the debate over the transition from world capitalism to world socialism remains open.

(iii) In the debate, Frank advances the proposition that an anti-statist strategy built upon "social movements" constitutes the alternative. I shall return to this proposition. But might we not remark that if polarization has characterized the world system for five thousand years, it must, so to speak, be the consequence of some anthropological characteristics of the human species transcending social formations? Why suddenly, today, should social movements be the answer?

3. Frank has therefore passed from one extreme to another. He had accepted the thesis that liberation could be obtained by delinking and building

socialism. He has now renounced direct action in this framework and adopted in its place a resolutely anti-statist and globalist trust in social movements.

In my opinion, the very category demands that one pull together movements of such an extremely diverse nature that it has hardly any relevance. In this sense, the social movement is nothing new. What else is one to call the religious movements and peasant revolts of the past, the workers' movement of the 19th century, and the national liberation movements in modern Asia and Africa? What is new is the eclipse of the particular forms of social movement that occupied the stage for a century at least—the political parties and the syndicates. But this eclipse, linked to the loss of legitimacy of the projects that these forms of organization promoted—the "socialist state," the independent state in the Third World—or more tenuously to the crisis of Western democracy, which gave to other forms of social movement the appearance of liberty and permitted them to reject the old disciplines of parties themselves sclerotic—Was it definitive or only conjunctural?

I myself claim that the movements in question, in their present form, will either crystallize into an alternative politics of contemporary capitalism or feed on negative and self-destructive regressions. I therefore do not partake of Frank's optimism, which is naive, in my estimation. For example, Frank writes apropos the religious movements (and cites the example of Islam) that they "refuse the prescriptions of modernism and increase cultural variety." This is just not true. The Islamic fundamentalist movements accept without discussion the participation of their societies in world capitalism and the "compradorization" that is their lot in this system. Their rejection of modernism, exclusively limited to the political and cultural aspects of models proposed by "the West," is fundamentally reactionary and antidemocratic and testifies to the crises of the ideologies that have been dominant in the recent past and to the disarray that has resulted from the lack of a viable alternative. The communitarian and ethnic (or ethnicist) movements are also party to the assault on the multinational (or pseudonational) state, about which I have proposed a reading quite different from Frank's. These "social movements"— and they are really the most powerful movements on the contemporary scene—seem to me to be completely manipulable (and are manipulated) by the dominant forces of capital, preoccupied in the short term with the management of the crisis and not with its solution.

It is true that other forms of social movement appear to be progressive, or really are progressive, like the ecology and feminist movements. Far be it from me to underestimate the importance of their struggle and, in the case of the feminist movement, to fail to see the place it must occupy in the whole project of human liberation. But it is necessary to see that this movement is not new or uniform or necessarily an obstacle to the pursuit of the hegemony of the merchant economy and all the alienations proper to capitalism. It cannot become such until it is embedded in a multidimensional anticapitalist alternative.

I do not reproach Frank for the emphasis he places on the globalization necessary for liberation. I share this perspective, but I believe it is not new, or at least it ought not be new for the Marxists. If despite the universalist vision of Marxism this point of view were to be sacrificed on the altar of building socialism within the frontiers of the state, this fact ought to be explained. We know that, in his day, Trotsky denounced the impossible "building socialism in one country." But if the world revolution he advocated did not transpire, what else could one do in the U.S.S.R. or China but to try to advance the nation in its struggle with the logic of capitalist expansion? Frank is not seriously interested in discussing this problem, which to me constitutes the central challenge.

I shall not repeat here the answers I have proposed to this question in my *Re-Reading the Postwar Period*. The recognition of the insufficiency of socialist attention to this question (that of historical Marxism included) imposes on our thinking about the possibility of a transition from world capitalism to world socialism a much longer horizon than that envisioned by historic Marxism. It implies that we must free our thinking from the capitalism-to-immediate-socialism construction in order to substitute for it a much more drawn out strategy of transition, combining the fight-capitalism-aspire-to-socialism forces that are deployed on various terrains. A dialectical vision of these contradictory relationships is necessary. This seems to me foreign to Frank's one-sided method, outdated from a global perspective cast in naive terms that he has not criticized sufficiently.

The differences between Frank and me lay not on the question of the "final goal," which we share in common, but on the strategies that are likely to achieve it and on the "lessons" that history has to teach us on this matter. Frank has defined the final goal in terms of the aspirations of the people expressed through a participative democracy. How could this general statement define anything other than the consequences of socialism? Then why is he unwilling to call it that?

The moment has come to reread the ideologies and strategies of development that have been pursued in the half century since the war. In this exercise, what appears to be most interesting is to reread critically those who have been critics of the development in question, among whom are Frank and me. I would like, in the second part of this chapter, to examine the various strands of this critique of development and of the critique of the critique of development. This will allow me at the same time to situate Frank's work and its evolution.

II

1. I use the term *social thought* (or *social theory*) in preference to *social science* so as to avoid the spurious identification of analytical social disciplines with the natural sciences. I find the presumption that the former could ever attain the epistemological status of the latter arrogant. For one thing, if the former were ever seriously to rival the latter, such a development would be harmful. It would reduce social governance to the level of animal husbandry and thereby abolish human liberty. Human social liberation and its twin, the control of nature by humans, necessarily imply resistance to the pretensions of self-styled rational management even when its claims are supported by social disciplines that proclaim themselves to be scientific, objective, and therefore effective.

It is, of course, a long-standing ambition of bourgeois thought—which postmodern critics confuse with modern thought—to make the social disciplines as rigorously scientific as the natural sciences. The social system that serves as bedrock for bourgeois thought (in plain words, the capitalist system) is a product of a worldview most clearly expressed in the economic sphere. Weber, who is enjoying a revival these days, presented this self-image of capitalist society in a formula of astounding naïveté. Capitalism, he argued, entailed the triumph of a rational ethos working to liberate the world from the thralldom of age-old irrational norms.

For some time now, I have been suggesting an alternative view of the differences between past systems of thought and modern (capitalist) thought. My comparative approach is based on the contrast between pre-capitalist (I call them "tributary" societies), with their stress on metaphysical interpretation of reality, and capitalist societies, with their stress on economic aspects. From this novel point of view, the difference between the metaphysical worldview of tributary societies and the thinking of a more advanced society (due to evolve after it resolves the economistic biases and contradictions of the bourgeois system) is not sharply oppositional. One might call such an evolved society socialist.

By enshrining its new economic rationality as an absolute value, bourgeois thought sought to legitimate the emergent form of social organization. In the process, it assumed the new organizational form to be an eternal construct somehow signaling, as certain commentators have recently written, the end of history. This was a worldview in which Progress (with a capital letter) became a surrogate for God, the basis for an everlasting scheme of things.

From my viewpoint, in two aspects capitalism and bourgeois thought, despite their limitations, represented a measure of progress (lowercase). They gave birth to forces that initiated prodigious material development and achieved unprecedented control over nature. (This control was by no means entirely a good thing; it now poses a threat to the survival of the planet.) Simultaneously, by freeing society from old metaphysical prejudices, capitalism and bourgeois thought prepared the way for the concept and practice of modern democracy. Here, I point out that such democratic practice was circumscribed by the nature of the capitalist system. The equation of the "market" with democracy is, of course, facile. But it is based on a real, tangible instance of progress.

The critique of capitalism is meaningless unless it sharpens our awareness of the limitations of bourgeois thought. To do this, it must examine capitalism both as a qualitatively new stage of historical development and as an instance of the unfolding of contradictions between the liberating aspirations the new system encourages and its inability to satisfy those aspirations on the scale of a global society. The critique of capitalism aims unambiguously at its transcendence. That means it must be prepared to transcend modernity when it is construed as a symbol for capitalism. To achieve this transcendence, the critique of capitalism must also put forward alternative rules for social organization, along with alternative values. In short, it has to present an alternative system of rationality. Does this mean the critique of capitalism will, like capitalism before it, inevitably be tempted to present the new rationality of its own as an eternal construct? I think this can be avoided.

But has the critique of capitalism truly outgrown the existing framework of bourgeois thought? That is the question. For the moment, this cannot be clearly answered. The new critique is still incomplete. It needs to be deepened and enriched with insights gained from interacting with new challenges thrown up by the very development of capitalism. Initially focused on moral values, the critique of capitalism reached its decisive stage in the work of Karl Marx. At that juncture, Marxism went through a series of gradual developments under the Second and Third Internationals. Along the way, it assimilated the economistic bias of bourgeois theory, yielded to the lure of its deterministic vision, and thus turned the "laws of history" into a set of implacable rules identical in kind to the laws of the physical universe. Marxism thus reached the point of advocating, in the name of socialism, a utopian system of rationalized management based on a knowledge of these laws and, in that process, threw the dialectic of human freedom in the dustbin of history.

Marxism, then, is obviously incomplete by any measure. Nevertheless, it would be totally unjust to reduce it to a particular form, that of Soviet ideology, which I have long considered to be closer to bourgeois ideology than to Marxism.

The critique of capitalism antedated the faddish critique now offered by postmodernist theoreticians. The point is to judge whether postmodern theory contributes any fresh insights. I regard postmodernism as an intellectual nonstarter, in the sense that, beyond its hype, it offers no conceptual instruments capable of transcending the capitalist framework, nor does it demonstrate any capacity to inspire an innovative design for social change. In short, the postmodernist critique is less radical than the critique whose seminal ideas were put forward in Marx's work.

No doubt, the exercises in the deconstruction of discourse, whereby Lyotard, Derrida, Deluze, Guattari, Foucault, and Baudrillard laid the groundwork for postmodernism (in the form advocated by American scholars and by Touraine in France), did serve some useful purpose. They had the merit of exposing the metaphysical nature of both post-Enlightenment bourgeois discourse and its extension in the prevailing schools of socialist thought. They laid bare the essentialist bias of that discourse—that is to say, its option in favor of metaphysical explanations in its search for the absolute. They shed light on its economistic prejudices, which subordinated every aspect of social life to the imperatives of economic rationality. They made explicit its implicit teleological thrust, according to which historical laws work with implacable rigidity in the steady forward march of Progress.

The insights of such postmodernists may therefore look fresh to readers previously impressed by the assumptions of bourgeois essentialism, economism, and teleology. For those who have never swallowed such assumptions, however, they represent nothing fresher than another trip along the boundaries of bourgeois thought. And on that journey the pioneer was Marx.

Postmodernist thinkers rediscovered the fact that the Enlightenment did not liberate humanity. From the standpoint of the precise strain of Marxist thinking that I share, that is merely axiomatic. Our school of Marxist theory highlights the realization that the economistic alienation peculiar to bourgeois ideology (including its so-called socialist variants) is an extension of and a functional surrogate for the metaphysical alienation typical of past world-views, in the same way that capitalist exploitation is an extension of and a functional surrogate for tributary exploitation. So when Lyotard says Auschwitz and Stalin meant the failure of the modernist dream, he left out the word *capitalist.* Imperialism and its virulent offspring, fascism, along with world wars and colonial massacres, are all precisely products of sharpening contradictions within the capitalist system, measures of the conflict between the promises of freedom it offers and its inability to deliver commensurate improvements. The Soviet ideology itself, with its economistic vision focused on "catching up" (which signified, in my opinion, a dream of capitalism without capitalists), was a variant of bourgeois ideology. As Maoist thinkers predicted thirty-five years ago, it was scheduled in the course of its natural development to lead to "normal" capitalism. Events of the past several years, themselves hardly surprising, have borne this out.

The postmodernist critique, pitched short of the radical perspectives attained by Marxist thought, fails to provide the tools needed to transcend capitalism. For that reason, its propositions remain ambiguous, hazy. Its penchant for the uncritical adulation of difference and the glorification of empiricism makes it quite compatible with conventional economistic management designed to perpetuate capitalist practices, still considered the definitive expression of rationality. That leaves the way open to neoconservative communalist ideologies of the kind common in Anglo-Saxon traditions of social management. In extreme cases, it may also lead to nihilistic explosions. Either way, the result is an ideology compatible with the interests of the privileged, those whom Galbraith, in his brilliant analysis, calls the "haves."

Still, the emphasis on the need for democracy is far from pointless. It might, in fact, turn out to be an effective stimulus for new advances in the theoretical and practical critique of capitalism, assuming the concept of democracy is understood in all its dynamic scope. Workers' struggles gave depth and meaning to democracy in past times; in much the same way, we should not overlook the possibility that the struggle for democracy might impart a progressive spin to the course of coming events. That is a hope shared by a substantial section of the postmodernist school. It is not my intention to accuse them of harboring "evolutionary" illusions doomed to frustration from the start. For I maintain that the dichotomy established between evolution, misconstrued as betrayal, and revolution, presented as the sole acceptable path of socialist transition, was a specific result of circumstances linked to the world wars and the Russian Revolution, not a logical inference drawn from the radical critique of capitalism. In the particular conditions of the time, such an interpretation might have reflected reality accurately enough. But what began as an expedient interpretation was subsequently raised to the level of an absolute principle by vulgar Marxists—an unwarranted shift. Similarly, the role assigned to the working class under the objective conditions created by capitalism at an earlier stage of its development now needs to be revised in the light of changes in the capitalist system resulting from the interplay of social forces both in their national environments and on a world scale. For some time now, strategies for a revolutionary break with capitalism have been pushed backstage. That does not mean there is no longer any need to transcend the capitalist system. All it means is that the time is ripe for the design of new strategies sophisticated enough to encompass current changes within the capitalist system itself.

The fact remains that the rejection of Marxism is fashionable these days. To facilitate such rejection, Marxism is first reduced to its Soviet manifestation and then is condemned for "explanatory overkill," by which is meant a tendency to explain reality in terms of a deterministic scheme that makes every event not only explainable by but also the necessary outcome of the laws of capitalist development. Many Marxists may deserve this accusation. When leveled at Marx himself, however, it is patently unjust.

Meanwhile, the issue of the relation between the economic and non-economic spheres—that is to say, of links between politics and culture—remains unsettled, both within the Marxist framework as it has been developed so far and within other frameworks, including the postmodernist scheme. The economistic idea according to which culture adjusts to economic imperatives does not come from Marx. Instead, it reflects prevalent bourgeois ideological perceptions from the Enlightenment to this day. But the contrary notion of cultures as nucleic constants, peddled by now modish cultural pluralists—some of them simply Eurocentic, some reverse Eurocentrists—seems to me even less tenable in the face of reality. What, then, of a middle position between these extremes, dictated perhaps by prudence? How satisfactory might it be, and how would it operate? The fact is that certain thinkers in the past have adopted just such an attitude yet shed no useful light on the issue. Weber is a good example. His theses, in particular those on the Protestant ethic and the rise of capitalism, seem to me to be rather unconvincing.

Similarly, the issue of the dynamics of social conflict, a simpler problem at first glance, has within the Marxist tradition itself continued to raise questions eluding definitive answers. How, for example, does a class *in* itself turn into a class *for* itself? On this issue, Lenin advanced a set of propositions asserting that theory is imported into the working class from external sources, an argument that others have characterized as non-Marxist. And how, for instance, does Gramsci's stratum of organic intellectuals emerge? Needless to say, any progress in solving these problems presupposes advances in the understanding of relationships among the economic, political, and cultural spheres. Here again, we might choose to stay on solid empirical ground and observe the many "social actors," to use the term in vogue. We might note that their plans, implicit or explicit, are piecemeal and cover domains different from one another; that there is no way to predict whether they will complement each other or clash, whether they are feasible or utopian; and that, for these reasons, the outcome of their confrontations is impossible to forecast.

Thus formulated, all of this is axiomatic. But it seems to me illogical to argue from these premises that social movements, because they are vectors of social change and because they express the aspirations of real human groups, all deserve respect and support in the spirit of democratic equity. Why should we respect and support any group if we have no idea where its plans may lead? Why exclude the possibility that established regimes may manipulate them? It seems to me that many of the ethnic claims advanced these days are subject to manipulation by governments more concerned with crisis management than with solving underlying problems. Such governments may manipulate a people's right to self-determination, not to increase their freedom, but rather to curtail it. And the option of "activism in the service of movements," an approach supposedly based on the analysis of social actors, carries the risk of an antitheoretical bias no less dangerous than its opposite, the prejudice of dogmatic theory.

2. Social theory comprises a range of loosely integrated skills and methods applicable to the analysis of social reality. The epistemological status of these disciplines varies widely from field to field. In economics, the prevailing obsession with management has imposed an agenda of specific issues, a selective approach to significant data, and a tunnel vision of reality narrowly focused on management goals. True, such options sometimes enhance efficiency. But then the so-called science of economics implies a latent ideological option that legitimates the kind of management involved and, by extension, the social system it perpetuates, the capitalist system. For that reason,

the discipline of economics sidesteps more basic issues related to social change and historical development, assigning them to the free play of imaginative thinking, a process it considers unscientific.

Marx sought, successfully I think, to expose the alienation engendered by capitalist society, by whose workings "economic laws" are supposed to operate "as inexorably as" natural laws and thus give to the regulation of the system a certain efficacy. He shifted the range of issues considered from this narrow domain to the much broader domain of social change. But this shift did not keep the Marxian tradition from developing an approach close to that of the economistic school in the definition of its problems.

In any case, the radical critique of capitalism formulated by Marx did not provide a guide for the regulation of a society liberated from economism. These questions present themselves as soon as radical movements seize power and begin to build socialism. The ambiguity of their project—socialism? or catching up with advanced capitalism?—is inherent in the objective conditions of their problem. The legitimation of the choices made by appealing to rationality (constructing a society regulated according to the principles of reason) had already been raised in the critiques that Engels addressed to the German social democrats, calling the whole project "capitalism without capitalists."

In my opinion, these questions are still unresolved. The global polarization inherent in capitalism implies long projects of transition that confront the double task, in part contradictory, of developing the forces of production and of constructing alternative social relations of production. The debate on these questions is therefore far from over.

Social thought, in short, cannot be kept within the narrow confines in which the economistic school would like to keep it. But understanding society in the totality of its movement cannot be kept separate from the desire to orient its development in one direction or another. Ideology (the value system underpinning the advocacy of a particular social program) and science (knowledge of the objective factors that bring about change) are here inseparable. I think, for example, that the concept of development is an ideological concept defined by the type of society the development process is to bring into being. And as I have tried constantly to make clear, development should not be confused with the realities of the modern world, which are geared, not to development, but rather to the expansion of capitalism. The blend of science and ideology practiced by the ideologues, politicians, and officials connected with the development in question is, in fact, the capitalist option that underlies their project. Similarly, the feminists have completely exposed the ideological basis of established social "science." They have shown how, through their definition of issues and their choice of ideology, the social disciplines manage to push feminist questions outside the framework of investigation.

The foregoing reflections, in turn, call for the clear differentiation of social thinkers according to the class perspectives driving their work. On the one hand are those whom Galbraith calls the "haves." From their viewpoint, all society needs is managers capable of changing the capitalist system in positive directions still to be defined. Anything beyond that is a public danger. On the other hand are those who say society's overriding need is for critical thinking leading to a better understanding of the mechanisms of change, and they are able to influence such changes in ways that free society from capitalist alienation and its tragic consequences. As far as the overwhelming majority of humanity—the peoples of Asia, Africa, and Latin America—are concerned, this need is vital because they experience actually existing capitalism as nothing short of savagery.

The distinction I propose here, then, separates those whom I call operatives, serving the established ideological apparatus, from the intelligentsia proper. The latter have no impact except to the extent that they are critical and competent. In other words, they have to be capable of inspiring liberating action within a sustained program of linked theory and practice. From this perspective, an assessment of Third World intellectuals ought to start from an analysis of the relationship between their confrontation with "actually existing capitalism" and the orientations of the actions inspired by their work. I shall return later to a more concrete interpretation of what I propose here.

3. Now that the critique of development has become a live issue, I think the time has come to examine the types of criticism leveled at the concept and practice of postwar development; to conduct a critical assessment of theories, concepts, and practices attendant on the process now in its crisis-ridden state; to review new analytical techniques used by these critics; and to evaluate the strategies they propose.

Critiques of development fall into two schools. According to the first, in the balmy days from the 1950s to the 1970s the experience of development, however uneven, was, on the whole, positive. Since then, the process has stalled. The point is therefore to kick-start it once more. According to these critics, the cause of the stall is the general crisis affecting the developed centers of the world economy. Some trace the root of this crisis to excessively nationalistic development policies incompatible with the imperatives of globalization. Others see the problem as the result of the combined impact of the two processes. Obviously, such critics consider development coterminous with the worldwide expansion of capitalism, although some would add that capitalist expansion needs to be channeled along adequate policy guidelines. In short, such criticism remains bounded within the managerial approach.

The critics of an opposite school think the development process under discussion is in crisis because it has defaulted on its promises; because it has led to increasingly unequal patterns of income distribution between the societies on this planet and within the societies in the periphery of the system, in the process worsening the poverty and marginalization of the disadvantaged instead of integrating all social strata into a steadily inclusive and more stable system; and because it has produced a dangerous waste of nonrenewable resources and caused a horrific devastation of the environment. My concerns coincide largely with such critiques. It might be helpful at this stage, then, to point out that articulate criticism of the development ethos antedated the crisis of the 1980s. And that brings us to the need to recapitulate the ideas of critics of the development process in its heyday.

I am well aware that current criticisms of past critiques of development vary in type and scope and that any attempt to pare them down to a few general statements will only compromise the clarity of ongoing debates. I shall do my best not to overgeneralize. It seems to me, however, that quite often our critics present summaries of our arguments lumped together under the general rubric "neo-Marxism in recent decades," which they present as a body of thought in a state of crisis. As a matter of fact, our critics have themselves been members of one or another such "neo-Marxist" school, and the criticisms and self-criticisms advanced by some of them have been inspired by the same preoccupations as in the past.

In this recurrent presentation, neo-Marxist schools of thought are classified under three main categories, depending on whether their theoretical emphasis is on modes of production, dependency, or the world system. The analyses presented are, of course, varied, with emphasis differing from author to author. But I confess that I am in agreement with many of the criticisms raised against these neo-Marxist schools. I think, for instance, the perennial fine-tuning of concepts related to modes of production is the expression of a donnish obsession with detail. Further, it seems to me that theories developed within the framework of dependency or that of the world system have sometimes been mechanistic, economistic, and deterministic. My list of reservations could go on and on.

Valid as these reservations are, however, I think no purpose is served by carrying them too far. It would be more useful to keep a clear focus on what, in my view, are the important contributions of the neo-Marxist thinking under discussion. One such achievement is the highlighting of links between the national and world spheres. All subsequent modifications of this theoretical insight have shown it was of vital importance and served as an antidote to the naive approaches of the ideologues and theorists of both the bourgeois and the dominant Marxist schools.

That said, let me point out that I do not see my own work as belonging to any of these "schools." My constant focus on historical materialism, understood in its totality and with special reference to the history of and the transition to capitalism, and my criticism of the economistic and Eurocentric vision of dominant meta-theories in these fields were at least an expression of a determination to avoid the kinds of faults now imputed—sometimes justifiably—to the neo-Marxist schools: their economistic and essentialist bias, their often sophomoric and dogmatic interpretations of Marxism, and their teleological tendencies, particularly obvious in the Soviet strain of vulgar Marxism.

The gist of my critique of the critical corpus, however, falls outside the scope of so-called theoretical works. Social thought is inseparable from the practical work it inspires. I would therefore rather examine and reexamine statements and analyses put forward within the framework of theoretical and policy connections on which they rested within the environment in which they were formulated. This was the task I set for myself in a recent reexamination of "The Unfolding and Erosion of the Bandung Plan" in my *Re-Reading the Postwar Period,* in which I emphasized the challenges facing theoretical thinkers on account of real-life conflicts. In this framework, there is no way anyone can overlook Soviet formulations, the rival formulations of Maoism, and the ambiguous stances of radical populist Third World nationalism, which has, alas, petered out entirely. I find this intellectual penury deplorable, and I think it is an outcome of the ivory-tower nature of most of these criticisms. I think a further contributing factor has been the U-turn executed by many Western left intellectuals in their retreat from a characteristically naive enthusiasm for the Third World to a pro-imperialist stance now hardly distinguishable from Third World bashing.

The main argument used in this self-criticism of Third World advocacy is that, given the wide range of developmental paths, it was foolhardy to insist on comprehensive assessments of capitalism on a world scale, to focus on the contrast between centers and peripheries, to highlight imperialism, and so forth. That supposedly was the fatal flaw in Marxism, shared by neo-Marxism as well. The diverse reality in question necessarily called for a subtly differentiated analysis capable of accounting seriously for internal circumstances governing the development of each society at all levels (economic, political, cultural) and thus determining the evolution—progressive or regressive—of each society within the world system.

Formulated thus, the argument strikes me as a truism. At no point in the analyses have I claimed that the worldwide expansion of capitalism leveled all differences. Quite the contrary: all efforts were focused on analyzing the nature and scope of differentiations occurring in the process of that expansion, the particular or national aspects of reality. The acknowledgment of diversity, perfectly normal in itself, does not absolve us from the parallel necessity to recognize the general, for in the absence of the general, diversity is meaningless. The real issue raised by diversity lies elsewhere, and it is often misperceived by the critics referred to here: Does modernization within the capitalist framework lead to "catching up"—that is to say, to the abolition of worldwide polarization? And if so, does the outcome depend on internal (national) conditions?

Now, as in the past, implicitly or explicitly, the question draws two contradictory responses. Yes, according to some; no, according to others. I share the latter view. Meanwhile, these polar positions take on new forms, in keeping with the new configuration of the capitalist system, different from that of the postwar boom years (1945-1990).

Other critiques are set in a framework fundamentally different from the Marxist and neo-Marxist traditions and in fundamental disagreement with them. Postmodernist criticism belongs in this category. As a matter of fact, it would be accurate to say the Third World does not interest postmodernist thinkers because they see it as a mere collection of "backward" states, in line with the bourgeois worldview, past and present. Some postmodernists are in the habit of projecting trends they discern in the developed world onto social movements in the peripheral countries. In my opinion, their extrapolations have little to do with reality. Far from expressing a rejection of modernity, the movements in question are, in fact, the consequence of the shattering of the promise of real modernization, a failure typical of peripheral capitalism.

The various development strategies, often hyped as new when the only novelty they possess is their packaging, remain vague and short on credibility. The repeated calls for democracy, given a high profile in contemporary discourse by practically unanimous consent, are certainly a positive change. It should at least help demolish such wrongheaded but widespread prejudices as the supposition that democracy follows automatically from development. For those of us who see *development* as a shorthand term for a progressive social design, the democratization of society is, by definition, an integral part of the development process. Without it, the liberation and empowerment of the people are only empty words.

Agreement with this viewpoint, however, does not mean the problem is solved. Beyond that, we need to analyze the practical ways in which peripheral capitalism acts as an objective obstacle in the path to democracy. That, incidentally, is why antidemocratic prejudices have characterized the approaches not only of so-called socialist technocrats but also of overtly capitalist establishments, a clear indication that real development clashes with the imperatives of capitalist expansion. Last, we have to be able to design practical action programs linking democratization with social advancement, with sufficient courage to deal boldly with the thrust of capitalist expansion. (This is the option I call *delinking*.)

Other strategic options currently in fashion, such as advances in women's liberation, increased cultural awareness, and concern with the environment, are undeniably important on their merits. Unfortunately, rhetorical outpourings on these issues are still often ambiguous and superficial. Development agencies have become extraordinarily clever in handling these issues, changing their rhetoric without ever challenging established regimes. There is constant talk of "women in development," of "respect for cultural values," and of "sustainable development." But rarely does anyone take the trouble to conduct a preliminary analysis of relationships nurtured by the expansionist capitalist system as far as male and female roles, extant cultural values, or the reproduction of the natural conditions of production are concerned.

Any design for development as a liberating process is bound to bring up extremely complex issues in these areas. And the typical evasive arrogance of development managers is a totally inadequate response. Here, too, the connection between the universal (especially the universalistic objective of worldwide transition) and the particular (which defines the stages of transition) raises a series of theoretical and practical dilemmas. Instead of facing them, development managers simply and shamelessly sidestep these problems with their rhetoric.

Under these conditions, strategic proposals put forward in scattershot fashion run a high risk of getting turned into simple crisis-management stratagems instead of serving as pointers to the resolution of the crisis. The risk is especially high because the managerial elites are not above manipulating potentially progressive but incoherently organized proposals and turning them into slogans helpful to the established regimes.

4. My intention, then, is to examine the analyses and strategies put forward by the Third World intelligentsia during the past several decades, interpret them, and thus clarify linkages between them and the real-life stakes involved in the liberation struggles of the time. I intend to conduct a similar assessment of the debate about ongoing transformations on the scale of the world system and of the various African systems as a way of identifying pointers to new stakes and appropriate strategies.

I propose an analysis of the half century following the Second World War as a long phase in the expansion of ascendant capitalism. That analysis will be founded on three bases: (a) the national social-democratic compromise in the developed Western countries, (b) the Soviet design for catching up with the West within a framework of disengagement, and (c) the bourgeois nationalist scheme to which I have given the name *Bandung Project* (see *Re-Reading the Postwar Period*). The steady erosion of the systems built on these bases, culminating in their collapse, has led to a phase of long-term structural crisis on a world scale. Meanwhile, the deepening process of globalization, which caused the erosion of the now outmoded systems in the first place, has resulted in a new definition of worldwide capitalist polarization. By the same token, it has defined the parameters of new challenges facing those committed to liberation struggles.

Within this framework, it is necessary to reexamine the analyses and strategies put forward by the Third World and African intelligentsia in the postwar period as expressions of the process I call "the unfolding and erosion of the Bandung Plan." That plan entailed a bourgeois nationalist modern-ization scheme designed to lead to the construction of relatively endocentric and industrialized national interdependence on the world scale, as opposed to the Soviet framework of disengagement. Needless to say, there were numerous variations on this plan, depending on internal factors, in particular the degree of radicalization of the anti-imperialist liberation front, in much the same way as achievements in the liberation struggle, as measured by effective industrialization and competitivity, have turned out to be uneven, depending on internal and external factors.

The way I see it, throughout the past half century the main divide between the principal opponents in this debate on the Third World and Africa was defined by the following question: Was the plan workable? In other words, would it facilitate the establishment of modern national capitalist societies striving to "catch up" with the advanced societies within a framework of interdependence on the world scale? Or was it utopian in the degree to which the objective sought would have necessarily required a radicalization of the plan that would carry it beyond the capitalist logic that had inspired it? Some asserted that the national bourgeoisie still had a historic mission to fulfill; others argued that this was an illusion. I was of the latter school, and I think history proved us right.

So, the time has come to define the challenges afresh on the basis of the achievements chalked up during the so-called development decades, while taking due account of the new configuration of the global system.

5. I propose, then, to analyze the diversity of what used to be called the Third World by using the capacity of the various partners in the system as a basic criterion. On this basis, the peripheral societies fall into two distinct categories. On the one hand are those whose manufactured products have achieved a competitive edge in the world market. On the other hand are those that, either because they still have not entered the industrial age or because their industries are still far from having achieved a competitive potential, remain trapped in the role of exporters of raw material, prisoners of an outmoded division of labor.

The first group comprises the countries of East Asia, Latin America, and to a lesser extent, India and Southeast Asia. In the jargon of development managers, these are the "real developing countries," meaning they are seriously engaged in catching up with the developed societies. In my opinion, they constitute the real periphery of the emerging world system. The pattern of their industrialization resembles a gigantic subcontracting enterprise controlled from countries at the center of the system and working through what I identify as the five new monopolies, which enable the latter group of countries to polarize the world for their exclusive benefit. The second group, comprising all of Africa north and south and sometimes referred to as the "Fourth World," faces the prospect of further marginalization in the new world order.

The various ideologies and strategies proffered by ruling regimes are the means they use to manage the crisis of the emergent system. Their management style leans heavily on a patchwork of rhetoric gleaned from disparate sources, haphazardly buttressed with arguments of varying degrees of validity, most of them presenting a moral veneer, all recycled in the service of the existing regime. For example, in the name of constructing a world system, attempts are made to justify using the United Nations as a fig leaf while beating down the states on the world's periphery that are incapable of resisting the onslaught of the world market. In the name of the environment, societies of the center accuse peripheral states of waste while they themselves are strengthening their monopoly over access to global resources and reaffirming their right to waste them.

It is the duty of the intelligentsia, especially those of the Third World and Africa, to "deconstruct" the new justificatory rhetoric and thus lay bare its functional connections with the tactical and strategic objectives of crisis management. We cannot do this, however, as long as we cling to time-worn formulas left in the dust by the renewed thrust of the world system. We need, therefore, here and now, to seize the progressive democratic issues now given a high profile in order to give the attention and the thinking focused on them a radical spin.

If the intelligentsia fail to do this, the cycle of spontaneous and inadequate reactions from the peoples crushed by the new worldwide polarization is bound to continue, and the energies will just as surely be harnessed by the dominant regimes in their determination to manage the crisis. I have in mind here the various ethnic and communal forces, the nostalgic cultural revivalists, and especially the religious antiquarians active these days, whose devastating impact, notably in the disillusioned Fourth World, has taken on such tragic dimensions.

In the face of these crisis-management ideologies and strategies, the intelligentsia ought to respond with alternative proposals offering real solutions to the crisis. I have no intention of offering ready-made nostrums. Still, I think it useful to outline in recapitulative form a few basic concepts that could help reshape effective strategies for resolving the crisis and prepare the ground for a people's international robust enough to deal effectively with the world-devouring appetite of capital. These suggestions would presuppose inputs from all levels, from the grass roots to the states, regions, and world system as a whole.

Their implementation would require the creation, perhaps in gradual stages, of anticomprador fronts in the peripheral societies because comprador-based social alliances are precisely those that fit into the capitalist design for a new world order. It would also call for programs aimed at restructuring the states capable of meeting the challenge, for there is no way monopolies over technology, finance, raw materials, the media, and weapons of mass destruction identified earlier can be broken without the creation in a major regional environment of a political, cultural, and military power strong enough to meet the challenge. The objectives of democratization linked with social advancement for the ordinary classes, with respect for ethnic, religious, and other differences coupled with the promotion of freedom and diversity in these areas, could provide a starting point for such a necessary reconstruction. In Africa, it is time to breathe new life into the concepts of pan-Africanism and pan-Arabism, pushed off the center stage by the earlier successes of the "development" process, now that the hollowness of those past successes is so clear.

Last, at the level of the world system, the struggle should aim at a reconstruction based on the negotiated creation of major regional blocs strong enough to meet current challenges. This reconstruction would cover the economic sphere: exchange connections and new international monetary, financial, scientific, technological, commercial, and environmental institutions designed to replace the World Bank, the International Monetary Fund, the General Agreement on Trade and Tariffs, the Agreement on Patents and Copyright, and so on. It would also be involved in political organization. For that reason, the role of the United Nations would have to be renegotiated in a process I see as a new multipolar strategy of delinking.

These proposals will, no doubt, be glibly dismissed as utopian. Utopian they certainly are, in the common sense of the word, meaning they look forward to changes toward which current trends will not necessarily lead. But in a sense they are far from utopian, because the first steps in this direction would trigger a virtuous cycle leading in their direction. Put differently, the utopia under discussion is a positive, creative one. But in any case, in the absence of such positive utopias, the peoples of the world invariably react to their desperate circumstances by reviving other types of utopias. Hence, the surge of enthusiasm for fundamentalist religious movements. The difference is that those other utopias are dangerous because they are inherently backward-looking. Worse still, the religious utopias are ineffective because their inherently culture-bound focus makes them perfectly compatible with supine capitulation to the imperatives of the capitalist world order.

The same critics who will dismiss my proposals as utopian will, as usual, keep intoning "there is no alternative"—the TINA syndrome. This position is absurd and criminal. All situations have alternatives. This is the very meaning of the concept of human freedom. It is amusing to see managerial types who dismiss Marxism as unduly deterministic preferring this other, vulgar determinism. Moreover, the social design they seek to defend with this argument— the market-based management of the world system—is utopian in the worst sense of the term, doomed to fall apart under the pressure of its own highly explosive charge.

6. In the current state of the world, the intelligentsia face a new set of daunting responsibilities. In previous phases of Africa's history, during the national liberation struggle and later during the "development decades," they fulfilled their mission quite honorably. In those days, committed academics struggled with and made a rich and fruitful contribution to the progressive forces. Admittedly, their work then was made easier by the fact that the intelligentsia could count on support from national liberation parties or from progressive forces making constructive contributions in the period after achieving independence. In other words, they were backed by real, organized social and political forces. Unfortunately, at times such connections engendered dangerous illusions and led to subsequent backsliding.

We live now in a different configuration. The ruling classes, misnamed the "elites," rationalize their collaboration with the scheme for the worldwide expansion of capitalism, which makes their people underdogs, in terms of "Afro-pessimism," a set of negative attitudes they affect in common with the managerial functionaries of the world system. Cut adrift from these false elites, the ordinary classes try to cope as best they can, sometimes coming up with creative feats in their daily struggles for survival. Meanwhile, the intelligentsia seem absent from the fray. It is high time they took back their rightful position.

Clearly, the crisis will not be resolved until popular democratic forces capable of dominating society get together again. But all effective hegemony depends on the presence of ideological and strategic instruments. It is the mission of the intelligentsia to establish bonds between their own productive thinking and the aspirations and actions of the popular classes and thus to make them social partners. If this is not done, each is doomed to social isolation.

Needless to say, in this first phase of reconstruction, the relevant task is not the immediate taking of power. The task ahead is first and foremost the reconstruction of the social power of the popular classes that has been eroded by the ongoing crisis.

REFERENCES

Amin, S. (1991). The ancient world systems versus the modern capitalist system. *Review, 14*(3), 349-386.
Amin, S. (1992). Capitalism and the world system. *Sociology and Societies, 2.*
Amin, S. (1994). *Re-reading the postwar period: An intellectual itinerary.* New York: Monthly Review Press.
Frank, A. G. (1962). Mexico: The janus faces of twentieth-century bourgeois revolution. *Monthly Review, 14,* 7.

4

⊞

Pathways Toward a Global Anthropology

ERIC R. WOLF

I am writing these lines to mark Andre Gunder Frank's sixty-fifth birthday and to congratulate him on that occasion. Gunder received his training in economics; my background is in anthropology. Yet, I have tried to relate my anthropology to an understanding of economic development, and Gunder has engaged issues of major significance for anthropological theory and practice. Gunder Frank has delineated the global processes of accumulation; here, I address the issues confronting an anthropology that wants to study the processes drawing societies and cultures into global relationships.

The first thing to note in such an endeavor is that we must not deceive ourselves into thinking we are about to discover something wholly new; this view of the task has always been implicit in the definition of anthropology as the comparative study of humankind. Indeed, some issues posed by a global anthropology have been around since the beginning of the discipline. Evolutionary perspectives assumed a unity of humankind and a unitary career for humanity that bound ancestors—past and contemporary—to their ever-improving descendants. The evolution of human culture was envisaged as a linear movement through successive stages or typological thresholds leading from primitive simplicity to civilized complexity. Each crossing of such a threshold opened a new innovative phase of enhanced complexity. Each particular society and culture was then treated as an independent example of cultural attainment and was slotted into its appropriate position on the ladder of progress. Once placed in this position, it could serve as a representative and illustrative example of thresholds crossed, positions attained, and accomplishments still to be faced and to be accomplished.

The diffusionists who followed criticized the conception of a linear route from initial ancestral brutishness to the achievement of civilization by the filial descendants. They cast grave doubts on the standard method of assigning present-day culture-bearing populations to the appropriate hierarchical and progressive rungs on the ladder of progress. They invoked instead the various phenomena of contact, interaction, exchange, and mutual learning among the various cultures past and present. There was a realization of a measure of commonality among humans, but seen this time as building up a multiplicity of cultures out of cultural donations proffered, accepted, or rejected. Many diffusionists did not reject evolutionary perspectives as such but, rather, made evolutionary pathways conditional on the accumulation and recombination of culture elements in the course of interaction in particular times and spaces. Evolutionary processes, leading to increased control of energy or producing more complex organization, came to be understood as outcomes of interactive relationships, not as independent breakthroughs by isolated societies with wholly self-enclosed cultures. The diffusionists saw cultures and societies as located in culture areas, in *oikumenes*, in interactive clusters, and in interaction spheres, and social and cultural processes as dependent on wide-ranging interaction. In a major way, present-day efforts at conceiving a global anthropology must build on the contributions of these much-maligned ancestors.

Put in another way, the evolutionists focused on the grand outcomes but gave little thought to the processes that led to these results; the diffusionists, in their turn, emphasized interaction as the source of culture change and culture growth. In their own time, each saw the other as an opponent. In our time, we can synthesize their contributions; both perspectives are required to construct a viable global anthropology. To do so, we should pay attention not just to the *fact* that cultures are made and re-made but also to the *how* of culture making. We have to understand that the processes of cultural construction and change respond to ever-changing and -shifting interactive contexts, at once ecological, social, economic, political, military, and ideational. Cultures are shaped by these contexts, react to them, incorporate these reactions, and carry these effects on even as they go forward to the encounter of new interactive contexts. The analysis of the single case needs to be placed in its surrounding situations and scenarios. Even instances of evolutionary advance or transformation must be understood as outcomes of interaction, and not as idiosyncratic breakthroughs.

If diffusionism arose as a critical response to linear evolutionary schemata, the functionalism that followed unfolded in a critique of diffusionism. The functionalists reacted against what they called "conjectural history" projected by studying the geographical distribution of culture traits. They wanted to see societies and cultures as comprehensively integrated systems answering to human needs, psychobiological, jural, or political. We still applaud their criticism of conjectural historical reconstruction, but we now also know that it has become possible to uncover important aspects of the past through disciplined use of documentary texts and oral testimony. We can now do history that allows us to understand much better than before how the peoples of the world were drawn into more extensive political, economic, and ideational relations with one another.

As a result, we can see more clearly the limitations of the extreme initial functionalist position that declared that because doing history was impossible, one should study each society and culture only synchronically and do this by visualizing it as a quasi-organism in which all elements were held in a tight functional embrace. Indeed, only the initial generation of functionalists insisted so wholeheartedly on the study of social structures or cultures in isolation. Later functionalists (e.g., Max Gluckman in Zambia; Edmund Leach in Burma; J. P. S. Uberoi in New Guinea) soon widened their vision to include more extensive intersystemic fields. We do owe the functionalists a major debt for teaching us methods through which functional relations can be ascertained. For us today, however, viewing social and cultural arrangements against the backdrop of flux and upheaval caused by global processes, integration should always be demonstrated before it can be assumed.

Yet, locating societies and cultures in interaction spheres and looking for the ways these arrangements cohere to some degree and for some measure of time is also not yet enough. Only in the rarest instances do interaction spheres occur in complete isolation from others. Generally, they are drawn together into larger networks, lattices, or zonations. Narrower spheres of interaction connect with wider spheres, and macrospheres with superspheres, and an adequate understanding must come to terms with these connections. This is not a new idea, but it needs emphasis. A hamlet in Yucatan is part of a larger municipality, and that municipality forms part of a state and a national entity;

marketing arrangements connect people in the hamlets and villages with towns and metropolises and with the continentwide trade spheres; people from the little village migrate to Guadalajara and Mexico City, but I also meet them in Chicago and New York. First radio and then television greatly enlarged the scale and scope of communication. In consequence, life patterns in the hamlet also change and differentiate as the sons and daughters of the village combine older resources initially drawn mainly from home with new resources encountered elsewhere, in different settings, controlled by unfamiliar power brokers and elites.

We need to remind ourselves that this point was raised more than sixty years ago when anthropologists began to extend their endeavors of participant observation and interviewing to hamlets, villages, and towns in complex, modern societies. Robert Redfield first explored in Mexico the relation between the folk in Tepoztlan with the "city," embodied for him in La Capital. He then (1955) went beyond this simple dualism to consider more differentiated arrangements of communities within communities, of wholes within wholes. And he sought, in the last decades of his life, to deal with entire civilizations, especially with the social and spatial distribution of their distinctive cultural systems of communication. In this endeavor, he manifests ideas of evolution moving through the successive incorporation of older and smaller "wholes" into new levels of integration (see Redfield, 1942). The idea of a succession of organizational types integrating and encompassing previously formed units also guided Julian Steward (1950) and led him to study Puerto Rico as a totality made up of several integrated parts, itself then integrated as a whole into the political economic orbit of the United States of America.

Although these approaches attained considerable sophistication and still have much to teach us, they also proved self-limiting. Their limitations owe much, I think, to the way the social sciences then justified their disciplinary autonomy by postulating a realm of the social sui generis and ascribing to social interaction a self-defining dynamic of its own. This led to treating social units—homesteads, yard groups, hamlets, villages, barrios, towns, regions, national entities—as circumscribed units defined predominantly by the social interaction taking place within them. Each such bounded scenario was conceptualized as producing a distinctive social universe of its own. Society could then be visualized all too easily as an edifice built up through the addition of such units as building blocks. And each culture could be treated similarly, as a domain of "custom" with its own dynamic and "carried" by these distinctive and bounded social units.

With this approach, one inevitably ends up with models of society or culture as static architectural entities. Exaggerating only slightly, these resemble housing projects composed of three-tiered structures. They rest on entities—villages or locations—arranged as so many compartments at ground level, in turn propping up a second floor of multi-village regions. The regions then support a third story, decked out with the trappings of national integration, the entity of the nation. The whole three-decker might then be seen as connected internally by communication channels or institutions reaching up and down, like so many stairways, elevators, and air ducts connecting level with level. Presented as such, the model remains "hollow," an architectural arrangement of numerous scenarios arranged collaterally or in tiers; we get to see the social interplay going on in each of these scenarios but do not learn what all that social interplay is about.

Julian Steward stood at the threshold between (a) a cultural ecology that sought explanations in cultural adaptations to particular environments and (b) a new problematic that might have understood the relation of local or regional ecosystems to transformative processes operating on a more encompassing scale. To make that transition, however, would have required a much more dynamic understanding of capitalist development and of the politics connected with it than he achieved in his study of Puerto Rico. A purely ecosystematic study of a sociocultural entity such as Puerto Rico inevitably emphasized the ways in which the inhabitants of the island drew energy from their particular and varied habitats. That knowledge by itself, however, would not lead you to understanding that the production of sugar or coffee or tobacco on the island might be *facilitated* by the island environment, but was not *dictated* by that environment. That particular choice of crops was governed and controlled by the operations of the capitalist market under the political aegis of the United States. It was not enough to look at production in its eco-systematic implications and consequences; under capitalism, its modus operandi is governed by a much wider, nonlocal dynamic. To understand systems like that of Puerto Rico, cultural ecology needed to come to grips with the Marxian understanding that, among humans, in contrast to societies of insects or birds, culturally constituted strategic social relations of production intervene between the environment and its occupants. These relations generate forces that do not stop at the confines of particular social scenarios, but rather reach through and beyond them. To the extent that such forces now dominate much of the world, a global anthropology must concern itself with them.

This lesson was brought home to anthropology in the late 1950s when economists, political scientists, and sociologists—notably in Latin America—began to address the issue of power differentials between entire societies, regions, communities, and of the people within them. This questioning initially took the form of *dependency theory,* which tried to address the asymmetry in markets and power between metropolitan powers and the "less developed" countries (LDCs). This attention to asymmetries in power and exchange developed in conscious contrast to current theories about the processes of modernization. Andre Gunder Frank then made a notable contribution by taking note of the enduring hierarchical and asymmetrical positioning of different coeval world regions in the global system. Frank (1966) also posed the question, only seemingly paradoxical, of what lay behind "the development of underdevelopment" in a world where everyone was supposed to be "developing." Many of us came to realize that answering Frank's question would require the development of a history oriented more toward understanding structures and less toward the elucidation of events.

The panoply of modernization theories, if theories they were, can perhaps be best understood as a revival of unilineal evolutionism. The theories, in fact, exhibited two major variants: one "Western" and capitalist, the other "Eastern" and socialist. Both versions agreed in taking West European development from feudalism to capitalism as the guiding scheme in the interpretation of history. They differed in their projection of the end stage of development: The Western variant saw capitalism as the ultimate stage of development; the Eastern model projected a transcendence of capitalism through "the building of socialism in one country." Both perspectives, however, embraced the notion that development lay in the liquidation of traditional ascriptive organizational forms that inhibited growth and change. Both sought the answer to growth and change through the development of industrialization and large-scale organization. Both saw development as the repetition in some form of the European "success story."

The two variants appeared in complementary and hostile distribution, each variant disregarding the salient conceptual focus of the other. This was especially pronounced as both versions became more "orthodox" under the imperatives of political competition. The Western variant emphasized individual choice making and mobility. It postulated an unlimited horizon of human needs that were to be satisfied through risk taking in the market. It traced social differentiation, including stratification, to choice making and risk taking in markets but disregarded issues of class structure and class hegemony in the state. The Eastern variant emphasized issues of class and class domination over the state. The range of needs was seen as limited and controllable through social and political sanction. It advocated industrialization and large-scale organization but paid little attention to the enhanced social differentiation and mobility that would accompany them. Defining politics only in terms of class, it also ignored the possibility of a competitive politics fought out among the developing interest groups.

Both variants suffered furthermore from their simplified and rigid interpretations of history. The Western variant disregarded the complex and conflict-ridden four centuries of state making and market differentiation that intervened between the "traditional" society of 14th-century feudalism and the advent of industrialism. It also excluded from its vision the interconnections of the European sphere with the socioeconomic formations on other continents. The Eastern variant oversimplified the course of development in its vision of a linear evolutionary movement through feudalism to capitalism and on to socialism, with a concomitant neglect of the complexities of interactions and developmental trajectories in all three Worlds—First, Second, and Third.

Expanding the limits of the discipline to address issues of political economy and questions of history, however, entailed a cumulative challenge for anthropology in the early 1960s. The concepts and methods of the discipline had been forged in the pursuit of participant observation among specifiable populations in demarcated localities. Now, anthropologists encountered a much larger universe of reference, characterized by much greater historical depth and much wider geographical scale. The return of evolutionary perspectives, whether in the guise of modernization theory or flying the flag of one or another Marxian variant, was one symptom of this challenge, as anthropologists were now called on to explicate the so-called Third World, presumably the world zones in which anthropology had accumulated special expertise. But they were also supposed to connect their understandings of this Third World with theories of "tradition" and "modernity" or with theories of capitalist or socialist development. They were expected to act locally but think globally; this was not easy for people trained in a highly localocentric methodology.

Just when anthropology confronted this new challenge to consider the wider implications of economics and politics in relationship to culture and society, however, it also underwent a major transformation from within. This initially occurred because of the advent of French structuralism and the influence of the work of Claude Lévi-Strauss. Anthropology had always been strongly influenced by linguistics, but what French structuralism accomplished was to install the linguistics of Ferdinand de Saussure as the guiding model for the study of culture. The notable distinction of Saussurean linguistics was that it treated language as a system or structure of signs whose ability to produce meaning was dependent on their relation to each other and not to any objects in the world outside language to which they may refer. French anthropological structuralism applied this idea to the comprehension of culture as a system of interdependent signs through which humans manage the worlds they inhabit. The world furnishes elements out of which mind constructs these systems but does not influence or determine the ways these systems are organized internally or the ways they impart meaning to the world. Thus, structuralism reversed understandings of causality that permitted explanations of the world through reference to its materiality: Culture could no longer be explained as an outcome of the human ecological relation to nature or of the ways humans organized their relation with each other. Both ecology and social organization were seen as mapped in the mind before human action could be deployed in the world. Mind created the relation of signifier to signifier and rendered it impossible to refer to anything in the real world without first going through the culturally created screen of interrelated signs. Although Lévi-Strauss formally acknowledged the "indisputable primacy of the infrastructure," the logic of this "linguistic turn" eliminated any causality outside the grip of the cultural system of signs. In this grammatological perspective on culture, there could be no "immaculate perception," as Sahlins (1985, p. 147) so quaintly put it.

Thus, just when the discipline was called on to expand its scale and scope to include more of what was going on in the world, anthropologists retreated into the study of particular cultures, this time understood not as functionally integrated quasi-organisms, but rather as independent and totalizing systems of signifiers. Each culture was now to be studied as a set of texts, rendered through such a distinctive system of mental constructions. Ironically, this coincided with an intensified surge in transnational migration, a worldwide outpouring of commodities across national boundaries, and a vast increase in the density and intensity of worldwide communication.

Ironically, also, anthropologists opted for a route into linguistics that emphasized closed and static grammatological systems and failed to heed the inspiration of an ethnography of speaking that was developing at about the same time. This emphasis on language in social action—which owes much to Bronislaw Malinowski's (1935) emphasis on language as played out in particular social contexts—has meanwhile burgeoned into a dynamic and expanding field that studies "discourse" as a necessary and important part of understanding the work of culture in social life.

Noting such ironies is not enough. We must also evaluate our intellectual tool kit, most especially how we think about "culture." First, we must really confront the logical impasse we have created for ourselves by visualizing mind as so totally determined by culture that it cannot perceive, observe, or experiment with anything in nature or in society that is beyond the limits of the sign system. Given that model of mind, there would have been no cumulative history anywhere in the world. Second, we must escape the grammatological trap by heeding theoretically sophisticated critiques of the total arbitrariness of sign systems (see Friedrich, 1979). Third, we should confront the idea of each culture as a separate master system of signifiers when it is historically evident that cultures have continuously borrowed from each other and when our ethnographic evidence demonstrates daily how boundary making is continuously challenged and upset by the ongoing interpenetration of social and cultural arrangements.

This last issue deserves emphasis. Whatever their shortcomings, and there were many, the diffusionists demonstrated for us that such interrelationship is much more common than isolation. The ethnology of Australian aborigines that so impressed the evolutionists describes wide-ranging networks of inter-marriage, exchange, and ceremonial participation. The diverse tribes of Plains Indians, studied by North American anthropologists, quickly adopted a common pattern of horse pastoralism and mounted warfare, together with common understandings of status rivalry, military honors, and dealings with the super-natural. Both New Guinea and the Northwest Coast of North America are described as regions in which men learned common ways of gaining renown through status displays and war. This work should remind us that assemblages and repertoires of cultural forms and meanings travel across group boundaries and create connections of convergent understandings even when (or perhaps because) the groups involved sometimes fight and at other times marry.

At the same time, it is also clear that these assemblages and repertoires of cultural forms and understandings are not the same for all categories of people within these groups. They differ by gender for men, women, and dually gendered berdaches; they differ by age and age set; they differ by occupational role and, within these roles, by knowledge and skill; they differ by rank and class; and so forth. These differences pose the question of what holds all these variant repertoires together. Participants in common social interaction need not share all or even most common understandings; interaction can go forward on the basis of only a few commonly understood criteria that define the frames of interaction (Wallace, 1961), as when patients interact with doctors in a medical clinic or when Cambodian gardeners interact with a homeowner in a California suburb. In "modern" cultures, a multitude of magazines are kept busy telling men how to understand women and telling women how to understand men, without ever producing an answer adequate enough to put them out of business.

This holds true not only of variations among social categories but also in response to variations in behavioral settings and contexts. Quite some time ago, some anthropologists involved in the study of North American Indian children began to refer to their "biculturation" (Polgar, 1960), their socialization in two cultures. One of these cultures was "white" and acquired in the context of school, government offices, and work; the other was "Indian" and learned in the context of home.

This kind of contextual learning and cultural acquisition has expanded and become ever more important, first with the intensification of rural-urban migration and then with the vast increase in the movement of people across national boundaries and entire continents. The migrant from Guerrero who works in a restaurant or car wash in New York returns to Chilpancingo with a repertoire of cultural understandings, some he or she learned as a child, some acquired in the course of work experience, some coming from *telenovelas* on the ubiquitous television or from tapes of fundamentalist Protestant preachers.

In 1948, Julio de la Fuente described the spread of what he called Mexican *pocho* culture to denote the cultural repertoires of socially and geographically mobile Mexicans in the U.S.-Mexico border zone; more recently, Ulf Hannerz (1987) has spoken of the growth of cultural creolization in the world, drawing the term *creole* from the simplified and composite languages that grew up to facilitate cross-cultural communication within the advancing world system of the recent centuries. Today, we are all pochos or creoles, although saying so does not yet mean that we really understand what we are saying. Raised in a tradition in which all elements of a culture were thought of as tightly interrelated, either functionally or structurally, we anthropologists are ill-prepared for situations in which cultural repertoires appear to be put together contextually, like Tinkertoys, and not like embodied forms of a unitary vision. We are all heirs to ways of thinking about cultures, especially those of the so-called primitive world, as totalities or organisms in which all aspects dove-tailed or were embedded in each other and were given comprehensive meaning through a common sign system dramatized in myth and ritual. Maybe even the "classical" anthropological cultures on which we cut our eyeteeth were never like this, but were held together rather by organizing processes of power, control, and influence that promised support in exchange for conformity and threatened loss of that support for nonperformance.

If so much of present-day cultural learning depends on situation and context, how do the resulting assemblages acquire an organized coherence? One way this issue is being raised in recent anthropology is through the concern with identity, whether defined as identity of the person of an ethnic group or of an entire nation. But identities do not swim about in the stream of social life like amoebas in fermenting banana soup. If definitions of identity involve a characterization of attributes and a drawing of boundaries around the units so defined, in contrast with other units, this must have a causal context. Moreover, we know that the search for identity varies historically, intensifying or slackening over periods of time. Thus, a major rise occurred in the demand for identity with the advent of the nation-state and the collateral development of nationalism, which hoped to create a unified and identifiable "people" out of diverse populations with distinctive identities of their own. Recently, the demand for identities has risen once again, precisely at a time when cultural repertoires are becoming again more heterogeneous, as people have responded to changes in the social division of labor, in their relation to governments, in reaction to new modes of communication.

These repertoires of cultural understandings and practices do not easily fit any traditional notion of culture as an integral and integrated set of forms and meanings. People amass repertoires in the course of their lives as they move from structural context to structural context. These repertoires will exhibit individual variation but are yet also partially shared by people who have moved and migrated through similar settings and contexts. One might call these sets of understandings and practices *cultural portfolios.* People who have learned them acquire with them also the ability to deploy contextually relevant knowledge in managing their behavior in pertinent situations.

With enhanced social and geographical mobility and intensified communication, not only have the portfolios so developed become more varied in response to the multiplication of contexts in which they are learned and dis-played, but also these contexts themselves are no longer learned and defined primarily in one-to-one personal and local interaction. Interaction is now threaded through with quite impersonal and only briefly tangent encounters in the market, in the offices of power-wielding institutions, and in the hallways of agencies that traffic in information.

Characterizing the problem in these general terms is, I fear, also not yet enough. For example, capitalist modes of production and distribution, and the politics that go with them, are reaching into many different areas of the globe. The results are fraught with contradictions not anticipated by our concepts. We are witnessing the development of new forms and processes of production that use the new information technology, explore new sources of energy, and employ new routes and systems of distribution to move their products (Rothstein & Blim, 1992). This development confronts the concentrated factory complex of earlier modes of large-scale production with the establishment of new, spatially separated locations of production and presages the return, on an organizationally higher plane, of "putting-out systems" that can combine features of factory production with that of the artisan workshop. Simultaneously, new and more flexible modes of financing are expanding well beyond the traditional core areas of capitalist production.

Socially, this expansion has led to the mobilization and recruitment of new kinds of laborers, as well as to the formation of new strata of labor recruiters, technical supervisory personnel, service trades, and financial mediators. Concentrated forms of production, in which centralized management marshalls large numbers of people, are being replaced by more dispersed and temporary organizational forms. In these new enterprises, functions are carried out by teams that now often recruit on the basis of kinship, friendship, or local acquaintance, supplemented by a pool of more casual workers, often recruited from immigrant populations. Capitalism thus expands, even as its productive base becomes more spread out and decentralized. Concomitantly, of course, cohorts of the newly unemployed join the ranks of the industrial reserve army. Thus, as social relations are reorganized in some contexts, they are simultaneously destabilized and disordered in others.

The rise of such new forms of "flexible" capitalism may simultaneously and quite paradoxically enhance appeals to a seemingly primordial, "ethnic" solidarity, even while mobilizing human resources for action in an intensifying capitalism. More segmented social and cultural scenarios may also give rise to a local or regional politics opposed to the demands of centralized governments that "tax and spend" the resources that people in the home domain want to retain for their own purposes.

This is, of course, where we cannot advance the cause of a global anthropology without breaking out of the dilemma created for us by the grammatological option in the linguistic turn. We need to find a way of conceiving culture that allows us to deal with the realities of a political economy in which diverse and quickly changing social and cultural arrangements are brought into ever new connections with each other. These arrangements have causes and create new settings of power and production. People experience these as both constraints and opportunities and shape these experiences into portfolios that meet the challenges of shifting contextual scenarios. In the process, they also encounter classifications and identities that are forced on them or assigned to them; they incorporate or contest these impositions; and they create new definitions of who they are or who they have become as results of their travails. Thus, the construction of identities, too, needs to be visualized in the relevant contexts of power and economy if indeed we see our mission as trying to explain the world and not merely to furnish exotic entertainment.

The genesis of signifiers in the mind, as well as their interlinkages, may indeed be governed by mechanisms and processes in the brain that seek out and define contrasts and analogies, but these signifiers also have work to do. They classify people and establish categories of inclusion and exclusion, equality or hierarchy, command or followership. They are, however, neither self-evident nor self-reinforcing; they require social consensus or opprobrium, persuasion or force to guarantee their stability and effectiveness. Even Lévi-Strauss (1966, pp. 234-235) recognized that explicitly societies needed "effective procedures" to limit possibly cumulative social antagonisms. When Hawaiian women swarmed onto the deck of Captain Cook's ship to traffic with the English sailors, they were discouraged from continuing, not so much by a play of signifiers in their minds as by the arrival of a chief in his war canoe. At the same time, although it is surely the case that, in the past, cultural portfolios in particular local settings were communicated primarily through local channels and sanctioned by local authorities, expansion of the scale of power and communication has nearly everywhere brought in outside agents and agitators—regional, national, and international—whose influence rivals and often outpaces the scope and competence of local claimants to power.

If nations are now diversifying or disintegrating into "ethnic groups," surely similar questions can be asked about the identities so formed. Each ethnic group may have its characteristic "just cause" phrased in its particular portfolio of cultural signifiers. But it is incumbent on us to locate this just cause in the power scenarios and productive modes to which identity makers and identity seekers respond and in which they must operate. We do have the intellectual resources and instrumentalities in an anthropologically sophisticated economics and in an economically informed anthropology to comprehend what is going on in the world, both on the level of global processes and in more restricted domains. We do know a lot; we need to know a lot more; so there remains work for many hands to do. Among the workers in this nabob's vineyard, Andre Gunder Frank has already made notable and important contributions. We owe him a lot; we hope he will continue his work for many, many years to come.

REFERENCES

De la Fuente, J. (1948). Cambios socioculturales en Mexico [Special issue]. *Acta Anthropologica,* *3*(4).
Frank, A. G. (1966). The development of underdevelopment. *Monthly Review, 18*(4), 17-31.
Friedrich, P. (1979). The symbol and its relative non-arbitrariness. In A. S. Dil (Coord.), *Language, context, and the imagination: Essays by Paul Friedrich* (pp. 1-61). Stanford, CA: Stanford University Press.
Hannerz, U. (1987). The world in creolization. *Africa, 57,* 546-559.
Lévi-Strauss, C. (1966). *The savage mind* (La Pensée Sauvage). London: Weidenfeld & Nicolson.
Malinowski, B. (1935). *Coral gardens and their magic: Vol. 2, Part 4. An ethnographic theory of language and some practical corollaries.* New York: American Book.
Polgar, S. (1960). Biculturation of Mesquakie teenage boys. *American Anthropologist, 62,* 217-235.
Redfield, R. (1942). Introduction. In J. Cattell (Ed.), *Levels of integration in biological and social systems* (Biological Symposia Vol. 8, pp. 1-26). Lancaster, PA: Jacques Cattell.
Redfield, R. (1955). *The little community: Viewpoints for the study of a human whole.* Chicago: University of Chicago Press.
Rothstein, F., & Blim, M. (Eds.). (1992). *Anthropology and the global factory: Studies in the new industrialization in the late twentieth century.* New York: Bergin & Garvey.
Sahlins, M. D. (1985). *Islands of history.* Chicago: University of Chicago Press.
Steward, J. H. (1950). *Area research: Theory and practice* (Bulletin 63). New York: Social Science Research Council.
Wallace, A. F. C. (1961). *Culture and personality.* New York: Random House.

5

Underdevelopment: Culture and Geography

PHILIP L. WAGNER

Andre Gunder Frank has done so much to both enlighten and change the world that even a friend and admirer of many years standing, such as myself, must feel honored but somewhat unworthy to contribute to a volume addressing his achievements. Nevertheless, Gunder and I have carried on sporadically, over nearly forty years, a wide-ranging discussion of matters that bear on his quest and mine, and it appears that our viewpoints are tending toward gradual convergence. I have come to appreciate more fully the importance of both the popular movements and the long-term world-system phenomena that he has worked on of late, as well as to share his growing mistrust of grand development schemes. In turn, he pays ever more heed in his work to the ecological and geographical considerations that comprise my own stock in trade.

A geographer, at least of my old-fashioned stripe, perceives the world in a way very different from that of most economists, even of an economist so original and learned as Frank. For one thing, a fairly traditional cultural geographer of my sort feels constrained to remain quite "down to earth," fixed often on the smallest concrete details and wary of large abstractions to such an extent that particularity may simply become triviality. A good number of

AUTHOR'S NOTE: Thanks to Paul Blank for comments on an earlier draft.

my colleagues in geography, attentive to development (although less to under-development) issues, have, to be sure, made significant contributions to the study and even partial solution of problems of the poorer countries, as I discuss below, but I can hardly claim as much for myself.

Cultural geographers have tended, in general, to express in their works a dependable awareness of and indignation over the plight of most people in the regions of want that have frequently served as their sites of research. For many years, however, they were left with a sense of frustration and impotency in the face of the deprivation they saw, and they found no practical vision that might inspire them to measures of help. Their focus fell more frequently on historical and ecological than on social and economic problems. A goodly number of such geographers did, to be sure, enlist in programs of technical improve-ment of a conventional sort and secured some advances here and there. It was, though, Gunder Frank's call for radical reexamination of the "development" situation that first awakened and armed another generation of geographers and other field scholars, in my opinion, in such a way as to redirect study and practical action. Ensuing pages cite some results of that call.

Even so, the inspiration and impetus given by Gunder Frank's new con-ceptions did not fundamentally change the way the geographer sees the world or conducts research. Understanding still comes from the ground up, out of the mud or the dust of a suffering world, or the litter and fumes of indigent cities. Development and its converse must therefore represent a reality some-what different for geographers than that apparent to other scholars. A clarifica-tion of how the geographer sees development is therefore required, and this vision can be exemplified by means of a brief, final survey of some major books on the subject by geographers, which will suitably summarize the relevant literature as a whole.

THE GEOGRAPHICAL VISION

In conjunction, the map and the landscape observed define the terrain—the one attesting geography's habit of graphic spatial abstraction, the other its stubborn fixation on first-order sensory data. Classification and measurement wed these two forms of cognition. Thus, the map abstracts and displays informa-tion selectively classed under categorical types and various magnitudes. Familiar examples include surface relief, differentiated by isohypes, or contour lines; human settlements distinguished by size; and routes of transport according to varied capacities. Virtually any sort of feature of interest can be represented in this manner, including such things as per capita income, religious affiliation, and frequency of floods. Dynamic as well as status conditions lend themselves readily to such portrayal, as illustrated in the daily weather map.

The map so derived can itself then reveal an infinity of further information of a spatial character. The inexhaustible array of relationships it contains are themselves, in turn, susceptible to classification and measurement. The map bespeaks varying properties of spatial arrangement such as density (e.g., of human population or usable hardwoods); connectedness and articulation (e.g., of road or stream networks); co-occurrence or association (e.g., such as might be shown to relate a given type of crop with certain soils); and above all and in general, regionalization.

For years, a majority of geographers assumed that distinguishing and describing plausible "regions" must be their main task. But that device, though highly important, by itself was lacking in both precision (a region has no absolute existence in nature) and theoretical implication. It failed to exploit sufficiently the map's enormous potentialities and likewise those of field observations. In recent decades, not only did geographical connectedness come into its own as a theme but also the problems it presented evoked a new kind of modeling. Hierarchical and serial relationships of elements in space (e.g., among marketing centers of different sizes or zones devoted to particular crops) began to attract attention. Temporal factors, often implied in the former relationships, also acquired a new prominence—for example, in studies of the spatio-temporal diffusion of technical or cultural innovations. Questions of spatial association, too, began to be addressed in a radically different way, probabilistic modeling replacing haphazard conjecture. Often, a map compiled from public data easily available, such as national censuses or trade statistics, could supplement or even supplant the older kinds of maps so painfully constructed on the basis of personal fieldwork, as a source of the data for manipulation. A new generation of geographers armed with adequate mathematics could keep their boots clean, be dispensed from the rigors of fieldwork, and think of themselves as theoreticians.

In fact, though, the somewhat occluded minority of physical geographers perforce had to continue their forays out into nature in the raw, and even the most cloistered of "spatialist" quantitative human geographers might deign on occasion to conduct fact-finding interviews. But field investigations of the previous "regional" sort fell into decline for a while, until the emergence of a vigorous social, behavioral geography.

SOCIAL GEOGRAPHY

The social geographers and their sympathizers began to be attracted back to the pathways earlier trod by traditional human or cultural geographers. But they arrived equipped not only with new and more sophisticated techniques but also with new sensitivities and a heightened social concern and commitment.

At about the same time as a concerned and competent social geography was coming into being, Andre Gunder Frank was issuing the first of his appeals for a radical new appraisal of the human condition and its historical foundations, specifically in the so-called developing world. Impulses from other sources, sometimes like Frank's, engendered in part by Marxist critique, were conditioning geographers to consider and reconsider their personal values and direct their attention as professionals toward issues identified by such reflections. Hence, Frank's lessons hit home and in due time could stimulate geographical research and discussion and evoke some properly geographical conceptions of underdevelopment as well as its possible remedies.

The circumstances in which the social subdiscipline arose, however, did not initially favor immersion in overseas work. In both Britain and North America, the movement recruited most of its members from among the ranks of urban and economic geographers of a quantitative and behavioral bent. The cultural geographers, still at that time the chief frequenters of foreign places, proved slow to respond to the new movements and challenges.

Social geography in the 1960s and 1970s focused mostly on problems of cities in the home countries. In addition, some number of researchers trained in quantitative methods and spatial analysis, along with colleagues of an earlier formation, went abroad to work with governmental and other developmental agencies. Gilbert F. White, for example, led a whole platoon of water resource specialists out into the Third World. Brian J. L. Berry and some of his students addressed urban hierarchical orders in several poor countries. Norton S. Ginsburg, then like the foregoing two scholars teaching at Chicago, even produced an *Atlas of Economic Development* (1961) that displayed statistical indices of relative standings among countries. Peter Gould worked on topics as diverse as adjustments in agriculture and public health in various tropical lands and sent forth his disciples to do likewise. Robert C. Mayfield applied diffusion analysis to rural situations, particularly in India and elsewhere, and went on to develop a practice of community economic initiatives. Many more names of such pioneers in development geography could be cited, but the work of such scholars hardly touched on the underlying structural conditions and historical antecedents of the poverty they sought to palliate.

Whole books also appeared in the 1970s devoted explicitly to the geography of development. Most notable among them, probably, were those by a Brazilian, Milton Santos (1975); the distinguished Nigerian, Akin Mabogunje (1980); and Harold Brookfield (1975), an English geographer with abundant field experience in New Guinea and the South Pacific. In the same period, too, a number of French and other European geographers pursued similar directions. The perspectives informing the writings of Santos, Mabogunje, and Brookfield were comprehensive, and they wrote in explicit awareness of Gunder Frank's ideas. Accordingly, some of those and other geographical books, which have proved of enduring relevance, call for more discussion below, in regard to the uses to which each puts geography and how they interpret not only development but also underdevelopment.

Subsequent book-length studies in development by geographers have been as diverse as rather vapid, timidly technical textbooks, rigidly ideological diatribes (something utterly alien, by the way, to Gunder Frank's work), specialized applications of various geographical concepts and practices, and cases at or above the country level. Relevant major works have appeared that deal with everything from long-wave prognostication to feminist critique, from demographic processes to spatial mobility, and from communication to cultural change and adaptation.

COMMUNICATION ON THE MAP

Among the maps that these and all geographers are wont to employ, the most revealing, I should maintain, are also the most common, prosaic ones, which depict the world's physical features only stingily. I refer to political maps. They revel in boundaries. They may also, somewhat grudgingly, accord some space to transportation routes, and they inevitably locate certain cities. Even in its most rudimentary form, this very familiar sort of map declares a great deal of fundamental, influential, frustrating truth. It always proclaims, in a word, tension and conflict. For the boundaries it shows constrain, obstruct, choke, and divert the potential free flow of people and goods, ideas and initiatives, among places and populations over the transportation routes also commonly depicted. The jurisdictions and sovereignties they proclaim, highly unequal in potency, themselves conflict and contend. The stronger can often regulate to their own advantage the currents of transport and communications, and even of human migrations, into or out of the weaker.

The world system to which Gunder Frank and others have devoted so much of their study now consists of a closed order of states, through and among which thread the communication and transportation routes just mentioned. The diversified traffic that pulses over those routes obeys strict controls imposed from all sides, but most particularly those maintained by the affluent, powerful states and the enterprises fostered by them. It has, presumably, always been so, ever since at least the Bronze Age, as Frank would have it. Some traffic does always irresistibly flow, and influences are universally shared out as "cycles" or waves of relative felicity or deprivation, as envisioned by Frank again. As particular powers wax and wane in history, the directions and volumes of flows over the routes and crossing the boundaries constantly take on new character, but humanity as a whole remains locked into that unity of interaction.

Look at the map once more and notice the principal cities in each of the countries. Those agglomerations, necessarily, stud the transportation routes. They live by connection, across those same boundaries, under those same diverse and unequally strong jurisdictions, and furthermore under controls responsive as remarked to relative power. The simple map here invoked can say little more, but once inside the actual city, a geographer or anyone else can better appreciate what all of this must mean.

Another defect of an ordinary political map resides in the fact that it does not reveal of what the particular traffic over its routes consists. What goes in and how much, and what and how much comes out? The geographer's term *commodity flows* covers that question, in part, and the notion of "input-output analysis" is commonplace in economics. Add to those two the kindred ideas of cultural diffusion and, indispensably, a model of entrepreneurial and administrative communication—respecting always the routes and the boundaries impinging on them—and I think you get a fairly accurate geographical picture of development and underdevelopment and how they relate.

SPATIAL FACTORS

An inherent contradiction thus obtains between the boundaries of a country, or sometimes even a province, and the routeways that unite and connect it into a larger domain. This feature affects even animal species, among many of which the security of the home territory, fiercely defended, is bought at the cost of a wider access to food supplies, for the terrain is all parceled out into familial fiefdoms whose boundaries cannot be transgressed. Despite claims to the contrary, however, I do not believe that humanity suffers the same rigid restrictions or territoriality that numerous other species do. Rather, human beings are able, through certain communicative behavior, to negotiate passage across such boundaries as still do occur.

A forthcoming book of my own (Wagner, in press) explores the implications of this fact. I contend that, unlike many or most other creatures, a human individual, throughout a lifetime, remains utterly dependent on the social group for protection, productive collaboration in livelihood activities, and permanent opportunity for lifelong learning, not just from experience in general or trial-and-error experimentation, but specifically from imitation of others' behavior. The learning procedures peculiar to people involve demonstration, deliberate instruction, coaching, and critique. Call this "culture."

Culture consists of certain consequences as well as of certain practices of communication. Among the latter cultural endowments, the forms of human interaction permitting negotiation of free spatial passage are especially crucial, though hardly much noticed because they appear in everyone's everyday rounds. Likewise essential are similar communicative devices that enable people to collaborate and exchange both ideas and material products.

Dissenting perhaps somewhat from Marx, I maintain that the fundamental means of production consist, not of useful objects as such, but of tokens, including even words, employed in communication. Money itself is obviously one such token, and so even is a mere reputation for wealth or any other striking personal attribute. Discourse directs decision and enterprise. It employs display behavior analogous to and continuous with the mating or aggressive displays of animal species, but much elaborated and enhanced through such devices as language and artifacts and, unlike the respective animal activities, it goes on constantly as people intermingle and interact, thereby regulating and directing social activity indispensable for survival.

Displays of this sort, of course, are the instruments used in negotiating boundary passage and spatial mobility. They furthermore function in structuring all social relationships and managing common activity. Necessarily, they always discharge a political function thereby. Communicative behavior of this kind attempts to allocate initiative, authority, and privilege. Someone, in effect, always comes out on top: These are the politics.

The material landscape itself embodies not only abundant display as such but also constructions and other constraints that concentrate, insulate, and channel communication, and hence controlling political power, into certain protected points and pathways whose boundaries are firm and hard to negotiate. In view of such artifactual, selective structuring of communication systems, any effective geography must have a political aspect.

From this standpoint, it becomes easier to conceive how underdevelopment develops. When, by conquest or otherwise, new communicative linkages, protected and preponderant, replace the former ones, those people who use and manage them can readily monopolize initiative and thus, to their own benefit, control the flows of circulation of all kinds, and even by this means reorganize a whole productive system; both means and relations of production thus become transformed.

COMMUNICATION AND CONTROL

Consider how these principles manifest themselves concretely in geographical space. The surface of a country is configured by integrated nodes and networks of communication, substantive elements of landscape grouped in characteristic, distinct complexes of actual buildings, roads, ports, and numerous kinds of other, often highly technical presences. Like the nerves of a body, insinuated into every organ, these "nerves of the world" reach deeply into the physical landscape and transmit the governing impulses that integrate and meter its functions, more or less in coordination with those of the system of humanity as a whole.

On the map, we can differentiate the various sorts of elements in such control systems, assigning to them proper magnitudes of relative importance, delineating their fields of effect, indicating their interconnections and order of precedence, and representing the barriers that insulate and protect them. A diversified yet unified communicative space becomes thus apparent. Control is clearly depicted. This situation may well have prevailed as a single grand pattern in much of the world since the Bronze Age or before.

Although specific impulses or messages the system will carry remain to be monitored, the potentialities they represent are already prefigured in the design of the system. And likewise, directions of flow are set in advance. Only human, physical actions can operate communication systems of the kind described, however technical they may be; but likewise, those same human actions are only effective as controls on either inanimate process or further human activity when performed by means of the physical complex of devices comprising the system of communication.

Regarding any particular province or country, then, it ought to be useful and enlightening to map the actual communications apparatus, ascertaining both whither and whence it leads and disclosing the actual people it empowers to exert control. Then one might see underdevelopment's visage.

Many serious writers equate underdevelopment with widespread poverty, illiteracy, inequity, and rampant injustice; or with a patent sluggishness in social and technical change; or with the obvious neglect of promising resources and labor potential; or yet more simply with dependence and subordination. All of the same conditions are found, however, in substantial sectors of almost any country's population. Most people in every modern country are totally dependent on forces they cannot control, and the only independent folk left may be the vanishing bands of primitive gatherers. Furthermore, "full employment" seldom if ever occurs, and technological advance is everywhere constrained and limited by circumstance.

Specifically geographical cases of underdevelopment may well prove easier to find. How much has human activity altered a given landscape, one may ask. But such a simpleminded conception surely exposes the fallacy that change, or even modernization, must always be beneficial. Ironically, one of the indices of underdevelopment in Third World cities and countries now consists of environmental contamination imitating and often exceeding the kind prevailing in so-called developed countries and identifiable as itself a product of vaunted development.

Underdevelopment, too, may be hardly the word for enormously lucrative, efficient commercial enterprise, such as widely occurs in many Third World countries. Mines, plantations, ports, and similar implants in such places frequently even lead in technological innovation, not to mention profitability—that is, according to some criteria, precisely in development. The abundance of good examples of this kind of incontestable development occurring right amid the misery of many poor countries demonstrates well that spatial connections and governing structures matter much more than do technical achievements alone in defining underdevelopment.

The part that foreign sojourners, individual or corporate, can play in underdevelopment is illustrated, yet not fully revealed, in such technical proficiency as just mentioned. The communicative aspect of their presence is crucial as well.

THE FOREIGN PRESENCE

One prominent aspect of underdevelopment is the common occurrence of a two-tiered ethnic stratification, over and above the tribal or even class distinctions among the indigenous people. Into the most favored position of effective communication and control, expatriates and transients from the United States, Europe, and elsewhere ensconce themselves: engineers, teachers, technicians, landowners, managers, and sales representatives. Between these exotic elites and the masses there enter more humble mercantile folk from China, the Levant, or India, as well as sometimes European refugees and likewise members of certain trading tribes of nearby provenience. Some fuse into the local society; some do not. It is often these latter people, hard bargainers and insistent creditors, who bear the brunt of native resentment.

The presence of these rather cohesive foreign "colonies" within a Third World country facilitates development in at least two respects. The outsiders introduce and maintain their own discrete communication arrangements, serving both cultural and business activities and linked with systems abroad. Their internal and external connections enable the humbler mercantile im-migrants to extend and intensify household consumption of basic goods among the local peoples; they operate, if necessary, as backpacking peddlers, going on later to open small shops near the marketplace and, eventually, powerful importing houses. Thus, these traders can stimulate an improvement of consumption at the household level, introducing credit possibilities in order to do so and reaping their goodly reward.

The North American, European, and now Japanese presence, in contrast, again provided with its own communication linkages and practices, exerts a powerful influence in the productive sector: agriculture, forestry, public utilities, and manufacture. Its enterprises dominate plantation activity, for instance. Furthermore, through intergovernmental or private assistance and technical missions, numerous resident or visiting foreigners of this type involve themselves directly in fomenting development according to their own established priorities.

In both of these instances, the advantageous connections accessible to implanted foreign social strata enable them to invigorate and diversify con-sumption on the one hand or to instigate and intensify production on the other. However, three objections can obviously be raised to the roles they assume: (a) Their nearly exclusive communicative arrangements have little or no place for native or "national" participants; (b) the foreigners within the country tend to enjoy superior living conditions, often the envy of and seductive model for natives; and (c) through distant connections, economic and even cultural control are transferred to external centers. All three of these grievances become potent political themes.

GEOGRAPHICAL STUDIES

Certain geographers have contributed excellent studies of some of the foregoing phenomena. The work of Janet Henshall Momsen, for example, has concentrated on the plight of Third World women (1991). Her geography highlights continuing exploitation and subordination even when female operatives find, as often happens, an eager welcome in industry (e.g., in *maquiladoras*). The burdens borne by women frequently become all the more onerous when unrelieved domestic duties are compounded with work in a factory. Women also tend, in the process of urbanization, to be drawn into the lowest levels of service activities, where miserable wages, excessively long working hours, and even sexual abuse are almost the rule. Both the altered spatial circumstances and the communicative options of the individuals concerned put them at a great disadvantage.

The disadvantageous position of women also becomes clear in Lawrence A. Brown's (1991) examination of the effects of development and urban or regional growth on selective migration patterns. Because, as he recognizes, such change is highly heterogeneous, and much conditioned by forces exogenous to the places concerned, Brown presents comparative data that, despite considerable variations, succeed in demonstrating a selective displacement of young females that both disfavors them and leaves their source areas out of demographic balance. In fact, the young and unskilled of both sexes are drained out of their quiescent home regions and do not necessarily gain security thereby.

Akin to Momsen's and Brown's approaches, some work of Wilbur Zelinsky has relevance to development. He has presented a model of what he calls the "demographic transition," postulating lengthened lifetimes, reduced natality, and greater per capita employment of resources as development proceeds. Applied geographically, this not altogether unfamiliar idea seems to accord well with other indices of underdevelopment.

Brian J. L. Berry, in his book on long-wave rhythms (1991), throws light on another possible factor in underdevelopment, in a manner strikingly compatible with recent ideas of Gunder Frank. And some other geographers have even gone so far as to offer not only diagnoses but even possible cures.

An Australian geographer, D. K. Forbes, for instance, has surveyed the literature up until the mid-1980s and come up with both a specific conception of underdevelopment and suggestions for overcoming it. In his book (1982), he asserts that underdevelopment is really a geographical issue, and he considers various geographical theses regarding the subject, beginning with old-fashioned environmental determinism and extending to the "dual economy" concept, growth pole theory, and macrolevel concepts in general. Forbes tends to agree with ideas expressed in the past by Gunder Frank in concluding that class struggle and social movements in the Third World may hold the best key to real improvement. His emphasis, too, on "articulation" of forces and agencies in development I find particularly salutary because it explicitly recognizes the spatial and communicative aspects of the issue.

Harold Brookfield, deploring the paucity of geographical contributions in this domain, rejects economistic thinking, Keynesian or Rostowian, but also casts doubt on geography's own central place theory. He stresses the universality of the underdevelopment problem throughout the world and the interdependence that characterizes the world system but opts in particular for sensitivity to local needs and know-how in coping with the inequalities of supposedly dual economies.

First published in 1980, and thus a pioneer work, Akin Mabogunje's book attacks "cultural colonialism" and the view of development as purely a matter of economics. Mabogunje espouses a program of major spatial reorganization centered on rural resources, populations, and their settlements and considers industrial growth and urbanization as properly subordinate in their importance to such a fundamental reshaping of the whole geographical structure of a country. He admits that such "mobilization" may be most easily accomplished under authoritarian controls (cf. Romania, Indonesia, or Ethiopia) but urges a redistribution of political power to assuage them and work toward resurgence of distinctive national cultures. For these ends, he maintains, new spatial structures are indispensable.

Mabogunje's critique and corrective construct of spatial reformation, tempered by his own and Brookfield's admonitions to respect and incorporate indigenous solutions, stand as the most profoundly geographical statements to date on development issues, as well as embody the most concrete and specific proposals for effective change. In view of the conceptions I have outlined already in this chapter, I must regard the spatial-cultural analysis and recommendations of these two writers as highly important and relevant. If indeed communicative structures, in the widest sense, do account for relative development and also dependency, then change in these structures seems obviously called for. This change would assign new meanings and functions to boundaries, require new patterns of interconnection, involve a different distribution of initiative and authority, and in general adjust development activities more intimately to local realities. It would seek to create a totally transformed geographical order.

It has slowly dawned on the planners and proponents of development that not all "native" methods of production deserve to be mistrusted as antiquated or inept; a growing tide of favorable ecological assessments—not a few by geographers—now focus on the success and even superiority of traditional farming and handicraft procedures in certain places, for instance. Often, the organizational and communicative apparatus affecting production and distribution, rather than the old techniques in themselves, account for the various systems' shortcomings and are often of extraneous origin.

Furthermore, as I have remarked in passing somewhere above, not every introduced institution in Third World countries merits dismissal as "backward" or "underdeveloped." The technical and economic efficiency of countless extractive enterprises under foreign control are impressive. Lamentably, too, development in some sense or other has achieved a resounding success in police and military domains; under American, Soviet, Chinese, and other great power patronage, national armies in a great many poor countries have eagerly mastered complex, advanced weapons technologies and the associated discipline. Their superior networks of communication, clear lines of command, and preponderant spatial mobility allow devastating application of their technology. This result carries a lesson for all development efforts.

The foregoing reasoning in this chapter has inevitably led toward one major conclusion. Although I might like to maintain that underdevelopment is primarily a geographical problem, I am obliged to qualify such a claim by pointing out the decisive role of communicative structure in the relevant kind of geography. Moreover, it is not the physical or technical properties of this structure in the geographical landscape that most matter; it is, rather, who operates them, to what ends, and with what results for the country and people concerned. In the end, it comes down to politics.

Politics, yes, but politics that operates through elaborate systems of both physical linkage and spatial exclusivity, detectable readily enough by geographers, at least, and absolutely decisive for human affairs. I find it regrettable and paralyzing, as Gunder Frank now likewise does, that so many discussions of underdevelopment concentrate still on ideologies, treaties and laws, and even personalities. Those factors, though they do count, are clearly subsidiary.

Real change, improvement, or emancipation can only occur when the actual, substantive structures of communication and control, the nerves of the world, receive their proper attention and the geographical order they exemplify is revolutionized.

REFERENCES

Berry, B. J. L. (1991). *Long-wave rhythms in economic development and political behavior.* Baltimore, MD: Johns Hopkins University Press.
Brookfield, H. (1975). *Interdependent development.* Pittsburgh, PA: University of Pittsburgh.
Brown, L. A. (1991). *Place, migration, and development in the Third World: An alternative view with particular reference to population movements, labor market experiences, and regional change in Latin America.* London: Routledge.
Forbes, D. K. (1982). *The geography of underdevelopment: A critical survey.* Baltimore, MD: Johns Hopkins University Press.
Ginsburg, N. S. (1961). *Atlas of economic development.* Chicago: University of Chicago, Department of Geography.
Mabogunje, A. (1980). *The development process: A spatial perspective.* Sydney, Australia: Allen and Unwin.
Momsen, J. H. (1991). *Women and development in the Third World.* London: Routledge.
Santos, M. (1975). *Underdevelopment and poverty: The Latin American geographer's view.* Toronto: University of Toronto Press.
Wagner, P. L. (in press). *Spaces of human display: The geltung hypothesis.* Austin: University of Texas Press.

6

⊞

The Debt Crisis Revisited

OTTO KREYE

CONTINUING CRISIS

It has recently been suggested that the debt crisis is coming to an end. In his concluding remarks at the 1992 conference of the International Monetary Fund (IMF) and World Bank, the director of the IMF, Michel Camdessus, declared that "the debt crisis has been tamed although a few indebted countries still have to make efforts to overcome their economic and other problems" (Nachrichten für Außenhandel, 28 September 1992). And in contrast to previous years, the annual conference of the Bretton Wood Institute made no mention of the indebtedness of developing countries. The then president of the World Bank, Lewis Preston, felt able to go as far as announcing to the World Bank governors from Latin America and the Caribbean at a meeting held on September 19, 1992, that "ten years after the start of the debt crisis it is now possible to celebrate its end" (epd-Entwicklungspolitik, 18/19 September 1992, p. 9).

The recent meetings of the heads of government of the Group of the Seven Industrialized Countries (G7), the summits held in Munich 1992 and in Tokyo 1993, did not pay much attention to the debt problem of the developing countries. The final declarations welcomed "the progress which many developing countries have achieved in overcoming debt problems and regaining their creditworthiness" and noted "that the international debt strategy continues to be valid."

William Rhodes, vice president of Citibank (the U.S. bank that is particularly involved in lending to Third World countries) and chairman of the Creditors Committee of the International Banks "announced in February 1992 that probably by August [1992] Latin America's debt crisis will have been overcome" (Börsen-Zeitung, 4 August 1992). The London *Financial Times* has also felt moved to note that, given the regaining of solvency by a number of countries, the worst at least may now be over (e.g., see "Nightmare Begins to Fade," 1992; "Solution Passes," 1992).

What do such announcements mean? Is the debt crisis really coming to an end, and if this is the case, for whom—for the creditors, for the debtors, or for both? It should be remembered that, from the standpoint of the creditors—that is, the international financial institutions (IMF and World Bank) and the international banking system—the suspension of debt service payments by Mexico in August 1982 marked the beginning of the debt crisis. And indeed it would appear that, ten years after the start of the debt crisis defined from this perspective, the problem of international indebtedness has indeed begun to lose its threat for major parts of the creditor side and in particular for the international banking system. The international banking system has not collapsed, and no breakdown is expected in the foreseeable future as a consequence of Third World indebtedness. The sums owed to the private banking system by debtor countries have been reduced without any notable losses for the banks, in part with public funds bearing the costs. And as a result of the implementation of structural adjustment and stabilization programs in many indebted countries, the remaining debts owed to the international banking system are being serviced relatively reliably.

However, the picture looks very different from the standpoint of the debtor countries. No mitigation, let alone a solution, to the debt crisis is in prospect for the debtor countries. The foreign indebtedness of the developing countries has almost doubled in the ten years since the generally acknowledged outbreak of the debt crisis—between 1982 and 1992—and is still rising. A growing proportion of gross domestic product (GDP) is being consumed in meeting debt service obligations. And the economic and social consequences of the structural adjustment and stabilization measures that guarantee or are intended to guarantee debt service are devastating.

Increasing evidence suggests that the measures that have proved useful for the creditors do worsen the debt crisis for the debtors—that is, for the peripheral countries. Citibank's Vice President Rhodes's statement, as quoted above, that Latin America's debt crisis will be overcome in 1992 actually meant that the banks (primarily U.S. banks) that had been in a state of some anxiety about the loans they had extended to Latin American countries thought that they, the banks, would escape largely scot-free from the financial debacle for which they themselves bear primary responsibility. However, Latin America's debt crisis is far from being solved.

Figures showing the development of the foreign indebtedness of the peripheral countries illustrate this point very clearly (see next section). The creditor banks and creditor countries continue to be in receipt of a steady stream of amortization and interest payments; as a result of those debt service payments, the debtor countries suffer an uninterrupted outflow of resources. Not only the financial crisis of many peripheral countries but also their economic and social crises are worsening yet further.

As a consequence, some international organizations, such as the United Nations Secretariat, the United Nations Economic Commissions, and the Organization for Economic Cooperation and Development (OECD), do not share the optimistic assessment of the heads of the IMF and the World Bank that the debt crisis has come to an end. Rather, they are pessimistic about the prospects for a solution to the debt crises and the remedying of its worst consequences.

The United Nations Economic Commission for Latin America (CEPAL) noted in its 1991 annual report that

> also for Latin America the problem of foreign indebtedness is far away from a definitive solution, even if it may have lost a little in explosiveness. Latin America's overall indebtedness continues to rise. In all countries the process of adjustment has been more or less a "regressive character." The gap between rich and poor is continuing to widen. (Nachrichten für Außenhandel, 1 October 1991, p. 5)

The OECD's annual report of September 1992 also observes the continuation of the debt crisis in the Third World even though the governments and banks may be getting an upper hand. It seems that the debt problem has not been resolved nor has it at all disappeared globally (*Financial Times,* 14 September 1992).

Even the experts of the World Bank do not entirely share the optimism of their president. For example, the head of the Debt and International Finance Division at the World Bank, Masood Ahmed, and the then Vice President of Development Policy and the Bank's Chief Economist, Lawrence Summers, wrote in the September 1992 edition of the IMF and World Bank's quarterly: "But the debt crisis is far from over for more than 40 developing countries, which continue to have difficulties in servicing their debt as originally contracted" ("Tenth Anniversary Report on the Debt Crisis," In *Finance and Development,* September 1992, p. 5). The Neue Zürcher Zeitung commented in August 1992: "Public interest in the debt crisis may have abated—but the economic crisis behind it has lost none of its immediacy" (Neue Zürcher Zeitung, 16/17 August 1992).

> The more debtors pay, the more they owe.
>
> United Nations
> Development Programme, 1992

THE DEVELOPMENT OF FOREIGN DEBT

According to the IMF, developing countries' foreign debt at the end of 1992 reached U.S.$1,390 billion (developing countries excluding Eastern Europe and successor states to the U.S.S.R.). The World Bank's figure for the developing countries (including Eastern Europe but excluding successor states to the U.S.S.R.) was U.S.$1,510 billion. And the OECD's total for the developing countries (excluding Eastern Europe and successor states to the U.S.S.R.) was U.S.$1,534 billion. The differences among these figures are attributable primarily to the use of different criteria (country grouping, number of countries, types of credit) and different methods for assessing the figures for foreign indebtedness (primary surveys, balance of payments statistics).

As far as the broad orders of magnitude are concerned, however, there are no significant differences among these figures. By the end of 1993, the IMF, World Bank, and OECD all expected developing countries' international indebtedness to have risen to U.S.$1,500 billion. This represents a virtual doubling since the onset of the debt crisis.

The foreign debt of Latin America, the most heavily indebted region of the Third World in 1982 in both absolute terms and in relation to GDP, increased from U.S.$331 billion in 1982 to U.S.$453 billion by 1992. A dramatic increase of foreign debt of Africa occurred during this period, from U.S.$122 billion to U.S.$222 billion, and also of some countries of Asia from U.S.$187 billion to U.S.$424 billion. India, which in 1982 was almost without any foreign debts, had joined the ranks of the most indebted Third World countries by 1992, with foreign debts of U.S.$74 billion. The World Bank expects a further increase to U.S.$93 billion within the next five years (see *Financial Times,* 20 August 1992). It seems to be merely a question of time until the devastating consequences of this development inevitably lead to a collapse in what are currently still relatively intact social structures. Perhaps only then will complaints begin about India's foreign indebtedness among the public opinion formers of the West.

The debt ratio of the peripheral countries (foreign debt related to annual GDP) and the debt service ratio (debt service payments in percentage of exports of goods and services) provide a clear illustration of the persistence and regional deterioration of the debt problem of peripheral countries. The debt ratio of peripheral countries has long since exceeded 25%, a figure generally regarded as bearable. Africa's debt ratio rose from 35% in 1982 to no less than 61% in 1992; that of the Asian countries from 22% to just 25%; and that of Latin America at 43% for both 1982 and 1992. In the intervening period, however, it exceeded 50% for a number of years.

Even a debt ratio of 25%, however, requires debt service payments at a level that inevitably exceeds the capabilities of virtually any economy. One numerical example might illustrate this:

> Assume a GDP of U.S.$100 billion, a debt ratio of 25%, and thus foreign indebtedness of $25 billion. Given an average maturity of debt of ten years and an average interest rate of 10%, then annual repayments of principal will be U.S.$2.5 billion and average interest payments will also be U.S.$2.5 billion; that is, the annual debt service payments in all will be U.S.$5 billion, or 5% of GDP. If these payments are indeed made, then resources will be denied to domestic savings equal in volume to the average increase of net investment in many economies, with grave consequences for investment, growth, and consumption. If due service payments are not made or only made in part, then foreign debts will continue to grow and the problem of indebtedness will be perpetuated.

In 1992, the Third World countries made debt service payments—that is, repayments of principal plus interest payments—of U.S.$170 billion. This represented an outflow of some 5% of peripheral countries' GDP of that year. In comparison, the core countries spent only around 0.35% of their GDP for official development assistance; that is less than one tenth of the proportion of GDP the peripheral countries have to spend to meet their debt service obligations.

According to the IMF, between 1982 and 1992 the developing countries have paid a total of U.S.$1,520 billion in debt service. By the end of 1993, this will have grown to a total of U.S.$1,700 billion. This sum is more than twice as large as the total foreign indebtedness of the peripheral countries in 1982, at the beginning of the debt crisis. Foreign indebtedness rose to U.S.$1,390 billion by 1992 and has further increased to $1,500 billion by the end of 1993.

On the basis of figures provided by the World Bank on the peripheral countries' foreign indebtedness, it is possible to draw up the following calculation:

Foreign debt 1982:	U.S.$745.1 billion
plus long-term credits 1982-1991:	U.S.$1,048.6 billion
less repayment of principal 1982-1991:	U.S.$681.1 billion
plus short-term credits 1982-1991:	U.S.$52.2 billion
balance	U.S.$1,164.8 billion

In fact, the World Bank puts foreign indebtedness for 1991 at U.S.$1,280.8 billion, some U.S.$116 billion higher. This is primarily explained by the fact that the nonpayment of interests is added to the total and that the dollar value of those obligations, which have to be paid in such currencies as deutsche marks, Swiss francs, or yen, have increased because of the depreciation of the U.S. dollar (a further additional burden for the peripheral countries).

The peripheral countries have had to suffer a permanent net outflow of resources every year since 1984 as a result of their foreign credit relationship. Only in 1982 and 1983 did a small net transfer to the peripheral countries occur (U.S.$25 billion). Between 1984 and 1991, the net outflow of resources was U.S.$243 billion from the peripheral countries.

Since 1982, the peripheral countries have not made interest payments of less than 5% of the foreign debt of the respective years. According to the IMF, the debt service ratio of the developing countries fell from 19.6% in 1982 to 14.2% in 1990. Whereas the debt service ratio of the African developing countries rose from 20.3% to 26.7%, it fell for the Asian developing countries from 12.7% to 7.9%, and for the countries of Latin America and the Caribbean from 53.6% to 31.5%. These data would appear to suggest, with the exception of Africa, a welcome development. In reality, however, the falling debt service ratios, given unchanged debt ratios, are simply an indicator of the fact that export ratios—in other words, the use of domestic resources for export—has increased. The apparent improvement in the capacity of these countries to service their debts has in no way reduced their financial burdens. Moreover, debt service ratios of 26.7% (Africa) and 31.5% (Latin America) indicate that more than one quarter (in the case of Africa, and just under one third in the case of Latin America) of export earnings are consumed to meet debt service payments and are therefore unavailable to finance imports of goods and services.

The scale on which debt service and the associated outflow of resources occur is illustrated particularly by Mexico, the country whose announcement of a moratorium on debt service in August 1982 "triggered" the debt crisis. Between 1982 and 1990, Mexico had to spend U.S.$114 billion for debt service payments, a larger amount than its total foreign debt in 1982. In the year in which it announced its moratorium, Mexico paid a total foreign debt of U.S.$86.1 billion, interest of U.S.$7.8 billion, and amortization of U.S.$4.5 billion. One year later, in 1983, a total of U.S.$14.8 billion was paid for debt service. In 1984, it was U.S.$16.9 billion. And in 1990, interest payments of U.S.$7.3 billion and amortization payments of U.S.$4.9 billion flowed abroad.

In all these years, debt service payments exceeded 5% of GDP. In 1988, they reached the record level of 7.8% of GDP. Interest payments actually made in 1982 amounted to an average interest rate of 9%; in the period from 1983 to 1985 to an interest rate of more than 10%; and in the period from 1986 to 1990 to an interest rate of between 7.5% and 9.7%. Between 1982 and 1990, Mexico recorded a total net transfer abroad of U.S.$52.8 billion through its credit obligations.

In recent years, a considerable portion of Mexico's debt service payments and those of other countries has been financed from the earnings that have accrued to the state from the privatization of public undertakings.

The use of foreign currency earnings from the sale of public organizations to foreign investors has occasionally been appraised as a particularly effective method for reducing debt. In fact, at best, it creates a short-term breathing space. In the long term, it means that the state forfeits the earnings from what were once public institutions and that more foreign currency is required in order to cover the transfer of profits and repatriation of capital.

The Secretariat of the United Nations Development Programme crystallized the entire dilemma of the peripheral countries in a pertinent phrase derived from Keynes's and Irving Fisher's observations of the 1930s: "The more debtors pay, the more they owe" (United Nations Development Programme, *Human Development Report 1992,* New York: Oxford, 1992, pp. 50-51).

In the efforts of the peripheral countries to earn the foreign exchange they need to make debt service payments by increasing their exports of goods and services, almost without exception the debt strategy pursued by the peripheral countries culminated only in even greater indebtedness. The increased supply of exports inevitably leads to a deterioration in the terms of trade for the exporting countries, possibly a full-scale price collapse, and hence a need for even greater export efforts in an ultimately self-defeating strategy. During the 1980s, the debtor countries found that, instead of higher earnings from increased exports, on balance their receipts were lower. Debt could not be serviced or could not be serviced in full, and indebtedness increased.

ECONOMIC AND SOCIAL
EFFECTS OF DEBT SERVICE

On July 30, 1992, the *Financial Times,* uncertain about the prospects of economic growth in Latin America, asked whether there is life after debt. It sees signs for a degree of recovery of economic growth in some of the most indebted countries in Latin America but is by no means certain that this growth is sustainable. Rather, it is skeptical that governments have anything with which to combat the catastrophic consequences of the debt crisis seen so far: primarily desperate impoverishment and the increasing decay of infrastruc-tures. The staff regards it entirely possible that the economic and social crises could be followed by political crisis in the form of military coups and civil wars. There are already ample indications of what this might mean in a number of countries, such as Brazil, Peru, and Venezuela.

Without a doubt, there will be no scope for an economically stable, eco-logically sustainable, and socially acceptable development should the peripheral countries continue to be compelled to make debt service payments at the current scale on their foreign debts. A permanent net transfer of resources from the debtor countries, as was the case between 1984 and 1992, denies the debtor countries not only capital but also, through the need to raise exports to meet debt service payments, real economic resources such as natural wealth, agri-cultural land, and infrastructure.

Per capita GDP is stagnating or falling. New investments can no longer be financed, and neither can replacement investments. Public revenues are consumed unproductively. Resources available for domestic markets and domestic consumption have to be used far beyond the level at which they can be sustained. Environmental destruction is on the increase, with social consequences in the form of unemployment, hunger, and homelessness.

The slow growth in GDP and the increase in poverty in the developing countries provide depressing evidence of this. In Latin America, the 1980s are referred to as a "lost decade." Between 1980 and 1990, GDP in the Third World as a whole rose in nominal terms from U.S.$2,493 billion to U.S.$3,683 billion. In the previous ten years, between 1970 and 1980, when there was a net transfer of resources to the Third World, it increased in nominal terms from U.S.$493 billion to U.S.$2,493 billion. The GDP of Africa, the region with the highest debt ratio, fell in absolute terms during the 1980s from U.S.$347 billion to U.S.$318 billion. During the 1980s, Latin America's GDP rose in nominal terms from U.S.$841 billion to U.S.$1,046 billion and hence virtually stagnated. The GDP of the Asian countries rose in nominal terms from U.S.$1,305 billion in 1980 to U.S.$2,319 in 1989, compared with a nominal increase in the previous ten years from U.S.$272 billion to U.S.$1,305 billion.

The rates of growth of the GDP of the Third World as a whole, which stood at an annual average of 5.5% during the 1970s, fell to an annual average 2.9% in the first half of the 1980s. During the second half, from 1985 to 1989, they rose on average to 4.2% per year. Growth rates of GDP in Africa fell from an annual average of 4.1% in the 1970s to 1.3% in the first half of the 1980s and 2.1% in the second half. In Latin America, the annual average rate of growth of GDP of 5.4% in the 1970s fell to an annual average of 0.6% in the first half of the 1980s and to 1.9% during the second half. Only the countries of Asia saw an increase in the average annual growth rate of GDP, from 5.7% in the 1970s to 7.2% in the first half of the 1980s and to 7.6% in the second half.

The only region in which per capita GDP rose during the 1980s was Asia. In Latin America, it remained unchanged in nominal terms and fell in real terms; in Africa, it fell dramatically. The proportion of world GDP accounted for by the Third World countries, which rose from 15.5% to 21.5% between 1970 and 1980, fell during the 1980s. By 1990, it stood at only 18.5%. According to the World Bank, in 1990, 4.1 billion people in the South, 78.5% of the world total of 5.3 billion, had to share 15.7% of world GDP (U.S.$3,479 billion). In contrast, 1.1 billion people in the North (21.5% of the world population) had access to 84.3% of world GDP (U.S.$10,094 billion) (see World Bank, *World Development Report 1992,* New York, 1992, p. 196).

The stagnation and decline in per capita GDP has been accompanied by growing social impoverishment. According to the World Bank and the United Nations Development Program, the number of people living in poverty in the Third World is larger than ever before. Some 1.1 billion people live under conditions of extreme poverty: They have an annual average per capita income of less than U.S.$370; 1.300 million people have no access to clean drinking water; 600 to 800 million are quantitatively or qualitative inadequately fed. Unemployment continues to grow; about 600 million people of working age are unemployed in the Third World, and hence, in most cases, entirely without income.

Of course, growing poverty and immiseration are not solely attributable to foreign indebtedness, debt service, and the associated net outflow of capital from the Third World countries. Debt service and net transfer of resources, however, make a major contribution to the fact that GDP is either stagnating or falling, that investments can no longer be financed and are therefore not undertaken, that public expenditure is being reduced, that inflation is mounting, that real wages are falling, and that unemployment is increasing. The prime victims of these developments are those people already living in poverty. The economic and social existence of many people in the Third World who have had access to moderate incomes and acceptable living conditions, however, is also increasingly at risk.

Without doubt, the continuation of the debtor-creditor relationship between the core and peripheral countries that has characterized the last ten years (1982-1992) will block any prospect of development in the debtor countries (that is, among the majority of the peripheral countries). The growing number of people who have become social victims of this relationship are left only with the alternative of migration; 70 million people from peripheral countries are already on the move. When this number rises, as it soon may, to 700 million, it should not surprise those living in the industrialized countries that have continued their remorseless insistence on the maintenance of debt service payments.

REFERENCES

Camdessus, M. (1992, September 28). *Nachrichten für Außenhandel.*
Financial Times. (1992, July 30).
Financial Times. (1992, August 20).
Financial Times. (1992, September 14).

Neue Zürcher Zeitung. (1992, August 16/17).

Nightmare begins to fade. (1992, April 6). *Financial Times.*

Preston, L. (1992, September 18/19). *Epd-Entwicklungspolitik,* p. 9.

Rhodes, W. (1992, August 4). *Börsen-Zeitung.*

Solution passes the test of time. (1992, July 30). *Financial Times.*

Summers, L. (1992, September). Tenth anniversary report on the debt crisis. *Finance and Development,* p. 5.

United Nations Development Programme. (1992). *Human development report 1992.* New York: Oxford University Press.

United Nations Economic Commission for Latin America (CEPAL). (1991, October 1). *Nachrichten für Außenhandel.*

World Bank. (1992). *World development report 1992.* New York: Oxford University Press.

7

Developmentalism

A Eurocentric Hoax, Delusion, and Chicanery

HERB ADDO

[The wise teacher] does not bid you enter the house of his wisdom, but rather leads you to the threshold of your own mind.

Khalil Gibran, *The Prophet*

ENCOUNTER WITH THE FRANK ESSENCE

Without doubt, Andre Gunder Frank (AGF) is a teacher in the Gibran vein. AGF is to be counted among the select few whom I consider to be my teachers because he "taught" me "nothing." For most of us, he teaches from a distance. Teaching is, by nature, chauvinistic and authoritarian. It is the few, the very few, who refuse to teach you, but who instead provide you with rich insights that release your imagination, who actually teach you in the true sense of the word. They encourage you to learn from them in your own ways. You come out of such teaching experiences convinced that although you have learned, you still emerged your own person.

The purpose of these brief observations is to adumbrate how I benefited from AGF's writings and thoughts at an early but crucial moment in my burdensome search for understanding of the development *problématique* in the early 1970s; how his thoughts contributed to the development of what I call neo-radical Third World perspective on the study of the development and transformation of the capitalist world-system; to raise some interrogations with respect to aspects of the reversals by AGF of his earlier thoughts and positions; and how I think I can explain these stunning reversals in ways that are satisfyingly conciliatory with my own evolving thoughts on the worsening plight of the Third World.

THE NAGGING QUESTIONS

Something, I was not sure what, had been bothering me for a long time. The double-barreled question that was not articulating itself well was this: Was this thing called development desirable; and was it feasible? Of course, everybody, and all that I had read, said an obvious yes to this. I myself believed that it could be so, except that I was haunted by this question precisely because I was not comfortable with my own stance with respect to the obviousness of the answer. If it were so, then how and why was it that I thought it was not possible or desirable, largely because not only was development happening so slowly but also, and worse, it was happening in perverse ways that seemed to be working against themselves.

I could not have been the only one bothered by the perversions of the processes of the development project. My problem, however, was to find some solid ground from which to answer such questions. Was "developmentalism" as it became known, patently Eurocentric and therefore possibly a Eurocentric hoax, delusion, and chicanery, in both the liberal and the Marxist modes of thought and praxis? Were Third World thinkers of all ideological views not being equally duped by cultural self-serving Eurocentric developmentalism? Did Third World intellectuals not have special responsibilities to go beyond the limits of Eurocentrically imposed developmentalist curiosities? Did Third World societies have to be like Western Europe in order to be said to have entered respectable modernities? Did Third World intellectuals have to subscribe to the progressivist universalist notion of historical developments and history itself, as attended by the notion of dialectical motions of history to the very enactment of the end of history itself? Must history be linear? Why must history end? Where were cultures, in their specificities, adaptabilities, durabilities, and corruptibilities in all this? Whose responsibility was it, any-way, to develop whom for whom, and why? But above all, was there an inherent debilitating contradiction in Euro-historical-humanism's underpin-nings of the developmentalist philosophy that should compel us to locate developmentalist futilities and inefficacies in its own very impossibilism?

MY METHODOLOGICAL PROBLEMS:
INTERNATIONAL POLITICS AND ECONOMICS
OR INTERNATIONAL POLITICAL ECONOMY?

My list of questions evolved over a long period. Before my initial en-counter with AGF's thought, I was involved in my Ph.D. dissertation, in which I was attempting to argue that the idea of underdevelopment was not the property of solely the Third World: that the development/underdevelopment contrast, as a property, belongs rightly to the international system. To the extent that the Third World, as an indelible part of the world, was under-developed, the international system was itself underdeveloped.

Empirically, the exercise was interesting. Using an array of measuring techniques, it was easy to establish the extent to which the Third World was comparatively grossly underdeveloped. But how could I jump from this obser-vation to relate it to the developedness of the other parts of the world in order to attribute underdevelopedness, as a property, to the international system?

The social sciences I was exposed to were of little help. International relations as part of the social sciences, which was supposed to focus on the international system, was even of less help. The general objection to my idea was that the international system was a system autonomously inclusive of all its different parts, however the differences were assigned or portrayed. The specific objection to this idea was that the North and the South were different parts of the international system. Everything separated them and nothing united them into a single system of any sort. And, in any case, I had to have an area of specialization within the international system to study, not the system itself, as a holistic entity, because such an entity did not exist. For me, the area of specialization was, naturally, Africa. Hence, the title of my thesis could not be the connotatively dangerous *Toward a Theory of International Development*. It had to be *Trends and Patterns in African Participation in International Relations, 1960-1970: Toward a Theory of International Develop-ment*. The proposed and accepted title showed that, in true philological style, I was empirically grounded in and about a part of the world.

Four things were happening about which I was not fully aware. First, I was being assiduously channeled toward the mainstream ahistorical dedication to "rate of growth" puzzle solvings, of closing the "North-South gap" in the dualist/diffusionist tradition, and away from historical-causal linkages between the North and the South. Second, in international relations, methodology had been reduced to the mere study of mere methods. There was no need for theories outside those of the causes, conduct, and management of the end of wars, and one war at that—the cold war. Third, I was not aware of the murky location of developmentalism in the causes of the cold war, nor was I aware of the fact that, in the post-war *Pax Americana,* international relations as a discipline was nothing but an American foreign policy science in the service of American (West European) interests in the waging of the cold war. In such circumstances, it is no wonder that history before 1945 was deemed an expensive luxury; theorizations outside wars were seen as irritating bother, and philosophy was considered a highly intolerable anathema. In such circumstances, the world before 1945 did not exist, and if it did, it did not have much to do with explaining the world of the cold war order (CWO). Fourth, and accordingly, epistemological considerations could not venture beyond the sacred confines of those raised by the liberal-Marxist confrontation. Both ideologies, we should all note, could therefore only be ahistorical, atheoretical, and aphilosophical.

But all was not lost. Johan Galtung's various structural theories—of violence, peace, aggression (1964), imperialism (1971), integration (1968), and so on—provided some initial answers. Galtung argued that systems left to themselves will remain at or return to the feudal state because this is the most stable system. He posits that, if we do not want systems to remain feudal, then at least one of two conditions must be fulfilled. The first is that the units of the lower stratum should increase their rank at the expense of some of the higher-stratum units. The other is that the lower-stratum units must associate more—that is, intensify interaction among themselves—to strengthen themselves relative to the units of the higher stratum. Thus, we see that a world that is becoming more egalitarian will be one where the poorer and weaker nations are gaining more of the system's output over a period of time and where the interactions between these nations are intensifying relative to other possible interactions.

I took Galtung's views to mean that an underdeveloped system is a feudal system and a developed system is an egalitarian system and that, hence, a developing system is one in which rank-concordance and interaction-dependence both tend from high to low over time. I therefore posited that (a) the international system did not develop between 1960 and 1970 to the extent that the system did not become less rank-concordant and less interaction-dependent and that (b) African nations did not develop during this period to the extent that they did not contribute to these desired changes.

At the final stages of that dissertation, a curious Ghanaian student friend, Kofi Hadjor, asked, "Why do you follow Galtung to depict the system as feudal?" I answered, "But it makes sense. Does it not?" He responded, "Yes, but only up to a point. The world is not feudal. It is capitalist!" Hadjor asked whether I had read Baran and Frank and others like them. "Baran and Frank who?" I asked. Hadjor said he would lend me Frank's powerful essay *Sociology of Development and Underdevelopment of Sociology.*

I had always wanted to do international political economy in the grandly wholesome ways in which the classical political economists—Rousseau, Smith, Ricardo, Marx, Mill, Bentham, and so on—did it, with the prospects of the development of Third World societies firmly in mind. But I had only managed to do political science and economics separately. There appeared to me to be a conscious determination to delink politics and economics. The term *political economy* had come to mean inorganically superficial slapdashing together of economics and politics. What I really wanted was a little initial "in" into international political economy, understood as the organic linkages between the political contexts, or underpinnings, of the justifications of actually existing economic realities on the one hand and the economic justifications of actually existing political realities, in which Third World societies found themselves at that level, on the other.

MY INITIAL ENCOUNTER AND
EMERGENCE AS A WORLD-SYSTEM ADHERENT

My first encounter with AGF's thoughts was his essay mentioned above. I was struck by its clarity. His criticisms of the dualists and the diffusionists were most informative in clarifying for me some of my most fundamental worries with respect to the unicity of the world. It made clear why, in studying development, the initial context should be the whole. The whole is surely greater than the sum of its parts, and the study of the development of any parts of it essentially meant the study of the impact of the whole on the parts. The proper appreciation of the nature of and the relationships among the many parts was, therefore, imperative. The whole was to be understood in the crucial terms of the forms or characters of its interrelating strands of processes and values, and the whole and its inner activities and logics must also be made historically specific. To my intellectual heart's delight, this is the profound meaning I made of AGF's essay. The proper name of the historical period within which the development/underdevelopment realities are located is *world-capitalism*.

After reading this essay, my appetite for AGF's writings became practically insatiable. AGF helped a lot in my emergence as a world-system adherent. His influence on the coherent development of my thoughts within the world-system was enhanced by the publication of his *World Accumulation, 1492-1789* (1978), *Dependent Accumulation and Underdevelopment* (1979), and "Crisis and Transformation of Dependence in the World-System" (1983), by which time I had gotten to know AGF personally as a dear friend. I read through a draft of the introduction to *World Accumulation*. I was beneficially impressed by his reference to Fairbank's constructive admonition to read history back-ward and the elegant parsimony of AGF's definition of theory in our field of endeavor: the *theory* = *history* formulation. This equation was altered in the printed form to read "theory equals history." When I later told AGF I did not approve of the change because it detracted from the full impact of this powerful equation of a statement, he said, "So?" So, you see what I mean when I say AGF refused to teach me "anything."

I read Baran (1957), Cox, Amin, Wallerstein, Hopkins, Aseniero, Kreye, Heinrichs, Frobel, and others, and I continue to read AGF. My methodological problems compelled me to gravitate toward this group of thinkers for precisely the same reasons that Charles Tilly wrongly condemns them:

> First of all, Frank [and others] incline to a very large definition of the capitalist sphere. They concentrate on capital accumulation via exchange for profit and tend to treat all parties to unequal exchange as part of the same capitalist world system. Thus for them the European creation of worldwide markets dominated by their principal centers of trade and capital marked the opening of our own system. That happened in the fifteenth and sixteenth centuries. Capitalism, then, is a mode of exchange; the principles of capitalist production follow from the requirements of capitalist exchange. (Tilly, 1984, p. 127)

This abridged version of Brenner's (1977) nonsense "neo-Smithian" criticism of world-system methodology notwithstanding, the terms of reference of these thinkers' thoughts are attractive to me simply because they are truly holistic and totally inclusive. They are historically precise by not being historically imprecise à la liberal historiography, or historically overprecise à la Marxist historiography.

By the early 1980s, I had come to accept the modern world-system as capitalist, initiated by Columbus's sadly successful 1492 (mis)adventure. The system is propelled by the historic motive of ever-increasingly efficient accumulation of global capital and its compulsive concomitant of the ever-increasingly efficient leakage of capital from the periphery of the system to its center by ever-changingly efficient mechanisms of ways and means.

The most attractive thing about the world-system methodology is that it provides a neat historic context within which to situate the apparent complexities of what is called the *development problématique*. Tilly (1984, p. 128) argues correctly that Frank and Wallerstein began the constructions of their world-system methodology by observing the influence of the core at the periphery, Frank mainly from Latin America and Wallerstein mainly from Africa. Then they moved to the core to understand its actions. Tilly goes on to praise Wolf (1982) for wanting to give "those people" back their history and then to rewrite the history of the core in consonance with that restitution. One can only say to this magnanimous gallantry, "If only this is possible and meaningful in any sensible way!" The intractable articulation between the "two histories" defies any such division of labor, no matter how genuine. This much must be clear. And from this we can make some discerning observations.

First is that, given its sources of initial inspiration, it is impossible to think about the world-system methodology without thinking about the Third World and the desirability and feasibility questions of the philosophy of developmentalism. Second, it should therefore be possible to refer to those who do not seek to tamper with the integrity of this methodology as sharing in common radical/critical Third World perspective(s) on the efficacy of the developmentalist project, regardless of the differences in the cultural-societies from which they come. Third, adherents to radical Third World perspectives must believe that their world-system methodology is the only valid mode of social analyses because it sees the non-European parts of the world as irremovable parts of world history, having been parts of it from the beginning. It is therefore the proper methodological framework within which to pose the question whether the developmentalist project is Eurocentric hoax, delusion, and chicanery, all rolled into one.

TOWARD A POINT OF DEPARTURE

CULTURE, HISTORY, AND DEPENDENCY

Quite correctly, Tilly (1984, p. 129) chastises Wolf for not asking (a) the extent to which European domination affected the character of "those people's" social organization and (b) what idea accounts for their variety. Tilly wondered why Wolf did not "use his encompassing comparisons to full advantage." One observation in this regard is that the world-system methodology surveys world history holistically, and convincingly so. This methodology, however, lacks the proper groundings for it to confront this very important question, by using it to "full advantage." It is too high flying, and so it runs the gross risk of being critically very limited, if not, in fact, empty. The idioms of radical Third World thinkers are broadly critical but not deeply critical enough. They betray strong beliefs in the feasibility of the developmentalist project, without the full consideration of all the critical observations and hard evidence. Their critical concerns are addressed to the presumed inner logicalities of this project, and they see illogicalities as if they were merely flaws in the universalist quest of a pretension that is the developmentalist project.

Another observation begins with the focus on the obviousness of material exploitation of the Third World. This, however, blinds world-system analysts to cultural-causal sources of the initiation and the continuously refining entrenchment of material exploitation. My argument is that material exploitation is a function of enforced and/or self-reinforcing cultural dependency. No matter how complex the concept of dependency may appear to be, it is, in the final analysis, a cultural phenomenon. The underdogs are forced, conditioned, or choose to depend on the top dogs because of the effects of cultural differences and imitations that create dependency.

The answer to Tilly's query of Wolf is the idea of practiced or practical culture, cultural dependency, and the expressed facts and effects of it in the many different ways. Not even in the most abbreviated abstracts of discourses should culture be reduced to the mere aesthetics of the complexity of social life, nor should history be equated with the perfunctory narration of victories and defeats. Culture and history are more than that. To world-system adherents, culture per culture should mean grand culture. It should mean the complex function of the totality of the various aspects of life, the daily and really lived aspects of life. Culture should always be seen in its complexity as the function of the politics, economics, laws, morals, mores, religions, intellectual forms, and styles, and not forgetting the aesthetic aspects of it—cuisine, song, dance, attire, art, and so on. Cultures are the worldviews they embrace and project, and the life-views they enact. To world-system adherents, history is nothing if it is not seen as the unfoldings of cultures in the motions of time. It is the resolution of the conflicts and tensions within and between cultures, over time, as cultures change into or stagnate in one form or the other.

Culture as depicted above should provide an "in" into the causal reality of dependency. Among the functional elements of culture as a daily lived reality are intellectual forms and styles. The question is what to do with them—intellectual forms and styles, that is. This is the question because we are yet to see that as cultures strain, collide, and/or impinge on one another, they undergo transformation and come to fall somewhere within the two extreme poles of authentic and corrupt cultural hybrids.

An authentic cultural hybrid is a culture that emerges stronger from its internal strains and encounters with other cultures than it was before. A corrupt cultural hybrid is a culture that emerges weaker than it was before its internal strains and encounters with other cultures. The authentic forms of cultures are stronger because they are internally oriented. They seem to know what they are about. The corrupt kinds of cultures are weaker cultures precisely because they are externally oriented. They see their strengths as located outside themselves. This is what makes them dependent to a large extent. As Galtung argued, Africa's problem is not so much the material exploitation of the continent as it is the misleading ideas that the European civilization has left with the Africans.

DISSENSION WITHIN THE THIRD WORLD RADICAL CAMP

Anyone who appreciates the Third World plight will have few difficulties in subscribing to the perspective depicted above. In doing so, most will nonetheless commit some gross methodological errors brought about by their subscriptions also to the fallacious Eurocultural epistemological notion of history as a dialectically programmed progressivist universalism on the march toward the Eurohumanist end. This complex fallacy buries human agency so deeply in the huge structure of global capitalism that it becomes nearly impossible to locate. It is in this context that misleading historical ideas and concepts such as universalism, Eurohumanism, determinism, developmentalism, progressivism, and dialecticism must be exposed and condemned for what they are: deceptive and dangerous from the point of view of Third World development in the dynamics of global capitalism on ascendancy.

The versatility of this set of fallacies, however, is not to be underestimated. It pervades the entire spectrum of Western-based political interpretations of present and future histories. Eurocentric progressivist universalism believes that History is necessarily a matter of progressing from one historical stage to another until History itself stops, dies, or ends; but not before final History has spread itself universally all over the world, obliterating all other histories and replacing them with itself totally.

The core belief in this piece of monstrous thinking is the absurd idea that history moves in a series of dialectical steps, whereby existing histories, by virtue of the resolutions of the conflicts and tensions within them, are vanquished by their supersedents and so on until World History stops. This march to finality is to be led by the West European socioeconomic political culture of liberal democracy. When this point is reached in Western Europe, the rest of the world would have no choice but to follow suit, either voluntarily or by compulsion. This view of history has some great names attached to it in Western social philosophy. They include Smith, Kant, Hegel, and a host of others whose lineage can be traced to the classical Greeks and can be carried on by our own modernization theorists of our CWO, and very specifically and especially Francis Fukuyama and his recent nonsense in *The End of History and the Last Man* (1992). Marx and Nietzsche, for different reasons, could not stand this ambition of History ending on a liberal democratic note, so they opted, respectively, for communism and fascism as the deterministic universalist notes on which history will have to end.

Fascism not being fashionable after the war, the CWO adherents to radical Third World perspective were to be found in the liberal and Marxist camps. Radicals in both camps subscribed to the notion of historical developments and History itself, as attended by the notion of programmed dialectical motions. These twin beliefs are too sacrosanct to be questioned because they are said to serve the Euro-historico-humanist end.

On these issues, the neo-radical Third World perspective begins to part company with the mere radical perspective. Commonly, radicals take too much of this mythology of a metaphysics for granted, which they must not be allowed to do, precisely because the questions that must be answered are the very ones, sadly, taken for granted.

A NEO-RADICAL THIRD WORLD PERSPECTIVE

TWENTY-FIVE THEOREMS IN
THE FORM OF RHETORICAL QUESTIONS

1. Why must history end?
2. Must history be linear?
3. Must it be progressive?
4. Where is culture in all this?
5. What will be the resultant cultural forms as the Western liberal democratic culture affects non-European cultural forms?
6. Or is it that these latter cultures are so benign that no possible interaction with liberal democracy, having totally vanquished all the other cultures, could result in any other mode than a global replication of itself?
7. Is the liberal democratic seedling so resistant that it can be transplanted successfully in any and every cultural environment?
8. Is it possible that some corrupt cultural hybrids can occur?
9. How seriously are we to take the notion of the dialectical motions of History?
10. How much does this notion account for, and how much does it conveniently leave out?
11. Is this notion of history unfolding in dialectical motions not two-dimensional, too mechanistic, and too rudely deterministic in its compass and therefore too shallow and sadly unhelpful in both its liberal and Marxist forms?
12. Can the notion of historical universalism not be a clever ruse to deceive some non-European cultures into permanent states of subservience and insecurity?
13. Would liberal democracy or communism not be a particularly good note for history to end on, if history had to end, were it not for the unmasked appearance that, in their quest for global dominance, they are both highly exploitative economic-cultural mediums in search of political and moral justification?
14. Judging by current semiotics, how can anybody be sure the "band of transition" is not preparing us for a new world (dis)order (NWO) wherein the confrontation for hegemony would be between modified fascism and modified communism and again largely at the expense of the Third World?
15. How do all of these questions impinge on the subjective desirability and feasibility of the Third World development project?
16. Knowing how badly the development project fared during the CWO, are we to be optimistic or pessimistic about the prospects of the project in the impending NWO?
17. Was it right for radicals to have believed, during the CWO, that the world-system should aim to develop the Third World?
18. Should we not now begin to think in terms of a Third World aim to develop itself within the global capitalist world-system? That is, should we not stop expecting development to be delivered to us like some Melanesian cargo from across some mirage of a horizon?

19. It is often said that even Third World radicals have captive minds. This being true, should they not attempt to retrieve their minds by revising their historical memories? By so doing, might they not hope to sharpen their acumens, improve their sights, hearings, touches, smells, and tastes for the benefits of appreciating the futilities inherent in uncritical developmentalist mimetism?

20. While criticizing the Other selves, should radicals also not criticize themselves as well?

21. Ever conscious of rising global consciousness and also conscious of the weaknesses of their own cultural-societies, where should radicals locate their strengths, all things considered: "home" or "outside"?

22. How should radicals understand the emerging idea of sustainable development?

23. Should radicals not leave the developmental future open, seeing that they must believe in the legitimacy and viability of multiple routes to multiple forms of comparable modernities?

24. Should radicals not avoid sensational titles such as "Capitalism in Crisis," "The World in Chaos," and "The World in Turbulence" because capitalism develops from crisis to crisis and the world is always in some kind of chaos, especially for the Third World?

25. Finally, but not exhaustively, should radicals not refuse to enjoin the screamings of such stupidly senseless and belated surprise-revelations as "Cascading Interdependence" and "Unstoppable Globalization," knowing that what is interesting about these actualities is not their voguish realizations at the end of this fifth phase of global capitalism, but how the seeds sown long ago enable them to bloom at this phase of it?

A perspective defined by twenty-five such questions must of necessity part company with the mere radical perspective. To part company is not necessarily to break all bonds, but the reader would agree that after such questions have been answered, any bonds that united the two perspectives must be, at least, fractured. I cannot respond in any satisfactory detail to all twenty-five questions raised here. The best way to proceed is to indicate the severity of the fractures in the bonds between the two variants of Third World radicalism by responding to only a few of the questions.

FROM DIALECTICS TO TRIALECTICS

Theorem eleven raises the matter of the inadequacy of the dialectical methodology. Its main faults are two. First, it compulsively, logically, and necessarily relegates some cultural-societies to the status of needing ordained exploitative tutelage in order to be deemed ready and so be allowed to join the presumed progressivist march of history toward its own self-consummation.

The problem here is that the judgments used are Eurocentrically derived and imposed. They therefore may not be valid in all aspects.

Second, the dialectical methodology is only two-dimensional, when what we need is really a three-dimensional methodology to enable us to get a proper and unprejudiced handle on historical movements. We need a historical methodology that does not divorce the struggle between the thesis and the antithesis from the verity of the expected synthesis. For these reasons, I propose the trialectical approach to the critical appraisals of historical motions and their synthesizing outcomes.

Trialectical methodology dwells not on mere claims to change, but on the meanings of such changes for the many whoms, defined in terms of economic, political, social, religious, and aesthetic aspects of the totalizing idea of Grand Cultures in this world of multiple cultures. This approach asks such questions as, Has the world really changed, or is the apparent change only an arrested variation of itself? Or, is it just a refined expression of its old self, an avatar of sorts? Or, have things changed only to remain the same, or get worse, for some and better for others? Or, has the world really entered a valid transition band wherein the texturity of its structures, processes, values, and mores are facing opportunities for the better for all?

Trialectics does not take the apparent dialectical resolutions of some major historical changes for granted, and it does not rush to praise or condemn such historical resultants. Instead, it subjects such claims to change to futuristic potentialities/depotentialities critique. Trialectics is critical thinking: Trialectical thinking = critical thinking, in the light of advancing the humanizing project.

Trialectical thinking, to illustrate, would ask such questions as:

1. Why did the formal ends of colonialism turn out to be different kinds of counter-finalities? Did colonialism really end, or did it merely change its forms by refining them?
2. Do or should all countries, cultures, and so forth have to industrialize to the same extent before they are deemed modernized?
3. Must we all follow Eurohumanist universalism blindly and be oblivious to its inherent contradiction, ignored so far, or must we be bold enough to raise it so that we can see what the real problem is: that we are pursuing self-serving Eurocultural humanism?

FROM VULGAR OPTIMISM
TO CREATIVE PESSIMISM

With respect to the development projects, theorem sixteen queried whether Third World radicals have good reasons to be optimistic or pessimistic. My neo-radical response is that because there is no good reason to be optimistic, I have to be pessimistic, but not pessimistic in the dictionary sense of the word. Rather, I am a "creative pessimist." A creative pessimist is not an abject pessimist who throws his or her hands in the air and cries, "Oh, there is no hope," and resigns from the struggle. On the contrary, creative pessimists are fully engaged in the struggle. The difference is that creative pessimists take neither victory nor claims of advancement for granted. They do not talk optimism just to gladden their own hearts.

Foolhardy optimism seems to be the order of the day. There is not a single conference, seminar, symposium, or colloquium on the human condition from which participants are not expected to emerge without optimistic cries, even when there are no grounds for such cries: "Conditions in Europe are very much reminiscent of Hitlerite Germany, *but I am optimistic,*" I heard someone say at a conference in 1992. "Conditions have worsened for the growing vast majority in the Third World in the past thirty years, *but I am optimistic,*" as I heard another person proclaim in 1993. Of course, there are always reasons for some degree of optimism. But in short supply are the autocritical appraisals for the proclamations of self-confident optimisms.

Creative pessimism is the antidote to such mindless and false indulgence in optimism. The emphasis is less on the pessimism and more on the creative. I believe that when things historical are not going well, one has every reason to be pessimistic, though not in the vulgar sense of debilitating disengagement, but in the critical sense of retreating to assess the efficacy/nonefficacy/inefficacy and even counterfinalities of accepted doctrines, premises, strategies, and the strategic ends themselves. This kind of critical pessimism borne of praxis and theoretical experience yields the creativity needed to redefine the goals, tactics, and strategies of the humanization project. The pessimism produces a renewed and engaged optimism: *nouvelle engagement.*

The *neo-radical Third World perspective* refers to new necessary ways that Third World elites have to look at the world, themselves, and their societies. These elites, while in fact corrupt, see themselves as authentic (Addo, 1987, 1993.) These elites, in actuality, are nothing but "ostentatious cripples," consciousness speaking, as the Ghanaian novelist Ayi Kwei Armah (1979) describes them. They are not authentic elites, because the historical forces that formed them also deformed them to serve against the real interest of their peoples. Why is this so? Because they have bought universalistic modernism, in the form of the developmentalist philosophy, without any critical considerations whatever. They have been only reactive, never proactive. Although global capital is generated globally, there is the fundamental logic in historical capitalism that such capital as could have accumulated in Third World societies must, by varying means and rationales, leak out of these societies to add to the accumulating capital owned and/or controlled by the center of the world capitalist system. This leaves the Third World impoverished and hopelessly dependent on the center, as an indubitable ever-widening and ever-deepening historical fact.

The mechanisms and rationales for exploiting the Third World are many and varied. At the conjunctural phases of changing historical capitalism, NWOs have been proclaimed, and the fortunes of the Third World have been promised vast improvements. Yet, these fortunes have remained relatively the same. The gradient of exploitation has remained relatively constant. Does it not look very much as though the more things historical-capitalist change, at best, the more they remain the same for the Third World? Why is it so, according to AGF?

A REVERSED FRANK ESSENCE?

FRANK AS A CREATIVE PESSIMIST?

It is obvious that AGF, like so many of us, is grossly disappointed by how things developmental, and dependency as a critical theory, turned out. The question is how AGF dealt with this. To some, perhaps to the many, he would appear to have taken the easy way out. He has thrown in the critical towel, thrown his hands in the air and screamed, "Oh, there is no hope." He seems bent on taking himself, and all that he has contributed, out of the critique of developmentalism. Or is it that he genuinely believes that a large part of his earlier thinking was wrong? If so, are the reasons he advances for this really convincing? In the section that follows, I pay a critical visitation to some aspects of AGF's reversal, from the points of view located in the theorems composing the neo-radical Third World perspective. Do AGF's reversals

advance the cause of the world-system methodology by sensible criticisms or
are they dangerous flights of fancy?

INTERROGATING ASPECTS OF "THE GREAT
REVERSAL OF THE FRANK ESSENCE"

I heard of AGF changes of mind from a number of sources, among them
an *FIU Newsletter* summarizing the essence of a talk given there recently.
Having now read AGF's own full account of the reasons why he had, of
necessity, to recant or modify many of his ideas of the past thirty years, I
proceed to point to some detailed aspects of the changes of mind noted in these
two sources in order to compile evidence for or against the validity of the
"great reversal."

AGF has said, or now maintains, among other things that:

1. I would no longer say that delinking is a solution. It is impossible. . . .
For Latin America, the option of getting out is either difficult or impossible.

Delinking has not been a solution for AGF for more than a decade. I heard
him make this argument at a conference where he presented his famous paper
on Kampuchea. His argument was that it is the system that delinks parts of it,
and not parts of the system that delink from it. Hence, it is impossible for parts
to delink wilfully from the total system. Purposeful delinking is not merely
difficult, it is impossible. Even if delinking were vaguely possible, the corrupt
cultural hybrid forms of Latin America cultural-societies preclude it as a probable option.

2. . . . the Achilles' heel of my work is that . . . I never said how it would
be possible to become non-dependent or independent.

AGF could not have said how. So long as independent development paths
mean nothing more than different means to the same developmental ends of
West/East European modes of development via industrialization, the Achilles'
heel remains vulnerable.

3. Development could be understood as a world technological process
where regions and firms participate for short periods of time until they are
out-competed. . . .

There is nothing to quibble with in this regard. This has always been the case. Whether development moves historically in a westerly direction or not is irrelevant and of no consolation whatever to those who are the subjects of the "development of underdevelopment" thesis. For AGF, therefore, the calls for responses to the increasingly generalized consciousness of crises in development and development thinking were all misplaced; and so upon reflection, he concludes that:

4. There is sensation of total bankruptcy in development policy, thinking, theory and ideology, indeed of development *tout court.*

5. . . . We are at the end of an era and need to look beyond development to the survival strategies of the people if we want to understand what is really happening in the Third World. . . .

6. No one left, right, or center, any longer has any practical solutions to offer regarding development. We should forget all these *isms.* . . .

The bankruptcy AGF refers to is a built-in part of the developmentalist discourse. All shades of radical opinion were blinded by the belief in the false efficacy and the imperative necessity of Eurocultural universalism. No account was taken of the many cultural conflicts, tensions, and distortions that could result. Exploitation was seen in the material superficialities of the phenomenon to the utter neglect of the effects of the phenomenon of grand cultural imperialism. This is particularly true of its intellectual components that subserve the material tip of the iceberg of entrenched and reinforcing grand cultural imperialism.

It is the survival strategies of the people that radical discourse should have looked into from the beginning. But the belief in the desirability and feasibilities of the developmentalist route of industrialization blinded us all to this. We criticized the thoughts of the "pioneers of development" but did not critique them. We shared in common with them their epistemological assumptions: development = Westernization via industrialization. We did not even pause to question the desirability and the feasibility of this vulgar equation.

But why should we, because of all this, "forget all these *isms*"? We should not, nor can we. The coinage of *isms* is unavoidable. I believe the coinage of *isms* called for in the theorems of the neo-radical Third World perspective is worth serious consideration.

7. . . . Social development would be a more equitable and better end. But then what is the measure of equity, let alone of efficiency?

8. . . . it now appears that if "development" has any operational sense at all, it is not in reference to a country. . . . Instead, the only meaningful development is of the world economy and society at one level and for much smaller social groups or individuals at another level.

It is nice for AGF to have moved from economic equity to social equity, but then, I thought this should have always been the case. I have two big worries here. Why does AGF make such a big thing about the mysteriousness of equity? Is not equity something you see when you come across it? Of course, there are, and will always be, disparities. Is the idea not to minimize them the best we can?

Why does AGF make such a wondrous and mystifying thing about "the only meaningful development is of the world economy and society"? I am bothered by this mystification. Is the central question in our world-system methodology not the development of the world and society and for whom? AGF is free to abandon the hyphenated "world-system" for the nebulous "world system," but does he have to go this far in the realms of mind-boggling marginality? Is AGF's present position not tantamount to an evasion of a very serious kind? Although we all live on this earth, is the problem not precisely that we, none of us, live all over it at one and the same time? Is our central *problématique* not the search for the explanation of the fact that, although we all live on this world, some, some few, live in this same world more than the vast majority of others?

9. The world system we live in is five thousand years old. It is still the same world. . . .

Well, this must be a cruel joke of sorts. Has this five thousand years world-system changed at all? Did "Columbus 1492" ever happen? Did the West European domination of the world ever happen? If it did, is it still a reality? And when Fairbank rightly advised that we read history backward, was he suggesting that we do so in search of final historical causes, or was he advising us to do so in order to hit on plausible, necessary, and sufficient historical explanations? To date, our world-system back five thousand years is to wish away the center-periphery axis of modern history. Or is AGF suggesting that we drop the word *modern* because it serves no useful purpose?

I should leave this matter at that, for if Abu-Lughod (1989) can date her world system back to the 13th century, why can't AGF argue for his five thousand years theory, even if I am still puzzled by this reasoning?

10. . . . a dual economy and society may now indeed be in the process of formation at this stage of social evolution in the world system. However, this new dualism is different from the old dualism I rejected. The similarity between the two "dualisms" is only apparent. According to the old dualism, sectors or regions were supposedly separate. That is, they supposedly existed without past or present exploitation between them before "modernization" would join them happily ever after. Moreover, this separate dual existence was seen within countries. I correctly denied all these propositions. In the new dualism, the separation comes after the contact and often after exploitation. The lemon is discarded after squeezing it dry. Thus, this new dualism is the result of the process of social and technological evolution, which others call "development." Moreover, this new dualism is between those who do and those who cannot participate in a world wide division of labor.

The distinction AGF draws between what one may call Dualism I and Dualism II when seen as historical processes is not surprising at all. It is a distinction whose time has come. This distinction shows clearly why developmentalism has all along been a Eurocentric cruel hoax and masked delusion, a clever chicanery masquerading all along as an elixir, in the multicolored pious garb of progressivist humanistic universalism. It hides its core contradiction of universalist impossibilism neatly and conveniently under its well-tailored garb.

11. However, I quarreled with orthodoxies more about their vision of development than with their idea of development itself. I did not then find it remarkable that I also shared an essentially similar vision of capital accumulation through industrial growth = development. Because, so did I! I had only managed to turn orthodoxy on its head. Doing so only evaded and rendered impossible any fundamental other sideways critique and reformulation, which I now regard necessary.

Here it is. The truth as it should have been known, if Third World Radicalism had not been dialectically silly to start with and had not compounded this silly error with the foolish nonsense of self-serving deceptive belief in the Eurocultural hegemonic ambition of Euro-serving humanistic progressivism. It is impossible for me to imagine a more fundamental confession of past errors. Bully for him!

COMFORTING CONCLUSIONS

Recalling my fortuitous encounter with AGF's works, my self-imposed immersion into the study of the world-system methodology, the twenty-five theorems framing my neo-radical Third World perspectives, and other aside derivatives, I can only conclude this chapter in honor of my teacher and friend, Andre Gunder Frank, on a comforting note.

I may appear to disagree with him here and there, but he continues to teach me by "teaching me nothing." I am still my own man, I would like to think, but I am obviously indebted to him. He has again led me to the threshold of my mind. From critically reading his chapter in this volume, I am more confident than ever that developmentalism via full-scale industrialization is open to only a few. The road, in this regard, is closed to the many. I am now more sure of my fledgling neo-radical theorems, my discussion of the numerous fallacies in African development thought, and particularly of the impossibilism inherent in Euro-imposed historical universalism, because of the inherent contradiction at its core, but above all, by the demonstration of his contribution in this volume that it is necessary to indulge in honest, creative pessimism at certain moments in a long career. I am encouraged by the support AGF gives to the view that we should release the development future from the straitjacket of Eurocentric closedness, or else we are doomed, for good. The development future should be open to allow in the serious considerations of multiple cultural routes to modernity (Addo, 1992). May AGF, in his retirement, live long to provoke and to help us all!

REFERENCES

Abu-Lughod, J. (1989). *Before European hegemony.* New York: Oxford University Press.
Addo, H. (1987). Crisis in the development praxis: A critical global perspective. In G. Schuyler & H. Veltmeyer (Eds.), *Rethinking Caribbean development* (pp. 17-26). Halifax: International Education Centre.
Addo, H. (1992). A Third World perspective on global justice and the new world order. In K. Tehranian & M. Tehranian (Eds.), *Restructuring for world peace: On the threshold of the 2lst century* (pp. 256-281). Cresskill, NJ: Hampton.

Addo, H. (1993). World-system and peripheral states. In J. Danecki (Ed.), *Insights into mal-development* (pp. 47-60). Warsaw: University of Warsaw Press.

Armah, A. (1979). *Healers.* London: Heinemann.

Baran, P. (1957). *The political economy of growth.* New York: Modern Reader Paperback.

Brenner, R. (1977). The origins of capitalist development: A critique of neo-Smithian Marxism. *New Left Review, 104,* 25-92.

Frank, A. G. (1978). *World accumulation, 1492-1789.* New York: Monthly Review Press.

Frank, A. G. (1979). *Dependent accumulation and underdevelopment.* New York: Monthly Review Press.

Frank, A. G. (1983). Crisis and transformation of dependence in the world system. In R. H. Chilcolte & D. Johnson (Eds.), *Theories of development: Mode of production or dependency?* (pp. 181-200). Beverly Hills, CA: Sage.

Fukuyama, F. (1992). *The end of history and the last man.* New York: Free Press.

Galtung, J. (1964). A structural theory of aggression. *Journal of Peace Research, 2,* 95-119.

Galtung, J. (1966). Rank and social integration: A multi-dimensional approach. In J. Berger et al. (Eds.), *Sociological theories in progress* (Vol. 1, pp. 145-211). Boston: Houghton Mifflin.

Galtung, J. (1968). A structural theory of integration. *Journal of Peace Research, 4,* 375-395.

Galtung, J. (1971). A structural theory of imperialism. *Journal of Peace Research, 1,* 81-117.

Tilly, C. (1984). *Big structures, large processes, huge comparisons.* New York: Russell Sage.

Wolf, E. (1982). *Europe and the people without history.* Berkeley: University of California Press.

PART II

On Peripheral Regions

8

Latin American Underdevelopment: Past, Present, and Future

A Homage to Andre Gunder Frank

THEOTONIO DOS SANTOS

Paulo Frank, Translator

The theme of underdevelopment, in various interpretations, has had an enduring hold on Latin America. In the 19th century, Latin American thought was largely defined by the debate over civilization and barbarism. National elites saw Latin America left farther and farther behind by a rapidly developing world under the dominance of West European cultural values. A non-European cultural, social, and ethnic presence seemed to be at the root of Latin American backwardness. Within the East-West framework, Latin Americans saw themselves as being nearer to the East than to the West.

This was also a debate over the dichotomies of modern and archaic, urban and rural, and progress and backwardness. Progress became one of the fundamental categories in the thinking of Latin American middle classes greatly influenced by positivist thought. *Positivism* views industry, technology, and science as the historic goals of civilization. The task of carrying out these goals would be left to an industrial class.

In the second half of the 19th century, progress—a progress in which Latin America failed to play a leading part—was seen to result from the importation of scientific knowledge and technology, rather than from their independent development. The ideology of progress was an expression of the outlook of a middle class that strove to keep pace with the middle and dominant classes in the countries at the center—countries to which Latin America exported raw materials and from which it imported industrial products.

These opposing views began to be revised and reformulated in the 1920s and 1930s, when a new perspective centered on industrialization gained ground in the region. As a result, these dichotomies were reformulated.

At the end of the 1940s and in the 1950s, intellectual developments within the United Nations Economic Commission for Latin America (ECLA) laid the foundation for the economic analyses, empirical groundwork, and institutional support that would later inform the search for the bases of Latin American development. These efforts led to the affirmation of industrialization as the key element of development, progress, modernity, civilization, and political democracy.

Industrialization was affirmed above all in Brazil, Mexico, Argentina, and, to a degree, also in Chile and Colombia. Industrialization was key to the most modern manifestations of development in these countries. Backwardness, archaism, and barbarism were the result of the specialization of Latin American economies that concentrated on the exportation of primary products. Some authors, such as Gilberto Freire, charged that monoproduction destroyed economic alternatives. Others denounced international capital, which had played an important role in the creation of export sectors in various countries, because in their view it produced virtual "enclaves" that had no effect on national economies as a whole. Foreign-sector investments did not create "external economies."

The view gained ground that underdevelopment was an economic, social, political, and cultural condition made up of negative processes, such as "enclave," "monoculture," the "racial" question, internal colonialism, and so-called economic dualism. These elements were interconnected and led to backwardness and underdevelopment. To advance from underdevelopment to development, it was necessary to break out of this vicious circle.

Meanwhile, a series of transformations associated with industrialization were subsumed under the rubric "bourgeois revolution." The problem of development was generally explained by pointing to the necessity of a bourgeois revolution in Latin America. Its absence accounted for the region's backwardness. The concept of bourgeois revolution was also directly connected to the agrarian question from two perspectives: (a) It supposed the destruction of the latifundio as the political and economic force that formed the basis of the dominance of rural oligarchies and sectors that depended on the export of primary products; consequently, (b) it had a political, social, and economic content in the struggle against the latifundium. Moreover, the latifundium was shown to be the generator of socioeconomic inequality and a block to the development of the peasantry and the creation of a domestic market.

Agrarian reform seemed, therefore, to offer a solution to these two great problems. There were important historical precedents, such as the Mexican Revolution, whose ideological influence was felt throughout the continent. The Mexican Revolution unfolded during the revolutionary struggles of the 1910s and the struggles to construct a modern, national, and democratic state. To this end, the Mexican Constitution of 1917 upheld the principles of agrarian reform, national ownership of minerals and national wealth, the state as a regulator of the economy, and progress tied to social, economic, and political transformations.

The ideals of the Mexican Revolution gained even greater prominence during the 1930s, when the Cárdenas government reinforced and radicalized them. Inspired by the Russian Revolution, this government broadened agrarian reform in an attempt to develop Mexican cooperatives and *ejidos*. By nationalizing the petroleum industry, Cárdenas sustained the principle of state monopoly of national resources; by instituting an economic plan, he defended the state's need to manage the process of industrialization.

The Mexican state's political support of peasant and worker centers contributed to the formation of a political framework in which liberal democracy was substituted by participatory democracy. Within this framework, the political and trade union organization of workers formed the basis for an alternative conception of democracy that was inspired by world socialist developments and found expression in Mexico through the idea of socialist education.

Developments in Mexico influenced men such as Haya de la Torre, founder of Peru's APRA, an organization that advanced the concept of Indo-America. When de la Torre and other political leaders in the region affirmed the autonomy of Latin American nations, they combined social, racial, ethnic, and cultural questions. Their autonomy thesis, rooted in the endorsement of indigenous peoples and influential among Communist Parties, eventually had to adapt the ideology of the Third International to the conditions of the Third World in general and to those of Latin America in particular.

In imitation of debates raging in Asia (mainly in India and China), efforts were made to identify an indigenous population that had fallen under the domination of Europe, colonialism, and imperialism. Indigenous populations thus appeared to be a wellspring for a social struggle that would also be economic and political. In the 1920s, Mariátegui sought to demonstrate that the Indian question was fundamentally an agrarian question. Whereas Mella emphasized the role of student movements, Ponce brought to the fore the necessity of education.

Yet, Latin American Marxism could not escape the more global context of Latin American intellectuals, such as Martí and Hostos in the 19th and especially at the close of the 19th century, who fought for an affirmation of the national, anti-imperialist, and anti-colonial in Cuba and Puerto Rico. Although there were debates over specific issues, there was a common frame of reference within which the need for a bourgeois revolution in Latin America was understood. The bourgeois revolution had to be led by a particular class—namely, the national industrial bourgeoisie.

Social forces and the left, especially the Communist Party, reached a peak in Latin America from the 1930s to the 1950s. During this period, intellectuals, large numbers of technocrats, and industrial (and even entrepreneurial) sectors came to see the Soviet Union—an industrial superpower and Second World War victor—as a model of planning to solve economic problems. Some authors adopted Schumpeter's concept of the innovative entrepreneur, who was to lead this revolution. An attempt was made to transcend a historical framework characterized by precapitalist "feudal remnants," variously interpreted. All the same, in the 1930s and 1940s, the condition of the exporter of primary materials, as well as of primary and agricultural products, came to be seen as the principal economic obstacle.

This viewpoint became more clearly articulated with the foundation, in 1947, of the United Nations Economic Commission for Latin America (ECLA) under the leadership of Raúl Prebisch. He carried further the argument that the role played by the export sector was the main obstacle to "economic development." It was a perspective that largely replaced the concept of bourgeois revolution.

ECLA was an organization that emerged from Latin American governments and that provided them with policy and technical advice. Its studies proposed policies designed to clear the road for the process of industrialization and to surmount obstacles in the way of development. Nevertheless, its political recommendations bolstered existing power structures.

The region's industrial development became dependent on the export sector through a process of import substitution. This process and its historical origins would later be systematized on a theoretical and conceptual level. As Andre Gunder Frank emphasized in his studies of Latin America, this process was the result of the global crises of world capitalism. In particular, the 1929 crisis had a negative effect on world trade. It fell, at the time, by about 50%, reducing the region's imports.

Celso Furtado also demonstrated how the policy of stabilizing the price of coffee stocks balanced average incomes and, therefore, internal demand. In other countries, the attempt was made to preserve domestic purchasing power to the fullest. In this way, a spontaneous protectionism was created, as a consequence of the world economic crisis, that made viable the development of a national industry that came to substitute a large part of the products that had previously been imported.

Although the effect of the First and Second World Wars was to curb imports, they also stimulated exports. Economic conditions during periods of war were extremely favorable to import substitution.

Some authors, among whom I count myself, called attention to the crises of the 1830s, 1840s, 1860s, 1880s, and 1890s, pointing out that if they failed to promote industrialization in any decisive way, it was because the manufacturing sector in the Latin American region was still exceedingly weak; this made it impossible to take advantage of the opportunities created by crises. The great world economic expansions of the 1850s and 1860s and of the 1895-1914 period, however, resulted in a fundamental restructuring of the Latin American region's economy in favor of the agricultural and primary products demanded by a rapidly expanding European (and later also a North American) economy.

The phenomenon of import substitution was a result of these crises and began to be the object of systematic investigation in the 1930s. Roberto Simonsen, the great Brazilian economic and industrial leader, was the first to describe it in a very important article in *Boletim do Ministério de Indústria, Comércio e Trabalho* (*Bulletin of the Ministry of Industry, Commerce, and Labor*).

In the 1950s, the ECLA carried out detailed studies of the process of import substitution. It began with the import substitution of consumer products, especially those consumed by the elites, that were soon saturated. In the 1940s, however, import substitution turned to durable consumer goods. Substitution in the machinery sector was only initiated during the final phase, the 1950s and 1960s. Industrialization based on import substitution causes industrial growth to depend greatly on earnings of foreign exchange generated from exports. The state adopted what were in some cases radical measures to appropriate or even expropriate the foreign exchange needed. The Brazilian case was typical: Here, state control of foreign trade was decisively put into effect in the 1930s by a government that took possession of foreign exchange earnings made from exports and that paid exporters with national currency.

This policy was opposed by landowners and commercial exporters, who denounced the so-called foreign exchange confiscation. The fortunes of the export sector were profoundly affected by a foreign exchange policy that fixed the value of the national currency in relation to foreign currencies through the manipulation of foreign exchange rates. Exporters received national currency for their exports and were forced to buy consumer products and make investments in the internal market.

The structural correlation between the survival of the export sector and industrialization would result in a particularly Latin American political alliance, a political alliance in which the industrial bourgeoisie supported policies aimed at ensuring the survival of latifundia. Consequently, the industrial bourgeoisie's revolutionary potential was limited, in that it abandoned any ambitions to confront traditional oligarchies and to work toward an income distribution in the countryside that would be conducive to the development of a healthier internal market. It proved unable to sell the means of production and consumer goods to the rural masses. Such an expansion of internal demand would have strengthened the productive capacity of Latin American countries. Instead, a structural obstacle was created that arrested the region's economic development.

This structural limitation was clearly reflected in the thinking of the ECLA. Being, to a great extent, a representative of the industrial bourgeoisie, it sought policies that did not touch on the agrarian question and permitted the nonconfrontational extraction of resources from the latifundia through state intervention mechanisms. One such mechanism was inflation, which permitted a price policy favorable to the industrial sector. Another mechanism, as mentioned above, was the nationalization of foreign exchange and a policy of exchange regulation. Last, the state intervened directly in the rural economy by subsidizing export production, protecting agricultural products for popular consumption, and through other means.

The bourgeoisie's capitulatory nature was also evident from its conciliatory attitude toward international capital. Although it recognized its exploitative character, the Latin American bourgeoisie relied on international capital because it controlled technology and international markets through powerful cartels and monopolies. International capital largely dominated the export-oriented sectors of the economy, energy, transport, communications, and in some cases the industrial processing of export products and even their marketing.

Within this framework, international capital appeared to be the ally of export-oriented latifundium production, mining, and the monoculture economy. It helped perpetuate relations of semi-servitude within the latifundium that were generally characterized as "precapitalist." Andre Gunder Frank played a very positive role when he argued that these economies were modalities of capitalism resulting from the growth of the world economy and the international division of labor. To be sure, this mode of dependent and subordinate capitalism lacked certain elements necessary for the development of capitalism, such as a wage regime and a modern working class. But let us not forget that the first working class to appear in Latin America was tied to the export sector. The first working-class demonstrations in the region were renowned for their ties to the mining sector. Such centers are associated with the growth of a relatively organized mining proletariat, most notably in Chile and Bolivia. The railroad sector, specializing in the transportation of export goods, gave rise to one of the Latin American trade union movements of greatest consequence. The rural salary workers of the United Fruit Company in Central America and the Caribbean made known their revolutionary presence in the 1920s and 1930s.

A small body of industrial workers was formed at the close of the 19th century and during the First World War. Being an artisan proletariat, these workers' ideological orientation was predominantly anarchist up to the end of the 1920s. National industry, as such, only began to take root in the 1930s, with the formation of the weaving and metallurgical industries, as well as urban trade unionism.

The Latin American industrial bourgeoisie, which emerged during the industrialization process of the 1930s and 1940s, existed in an uneasy relationship with international capital. It aspired to replace it, but it lacked the technological know-how and financial weight to make the large investments that were required during the advanced stages of technological development. Consequently, it relied on the state to perform this task, especially in those sectors of the economy in which international capital was reluctant to invest. The case of Latin American oil was archetypical. The world centers of decision making looked on it more as a U.S. reserve than as a resource to be exploited. Accordingly, international capital was not interested in investing in petroleum, except in the case of Venezuela, where it was plentiful, close to the surface, and inexpensive. It is therefore not surprising that international capital was viewed as an impediment to the region's industrialization. Instead, it seemed to bolster the export sectors, as well as the rural, mining, and export-oriented commercial oligarchies.

Attempts therefore were made to redirect international investment. The ECLA confronted this question in theory and practice and identified international capital as a key element in the economic and industrial development of our nations. International capital seemed to complement the internal savings necessary for industrialization. In practice, international capital had the capacity to secure from abroad the machinery, production systems, and technologies that national capital lacked. But it was rarely prepared to provide the resources needed for their proper functioning in the local economy. To the contrary, when international capital invested in a country, it tended to rely on its foreign reserves alone to finance the installation of machinery, production systems, and technologies. It was left to the host countries to meet the need for energy, railroad, and communications networks. In the postwar years, the United States undertook numerous missions aimed at promoting the creation of energy and transportation networks that would sustain a massive influx of foreign investment in the 1950s and 1960s.

Economic thinking within the ECLA paralleled these historical tendencies. In the 1950s, the ECLA criticized the export of primary products, underscoring that declining terms of trade proved the historical limitations of such trade. It demonstrated that the existing export sector stood in the way of industrialization. It also demonstrated that it was necessary to extract surplus from this sector and redirect it to industry. This tack required either indirect intervention mechanisms, such as inflation, allowing for pricing policies favorable to the urban industrial sector, or alternatively, direct state intervention (sometimes producing deficit-based revenues).

We are therefore in a relatively new context. Development theories moved beyond the debate that emerged in the 1950s and 1960s under the influence of the ECLA and centered on civilization and barbarism, modernity and archaism, progress and backwardness. In its place, a more consistent debate emerged over development and underdevelopment on the one hand and a modern industrial structure, with all of its social and political consequences and an agrarian or mineral export structure that needed to be progressively replaced, on the other.

The left, especially the Communist Party, saw the same issues in terms of a "democratic-bourgeois revolution." It argued that regional progress had to be led by a national bourgeoisie with the support of industrial-proletarian, urban and rural movements. The working-class movement was to assert itself within this new democratic society. This vision of a democratic revolution was sometimes more and sometimes less radical in its focus. Some argued that the bourgeois democratic revolution had to be led by the national bourgeoisie; others would have the working-class or peasant movements take the lead, either propelling the bourgeoisie or directly fulfilling its revolutionary tasks. This *problématique* culminated in the 1950s and 1960s with the introduction of the question of international capital and the new role of imperialism.

Reasoning on this issue took on complex dimensions. If the bourgeois democratic revolution was to succeed as both a national and a democratic revolution, imperialism, in its role as supporter of the oligarchic and anti-industrial sectors, had to be checked. But what was the correct response to an imperialism with links to industry—namely, to international capital that invested in the industrial sector? On this issue, there was still much hesitation and confusion. The general tendency was to accept international capital but to control the outflow of its profits and force it to play a subsidiary role in regional industrial development.

In this context, the bourgeois revolution in the region and the role played by so-called precapitalist economies began to be reinterpreted. It became necessary to reexamine the role of capitalist development in the region and to situate its economic evolution within the expansion of European mercantile capitalism, particularly that of Portugal and Spain. The subsequent displacement of mercantile capital by Dutch, French, English, and American manufacturing capital, and later industrial capital, also called for a fundamental revision of historical focus. New studies sought to demonstrate that slave and servile relations were brought about by a commercial capital whose interests would later merge with those of a modern industrial capital in need of raw materials and cheap agricultural products. The types of modern servitude and slavery that emerged from this new context differed fundamentally from those that characterized the classic feudal slave regime. Consequently, the region's supposed feudal past had to be fundamentally reexamined.

By the 1960s, studies produced from 1930 to 1950 by scholars such as Roberto Simonsen on economic history, Sergiu Bagu on colonial society, Luis Vitale on capitalism in Chile, Caio Prado Junior on colonization and the agrarian question, and Celso Furtado on the agrarian sector already constituted a powerful body of critique of the feudal colonial economy thesis. Andre Gunder Frank built on these studies to produce a paradigmatic shift. He argued that it was mistaken to speak of a feudal economy in the region and pointed instead to modes of commercial capitalist and later industrial capitalist expansion.

Frank offered an interpretative model of international relations that sought to explain different degrees of internal colonization, as well as the export of surplus. This cycle began in the most distant local, regional, and national centers and ended overseas in the hands of international capital. Frank denounced the brutality of a process of surplus extraction that prevented the region's economic development. Contrary to existing opinion, he argued that rather than supplying capital or contributing to the economic development of the region, international capital initiated a process of expropriation of its riches.

This argument was articulated and reexamined again and again by Latin American intellectuals who tried to escape from Frank's initial radical perspective. An attempt was made to reach a conceptual balance between the import of international capital, through machinery, technology, and the like, and the extraction of wealth from the region through the withdrawal of profits and prices unfavorable to the agrarian and mining sectors. This reformulation had profound implications with regard to the role of international capital. Some authors, including Frank, sought to demonstrate that there was no national bourgeoisie; others, including myself and Fernando Henrique Cardoso, emphasized the development of compromise between the national bourgeoisie and international capital.

I and the research group in which I worked (see Vânia Bambirra *El Capitalismo Dependiente de América Latina,* Siglo XXI, Mexico) opted for the second interpretation. We tried to demonstrate that, between the 1920s and the 1950s, the national bourgeoisie attempted to gain an industrial foothold in the region. Cardenism, ECLA thinking, and more sophisticated ideological models, such as that of the Instituto Superior de Estudos Brasileiros (created in 1955 by the Kubitscheck government and closed by the coup d'état of 1964) in Brazil all had roots in the national bourgeoisie. The national bourgeoisie exerted considerable influence on petty bourgeois perspectives, such as the Peruvian APRA and its various equivalents in the region. It also provided inspiration and support for populist and national-democratic movements, ranging from the radicalism of the Mexican Revolution, and above all of Cárdenism, to the conservatism of figures such as Perón or Vargas. Yet, all these political movements shared a nationalist and democratic vision. Nationalism and democracy were seen as both instruments and sine qua non for the affirmation and economic development of peoples.

This critical historical approach was developed as part of dependency theory in works undertaken by me and others at CESO at Universidad de Chile. Among its most brilliant examples was Ruy Mauro Marini's 1967 study of sub-imperialism, which demonstrated that the implantation of industrial economies in a number of Latin American countries gave rise to the growth of finance capital in the region. Rather than restricting its development to the local level, finance capital pursued national and Latin American development, the expansion of capital outside its borders, and the formation of alliances with international capital designed to strengthen its position as finance capital. Brazil took a clear lead in this process.

My aim at that time was to identify the close connection between Latin American economic cycles and world economic cycles up to the 1950s and the changing effects of these cycles on agricultural and mineral production beginning in that decade. It became evident to me that the advance of industrialization had produced increasingly endogenous four- and ten-year cycles that reflected the growth of domestic machine industries and technologies. I also tried to demonstrate that the growth of the industrial sector necessitated a new political approach toward international capital. International capital replaced national capital in the process of industrialization, importing technology, financing, and competitive patterns from economies that already produced technologically advanced products. It was therefore inevitable that international capital would force national capital to submit to the growing world economic power it wielded by a new type of multinational company. I was the first to analyze its expansion in Latin America, especially in my book *El Nuevo Carácter de la Dependência.*

These new studies led to a theoretical reformulation on a global level and underscored the need for an analytical methodology that would situate the history of Latin America in the context of the expansion of the world capitalist system. It was argued that emergent nationalist economies were the manifestations of the expanding world capitalist system. Nevertheless, as the economic and social structures of each country, region, and locality penetrated by colonialism differed, so did the specific manifestations of the world capitalist system. The attempt to overcome the limitations of local economies resulted in the African slave trade—that violent transplantation of much of the population of Africa to Latin America, the Caribbean, and the South of the United States—giving rise to an export economy that spanned from the Caribbean to the South Atlantic.

Thus, a great economic system dominated by commercial and manufacturing capitalism was formed, out of which a modern export-oriented, agrarian manufacturing system emerged. Sugar mills and plantations (*engenhos*) cannot be considered to have been simply part of a traditional or feudal agrarian system; rather, they were part of a modern economy oriented toward export and large-scale mercantile production. The regional economy entered a new phase of adjustment to the demands of expanding European capital undergoing the process of industrialization.

The result of this new global context was a redefinition of perspectives in Latin America. Those countries that attempted to escape from this context through the development of their internal economies, devising native and creative solutions to the problem of income distribution and the creation of internal markets, were simply destroyed. Such was the case with the Jesuit Indian missions destroyed by the Spanish crown, rebellions in manufacturing centers throughout Latin America in the years 1840-1852, and the Paraguayan manufacturing economy, which was devastated by a bloody war known in Brazil as the Paraguayan War. Nascent manufacturing regimes simply lacked the power to survive the expansion of the world economy, particularly during its boom from 1850 to 1871-75.

Internal local markets only produced stronger economies during the 1870-1895 world economic crisis and, later, during the global crisis that began in 1914 with the First World War and that grew into the 1929 crisis and the Second World War. As stated above, during these periods, conditions were favorable to the emergence of an industrialization process based on import substitution. After the Second World War, however, these industrial economies confronted a restructuring of the world economy under the hegemony of the United States.

The foundations for this restructuring were a scientific-technical revolution and a global expansion and diffusion of mass production technologies, especially in the durable goods sector. With the expansion of these technologies, a new phase of investment, spreading outward from the centers of technology production, was initiated. Considerable efforts were made to modernize these centers and to make them more competitive by renovating an industrial landscape that had grown decrepit in the years of economic depression from 1918 to 1940-1945. At the same time, newly created durable goods industries sustained a new drive for foreign investments.

During the 1950s and 1960s, the process of industrialization in dependent countries continued to be one of import substitution. Yet, in many of these countries, completely new products were produced because of innovations introduced by international capital. The strengthening of tariff barriers established in the 1930s and 1940s created conditions favorable to nascent industries in developing countries. At the time, international capital made no attempt to circumvent customs barriers to invest in and benefit from these protected markets. In effect, international capital abandoned its traditional investment base in the primary export sectors and turned its investments toward domestically oriented manufacturing in dependent and underdeveloped countries.

The appearance of international capital on the industrial arena led to a reconfiguration of the Latin American ideological and intellectual landscape. It also resulted in a realignment of forces during the struggles of the 1950s. These struggles culminated in revolutions in Bolivia (1952), Ecuador (1954), Venezuela (1958), and Cuba (1958-1959) and were directed without exception against old oligarchies engaged in the export of primary products or against the authoritarian regimes that supported them. All of these revolutionary processes faced bloody opposition from international capital and especially the United States government. This was also a time when forces allied to international capital stepped up their campaign against populist movements that pursued a national-democratic agenda. Two striking examples are the deposition of Perón (1955) and the attempt to impeach Vargas that led to his suicide (1954).

At the close of the 1950s, the view gained ground in the United States that a development process could only be transplanted with the aid of strong modernizing regimes supported by military, entrepreneurial, and even trade union elites. Johnson expressed this view in a book about Latin American middle classes. It was also an integral part of a project of political intervention in the region, whose principal proponents were at Stanford University in California.

The 1964 coup d'état in Brazil marked the foundation of the new model. The Brazilian national bourgeoisie, the most important in Latin America because of the size of the national territory and its natural resources, saw its ambitions for international, or at least regional power, status thwarted by this model. The military regime instituted in 1964 abandoned a national project for a modernization drive based on the alliance and integration of the national bourgeoisie with multinational capital. It consecrated a dependent industrial development subordinate to the expansion and organization of international capital, effectively submitting the centers of regional accumulation to the logic of expansion of the world's hegemonic centers. During the course of successive military coups, Latin American bourgeoisies would become junior partners of international capital and would abandon their ambitions for national independence and autonomous technological development.

These coups d'état were founded on brutality, torture, and ever more ruthless forms of state terrorism. It was a new modality of fascism. The concept of fascism has nothing to do with the existence of fascist parties or movements. Fascism gained ground throughout Europe in the 1930s without significant party representation in most countries. Fascism is, rather, a monopoly capitalist regime based on terror. This is precisely what occurred between 1964 and 1976 in Latin America and other regions of the Third World. In response to these expressions of fascism, in which some democratic conditions prevailed, united efforts were made to seek better negotiating terms for dependent countries within the world economy.

Under the inspiration of Raúl Prebisch, UNCTAD was founded in the early 1960s to articulate the economic claims of the Third World. The Venezuelan government of Andrés Peres nationalized Venezuelan oil and founded OPEC, an organization that increased the price of oil and thus shook the world economy in 1973. President Echevarría of Mexico, seeking to recapture the principles of Cárdenism, successfully promoted the United Nations' adoption of the Charter of Economic Rights of Nations and created the Latin American Economic System (SELA).

These changes coincided with the appearance on the world scene of postcolonial regimes committed to Third World progress. Closely tied to this process was the advancement of socialist countries, which tended to drive the Third World closer to a socialist transition. The most prominent expression of these transformations was the movement of non-aligned nations, aimed at giving a political voice to the Third World. Its ideological foundations were articulated at the 1955 Bandung Conference. At this conference, an ideological, diplomatic, and political movement was launched to rethink the world from the perspective of countries that had been subjected to centuries of colonialism. These countries sought to reenter the international arena as modern states founded on great civilizations. If this enterprise was to succeed, the world economy had to be fundamentally reorganized.

During the 1970s the Trilateral Commission launched a counteroffensive aimed at uniting the United States, Europe, and Japan against the Third World and the socialist camp. The foundation of this counteroffensive was the "human rights" policy of United States President Jimmy Carter. The United States and its allies now sought to cut ties with military dictatorships they had only recently supported. Having fulfilled their repressive roles, these regimes' nationalist pretensions now proved unacceptable to an expanding global economy.

The politics of conservative liberalization was continued during the 1980s under the aegis of the conservative governments of Ronald Reagan and Margaret Thatcher, with the support of Germany's Helmut Kohl, as well as the neoliberal agenda of the "Washington Consensus." The International Monetary Fund (IMF), the World Bank, and other international agencies shared in this consensus. "Economic adjustment" was imposed on dependent countries. Confronted with the harsh reality of rising international interest rates and large foreign debts draining their economic reserves, these countries sank into economic stagnation or even depression.

The depth of the transformations experienced by the world economy in the 1980s remains to be assessed. In a number of articles, I have tried to explain the origins of the world economic recovery that took place from 1983 to 1987, buoyed by the U.S. trade deficit. Raising demand by hundreds of billions of dollars, the deficit opened up the possibility for a world economic recovery. As an issue, this was submerged during this economic recovery, but when the deficit resurfaced, it did so with consequences, including the 1989-1994 crisis in the world economy, that are still being felt.

In this context, dependency theory was attacked from both the right and the left. On the left, this attack came from those who maintained that it grew out of CEPAL thought, insofar as it emphasized the importance of international capital, the export economy, and the international division of labor. These critics argued that dependency theorists attached too much importance to circulation. They contended that the debate should center on such issues as the mode of production, the development of social classes, and class relations.

The left's critical reaction to dependency theory was, in fact, greatly influenced by the Chinese Cultural Revolution and its concept of cultural revolution as it replaced the Marxist view of the role of the modern proletariat. These critiques sounded the death bell of the view that feudal regimes and traditional rural economies played a central role in the economies of Latin America and the Caribbean. Ironically, during the 1980s, what remained of the rural economic systems oriented toward domestic consumption in Latin America, Africa, and large parts of Asia were destroyed. The 1980s and 1990s were characterized by the destruction of economies focused on domestic consumption and on mass migration from rural to urban areas in the Third World, resulting in growing urban marginalization in the great metropolises of the Third World.

The fact is that the left's critique had nothing to offer. There was, however, also a global and conservative reaction. Based on the Reagan-Thatcher offensive launched during the American economic recovery from 1983 to 1989, it remodeled the world economy. Yet, even by the end of the 1980s, a new global economy had not necessarily come into being. On the contrary, the process of globalization was marked by wide shifts in course during this period—none more momentous than the growth of a huge international financial bubble. The transformations of the socialist bloc, exemplified by the collapse of the Soviet "empire" at the close of the decade, were trumpeted as expressions of the complete victory of neoliberal thought in the economic and political spheres. This ideological euphoria reached a peak with the publication of Fukuyama's *The End of History*. Fukuyama devotes a chapter to dependency theory and identifies it as the great enemy to be destroyed: the last obstacle to the end of history and the final victory of capitalism and liberalism in the world.

The conservative global reaction of the 1980s, until recently in some measure tied to liberal principles, is currently in the midst of a full-blown crisis not only because economic recession renders the conservative model unworkable but also because neoliberal ideology has been increasingly eroded and replaced in conservative thinking by fascist tendencies that have gained ground the world over since the 1980s.

Let's review this historical process. The Carter government, as we have seen, made human rights a central foreign policy objective and ran into direct confrontation with military regimes that had been created by the United States in the 1960s and the early 1970s. This confrontation had two basic causes. First, on a fundamental level, there was a growing contradiction between the process of globalization and resistance to it on the part of national governments backed by their armed forces. The most extreme case was the Peruvian Revolution, during which a military-led left-wing regime took power. Similarly, the Brazilian military regime that emerged during the Medici government, displaying the nationalist stripes and great power ambitions of right-wing radicalism, was considered to be extremely dangerous. This tendency was, to a degree, still evident during the Geisel government, which produced a Brazilian-German nuclear agreement and pursued other nationalist right-wing policies. The process of globalization was characterized by a conflict of interest between multinational companies on the one hand and the Pentagon's geopolitical agenda on the other. Second, this confrontation worked to the benefit of U.S. mobilization efforts. The human rights policy was designed as an ideological justification for a confrontation with socialist countries and Third World regimes that were generally not organized along liberal-democratic lines.

By linking the notion of human rights to liberal forms of governments, the stage was set for an ideological offensive against the very governments that, as we have seen, were created by international capital. In fact, international capital provided the arms and support for the coups d'état that gave birth to these regimes. While military regimes deprived of support were destabilized, liberal governments gained sustenance from policies that opened the way for the construction of a new liberal-democratic system in Latin America.

In an international context that tended to strengthen this current, dependency theory and its first proponents were subjected to strident criticism. The next step was an attack against analyses indicating that, under dependent capitalism, it was increasingly difficult for democratic governments to be consolidated. Ruy Mauro Marini, Vânia Bambirra, and I maintained a critical stance toward monopoly and dependency capitalism; but during the 1970s, we came to understand that shifts in the world capitalist system would eventually make possible democratic advancement within dependent capitalism. We disagreed less with the current assertion that democratic progress was possible than with theory that it was compatible with the survival of dependent capitalism. This is the defining point of divergence. As I see it, accumulation and democratic progress in the region are increasingly bound to destabilize dependent capitalism in the region. In fact, the democratic movement increasingly threatens the survival of dependent capitalism.

Another direction taken by dependency theorists in the early 1970s was a concerted effort to deepen the study and analysis of the world system. Frank has referred to the position he took (citing Samir Amin and me) at the beginning of the 1970s, when he was made conscious of the need for theory that would explain the world economic system. The 1970s saw the emergence and maturation of Immanuel Wallerstein's work on the historic formation of this world system under the influence of the thought of Fernand Braudel.

André Gunder Frank carried further his analysis of the world system. He argued that the world system extended back over a very long historical period, beginning some five thousand years ago. Frank's theses are highly interesting, but they raise the need to examine breaks in continuity during this process. I would accept the proposition that historic accumulation occurred within a world system that brought empires together in the Mediterranean, North Africa, India, as far as China, and along the Silk Road. This line of analysis is, beyond doubt, highly significant. Yet, it pulls us away from a purely Latin American toward a more global perspective. When Darcy Ribeiro in the 1970s and Wolf in the 1980s attempted to examine the history of civilizations from a global perspective, they included Latin America; but a discussion of these works would take us too far afield.

In the 1970s and 1980s, Raúl Prebisch experienced a fundamental evolution. On leaving UNCTAD, he founded the CEPAL journal, to which he contributed a series of essays that would form the basis of his book on the center-periphery economic system. In this study, manifestly influenced by dependency theory, Prebisch thoroughly revised his economic vision. CEPAL also began to show a persistent concern for the need for more thinking about the world system. The best expressions of this evolution were Fernando Franzylbert's analyses of arrested industrialization, transnational companies, and the need for a new development system founded on equity and a new integration in the world economy. At the same time, Oswaldo Sunkel sought to reanimate development theory in the context of "neostructuralism."

The 1980s were marked by a powerful liberal offensive arguing for the readjustment of Latin American economies to service the foreign debt. It was a period of soaring interest rates, when Latin America was bled to produce an export surplus. A large trade surplus was produced to pay what amounted to extortionistic rates of interest. During these years, the thesis we had defended, as had most notably and with great vehemence Andre Gunder Frank, became self-evident—namely, that the function of international capital and the world economic system was the relentless appropriation and extraction of surplus from our and other dependent regions. It was no longer necessary to make critical studies of balance of payment statistics, as had Caputo and Pizarro in the late 1960s, because during the 1980s even official statistics revealed that Latin America was an exporter of surplus and reserves.

The production of an ever greater surplus destined, not for internal investment, but rather for the payment of interest and other colonial tribute forced an increase in the negative distribution of income. This surplus could only be generated through the stringent reduction of wages and their share in national revenues. The result was social marginalization, poverty, and even destitution in the Third World and in Latin America. A contrasting situation during this period was presented by the modest but successful cases of South Korea, Taiwan, and Singapore, later known as the Little Asian Tigers. Official propaganda touts these countries as a demonstration that there is nothing perverse about the world economic system. During the 1970s, the so-called Brazilian economic miracle played the role of the Asian Tigers of today. In the 1990s, new models will have to be found, given the present economic difficulties of the Asian Tigers. In Asia, the success of the People's Republic of China under the leadership of the Chinese Communist Party is becoming more evident by the day. The models of the Asian Tigers are not founded on an economic or social theory. They are founded on ideological constructs and political propaganda designed to provide justification for historical conditions and the process of exploitation of peoples. The aim is to move the debate away from the central issues of our time—a time characterized less by balance and convergence among the regions of the world and more by a growing gap between the rich and the poor, the destitute, and the marginalized.

The process of structural adjustment has had a debilitating effect on Latin American states. These states have surrendered their resources to the world economic system and thus created a gigantic internal debt that requires enormous resources to be siphoned at exceedingly high rates of interest. Initially, these resources were appropriated by national financial capital. Currently, however, with the extensive influx of international capital on a short-term basis, they are being channeled to international capital. International capital, meanwhile, is increasing its presence in the region, aiming to obtain high returns from interest on public debts, stock market, and other methods of speculation.

Latin American history continues to be defined by the redirecting and restructuring of its economies to meet the demands of the world economic system. To reinforce this system of dependency, dictatorial regimes have been imposed on the region; this has resulted in mass destitution and increasing underemployment of labor. Democratization was established from above when these dictatorships were no longer convenient. Under these circumstances, political opposition to this economic system has been difficult. Moreover, the region's capacity to function within the world economic system has been hampered. Employment opportunities are reduced by advancements in automatization and robotization, coupled with globally oriented industrial development. The price for regional industrialization is ever-increasing mass unemployment and social destitution.

This complex of circumstances makes a political response extremely difficult. It also affects intellectual life and social science research because working conditions and resources are lacking. The weakening of the state has a direct negative impact on research and development in the exact sciences as well as in the social sciences and humanities. This is a discomfiting state of affairs; nevertheless, the intellectual and economic climate may improve significantly during the 1990s as the world economic system entered a process of recovery beginning in 1994.

Renewed economic growth may well result in a more favorable political climate and a remobilization of people committed to solving the great problems of poverty, illiteracy, and deprivation that afflict most human populations. The challenge will be to draw on the products of the scientific-technological revolution of recent decades to turn them to the service of the working peoples of the world.

The nations of the Third World must play a very significant role in the reconstruction of the world system. Taking advantage of their tropical climates and abundant sources of solar energy, technological development can turn these countries into mainsprings of wealth and of sustainable development. Yet, this is also a time when the ecology movement is posing a challenge to a capitalist civilization in the midst of a severe production and energy crisis. In one way or another, the emerging powers of the Third World, China, India, and Brazil, together with other important Third World centers, will be well positioned to correct the course of the world economy.

Even so, this is going to be a long and complex process, calling for a deep reform of scientific and technological development. For example, advancements in biotechnology may greatly facilitate a more rational use of the biodiversity of tropical regions.

In the 21st century, the question of development will be reassessed the world over. Development will no longer be confined to the acquisition of technological prowess, as it was during the second industrial revolution from the mid-19th century to the 1960s. Instead, driven by the technological revolution—whose economic, social, political, and cultural ramifications have transformed the world since the Second World War—development will turn to the acquisition of knowledge and increasingly quality-oriented economic initiative.

Linked to this change of focus is a revaluation of the way global civilization has been ordered and of the very foundations of liberal capitalist ideology. A new foundation of collectivism must be laid—a collectivism that recognizes the historic victory of a society based on the individual. The new individual who is emerging is no longer the product of capitalism and liberal doctrine, but rather recognizes the historical, social, political, and cultural roots of his or her own development. This change presupposes a recognition that individuality is in no way in conflict with social relations; on the contrary, it is the historical realization of social relations. In this new mode of civilization, the relationship between individual and society will be restructured. Society will strive to serve the needs of individuals to enable them to develop to their full potential.

The new society of the 21st century must open itself to all individuals. This process must not be confused with egalitarianism, one of the ideals of liberal bourgeois civilization. It is not a matter of egalitarianism, but of respecting and promoting individual diversity within a society that gives to each according to his or her need and asks each to contribute according to his or her ability.

This new society will configure a new planetary civilization. Within this new civilization, the question of development will need to be reevaluated—as will the role of the individual in the context of relations between men and women, in the context of economy and society, and as members of diverse ethnicities whose cultural and physical differences will have to be respected. Above all, the interactions among different civilizations, representing fundamentally different historical, economic, and social conditions, will have to be reevaluated. In the end, what is called for is a concerted effort to transcend the economic, social, political, and cultural framework created by a bourgeois liberal civilization that first came to be identified with European world hegemony and later with that of the United States. Historically, many social, economic, and cultural characteristics specific to Europe were identified with civilization proper and thus created Eurocentrism. These were used as instruments in the domination, subordination, and expropriation of some regions by others. Thus, centers, or poles, of accumulation forced centers, or poles, of dependency to produce surplus for their own sustenance.

Fundamental change will necessarily come. For a long time to come, the great civilizations will serve as points of reference in the construction of a pluralistic society and a truly planetary civilization.

BIBLIOGRAPHICAL NOTE

A bibliography on the debates on development theory, its Latin American version, dependency theory, its present manifestations in world system theory, the recent debate on development in the post-cold war period, neoliberal hegemony, and the Washington consensus would lie beyond the scope of this chapter. The interested reader may wish to consult the following works:

On the debate up to 1977, especially in Latin America, see Chapter 9 of my book *Imperialismo e Dependência* (Mexico: Era, 1978). For my recent reflections on the subject, see *Democracia e Socialismo no Capitalismo Dependente* (Petrópolis: Vozes, 1991). Cristobál Kay's *Latin American Theories of Development and Underdevelopment* (London: Routledge, 1989) is the best summary of the period. For a perceptive discussion of the current debate, see Kay's article "For a renewal of development studies: Latin American theories and neoliberalism in the era of structural adjustment" (*Third World Quarterly,* Vol. 14, No. 4, 1993). Both of Kay's works contain detailed bibliographies. Among other attempts to revive the theoretical debate, I recommend C. P. Oman and G. Wignaraja, *The Postwar Evolution of Development Thinking* (London: Macmillan, 1991); Magnus Blomström and Bjorn Hettne, *La Teoria del Desarollo en Transición* (Mexico: Fondo de Cultural Económica, 1990); and other sources cited in the bibliographies contained in these works. André Gunder Frank's *El Desarrollo del Subdesarrollo: Un Ensayo Autobiográfico* (Caracas: Nueva Sociedad, 1991) analyzes much of the literature. Ronald Chilcote followed the debate in *Theories of Development and Underdevelopment* (Boulder, CO: Westview, 1984). A. Y. So discusses theories of development, dependency, and world system in his *Social Change and Development: Modernization, Dependency, and World System* (Newbury Park, CA: Sage, 1990). See also W. Hout, *Capitalism and the Third World: Development, Dependency, and the World System* (Aldershot: Edward Elgar, 1993).

9

Asia in the World-System

GEORGE ASENIERO

The world economic crisis, whose arrival Andre Gunder Frank was among the earliest to announce and systematically analyze to a disbelieving world, rather imperceptibly left the sphere of controversy ("Crisis? What crisis?") some time ago and entered the realm of fact acknowledged by all: By all indications to date, it seems to be here to stay. In a two-page "public service" advertisement for Citibank, MIT economist Lester C. Thurow writes:

> In the last four decades, the real growth rates of the capitalist world have fallen from 4.9 percent per year in the 1960s, to 3.8 percent in the 1970s, to 2.7 percent in the 1980s, and to about one percent in the first four years of the 1990s. Japan is in a recession and much of the Pacific Rim is slowing down. China and those economies closely linked are thus far an exception to this slowdown, but it is only a matter of time until the slowdown reaches everyone on the Pacific Rim.[1]

Let's focus on the region that has so far been an exception to the world economic slowdown: the Asian arc of the Pacific Rim. By any measure, the economic performance of East Asia from north to south is indeed exceptional. But it is exceptional in more ways than one.

171

Through those thirty years of steady deceleration of the world-economy, the economies of East Asia have seen their growth rates surge ahead. Japan, already remarkable for its immediate postwar reconstruction achievements (not to speak of the rapid modernization that enabled it to wage the Pacific War in the first place), embarked in the 1960s on a manufacturing revolution that increased real income per head fourfold through the quarter century that followed and that, by the advent of the 1990s, made the Japanese in dollar terms the richest people on earth. Following the path of that Asian industrial forerunner, the four "tigers"—the two Japanese former colonies South Korea and Taiwan; and the two islands Singapore and Hong Kong, the first a city-state, the other still a British colony, soon to revert back to China—embarked on their own export-led manufacturing revolution, doubling real gross domestic products (GDPs) every eight years from 1960 to 1985 (an eightfold increase in all). In the late 1970s, China accelerated its massive modernization program, introduced market mechanisms, and welcomed foreign investment; since the 1980s, it has been the world's fastest-growing economy, averaging almost 10% yearly in the last fifteen years. And during that same period, three Southeast Asian countries—Indonesia, Malaysia, and Thailand—have proved that they, too, can sustain growth rates of more than 7% a year, a speed that doubles the size of an economy each decade. These economies of East Asia have been growing, since the 1980s, three times faster than the OECD economies, twice as fast as the rest of East Asia, three times as fast as Latin America and South Asia, and five times as fast as sub-Saharan Africa. Their export performance has been particularly impressive, with their share of world exports of manufactures shooting up from 9% in 1965 to 21% in 1990 ("A Survey of Asia," 1990; "A Survey of Asia," 1993; "A Survey of Asia," 1991; World Bank, 1993). Those are the indicators behind the phenomenon that has variously been called "Pacific Shift," the "Rise of Asia," the "Pacific Century," or as the title of a recently published World Bank study (1993) puts it, "The East Asian Miracle." Understandably, a sense of triumphalism accompanies this phenomenon, a touch of smug self-affirmation that, naturally enough, spills over into the realm of theory—and ideology—as well. Not surprisingly, Andre Gunder Frank's works figure prominently in the fray.

The East Asian phenomenon is advanced, first, as living refutation of dependency theory. In this part of the world, *dependencia* is broadly taken to imply that industrial development is precluded to the Third World because of the polarizing and marginalizing dynamics of global capital accumulation that the "Latin American" Andre Gunder Frank understood, articulated, and popularized so well. That may well be the case in Latin America and Africa, it is argued, but industrialization took off in East Asia, and today this area is outcompeting Western firms in the world export market for a vast range of mass consumer goods.

Second, Frank continues to speak of a continuing world economic crisis that he sees as having begun in 1967, with each global recession (the third started in 1990) being more severe and geographically more encompassing than the previous one and with no end in sight. That may well be the case elsewhere; the Western economies are certainly in disarray, Eastern Europe's socialist economies and their political structures have collapsed altogether, and the rest of the Third World is in "permanent crisis" anyway. But in booming East Asia, the question is "Crisis? What crisis?" To observers of the East Asian achievement, the boom in the western Pacific Rim either proves that it is not, after all, a *world* crisis or that East Asia can be an engine for reaccelerating the world-economy as a whole out of its doldrums.

This brings us to the third point of contact between what is being said of the East Asian phenomenon and Frank's theoretical works. In his recent essays aiming to set some theses and a research agenda for five thousand—and not just five hundred—years of world-system history, Frank argues for a reassessment of the systemic relationships among the world's major regions over time; now, insofar as the relationship between the West and the East is concerned, current East Asian discourse has a good deal to say on the matter. Frank lays great store by the fact that the "rise of the West" over the last five hundred years had been preceded by the "decline of the East," which resulted in a hegemonial shift from East to West. "The 'Rise of the West,' " he concludes, "including European hegemony and its expansion and later transfer to the 'New World' across the Atlantic, did not constitute a new Modern World Capitalist System as much as it represented a new but continued development and hegemonic shift *within an old world system*" (Frank, 1991a, pp. 20-21). Moreover, Frank's recent studies of early modern world history stress that this shift did not occur until 1800. Before that, the Europeans spent three centuries and tons of American silver trying to buy their way into the flourishing Asian markets. According to Frank and contrary to received Eurocentric wisdom, the main centers of manufacturing productivity and competitive success, and therefore also of the destination of world bullion flows and of capital accumulation, were not in Europe, but remained in China and India until the end of the 18th century. Frank suggests that, from this world historical perspective, it should not be so surprising that the center of the world-economy, which then (only briefly) circled the globe westward, is now shifting back to its (rightful?) place in Asia.

Today, East Asian discourse is replete with allusions to the reemergence of Asia to its rightful place in world historical development, and extrapolations into the next century of global demographic and economic growth trends point to an overwhelming presence of East Asia in world affairs. With such high-flying rhetoric and soaring statistics, the view from the other side of the world is, not surprisingly, tinged with trepidation. *The Economist* expresses succinctly (but then goes on at some length to dispel) that view:

> It is now likelier than not that the most momentous public event in the lifetime of anybody reading this survey will turn out to have been the modernization of Asia. Many Americans and even more Western Europeans cannot believe this is true but they are scared that it might be, thinking that if Asia rises the West—or at least its jobs and wages—must fall. ("A Survey of Asia," 1993, p. 1)

The competitive logic of global capital accumulation being as it is, the dynamism of East Asia has expectedly provoked a backlash, resuscitating protectionist impulses everywhere—for example, Japan-bashing on both sides of the Atlantic, the occasional threat of sanctions against South Korea under Super 301 of U.S. trade law, President Bill Clinton's continually reassessed option to deny most favored nation (MFN) status to China, persistent talk in Europe of modern capitalism's version of the yellow peril. It is in view of countering such reactions abroad that ultimately the East Asian phenomenon is presented with some ideological fervor by its admirers as a momentous achievement of capitalism itself, hence a vindication of the world capitalist system as a whole despite the sorry state it is in. If the Asians are able to succeed in this system—the message goes—the rest of the world (including the decadent West) should take heart, learn from their experience, and redouble their efforts. "If the Asia that many clucking westerners in 1960 assumed was doomed can pull it off," asks *The Economist* (1991, November 16), "why can't everyone else?"

There lies the question: How did they pull it off, and can others do it too?

In *The East Asian Miracle* the World Bank (1993) attempts to answer this question via a detailed survey of a set of factors and indicators across eight countries—those it calls the "superstars" of the region: Hong Kong, Indonesia, Japan, Malaysia, Singapore, South Korea, Taiwan, and Thailand. Conceding the obvious—that in some countries state intervention worked, whereas in

others it did not—the Bank insists that the one thing they have in common is
that they got the economic fundamentals right (low inflation, sound fiscal
policies, high levels of domestic saving, heavy investment in human and
physical capital) and that they have kept their economies open to foreign
influences (foreign technology, foreign investment, export market signals);
but, all said, the Bank points out that, in fact, there is no single Asian economic
model, so there is no simple remedy for success. What the Bank barely
succeeds in obfuscating, however, is the fact that, as MIT economist Lance
Taylor put it, "the standard Bank line is not consistent with the East Asian
experience" (quoted in *Far Eastern Economic Review,* 1993b, p. 79).

One more miracle still, in the World Bank's view, is the fact that, consistently over a thirty-year period, the East Asian phenomenon has displayed a
geographical concentration of success so extraordinary that, in the Bank's
reckoning, there is only one chance in ten thousand that it happened at random.
Now here indeed is a marvel of marvels, for if the World Bank were to jettison
its country-by-country approach, which takes the eight cases as separate and
parallel entities, and instead considered them as pertaining to a *system,* with
structured relationships to each other, then the question might not even arise;
it would, in fact, provide a key to comprehending the "miracle."

East Asia, I shall argue here, is an integral part of the world-system, and
only in terms of the functioning of that system—and this over a period of time
that is considerably longer than the thirty-year time frame of the World Bank
study—can the East Asian phenomenon be understood. Andre Gunder Frank's
contribution to world-system theory thus takes on renewed relevance to the
task at hand.

EAST ASIA IN THE WORLD-SYSTEM

JAPAN'S ASIA, 1895-1945

Back in the 1930s, the Japanese economist Kaname Akamatsu viewed the
pattern of industrial development of the entire East Asian region as a flock of
flying geese, with Japan leading the way. That model was a precursor of
today's product-cycle theory of industrial development; it was also an attempt
to legitimate, in social scientific terms, Imperial Japan's hegemonic ambitions
over the region as a whole. What matters to us now is that, during its time, it

was, in fact, descriptive of a process taking place in the northeast Asian region, where a "natural economy" had been rapidly developing since the turn of the century when newly modernized Japan expanded the borders of its dynamic economy to absorb the militarily conquered colonies of Korea and Taiwan. By the 1930s, more geese were to fly with the flock as Japanese imperial designs on the rest of East and Southeast Asia began to take shape under the Greater East Asia Co-Prosperity Sphere. In today's terminology, that planned regional integration would be characterized as a pyramidal structure with a center (Japan), a semi-periphery (the two colonies Korea and Taiwan), and a vast periphery (the rest of East and Southeast Asia), with the two latter categories having distinct functions to fulfill for the benefit of the center.

To consider the semi-periphery first: Uniquely in history, this was a case of a "late-industrializer" industrializing, in turn, two contiguous territories (the Korean peninsula is barely a hundred miles west across the strait, the island of Taiwan just over six hundred miles south) as integral parts of an economy that was seen to be too restricted, in geographical space and natural resources, to feel secure enough to survive in an age of heightened inter-imperialist rivalry. It was understood early on in Tokyo that Japan could survive in the modern world only by being at the center of a *developed* and tightly integrated Northeast Asian regional economy. Thus, between 1895 and 1945, both colonies underwent agricultural modernization (preceded by land reform), extensive infrastructural development, and a veritable industrial revolution as the Japanese relocated industries to both colonies: coal and iron mining, metal processing, chemicals, hydroelectric power, machine tools manufacture, and even, for a while, automobile production farther afield—in Manchuria. As war clouds gathered over the Pacific, the pace of industrialization accelerated as both colonies became vital planks in a war economy. Afterward came defeat and utter destruction. But even though the world war and the more devastating Korean civil war destroyed much of the physical infrastructure and industrial plants, the social impact (the "societal learning process," in current parlance) of that historical experience, including that of "administrative guidance" of the development process that was totalitarian to the extreme, was incalculable. That half century of breakneck modernization and industrialization, wrought at great human cost and suffering and carried out with extreme brutality, transformed both colonies beyond recognition and must be taken as indispensable to any understanding of how, from the 1960s onward, both South Korea and Taiwan pulled ahead of everybody else of the decolonialized Third World to become the so-called NICs. "Newly industrializing"? "Late industrializers" they certainly were, relative to the Western world, but industrialization began in earnest in these areas much earlier than anywhere else in the Third World, and that sustained fifty-year head start has made a crucial difference (Aseniero, 1994; Cumings, 1987).

The rest of East and Southeast Asia was to be treated differently because its function was distinct. This was to be the *real* periphery of the classic pattern—immense territories that would be exploited for their natural resources and labor and that would serve as a captive market to the Japanese economy; a kaleidoscope of Asian cultures that would be uniformly Japanized; a diversity of colonies of Western powers that would have to be turned around to repel the Western imperialists out of Asia; and the greatest prize of all, China: a continent unto itself and the matrix of East Asian civilization, now disdainfully fallen so low in the Japanese order of things. Such was the grand design of the Greater East Asia Co-Prosperity Sphere. It could obviously be carried out only by war, and war indeed there was for the asking—bringing ruination, at its end, on one and all: the impoverished periphery, victims, as always, of great power conflicts; the semi-periphery that had been compelled to fight somebody else's war; and finally the center itself, destroyed at its core by nuclear holocaust.

AMERICA'S ASIA, 1945-1985

The second half of the century saw the emergence, out of the chaos of the Second World War, of a new regional order in Asia, with the victor of that war as the new hegemon. Unlike Japan, the United States was not just a regional hegemon; it stood supreme at the center of the world capitalist system. It was also the superpower that took on, as its overriding political and military objective, the extirpation of Soviet influence all over the globe, the containment of the communist challenge wherever it might assert itself outside the Soviet bloc.

The communist challenge was particularly powerful in Asia. The victory of the Chinese revolution radically altered the balance of power in the Western Pacific and decisively influenced the course of events in the liberation of the old Japanese semi-periphery: Taiwan became the refuge-island of the vanquished Kuomintang, and the Korean peninsula split into two states that since then have been mortal enemies of each other.[2] And all over the periphery, one by one the newly independent states of Southeast Asia found themselves compelled to confront a diversity of socialist-inspired nationalist social

movements in their midst seeking fundamental socioeconomic change and
not just formal political autonomy from the old colonial powers.

Japan: From Antagonist to Ally

Under Pax Americana it was decided early on that, with China "lost" to
the other camp, a thoroughly reformed and demilitarized Japan would be the
crucial ally in both the cold war and the reorganization of the capitalist regional
order in the Western Pacific; henceforth, its functional role in America's scheme
of things would be that of junior partner in the region, properly Americanized
as to its political ways but totally free to follow its native instincts in
rehabilitating its distinctive form of capitalism. Doing it "the Japanese way"
did not bother laissez-faire America much. Better the bureaucrats plan the
economy with their trade and industrial policies and targets and intervene as
they see fit in the capital accumulation process than plan war games in the
Pacific and intervene in the affairs of other nations again.

Left to concentrate fully on itself under the U.S. military umbrella, Japan
quietly went on to reconstruct its economy, a "late industrializer" twice over,
leapfrogging over sequences of technological development by borrowing and
imitating the latest technologies and production processes wherever from, as
it had done before, but this time without inter-imperialist pressure from abroad
(except for the war reparations to pay). Having sacrificed so much for war,
the working classes proved willing to sacrifice as much for peace. Labor's
subservience to management was, after all, of a pattern, from fealty to the
shogunate to patriotism in the war and now loyalty to the corporation. With a
saving rate among the highest in the world—thanks to sound fiscal management and a cultural predisposition—and thus with a great capital-cost advantage, Japan saw its investment rates shoot up and the number of industrial
firms big and small multiply. Over the social consensus that prevailed between
capital and labor, and over the interlocking corporate concerns of the *keiretsu*,
once again the state bureaucracy, financial institutions, and industrial corporations worked in tandem, duplicating their feats of rapid modernization of an
earlier epoch and then surpassing those by good measure.

Dependent on imports for its basic materials, Japan found itself equally
dependent on exports just to keep moving. The advantage was that those
resources it had planned to extract from the periphery under its imperial order
were now abundantly available in exchange for manufactured goods. Being
then the only industrialized country in this vast part of the world, Japan had

little competition, other than from the high-cost countries of the West, in penetrating this immense market that spread before it like a fan. In a continuously expanding postwar world-economy hungry for inexpensive manufactured goods, the dialectic of unequal exchange worked out its miracle for the land of the rising sun.

South Korea and Taiwan:
From Client-States to NICs

What their former colonial master did in the immediate postwar years, South Korea and Taiwan sought to follow a decade or so later. That they could, in fact, do so this time was thanks not only to their previous half century of experience of Japanese-style economic development but also to the special circumstances in which they found themselves under Pax Americana. As frontline states in the cold war confrontation in Asia, both were treated by the United States as special client-states to be saved at all cost, to be militarily equipped and economically aided like no other states in the world; as such, they were a category *sui generis* in the capitalist world-system.

U.S. economic and military aid to these client-states was of such magnitude and importance to their survival and long-term development that it was a veritable Marshall Plan exclusively for two. In the 1950s, U.S. aid financed more than 80% of South Korea's imports and 95% of Taiwan's trade deficit. By 1978, the cumulative economic aid received by South Korea alone was almost as much as that received during the same period by all African countries combined, and 41% of the Latin American total; in three decades of sustained U.S. military spending on the peninsula, South Korea's total military aid was nearly 3.5 times that of the whole of Latin America and nearly 9 times that of all Africa. And both client-states benefited greatly from U.S. spending in the region connected with the Vietnam War.[3]

When U.S. aid started to taper off, the dollar continued to flow in the form of direct foreign investments and loans. The United States was the main source of foreign investments that entered Taiwan between 1951 and 1985 (amounting to 43% of all non-overseas Chinese sources), followed by Japan (28%) and European sources (13%). Along with Mexico on the other side of the Pacific, Taiwan benefited from the first wave of relocation of U.S. assembly operations to low-wage sites for products that would be reexported to the U.S. market; by the late 1960s, roughly half of such U.S. "imports" came from U.S.-owned factories in Mexico and Taiwan. When the Japanese countered by themselves relocating certain operations to Taiwan, the island took on its specialized function as a receptacle for declining Japanese industries at every stage of that dynamic economy's industrial restructuring process. (Joining in this product cycle game, Singapore and Hong Kong quickly transformed themselves into veritable industrial platforms for transnational capital.)

Ever the nationalist, South Korea's preference (until the mid-1980s) was for foreign loans over direct foreign investments. Following a sharp rise in the early 1970s, the country's total foreign loans soared in 1978 and remained at nearly $3 billion a year for almost a decade. The state's total control of the banking system and its complete autonomy in the allocation of subsidized credit enabled it to concentrate capital on a handful of favored conglomerates, the *chaebol* the backbone of Korean industry. With heavy deficit spending, South Korea in the 1970s embarked on a public-sector heavy industry and chemicals development program in defiance of World Bank protestations; Taiwan did likewise.

The trade policies pursued by Seoul and Taipei ran parallel to each other through the decades: initially, stringent import substitution and other protectionist strategies, which Washington chose to benignly overlook; then a determined export promotion program while still behind protectionist walls; then, with an eye to full access to the U.S. market, some sort of liberalization and a full-speed drive for exports. The market was ready even before the exporters were: it was the United States itself. With an unprecedented worldwide export expansion that followed in the 1980s, "NICs" became a household word.

Southeast Asian Periphery

As for the periphery, it was assumed that with decolonization would come modernization, deeper integration into the capitalist world-system, and economic development. But what took place instead was, in Andre Gunder Frank's now classic phrase, "the development of underdevelopment." Decolonization had merely given way to neocolonialism, and the same polarizing dynamics of dependency, unequal exchange, and uneven development between metropole and satellite that Frank had analyzed for Latin America were at work in the periphery in Asia.

The more articulate nationalist leaders of the newly independent states understood their common structural predicament early on; at their historic Afro-Asian conference in Bandung (Indonesia) in 1955, they asserted the goal of national development for the peoples of the Third World, one that would bolster national autonomy, rather than compromise it, and that would solidify the process of nation-building, rather than tear society apart. A strong governmental intervention in the economy was common logic; and common practice everywhere were import substitution and various other protectionist policies, foreign exchange controls, and heavy infrastructural investment by the state, all these understood as being essential for industrialization to take root and thrive. Development, however, proved to be elusive and contradictory. The results produced by those policies perversely turned out to be the opposite of what had been intended—a dialectical contre-resultat, to use Jean-Paul Sartre's concept. Development in the periphery was fully dependent on the center and thoroughly circumscribed by it.

Dissatisfaction with the outcome of the development policies of the national elites led, by the mid-1960s, to fundamental rethinking of the nature of government, the class structure of society, the colonial legacy, and the national consequences of the U.S. hegemonic order in Asia. Theories of imperialism, revolution, and social change became the dominant themes of social science research and defined the political thinking of nationalist intellectuals in Southeast Asia, with Mao's China as a contrasting paradigm just across the cold war divide. Here again, radical thinking from the other continents of the Third World found a loud resonance in Asia, with Andre Gunder Frank's works on revolution and social change being among the most influential.[4] That year of political effervescence the world over, 1968, saw a deepening radicalization of nationalist intellectuals in Asia and the social movements they either led or gave articulate voices to. Vietnam and the Chinese Cultural Revolution fired the imagination and inspired movements for national liberation in Southeast Asia.

The Bandung Project of the national bourgeoisie—to give a name to that aspiration to national autonomous development—was thus torn between the radical challenge to it from the left and the objective impossibility of pursuing its program under the conditions by which the economy was integrated into the capitalist world-system. In effect, it rapidly reached an impasse, and it was not the left that undermined it. The removal from power in Indonesia in 1967 of President Sukarno—the host at Bandung—by the military under General Suharto with the backing of the CIA, following a horrendous bloodbath all over the archipelago in 1965, was a turning point not only for Indonesia but also for what could now be called, with an air of finality, the Era of Bandung. In its stead came the program of transnationalization (see Amin, 1988).

The abandonment of a nationalist economic development program and its replacement by policies designed to lay open the economy to transnational capital—transnationalization, in short—was in response to changes in the world-economy, which through the 1970s saw the progressive relocation by transnational corporations of segments of their industrial production from the high-wage center to low-cost production sites in the periphery. This restructuring of the world-economy required, for its implementation, the progressive dismantling of autocentric national production systems (the Bandung Project) and their recomposition as constitutive elements of an integrated world production system.

The program of transnationalization was effected by a new type of regime in Southeast Asia. Indonesia's "new order," installed with extreme violence on a confused and terrorized populace, brought together the military top brass and U.S.-trained technocrats under the absolute power of one man, Suharto, beholden to no one, who equated the state with himself. In the Philippines, with excuses to save the republic from the left, President Marcos waged a coup d'état against his own elected government in 1972, transforming the state through martial law into the same authoritarian system as Indonesia's, henceforth with the military échelon and U.S.-trained technocrats on either side of the supreme leader of the "New Society." This reconfiguration of state power was nothing new for Thailand, where rule by military men, often succeeding each other by coup, had been traditional since 1932, when the absolute monarchy was overthrown by the armed forces. In the new wave of transnationalization, the formality of constitutional monarchy was thus easy enough to uphold as the Thai military elites took turns in appropriating political power (with more than half of the seats of the National Legislative Assembly constitutionally reserved for them) and exercising corporate control over key sectors of the economy. The Malaysian political elites could shift economic policies as they saw fit, untrammeled as ever in the exercise of political power simply because the ruling party, UMNO, had succeeded, through its dominance over the National Front coalition, to make Malaysia practically a one-party system since independence from Britain in 1957. In a league of its own, the People's Action Party of Singapore, with authoritarian-technocratic efficiency by which it managed the affairs of a tiny city-state, opted for development through transnational capital ahead of everyone else in the region. The People's Action Party of Singapore under Lee Kuan Yew, in absolute power since 1965, charted the city-state's developmental trajectory after the island broke away from the Malaysian federation.[5]

Brooking no opposition to their rule, these regimes brought the full strength of state power on the opposition left, right, and center—and abroad, against the foreign media that dared decry the violation of human rights, especially "touchy" Singapore. Except for the Philippines, where the left gained strategic power during the dictatorship despite (or because of) the repression, revolutionary peasant and workers' movements everywhere were dealt a mortal blow. The old industrial development programs of the national(ist) bourgeoisie were dismantled, accompanied by the political (and often personal) annihilation of their more articulate proponents, and the slate of economic policy was wiped clean.

With the fate of the national economy tied to the fortunes of transnational capital, development policy consisted primarily of constructing a "favorable investment climate" for multinational corporations. Export processing zones were set up; large-scale infrastructural projects were undertaken, financed by foreign loans; a range of tax incentives and repatriation guarantees were offered to foreign capital; "competitive" wage rates and labor discipline were assured; and a host of partnership arrangements between local and foreign capital for the exploitation of the country's natural resources were proposed—all this in competition with what the other states in the region could offer to transnational capital on their own.

Crucial to the entire enterprise was the management ability of the regime itself, its ability to run the state that would promote macroeconomic stability, administrative efficiency, and overall investor confidence in the country. The method of governance adopted by all the regimes in Southeast Asia to achieve those goals was authoritarianism. Under this political system, legitimacy was not established by mandate through free elections (although elections there were, from time to time, never mind the incongruity of there being only one candidate, or only one party with any serious chance of winning, each time). "Developmentalist authoritarianism" sought its legitimacy from the rate of capital accumulation. The rate of growth of the GNP was all that mattered, and everything else would come in line.[6]

Given their absolute power, absolute corruption came to the autocrats easily. Perhaps with the sole exception of Singapore, but certainly including Japan, systematic corruption became endemic to all of the western Pacific Rim. As state managers in partnership with transnational capital, the autocrats rewarded themselves handsomely, amassing immense fortunes for themselves and their kinsmen and cronies through means fair and foul. Often, this was through the connivance of transnational corporations that early in the game came to adapt their business practices to a political culture that appropriated officialdom as a fiefdom for pecuniary gain and self-aggrandizement. The Marcos kleptocracy in the Philippines might have been the most notorious, for being also the most flamboyant and utterly destructive of the economy, but the Suharto family's steadily expanding corporate control of key sectors of the Indonesian economy through power-brokering is no less far-reaching and enriching, which makes Chun Doo Hwan's sideline collections in South Korea a pittance (but cost him a disgraceful resignation all the same). If it is not a family dynasty that exercises public power for private ends, it is a monolithic political party that convolutes national development with its own capital accumulation for political patronage and, as a business concern in its own right, for oligopolistic corporate growth: hence, the self-perpetuation of political power and economic dominance of UMNO in Malaysia, and of the various political party guises of the military in Thailand, with its business interests from airline to television stations.

Except for the Philippines, however, the economic pie steadily grew through the 1970s and into the 1980s and allowed the regimes in power to stay the course while co-opting a broader range of social groups, appeasing an expanding middle class, and generally silencing the critics. The transnationalization of their economies was moving full-speed ahead, bringing in large infusions of capital as a steadily globalizing world-economy accelerated a massive industrial restructuring process that brought about in its wake a new international division of labor.

U.S.-JAPAN'S ASIA, 1985 TO PRESENT

The following quotation, from the initial draft of Frank's autobiographical essay "The Underdevelopment of Development," not only introduces this section of our study but also could just as well have enunciated, in theoretical terms, the content and thrust of the entire essay itself; if I have chosen to cite it here and not at the start, it is because it is in the last quarter century that these theses, true of the world-system throughout its history, have been self-evidently borne out (once again, cyclically) in our time:

> Real world system development has never been guided by or responsive to any global and also not to much local "development" thinking or policy. In this world-economy, sectors, regions and peoples temporarily and cyclically assume leading and hegemonic central (core) positions of social and technological

"development." They then have to cede their pride of place to new ones who replace them. Usually this happens after a long interregnum of crisis in the system. During this time of crisis, there is intense competition for leadership and hegemony. The central core has moved around the globe in a predominantly westerly direction. At the sub-system levels of countries, regions or sectors, all "development" has occurred through and thanks to their (temporarily) more privileged position in the inter"national" division of labor and power. (Frank, 1991b, p. 57)

Frank has written volumes to expound on each of these theses; no doubt, several of them have been thematically taken up in the other contributions to this festschrift. Of particular relevance to us here is how this complex theory of world development, encapsulated above, helps us understand contemporary developments in the Pacific Rim.

Frank's analysis of the present world economic crisis is fundamental to comprehending the global transformations that have been taking place in the last two decades. The decline of profitability rates in the center (the OECD countries) exerted relentless pressure on industrial firms there to go "transnational"—if they were not already—in their production and not just in the marketing of their products: Automation or relocation were the two options facing corporate decision makers from the early 1970s onward. Technological breakthroughs in the production process, transportation, and communications (robotics, the computer revolution, telecommunications) emerged in response to the first option while also making the second option a viable technical possibility. The question, then, was where to relocate: Worldwide sourcing of cheap, reliable, and easily trainable if not already skilled labor went hand-in-hand with a strategic assessment of political stability and long-term local or regional market growth potential of the prospective production site. The countries of the western Pacific Rim figured highly along these indices.

For those countries that had enjoyed a manufacturing head start—South Korea and Taiwan, and the mini-economies Singapore and Hong Kong—the dislocations in the world-economy provided the opportunity to break into the world export market with their own products at the same time that these economies of the semi-periphery themselves became favored sites for relocation of transnational industrial firms. Soon, with even cheaper wages and a range of natural resources to offer, the Southeast Asian periphery also began to participate in the emerging "new international division of labor."

What is "new" in this restructured world-economy can hardly be gainsaid: Whereas in the (neo)colonial dependency structure industrialization was precluded to the periphery, relegating this to agriculture and mineral production, now industrial production processes were being transferred to selected sites in this vast zone in the interest of the center. It remains, however, (a) a *dependent* form of industrialization all the same, with weak linkages to the rest of the national economy (export processing zones being, in this sense, the contemporary version of colonial enclaves), partial because segments thereof and not entire industries are relocated, and (b) strategically transitory, its location at any time in the world-system being dependent solely on the international corporate strategies of the parent firm and having nothing to do—as Frank notes above—with any national development program of the "host country." Globalization, under the terms of transnational enterprises, has, as its obverse side, the *de*nationalization of the periphery's economy.

The world economic crisis continued to deepen in the 1980s, however, despite this massive industrial relocation that took the ever-intensifying competition among firms farther afield in the periphery while adding to the structural unemployment in their home countries brought about by automation. Singularly for the United States, the economic crisis became a crisis of hegemonic leadership as the world's largest creditor became, in 1985, the largest foreign debtor instead. The "international currency" country lost all means of controlling its domestic budget deficit, which fueled even more its ballooning foreign trade deficit.

Westward across the Pacific stood the erstwhile junior partner with whom the United States now ran the gravest imbalance of all its bilateral economic relations. That same pivotal year of 1985, when 240 yen bought a dollar, Japan had a global trade surplus of $46 billion, sent a net $64.5 billion in long-term capital abroad, and made direct investments abroad worth $12.2 billion. The contrast between the two partners convinced many that unless something drastic was done, the U.S. hegemonic position would slide further and the center of the world-economy would move on westerly still and usher in a new hegemonic order in the Age of the Pacific.[7]

In a move to redress that imbalance, the 1985 Plaza Hotel Agreement of the finance ministers of the Group of Five sought to reduce America's trade deficit by making U.S. exports less expensive through a realignment of exchange rates and sent the yen soaring to eventually double its initial value in three years. The effect on Japanese capital was a tremendous outward pressure to relocate manufacturing operations to cheap-labor areas on a scale never attempted before; that firms could do so now with the unprecedented advantage of a currency double its value not only made that move easier but also was a positive incentive to acquire bargain-priced assets all over the globe. In the immediate years that followed, Japan invested less in Asia than it did in Europe and the United States, but that was enough to redefine its role in the entire western Pacific Rim. If it did not quite singlehandedly transform the regional capitalist order into a "yen bloc," as many observers contended and many more do now, it certainly stepped into the role of senior partner with the United States: Since 1985, a dual U.S.-Japan hegemonic order has prevailed over East and Southeast Asia.

Japan in Asia

For all the ubiquity of Japanese goods around the world, only 3% to 4% of them were, until the mid-1980s, being produced abroad. By comparison for that same period, 18% to 20% of U.S. products were not "Made in USA" but elsewhere. Despite Japan's towering presence in its home region, Japanese direct investment in Asia trailed after that of the U.S. for years and only roughly matched it in the early 1980s. Then, it surged ahead: between 1984 and 1989, the annual flow of Japan's direct investment to East Asia leaped fivefold, whereas that going to Europe and the United States grew even faster—ninefold in each case. But profitability rates varied greatly: 1992 figures from the Ministry of International Trade and Industry (MITI) indicate that whereas Japanese affiliates in Europe were doing just slightly better than break-even and those in the United States were incurring losses, those in Asia were bringing in enormous profits. Consequently, when Japan's total new foreign direct investment began to shrink as a result of its recession, the share going to Asia continued to rise. Of the $34.1 billion invested abroad in the year ending in March 1993 (barely half the total four years earlier), $6.4 billion were invested in Asia, up from $5.9 billion the year before. Asia now accounts for 19% of Japan's outstanding foreign direct investment, up from 12% in 1990. By contrast, U.S. and Europe's shares have fallen from 46% to 40.5% and from 25% to 21%, respectively, over the same period.

The trend is likely to continue. Forecasts of long-term growth put Japan's at 3% to 4%, around half that of East Asia's; Japanese companies are therefore interested in this region not only for production cost advantages (which grow as the yen strengthens) but also as consumer markets (which grow as the yen weakens). There is plenty of room to expand because only 9% of Japan's manufacturing industry's total productive capacity was located abroad at the end of 1991 (that for U.S. industry is two or three times bigger).

Worldwide, Japanese firms added $325 billion of investments abroad in the past decade. Earnings from those investments shot up from $1 billion to $23 billion annually between 1980 to 1990 and will exceed $60 billion by the end of the decade—more than half of Japan's current account surplus at today's levels.

The Four "Tigers" of the Semi-Periphery

The precipitous climb of the yen benefited the East Asian semi-periphery twice over: Their exports became more competitive relative to Japan's, and more Japanese industries relocated to them as their production cost advantages became more attractive than ever before. With the United States their main export market, the four NICs—South Korea, Taiwan, Singapore, and Hong Kong—saw their combined trade surpluses with this country grow to take up 22% of the U.S. trade deficit by 1987. The second half of the 1980s were years of supergrowth for them, with an amazed world their export market.

By the 1990s, however, rapidly rising wages (a 20% annual rate of growth for South Korea), appreciation of their currencies (the Taiwan dollar rose by 50% against the U.S. dollar between 1985 and 1992), a shrinking world export market, and a weakening yen began to hurt the tigers' competitiveness in turn. Like a torrent rushing toward lower ground, Japanese foreign direct investment shifted to the cheaper wage zone of the periphery, followed this time by investments coming from the NICs themselves. Just as industrial firms from the center had to relocate in hordes to survive a decade earlier, now the NICs' own industrial conglomerates had to move production offshore, while also trying to move upmarket, in a bid to maintain their competitive edge. In this new wave of industrial relocation, the NICs overtook Japan in the magnitude of new investments into the Southeast Asian periphery. In 1991, Japan accounted for 15.2% of investment in the Association of Southeast Asian Nations (ASEAN) countries, compared with 15.4% for Taiwan alone and 29.5% for all four tigers.

Having neglected Asia for years, U.S. firms came to realize that this was a region they could not afford to be absent from; between 1989 and 1992, U.S. foreign direct investment in Asia rose by 120%, more than twice the rate of increase for the rest of the world. Stoked with so much capital, Southeast Asia boomed.

The Southeast Asian
Periphery: The Next-NICs

We thus arrive at that rare phenomenon: the high-flying "next-NICs" of the Southeast Asian periphery enjoying in the 1990s even higher growth rates than the NICs of the semi-periphery, which in turn are growing faster than the Japanese economy at the core. Like kites lifted by the industrial dynamism of the economies to which they are attached, they, too, have flown, but not on their own: Akamatsu's flying geese imagery does not show the strings that pull these peripheral economies higher up, or may yet pull them down.

Until now, Southeast Asia has been flying high chiefly by playing on its low-wage advantage to transnational capital. This is, however, the most transitory competitive advantage in the world today, given the practically inexhaustible reserve army of labor in the Third World (or the South), the growing masses of highly skilled unemployed workers in the center itself (or the North), and the millions in the former socialist countries (or the East) desperately trying to survive in a capitalist system they thought they wanted but they're not sure about anymore. The developmentalist regimes in Asia can claim, however, that whereas chaos has broken loose elsewhere in the world, order remains in force over their societies and that there lies their edge; hence, the maximalist stance of these authoritarian states in their control of civil society, notwithstanding any concessions to "democratization" they might have been obliged to make in recent years. (The political and economic trajectory of the Philippines differed from those of its high-performance neighbors precisely because this country, never politically stable through those crucial decades, missed out on the successive waves of foreign industrial relocation; consequently, it is the only "nix" among the NICs and next-NICs of the World Bank's East Asian miracle and is only now, under a new leadership, desperately trying to catch up with the others but with little northeasterly wind on its sails.)

Will the western Pacific Rim boom continue? The crisis caught up with Japan, bursting its bubble economy and putting a definite end to the long boom years (see Emmott, 1989; Wood, 1992). But its dominance over Asia is undiminished. Indeed, it leans even more on this region in order to come out of its recession, with the NICs acting as a built-in stabilizer for its economy. When a stronger yen slows Japanese exports, shipments to world export markets from manufacturers in Southeast Asia—many of them Japanese subsidiaries— soar, spurring exports of Japanese capital goods and components to these countries.[8] Hence, the doubling of Japan's trade surplus with the four tigers between 1987 and 1993 and the paradox that the more the tigers export, the bigger their deficits with Japan become—these deficits being an indicator of the tigers' technological dependence on Japan.

The economies of the semi-periphery now find themselves in a structural squeeze between a center on which they are too dependent both for technology (Japan, and also the United States) and export market (chiefly the United States, as they have had little success in penetrating Japan) and a periphery that, as it increasingly participates in the industrial product cycle, gradually erodes their competitive edge.

In all this, the periphery remains true to its nature—that is, peripheral and dependent. These countries have not quite got their grip on sustained and cost-conscious productivity growth (unit labor costs in these countries have been rising at an annual rate of 3% for Malaysia, 3.7% for Thailand, 11.1% for the Philippines) and consequently run the risk of seeing transnational capital shift away from them to still lower-cost areas in the neighborhood, such as Vietnam and the rest of Indochina. Having started a revolution in rising expectations, they can hardly countenance a decline in their growth rates now; after all—to put those impressive growth rates in perspective—only in the past three years has the combined income of the six nations (counting Singapore) of Southeast Asia (322 million people) surpassed that of their neighbor down under, Australia, with a population of 17 million.

In the event of a further slowdown of world trade, can the export-oriented economies of the western Pacific Rim make up for lost markets by selling to each other? In fact, they already do, such that intra-Asian trade is expanding faster than Asia's trade with the United States. But much of intra-Asian trade is in assembly components and intermediate goods of products for which the final demand by far still is in the West. Whereas, half a millennium ago, the rise of the West became possible with the decline of the East, now the rise of the East will not be possible if the West continues to decline, or declines to buy what the East wishes to export.

But the factor with the greatest bearing on the future of the tigers and would-be tigers of Asia is the giant that in centuries past was *the* center of the

East Asian world-system and today remains little understood to the rest of the world: China.

ENTER THE DRAGON: CHINA
IN THE WORLD-ECONOMY

In Asia, China has had the fastest growing economy, averaging 10% yearly over the last thirteen years. It is by far the biggest in geographic and demographic terms and, if World Bank projections are to be believed, will be the biggest in the world in economic terms early in the next century. And it is the only one to claim that its system is not capitalist, but rather a "socialist market economy" since 1978, when the Communist leadership decided to allow the market mechanism to play a greater role in their modernization program and opened up China to foreign capital.

All the reasons that have made the NICs and next-NICs attractive to foreign capital were ipso facto valid for China, but on a vastly greater scale, making this giant the runaway favorite site for industrial relocation. In little over a decade, $20 billion of foreign capital poured into the coastal province of Guangdong alone, starting up 15,000 ventures there; capital inflows to China have not ceased growing by the year since then. In 1992, inflows of direct investment were more than $11 billion, bigger than what went to any other peripheral country; in 1993, these rose to $26 billion while approvals for future investment increased to more than $110 billion. Even as total Japanese direct foreign investment declined in 1992 because of economic woes at home, inflow to China increased by 83% over the previous year; in 1993, more yen went into China than into any other Asian country. If U.S. foreign direct investment in Asia has risen sharply since 1989, its highest increase has been in China, where year-on-year new U.S. investment jumped 95% in 1993. But now the greatest source of capital—comprising some 80% of total investment in China—is the network of overseas Chinese in Hong Kong, Taiwan, Singapore, and beyond.[9]

The question arises how China is being transformed by all these developments. To begin with, its trade with the rest of the world has become dangerously dependent on, and therefore vulnerable to, transnational capital. Although foreign-owned firms and joint ventures accounted for less than 5% of China's output in the past two years, they were the source of two thirds of its exports. Should these firms pull out en masse for any reason, China's economy would be severely affected (in 1989, GDP growth plunged to 3% as foreign investors waited out the crackdown on the pro-democracy movement). This extreme dependence also shows that, as in the case of the Southeast Asian periphery, the kind of industry brought into China by foreign capital is, in their great majority, only loosely linked to other sectors of the economy.

As a consequence of this type of extraverted industrialization, growth has been taking place mostly in the coastal provinces, where the export processing zones are; the result is sharply diverging relative growth rates between agriculture and industry and between the coastal areas and the hinterland. Left out of the boom, a "floating" population of some 50 million migrant peasants find their way to the cities but find no ready jobs there; many of them ended up at Tien-an-men in 1989. Many more try to migrate overseas. A political consequence of the utmost importance is the steady loss of control by the central leadership in Beijing of the provincial periphery that was once marginalized but that has now become the booming periphery of transnational capital instead. The central government's revenue has shrunk from 34% of GDP in 1979 to 19% today, and attempts by Beijing to reform the tax system in its favor (and for the welfare of the poorer hinterland) are thwarted by the increasingly rebellious coastal provinces. Attempts to curb inflation (now galloping at 30% in the industrial regions), cut the budget deficit (now nearing $15 billion, over a quarter of government revenues), and rein in the runaway growth of both money and credit supplies to halt speculation in property, foreign exchange, and shares are met with opposition and circumvention by the provincial governments, in a convoluted power play reminiscent of the endless feuding of warlords in the celestial empire.

Indeed, the danger now is that the simultaneous processes of economic decentralization within China initiated by Beijing and the economy's integration into the world-economy through the operations of transnational capital might build up centrifugal forces tending toward the political disintegration of the country in the end. The integrative thrust of transnational capital exerts an outward pull on the coastal regions and thus reorients them away from Beijing toward what is now being called "Greater China"—a "natural economic territory" integrating those parts of the mainland with Chinese communities across the seas.

What is the economic reality of Greater China? The economic motive of businesspeople is fast outpacing the political will of the governments involved. Hong Kong may well be "going back" to China, but Guangdong has certainly gone to Hong Kong: Three quarters of the workers employed by

Hong Kong firms live there, and a quarter of Hong Kong's currency circulates in China, much of it in Guangdong. Taiwan has its Fujian, where it has invested most of the $20 billion it has transferred to the mainland; indeed, Taipei fears that, with linkage at that scale, the island risks becoming an appendage to the mainland instead. Singapore's most ambitious project is to clone itself, at a capital outlay of $20 billion, and arise as "Singapore II" in Suzhou near Shanghai. And ethnic Chinese capitalists in Indonesia, Malaysia, Thailand, and the Philippines now account for some 10% to 15% of foreign capital entering China. Combined exports from the economic areas of Greater China were as large as Japan's in 1992.

But if Greater China means economic integration into the world-economy, it also portends political disintegration of the People's Republic of China. Hence, the maximalist stance of the central leadership is nipping at the buds of all political opposition.

The government may have the upper hand on the political front for now, but it risks losing the economic battle. Its macroeconomic policies have not made any headway in dealing with the overheating economy, now rapidly acquiring the looks of a bubble economy. On top of its spiraling inflation, budget deficit, and trade deficit (exceeding $12 billion in 1993), it now has to contend with capital flight as well, as shaky speculators seek safer havens abroad after the renminbi lost half its value in just a few months in the summer of 1993. Significantly, Taiwan has begun to scale back investment plans for the mainland, citing the overheating economy, corruption, deteriorating social order, and the difficulties of cracking China's domestic market; other investors could well agree and do the same.

As China tackles all of these problems, the power struggle for Deng's succession goes underway in Beijing, pitting yet once more the "free-marketeers" against those in favor of greater central planning. This time, the problems are vastly more complex, as China contends with the "successes" that have come round, in dialectical fashion, to perplex it from within and from without, and does so under the eyes of the whole world. If China succeeds in dealing with these problems, the world will have to deal with the enormity of that success. The global economy has accommodated the NICs by and large, but the full-scale industrialization of the dragon economy will be certain to destabilize the global balance of power. If China fails and plunges into chaos instead, the world will have to deal with the horror of that failure. Either way, it is the dragon—not the East Asian tigers or the Japanese flying goose or the American eagle—that will spell the future of the Pacific Rim.

THE OTHER ASIA: INDIA
IN THE WORLD-ECONOMY

If not China, with all its attendant uncertainties, surely Indonesia, the smaller and less complicated giant, would be just fine. This is how Jakarta has hoped the options would be defined by migrating transnational capital. But lately, those options have been considerably widened to include not just the other Southeast Asian countries of Vietnam, Laos, and Cambodia, with labor costs lower still than those of their ASEAN neighbors, but also a whole new world opened up to foreign capital: India.

Like Mao's China, post-independence India had set out to develop itself largely with its own resources and fundamentally on its own terms. That was the vision of its first prime minister, Jawaharlal Nehru, whose advocacy of economic nationalism (and political neutralism in cold war politics) made him a spokesperson, at Bandung, of the Third World. Although never determinedly isolationist, India's reliance on central planning and state monopolies—a legacy of British social democrats—and its nationalist striving for self-sufficiency, as expressed in Mahatma Gandhi's concept of *swadeshi* (the use of all homemade things to the exclusion of foreign things), predicated protectionism as a condition for national development. Restriction on the operations of foreign enterprises in the interest of national industries reached its peak in the early 1970s, when worldwide the achievements of OPEC and aspirations of the new international economic order fueled hopes that a vigorously protected national industrialization drive could succeed in the Third World and certainly in a country as technologically advanced as India.

Not long past that peak, however, India began to restrict its own economic nationalism instead, gradually—if haltingly—relaxing controls on foreign capital since Indira Gandhi's Emergency Rule in the mid-1970s. Rajiv Gandhi's tentative attempts at administrative reform of the "permit raj" in the mid-1980s and increasing dependence on external financing to bring India "into the 21st century" were accompanied by increasing concessions to foreign capital. The clearest signal to foreign capital that the page had been turned in India's economic policy came finally in mid-1991, when a severe financial crisis (ballooning budget deficits, mounting foreign debts, massive capital flight) sent the present Premier P. V. Narasimha Rao running to the IMF for an immediate bailout. The requisite changes—wide-ranging free market and fiscal reforms—imposed as a condition by the IMF and dutifully implemented by Rao made India finally "acceptable" to transnational capital.

The "discovery" of India—the world's fifth largest economy based on purchasing power parity, a middle-class market of some 150 million to 200 million Westernized consumers, an English-speaking society with a British legal system—by transnational capital was quickly translated into soaring figures. Total direct and portfolio foreign investments (the latter nearly seven times larger than the former) reached $4.7 billion in fiscal 1993, an eightfold increase from a year earlier. In a reversal of the East Asian pattern, the Americans, not the Japanese or the Asian NICs, have supplanted the British as the biggest investors, accounting for nearly half of the approved investments. But if Singapore gets its way, the island-state may not be far behind. Already there are plans that, just as Singapore II is arising in China, a mini-Singapore urban development complex will emerge near New Delhi.

Rao is India's Deng Xiaoping, so said Singapore's Lee Kuan Yew in effusive praise. But Rao's India is no China. If China is the dragon-economy—restless, growing by leaps and bounds, consumed by consumerism and overheating at the risk of burning itself—India is rather more of an elephant-economy—gigantic and ponderous, slow-gaited, a creature set in its ways. The economy grew at around 4% in 1992-93, and less than that in 1993-94. The 1994-95 growth target of 5% may well be within reach, but as reform-architect Finance Minister Manmohan Singh reckons, India needs a sustained growth rate of 6% to 8% to "take the harsh edges off extreme poverty" by the end of the decade—and *that* is far from certain. What is certain is that changes in government policy are generating losers on a large scale, from the sprawling and inefficient family-owned business empires, hardly changed in outlook from the Raj, to the small manufacturing firms of wide diversity, to the rural poor. Today, industry is stagnant. Even as the economy strains to attain the present growth target, opposition to the Rao-Singh liberalization policy grows—while religious strife and caste rebellions break out in far-flung areas.

As in the fable of the blind men and the elephant, India's political economy under Rao is different things to different interests. Is the ongoing liberalization irreversible? Transnational capital hopes it is but can never be too sure of Rao's Congress (I) Party surviving its own internecine factionalism while facing down the Hindu nationalist challenge from the Bharatiya Janaya Party, which quite expectedly has revived the call for *swadeshi.* To the countries of the Asia-Pacific region, into which it seeks integration as eventually a full-fledged member of APEC, India remains enigmatic—or they would rather have it so. Does India really belong in the grouping? Some members say not, if the criteria for membership include location in the Asia-Pacific Rim and economic engagement with the region, never mind Singapore's inroads into the subcontinent. To China, security matters with India remain a matter of concern; while to Indonesia, until as late as five years ago, New Delhi has posed a looming threat in the Indian Ocean. The Northeast Asian NICs are even more reluctant than their southern neighbors to allow India in. Japan, mildly favorable but only so toward eventual Indian membership, asserts its leadership in the region by typically letting matters be as they are. India may well have opened up to the world-economy, but APEC has yet to show that it wants the elephant in. Decidedly, one dragon is enough for now; indeed, to the aspiring tigers of Southeast Asia, it could already be one dragon too many.

CONCLUSION: FRANK ON ASIA

The rise of industry in East Asia has given rise to a burgeoning research industry on the phenomenon itself. Cultural explanations (Confucianism), political theories (authoritarian developmentalism), business strategies (lean-and-mean approach, shop-floor focus), economic history (late industrialization), and macro-historical postulates (Spengler's "decline of the West" updated) have been elaborated in best-sellers and fashionable MBA courses to account for the ascendancy of the Pacific Rim.

In Frank's order of things, such theories would provide no more than a secondary order of explanation, further elaborations of specific aspects of a phenomenon whose historical determinacy has to be sought in the deeper structures of the world-system. He has been consistent in his insistence on the primacy of global economic conditions in understanding specific developments anywhere in the world. Economic determinism is a charge that he would not be averse to accepting if properly understood as to the fundamental meaning he imparts to it.

In writings strewn over the last two decades, Frank analyzed, and in some instances anticipated, broad global developments that have come to shape the present reality of East Asia. The restructuring of the world-economy under the pressure of the current crisis resulted in the emergence of a new international division of labor that propelled the rise of the NICs. State intervention in the NICs clearly mattered in responding to those global dislocations and opportunities, but if it did, it was thanks to transnational conditions (prewar Japanese colonialism, postwar U.S. patronage, cold war subsidies) uniquely affecting them. Frank advanced the thesis—well before *perestroika* and *glas-*

nost became household words—that the brave new "transideological" partnership between transnational capital and the centrally planned economies,
including China, would render decreasingly relevant East-West ideological
differences and, in time, would redefine their relationships along the hierarchical North-South axis instead. Earlier than most, he saw the possibility of
regionalization or bloc formation in the world-economy as attempts to deal
with the global crisis, including the accelerated Japanization of Asia as the
United States sank deeper into the predicaments of a hegemonic power.
Effectively, the cold war is over and, as Frank notes with no surprise, in Asia
it is Japan that has won. Those who had not anticipated these developments
may proclaim that, with the fading away of the East-West conflict and the
complete reintegration of the Eastern Bloc into the world capitalist system,
history—after a seventy-year detour—has come to an end. East Asians, for
their part, may additionally proclaim that, with the advent of the Pacific Age,
history—after a five hundred-year detour—has come full circle as the East
rises again and the West declines. To Frank, who has always insisted on the
primacy of the axial division of labor and economic exchanges as defining
the interrelationships of nations, history continues to be what it has always
been, as fundamentally the history of the cumulation of accumulation within
the world-system, within which nations and regions have their rise and fall.
The current global economic crisis, which has engendered momentous developments, including the emergence of an industrialized East Asia, continues to
delimit the possibilities of history but poses no end to it.

NOTES

1. "Citibank Leadership Series," a paid advertisement that appeared in *Far Eastern Economic
Review* and other business magazines in 1993.
2. Cumings (1981) argues that the social and regional conflicts that racked Korea from 1945
to 1953 have their origins in the immensity of social disruptions brought about by Japan's
breakneck transformation of that colony.
3. See Aseniero (1994) for the sources of these data and those in the following paragraphs.
4. As taught in Southeast Asian universities in the 1960s, modernization theory characterized
Southeast Asian societies as transitional from traditional to modern, the incompleteness of the
process accounting for the "dual economy," which was what underdevelopment was all about;
mainstream economics—integrating Keynesian and neoclassical economics, as expounded, for
instance, in Paul Samuelson's textbook—exuded confidence in completing the modernization
process, provided that the national economy remained open to foreign capital and trade. Frank's
devastating critique of all variants of modernization theory in *Sociology of Development and
Underdevelopment of Sociology* (1971), widely read on Southeast Asian campuses, was a veritable

eye-opener in the progressive debunking of those approaches. His studies of Latin American political economy were particularly of interest in the Philippines, Asia's "Latin American country" with agrarian relations dating back to Spanish colonial times, where the apparent coexistence of different modes of production led the local Maoists to conclude that theirs was a "semi-feudal, semi-capitalist" society. Frank's postulation that this heterogenous social formation was the result of, and not the impediment to, modern capitalist development helped define the content and orientation of Third World studies in the region.

5. In *Crisis: In the Third World* (1980), Frank discusses some of these regional political economic developments of the 1970s in their world-system context. For a discussion of these political economic developments through the 1980s and early 1990s and other issues discussed in this section, see Aseniero (in press).

6. For a critique of developmentalism as the philosophical underpinning of the modern world capitalist system and as the inherited ideology of the contemporary Third World, see Aseniero (1985).

7. Figures for this entire section come from the Japanese Ministry of International Trade and Industry (MITI), the World Bank, Export-Import Bank of Japan, and Nomura Research Institute, as cited in *The Economist* (1993a, 1993b) and *Far Eastern Economic Review* (1993a).

8. It is estimated that 30% to 40% of Japan's trade with ASEAN (the Association of Southeast Asian Nations) is done between Japanese firms and their ASEAN affiliates.

9. Figures in this section come from studies done by the London-based International Institute for Strategic Studies; the Washington-based Institute for International Economics; the World Bank; the business periodicals *Far Eastern Economic Review, The Economist,* and the *Wall Street Journal;* Hornik (1994); and Segal (1994).

REFERENCES

Amin, S. (1988). Bandung trente ans aprés. In *L'échange inegal et la loi de valeur.* Paris, France: Economica.

Aseniero, G. (1985). A reflection on developmentalism: From development to transformation. In H. Addo et al. (Eds.), *Development as social transformation: Reflections on the global problématique* (pp. 48-85). Boulder, CO: Westview.

Aseniero, G. (1994, Summer). The transnational context of South Korean and Taiwanese development. *Review,* pp. 275-336.

Aseniero, G. (in press). El estado y el desarrollo en el este y sureste Asiatico. In P. González Casanova (Ed.), *El estado en el tercer mundo contemporaneo.* Mexico: Siglo XXI.

Cumings, B. (1981). *The origins of the Korean War: Liberalization and the emergence of separate regimes.* Chicago: University of Chicago Press.

Cumings, B. (1987). The origins and development of the Northeast Asian political economy: Industrial sectors, product cycles, and political consequences. In F. Deyo (Ed.), *The political economy of the new Asian industrialism* (pp. 44-84). Ithaca, NY: Cornell University Press.

The Economist. (1991, November 16).

The Economist. (1993a, April 24). pp. 27-28.

The Economist. (1993b, June 12). pp. 72-73.

Emmott, B. (1989). *The sun also sets: The limits to Japan's economic power.* New York: Simon & Schuster.

Far Eastern Economic Review. (1993a, June 3). p. 44.

Far Eastern Economic Review. (1993b, July 22). p. 79.

Frank, A. G. (1971). *The sociology of development and the underdevelopment of sociology.* London: Pluto.

Frank, A. G. (1980). *Crisis: In the Third World.* New York: Holmes & Meier.

Frank, A. G. (1991a). A plea for world system history. *Journal of World History, 2*(1), 1-28.

Frank, A. G. (1991b). The underdevelopment of development. *Scandinavian Journal of Development Alternatives,* special number, X(3), 5-72.

Hornik, R. (1994, May/June). Bursting China's bubble. *Foreign Affairs, 73*(3), 28-42.

Segal, G. (1994, May/June). China's changing shape. *Foreign Affairs, 73*(3), 43-58.

A survey of Asia. (1991, November 16). *The Economist,* p. 1.

A survey of Asia. (1993, October 30). *The Economist,* p. 6.

A survey of Asia's emerging economies. (1990, October 2). *The Economist,* p. 29.

Wood, C. (1992). *The bubble economy: The Japanese economic collapse.* London: Sidgwick & Jackson.

World Bank. (1993). *The East Asian miracle: Economic growth and public policy.* New York: Oxford University Press.

10

On the Origins of the
Economic Catastrophe in Africa

SAMIR AMIN

W. H. Locke Anderson, Translator

I

At the end of four decades of development in the postwar period, the balance of results is so uneven that one is tempted to drop the general expression "Third World" as a designation for the countries that have been the objects of the politics of development during these decades. One now contrasts, not without reason, a newly industrialized and competitive Third World with a marginalized "Fourth World" that includes the whole of Africa. One must remark, though not without inviting argument, that the countries of the first of these two groups have not been struck by the general crisis of contemporary capitalism, that they have registered high rates of growth, particularly in East Asia, whereas those of the second, devastated by the crisis, appear to be incapable of responding to the challenge that confronts them.

The objective of the politics of development deployed in Asia, Africa, and Latin America in the course of the entire postwar period (beginning in 1948-

1950, or in 1960 for sub-Saharan Africa, the time of independence for most of the states that comprise it) has been identical in its essentials for most of the states despite differences in the ideological discourse that has accompanied it. It has everywhere set into motion a nationalist project that has assigned itself the objective of accelerating modernization and enriching the society through industrialization. One comprehends this common denominator without difficulty if one simply recalls that in 1945 practically all the countries of Asia (Japan excepted), of Africa, and with a few nuances, of Latin America had been deprived of all industry worthy of the name, save for some mineral extraction here and there, were largely rural in the distribution of their population, were ruled by archaic regimes (e.g., latifundial oligarchies in Latin America, monarchies under the protection of the Islamic Orient, China), or were colonies (Africa, India, Southeast Asia). Despite their great diversity, all the movements of national liberation assigned themselves the same objectives: political independence, modernization of the state, and industrialization of the economy.

It would not be correct to say that they did not struggle as soon as they were in a position to do so. Certainly, the variations were almost as numerous as the countries, and it is legitimate, in view of this fact, to attempt to classify them on the basis of their models. But one thereby risks being the victim of criteria chosen on the basis of function, not necessarily on the basis of ideological preference or the ideas that were worked out from the experience of the epoch, from the unfolding of the experiments in question, and from the possibilities and constraints, internal and external.

On the contrary, by accenting the common denominator that links them together, I invite one to step away a bit, to examine these classifications and see this history from the vantage point of the present, and to reread it by the light of where it led.

To industrialize implied, first, to construct an internal market and to protect it from the ravages of competition. To do this, one began with commonsense observations. One had at one's disposal primary products of agricultural origin (e.g., cotton, foodstuffs, timber) or minerals, natural resources that would permit the production of energy, of construction materials, of steel, of essential chemical products, for which there already existed an internal market, supplemented by imports of manufactured products for current consumption (e.g., textiles, furniture, utensils, clothing). There was no reason not to profit from these possibilities to bring about what the West had done in its time: make an industrial revolution. The formulas could vary according to circumstances—

the extent of the internal market, the availability of resources—or even according to theses more or less rhetorical or ideological, giving priority to the production of light consumption industries or to those products allowing later acceleration of other industries. (They proposed the thesis of "the industrializing industries," which rationalized those of the Soviets.) The final objective was identical.

This good sense, expressed in the common language of all technocrats of the epoch, inspired pragmatic choices. The necessary technology for industrialization could only be imported, but it was not necessary to own installations built with foreign capital. That depended on the power of negotiation that one had. Finance capital ought therefore to be invited to invest in the host country even if it had to be borrowed. Here once more, the formula— foreign private property, public financing guaranteed by the national bank, foreign aid in grants and credits—could be tailored to the estimates one made of costs and benefits.

The required importation that was built into these plans of accelerated growth through industrialization implied, fatally, the export of known, traditional products of the farms and mines. No known strategy of development has been oriented at the outset toward exportation—that is, determined principally by the objective piercing the world market through the exercise of imagined comparative advantages. The reading that the World Bank proposes today, associating success of some countries with a choice "open to exportation" and the failure of others that fell back on the internal market is a reading a posteriori, which was not been made during the period, neither by the local officials who made the choices nor by the World Bank itself. The first attention in all these cases was on the internal market.

Experience moreover demonstrated that this reasoning was correct. During a phase of general growth like that after the war, the demand for almost all products was growing continuously, whether for energy, primary mineral products, or specific agricultural products. The rates of exchange fluctuated, but not systematically, canceling the effects of a growing volume of exports. "Natural" comparative advantage, resting on mineral resources or agricultural specializations, made some sense. More than that, moreover, the expansion of world markets opened some cracks that permitted one to exploit the "advantage" of cheap labor in certain ranges of manufacturing production for those who had not lost their advantages based on natural resources. The multiplicity of free zones at the end of the period of postwar growth testifies to the realities of these calculations.

The construction of the internal market, axis of all politics of development during the period, is only a synonym for a strategy of industrialization through import substitution, as opposed to a strategy oriented toward export markets that do not exist. The industry that is envisaged opens a market for itself by displacing former imports. Like the demand for final consumption, itself always expanding, the market adds to itself intermediate goods, sometimes simple equipment that one can envisage being built locally, and finally that occasioned by public outlays and work on infrastructure.

Modernization, though its axis rests on industrialization, cannot be reduced to that. Urbanization, infrastructure for transport and communications, education, and social services have for their objective, in part, to provide industry with suitably qualified labor. But such objectives are equally pursued for their own ends, to construct a national state and to modernize attitudes, as one sees in the discourse of trans-ethnic nationalism.

It is well understood in this period that the opposition one often creates is between "the intervention of the state"—always negative because it is in conflict with the spontaneity of the market—and "private interests"—always associated with this spontaneity. This opposition was neither a matter of fact nor noticed. On the contrary, the good sense displayed by the parties in power saw the intervention of the state as an essential element in building the market and modernizing. The radical left, socialist in its ideology, associated the expansion of the state with the gradual abolition of private property. But the nationalist right, which did not share this objective, was nonetheless interventionist and statist: It believed that the construction of private interests it proposed required a vigorous statism. The rubbish that nourishes the dominant discourse of today has no echo of the thinking of this earlier epoch.

Today, the temptation is very great to read this history as a stage in the expansion of world capitalism, which accomplished, more or less, certain functions attached to national primitive accumulation and thereby created the conditions for the following stage into which the countries involved now move, marked by their entry into the world market and competition on this terrain. I do not propose to give in to this temptation. The dominant forces of world capitalism have not "spontaneously" created the models of development. This "development" imposed itself on them. It was a product of the national liberation movements of the Third World in that epoch. The reading I propose, therefore, places the accent on the contradiction between the spontaneous and immediate tendencies of the capitalist system, which are always guided by the financial calculus of the short term (this is characteristic of capitalism's mode of social development) and by long-term visions that animate the emergent political forces (which are always in conflict with the immediate tendencies). To be sure, this conflict is not always radical. Capital makes adjustments, to its profit even. But it only responds; it is not the originator of the movement. I have for this reason proposed to call the postwar period, especially the two decades 1955-1975, the period of "the ideology of development," or the period of "the national bourgeoisie of Bandung" (in reference to the Bandung Conference that inaugurated the period). In this framework, the conflict between the dominant forces of world capitalism and those that animated the "developmentalist" project of Bandung had been more or less according to whether the statism put into place was envisaged as prior to supplanting capitalism or intended to sustain capitalism. The radical wing of the movement rallied around the first of the visions and by this fact entered into conflict with the immediate interests of dominant capitalism, notably through nationalizations and exclusion of foreign capital. The moderate wing, by contrast, attempted to conciliate the interests in conflict. On the international level, this distinction attached itself rather naturally to the East-West conflict between Sovietism and Western capitalism. We therefore find on this terrain both (a) the elements of the common denominator of national bourgeois development and (b) the characteristics of the opposition between its radical and moderate tendencies.

All of the national liberation movements in Africa partook of this modernist vision, capitalist and bourgeois. This did not in any sense imply that they were inspired by, much less directed by, a bourgeoisie in the full sense of the word. This class hardly existed at the moment of independence, and thirty years later it still exists only in an embryonic state. But the ideology of modernization exists and constitutes the dominant force giving sense to the revolt of the people against colonization. This ideology has been the bearer of a project for which I propose the seemingly curious name "capitalism without capitalists."

Capitalism, in the sense that it carries out modernization, calls into being the relations of production and the social relations essential and proper to capitalism: the wage relationship, the management of enterprise, hierarchical education, the concept of national citizenship. Without doubt, other values characteristic of evolved capitalism were cruelly absent, such as political democracy. One justified this absence in terms of the exigencies of the preliminary stages of development. All countries of the region, radical and moderate, opted for the same formula of one party, farcical elections, the founder-leader of the nation, and so forth.

"Without capitalists" has the sense that, in the absence of entrepreneurs, the state and its technocrats were called on to substitute for them. Sometimes, the emergence of a bourgeoisie was suspect because of the primacy they gave to their own immediate interests in preference to others that were more long term in coming to fruition. This suspicion became, in the radical wing of the national liberation movement, tantamount to exclusion. This radical wing then naturally conceived its project as that of "building socialism." It then redis-covered the discourse of Sovietism. This, too, became, by the logic of its own dynamics, the project of capitalism without capitalists, having made the objective of "overtaking" the Western developed world the center of its preoccupations.

In Africa, as elsewhere, the national liberation movements partook both of the tendencies toward a radicalization called "socialist" and the tendencies toward moderation. This break, sincere and clear-cut in certain cases, divided a movement that was outwardly unified in other respects. The opposition was based on a complex set of causes, resting for some on the social classes that were the basis of the movement—the urban popular classes, the peasants, the favored classes—and for others on the traditions of their political and organi-zational formations (e.g., urban Communist Parties, syndicates, churches). The rush with which the principal colonial powers of Africa—England and France—had conceived the project of "decolonization" in 1960 had accen-tuated this opposition in the short run. Africa in 1960 was split into two blocs: the Casablanca Group, under the flags of Nasserism, the Algerian FLN, and Nkrumahism; and the Monrovia Group, constituted in the first instance by the faithful pupils of Gaullist France and liberal England (e.g., the Ivory Coast, Kenya). Lumumba, in the then Congo, gravitated toward the first group, but important forces within his country were more inclined toward the second. The procrastinations of Belgian power, which refused until the last minute to draw from the lesson that France and Great Britain had had to learn, had been largely responsible for sustaining the conflict on the terrain of the Congolese themselves. In response to the establishment of a fragile Lumumbaist power in Leopoldville—then in Stanleyville—the "moderate" forces, supported by Brussels and others, notably South Africa, opted for the secession of Katanga and Kasai. Installed in Leopoldville, at first under the shadow of Kasavubu, Mobutu (reconciled with Tshombe and "Emperor" Muluba of Kasai) played the reconciliation card to which his masters had finally decided to rally. The Congolese example had therefore inspired a new politics, called "to smooth the edges" in an earlier time, to reconcile the radical and moderate camps, in order progressively to undermine the first. The genius of Emperor Haile Selassie had been to understand that the moment had come to confirm the reconciliation between the Monrovia and Casablanca Groups through the creation at Addis Ababa, precisely in 1963, of the Organization of African Unity.

The rapprochement created new conditions for the Bandung Project in Africa. Formally, all the states rallied to it and thereby became members of the "nonaligned movement" even while they remained in the lap of the Western powers and under their direct military protection in some cases. But suddenly they acquired a certain capacity for maneuver not envisioned in the neocolonial scheme. This event explains why, after the initiators of "African socialism"—Ghana, Guinea, and Mali—successive generations of radicalization from the same source of inspiration had been able to succeed in Africa (e.g., Congo-Brazaville, Benin, Tanzania), a strange fact when account is taken of the fragility of the states of this continent under imperialist pressures.

II

Whatever the common objectives of the era of Bandung—its ideology of development, its national and bourgeois project of capitalism without capitalists, the modalities of its undertaking, the vicissitudes of its relations with the conflict of the superpowers—the results were not so different from one group of countries to another.

The evaluation of these results is evidently a function of the criteria chosen to define *development,* an ideological concept whose meaning is always vague. If one sticks to the criterion of national liberation—that is, "nation building"—the results are arguable. The reason is that although the development of capitalism in the earlier period sustained national integration, globalization operated on the periphery of the system in the opposite way: to disintegrate these same societies. But the ideology of the national movement ignored this contradiction, remaining trapped within the bourgeois concept of making up for a historic delay and conceiving this catching up through participation in the international division of labor (and not through its negation, delinking). Without doubt, according to the specific characteristics of the precolonial, precapitalist societies, the effect of this disintegration was more or less dramatic. In Africa, where the artificial colonial carving up accorded no respect to the prior history of the peoples, the disintegration produced by capitalist peripheralization permitted ethnism to survive despite the efforts of the ruling classes in power after national liberation to avoid its manifestations. When the crisis took place, brutally wiping out the surplus that had permitted the financing of the trans-ethnic policies of the new states, the ruling class itself broke into fractions that, having lost all legitimacy based on the realization of "development," tried to create for themselves new bases that were often associated with an ethnicist response (Amin, 1993a).

If we hold on to the criterion of socialism, the results are still more mixed. Granted that we must understand the word *socialism* according to what populist ideology makes of it, it is a question of a progressive vision, putting the accent on maximal social mobility, the reduction of inequalities in income, some sort of full employment in the urban areas, and some sort of a poor welfare state. From this point of view, the achievements of a country such as Tanzania, for example, offer a striking contrast to those of Zaire, the Ivory Coast, or Kenya, where the most extreme inequalities persisted for thirty years, through periods of rapid economic growth and periods of stagnation. But the criterion conformed to the logic of capitalist expansion—a concept logically different from development—and to that of the capacity to be competitive in the world market. From this point of view, the results differed in the extreme and brutally contrast the principal countries of Asia and Latin America, which became competitive industrial exporters, to those of Africa, which were trapped into the exportation of primary products. The first constitute the new Third World (the modern periphery in my analysis); the second comprise the Fourth World, marginalized in the new stage of capitalist development (Founou-Tchuigoua, 1993).

The explanation of the defeat of Africa in its entirety must begin with the complexity of the interactions between specific internal conditions and the logic of the world expansion of capital. Because these interactions are often ignored, current expectations, such as those advanced by the economists of the "international economy," who are as conventional as the nationalists of the Third World, remain superficial.

The first group accents the phenomena that isolate the Third World countries from the logic of the system as a whole, such as the corruption of its political class, the fragility of its economic bases, the low productivity of its agriculture (still dependent on animal traction), and the ethnic chaos. Their solution leads inexorably to a greater integration into world capitalism. Africa will have to have "real" capitalist entrepreneurs; it is necessary to end the dance of self-sufficiency of the rural population by the systematic promotion of commercial agriculture. It is a matter of short arguments because it abstracts from the whole framework within which the reforms propose to operate. It ignores, for example, that the capitalist path in agriculture produces gigantic masses of surplus people, who—given the current state of technology—cannot find employment in industry the way they could in 19th-century Europe. History does not repeat itself.

The second group places the accent on other phenomena, no less real, such as the fact that the prices of primary materials on which the capacity to finance industrial development depends are systematically deteriorating. The nationalists of the Third World invoke also, with good reason, the innumerable political (and sometimes military) interventions of the Western powers, always hostile to the forces of progressive social change. But these arguments are not structurally tied to the logic of internal conflicts and similar matters, opposing the "outside" to the "nation" in which one must juggle the contradictions. The analysis of the impasse I propose recalls the responsibilities both of colonization and of the pursuit of its project by the ruling classes linked to neocolonialism, integral to the geostrategic considerations of imperialism.

The international division of labor that created the contrast between the industrialized centers and the non-industrialized periphery dates back to the Industrial Revolution at the beginning of the 19th century in Europe. It implied that the periphery countries would participate in world trade through the export of products in which they had an advantage derived from nature, rather than from the productive skills of their labor. This rule remained in force for Africa from the time of its colonization until the end of the 18th century, as well as for the other peripheral areas of Asia and Latin America, which from this point of view were not differentiated until the time of the Second World War.

One understands, therefore, why the European powers took part in the assault on the African continent, which they partitioned at the Berlin Conference in 1885. It was not a question, as it has too often been claimed, of an "erroneous" calculation whose absurdity history eventually demonstrated, Africa having turned out to be a dead weight on the colonizing powers. It was simply a matter of the powers' having acquired a right of preemption over the natural riches of the continent.

Once it was conquered, it was necessary to valorize the Africa in question. At this point, the logic of world capitalism intervened: What were the natural resources of the different regions of the continent and the prior histories of these regions? It appears to me that, in this body of analysis, one can discern three models of colonization: (a) the economy of trade incorporating small peasants selling tropical products in a world market of controlled monopolies and thus making it possible to keep the remuneration of peasant labor to a minimum and to squander the productive value of the soil; (b) the economy of southern Africa organized around mineral extraction, fed by a cheap migratory labor force from the "reserves"; and (c) the economy of pillage in which concessionaire companies were free from the imposition of any tithe. The Congo basin essentially belonged to this category (Amin, 1976, pp. 317-333; Amin & Coquery Vidrovitch, 1969). The statute establishing the Belgian colony (originally the private property of the Belgian king) with the mineral riches of Katanga had permitted a colonial development categorized as "brilliant" by its promoters—and beneficiaries—Belgian capital and the associated foreign capital. Moreover, notwithstanding appearances, the results of this insertion into global capitalism were an out-and-out disaster for the African people. This insertion is, in fact, responsible for the two major weaknesses that even today weigh heavily on the destiny of the continent.

First, it retarded for a century the beginning of the agricultural revolution. A surplus could be extracted from the work of the peasants and the bounty of nature even without investments in modernization (neither machinery nor fertilization), without really paying for the labor, without even promising to maintain the fertility of the soil in farmlands and forests. In the regions in which the economy of pillage operated, the regressions occasioned by its mode of realizing value were maximal. This destructive effect was nevertheless partly compensated for in the Belgian Congo by the creation of an embryonic industry more precocious than elsewhere. I refer here to the import-substitution industries established in Kinshasa (in the epoch of Leopoldville) after the Second World War, which are explained by the opening of Belgium to foreign commerce at a time when France and England were protectionist. The previous history nonetheless demonstrated that it was not a question of a fragile embryo, but rather of furthering an industrial revolution.

Simultaneously, this mode of realizing the value of natural resources, exploited in the setting of a world of unequal labor, excluded the formation of any local bourgeoisie at all. To the contrary, each time one started to coalesce, the colonial authorities suppressed it (Amin, 1969, 1973).

The weakness of the movements of national liberation in the states that were the heirs of colonialism can be traced back to this form of colonialism. They are not, therefore, remnants of precolonial Africa, vanished in the storm, in which the ideology of world capitalism tries to find its legitimacy—deploying its habitual racist discourse. The "critiques" of independent Africa, of its corrupt political bourgeoisies, of the absence of any sense of economics, and of the tenacity of its rural communalist structures forget that the character of contemporary Africa was formed between 1880 and 1960.

It is no wonder, therefore, that neocolonialism has perpetuated these characteristics. The political gangs that are found responsible for independent Africa were not necessarily agents of neocolonialism. Their weaknesses were those of peripheral capitalism. But this does not absolve them from responsibility. For despite the weaknesses of the colonial societies, the movements of national liberation had produced elites potentially capable of going farther. Yet, all their efforts were conjoined to make Africa's attempts to get out of the rut fail.

The form this weakness took was entirely defined by the famous accords of Lomé, which linked—and continue to link—sub-Saharan Africa to the Europe of the EEC. These accords have, in effect, perpetuated the old division of labor, relegating independent Africa to the production of primary products at the very moment when—in the period of Bandung, 1955-1975—the Third World elsewhere was engaged in an industrial revolution. Thus, Africa lost thirty years in a decisive period of historical change. Certainly, the ruling classes of Africa share in the responsibility because they were arrayed in the camp of the neocolonials against the aspirations of their own peoples, whose weaknesses they exploited.

The collusion between the African ruling classes and the strategies of global imperialism is, therefore, the ultimate cause of the impasse. One rediscovers, in the carrying out of these collusions, all the dimensions of the strategies of the imperialists in the postwar period (1945-1990), in particular their geostrategic dimensions. Being connected to Katanga in the configuration of southern Africa, Zaire had paid the price of the geostrategy of the postwar imperialisms. The entire region, from Katanga (today Shaba), Northern Rhodesia (Zambia), and Southern Rhodesia (Zimbabwe) to South Africa, constituted for the United States of the cold war a unique strategic zone because of its mineral resources and its location controlling communications between the Atlantic and the Indian Oceans. The U.S.S.R., during the period, attempted to break these strategic positions of its adversary by making alliances with the movements of African national liberation, notably the more radical among them in Angola, Mozambique, Zimbabwe, and South Africa (Amin, 1994, chap. 5). The Western powers responded by supporting almost unconditionally the regimes of Mobutu in Zaire, Banda in Malawi, and Kenyatta then Moi in Kenya, despite their notorious corruption and their extreme antidemocratic practices, like those that sustain Savimbi in Angola to this day and Renamo in Mozambique, and pushed for the federal compromise in South Africa, however undemocratic it might be (Amin, 1993b, chap. 4). At the same time, evidently these geostrategic considerations of Washington, with which the Europeans were always aligned, gave Mobutu some room to maneuver (more apparent than real), which he exploited through his "nationalist" discourse of "authenticity," sometimes even through measures of nationalization, which in fact did not essentially intrude on imperialist interests (Yachir, 1987).

Analogous geostrategic considerations explain the hostility of the Western powers to the bourgeoisies of northern Africa and the Middle East—that is, of the Arab world. Here, the importance of the region lay in its petroleum resources and its geostrategic position on the southern flank of the U.S.S.R. These strategies also had a part in keeping the Arabs in check. In a sense, these geostrategic considerations constrained the Western imperialists to support, or at least tolerate, the initiatives of the bourgeoisies of East Asia, which explain, in part, the "success" of this region in the postwar period of capitalist expansion.

But today, the page has turned. The anti-Soviet geostrategy no longer has any basis. The hour of the recompradorization of the peripheries has sounded and put to an end all the illusions of the era of Bandung. This recompradorization nonetheless operates on terrains made different by the uneven results of the deployment of the Bandung project.

III

A new stage of polarization is even now under way, in which the logic of the expansion of capital wills that the African Fourth World should be provisionally "marginalized." I believe also that the debate on these new forms of polarization should commence with the discussion of what is new in the world system, a product of the erosion of the previous system, that of the postwar period (1945-1990) described above. In my thinking, these are the new elements:

1. The erosion of the self-centered national state and the concomitant disappearance of the close association of the space of reproduction of accumulation and the space of political and social rule, which has until this time been defined precisely by the frontiers of the national autocentered state

2. The erosion of the contrast "centers = industrial regions; peripheries = non-industrial regions" and the emergence of new dimensions of polarization

The position of a country on the global pyramid is now defined by the level of competitive capacity of its products on the world market. This competitivity is the complex product of an ensemble of conditions—economic, political, and social—and in this unequal combat the centers put into place what I call the "five monopolies" that govern the effectiveness of their actions:

1. *The monopolies that benefit the contemporary centers of technology and that require gigantic expenditures that only the state—a great and rich state—can envisage undertaking.* Without this undertaking, which liberal discourse always passes over in silence—particularly for the sustenance of the military—the majority of these monopolies could not survive.

2. *The monopolies that control the financial flows of global large-scale enterprises.* The liberalization of the major institutions operating in the world financial market has given these monopolies an influence that is without precedent. It is no longer true that the major fraction of a nation's money can circulate only within the space—generally national—commanded by its financial institutions. This circulation is centralized by the intervention of institutions whose field of operation is the entire world. This privilege of worldwide circulation rests on a political logic that makes financial globalization acceptable. It is the logic of finance capital, the most globalized segment of capital. This logic can be suspended by a simple decision to delink. Elsewhere, the free movements of finance capital operate, one must know, within the rules defined by a world monetary system that I believe is already in decline. This system is based on the free fluctuation of value on the market (conforming to a theory according to which money should be a commodity like any other) and on a relationship to the dollar as the de facto universal currency. The first of these bases is without scientific foundation; the second only functions for lack of an alternative. A national money cannot replace the functions of an international money in a satisfactory fashion unless conditions of international competitivity produce a structural surplus of exports by the country whose currency fulfills the monetary function, ensuring the financing by this country of the structural adjustments of the others. This was true of Great Britain in the 19th century, but it is not true of the United States today, which finances its deficit by forcing other nations to lend. It is no longer the case that the deficits of the United States and the surpluses of Japan (those of Germany

having disappeared with unification) are of a common measure with the financial needs that the structural adjustments of the other nations require. In these conditions, financial globalization, far from imposing itself "naturally," is, on the contrary, fragile in the extreme. In the short term, it can only engender a permanent instability and not the stability needed for the processes of adjustment to operate efficaciously.

3. *The monopolies that operate within a framework of access to the natural resources of the planet.* The dangers of senseless exploitation of these resources are always afoot, and capitalism—which is based on a short-term social rationality, nothing more—is unable to surmount them; this reinforces the range of the monopolies of the already-developed countries, which simply ignore the fact that their profligacy cannot be imitated by others.

4. *The monopolies that operate in the fields of communications and the media.* They not only homogenize the basis of the world culture they carry but also invent new means for the manipulation of politics. The expansion of the modern media market is already a major component of the erosion of the concept and practice of democracy even in the West.

5. *The monopoly that operates in the domain of armaments of massive destruction.* Limited by the bipolarity of the postwar period, this monopoly is again the absolute arm of American diplomacy, as it was in 1945. If "proliferation" carries evident dangers, there is no other means by which this unacceptable monopoly can be combatted.

Taken together, these five monopolies define the framework within which the globalized law of value expresses itself. Far from being the expression of a "pure" economic rationality that one can detach from its social and political framework, the law of value is the concentrated expression of conditions that prevent the export of industrialization to the periphery and devalue the productive work incorporated in its products while they overstate the value attached to the activities by which the new monopolies operate to the benefit of the centers. It reproduces, therefore, a new hierarchy in the division of revenue on a world scale, more unequal than ever, and subalternizes the industries of the peripheries. The newly industrialized countries are not on the way to "overtaking" the dominant centers, while those of the Fourth World simply fall behind. Rather, the first constitute the heart of tomorrow's periphery, while the second are simply "provisionary tenants" on the margins of the system.

In contrast to the dominant ideological discourse, I maintain that "globalization by means of the market" is a reactionary utopia against which one must develop theoretically and practically an alternative humanist program for globalization from a socialist perspective. The realization of such a project implies the construction of a world political system, not "at the service" of the world market, but defining the limits of its operation, as the national state has historically represented, not the field of operation of the national market, but the social framework in which it operates. A world political system would therefore have major responsibilities in each of the following four domains:

1. The organization of global disarmament at the appropriate level, liberating humanity from the menace of holocausts, nuclear and other.
2. The organization of equitable access, more and more equal, to the use of the resources of the planet and the establishment of world decision systems in this domain, which covers the pricing of resources so as to reduce waste and redistribute the value and the rent assessed for the use of these resources, initiating by this means the elements of a world fiscal system.
3. The negotiation of economic regulations, flexible but controlled, among the great regions of the world, progressively reducing the technological and financial monopolies of the centers. This implies, it goes without saying, the liquidation of the institutions presently charged with the regulation of the world (e.g., the so-called World Bank, the IMF, the GATT).
4. The organization of negotiations permitting a correct resolution of the global/national conflict in the domains of communication, culture, and politics. This resolution implies the creation of political institutions that permit the representation of social interests on a global scale, and some kind of "global parliament"; this goes beyond the concept of the interstate institutions in force today.

It is more than evident that today's world is not headed in these directions and that the objectives of the humanist project do not constitute the stakes of the ongoing conflicts. The erosion of the former world system by globalization does not prepare the way for its own succession but can only lead to chaos in the immediate future. The dominant forces inscribe their acts in this chaos, searching only to protect their profits in the short term and aggravating the chaos by their actions. Their attempt to justify their choices through the ideology of the "self-regulating" market, by affirming that "there is no alternative," or by cynicism pure and simple is not a solution, but part of the problem. The immediate responses of the peoples to the degradation of their condition are not necessarily positive at first. In the confusion of illusionary responses, such as fundamentalism and chauvinism, important forces are able to mobilize. It remains to the left—this is its historic vocation—to construct in theory and in practice the humanist response to the impasse. By default, and until the left comes forward, regressive and criminal retrogressions are the most probable order of the day.

The logic of the dominant interests has no answer to the continuing moral and material degradation in which the popular majorities of the periphery are trapped. The structural adjustment it proposes is quite simply the unilateral adjustment of the periphery to the requirements of central capital, when what we need are mutual adjustments articulating the great, unequally developed regions of the world, based on collective negotiations subjugating the global interdependencies to national and regional strategies that take account of the inequalities inherited from polarization.

If certain countries can still nourish the illusion that structural adjustment will permit them to ascend within the global system because these countries have a certain bargaining power, for the Fourth World this adjustment can only accelerate pauperization and involution toward poverty and marginality. The adjustment in question cannot result in a resumption of growth, but on the contrary must lead to disinvestment and dismantlement of industry, without, however, having created conditions favorable to the beginning of an agricultural revolution. Stagnation of agricultural productivity (despite the gigantic potential that tropical agriculture promises in principle) brings, in turn, accelerated migration to the cities without any means to finance industrial development. The erosion of the fruits of independence—in the areas of education, health, and administration—are then inevitable. The pursuit of an equilibrium of public finance and external balance—the sole objective of adjustment—becomes an illusion. This objective is never attained in the involuted spiral that follows adjustment.

The adjustment processes that conform to this dominant logic nevertheless create political conditions contributing to their own perpetuation. In the most fortunate countries of the Third World, they reinforce the position of a comprador bourgeoisie that benefits effectively from its insertion in global capitalism. But if in those countries of the Fourth World they hardly succeed at all, they nonetheless create conditions unfavorable to the crystallization of appropriate, popular responses. These involutions then feed explosions that lead almost naturally to the collapse of the nation, its breakup into ethnic or pseudo-ethnic regions, and the loss of legitimacy of the state. Africa already presents us with some examples—in Chad, Somalia, Liberia, Rwanda, and Burundi. Other countries are not far from the brink of this kind of involution. The marginalization accentuated by each such collapse is, unhappily, dramatic only for the people concerned; they do not "menace" the "world order."

An alternative exists nonetheless, even if the realization of its preconditions is difficult. It implies, first, the building of a national, popular, and democratic front worthy of the name. But it implies, second, at the level of the world system, that the evolutions in the direction of a multicentered world that I have described above begin in a manner that recognizes the constraints that, in the world as it is, press all their weight against a popular democratic alternative.

REFERENCES

Amin, S. (1969). *Monde des affaires Senegalais.* Paris, France: Minuit.

Amin, S. (1973). *Neo-colonialism.* New York: Penguin.

Amin, S. (1976). *Unequal development.* New York: Monthly Review Press.

Amin, S. (1993a). *L'ethnie a l'assaut des nations.* Paris, France: L'Harmattan.

Amin, S. (Ed.). (1993b). *Mondialisation et accumulation.* Paris, France: L'Harmattan.

Amin, S. (1994). *Re-reading the postwar period: An intellectual itinerary.* New York: Monthly Review Press.

Amin, S., & Coquery Vidrovitch, C. (1969). *Histoire economique du Congo 1880-1986.* Paris, France: Anthropos.

Founou-Tchuigoua, B. (1993). Afrique subsaharienne: La quart mondialization en crise. In S. Amin (Ed.), *Mondialisation et accumulation* (pp. 179-190). Paris, France: L'Harmattan.

Yachir, F. (1987). *Mining in Africa today.* Paris, France: Karthala.

PART III

On the World
Historical System and Cycles

11

⊞

How to Think About World History

WILLIAM H. MCNEILL

There is no doubt that world-historians and would-be world-historians have proliferated in recent decades and that the publication of the book *The World System: Five Hundred Years or Five Thousand,* edited by Gunder Frank and his colleague, Barry Gills, constitutes a notable contribution to the resulting discourse. How to understand human history as a whole is problematic. Indeed, some historians even deny that the subject is a proper object of attention because it is not possible to know the personalities, institutions, and other relevant facts about the history of every part of the inhabited earth. Such an observation about the unmanageable bulk of historical information is accurate but irrelevant. If it were relevant, national and all other forms of history would also be impossible because personalities and other facts of local history of each part of a nation, not to mention the fleeting states of consciousness of individuals that constitute the ultimate ground of all history, are also too numerous for anyone to know.

Words, however, can extricate us from an excess of data by generalizing experience. Using words appropriately, we habitually and as a matter of course

This chapter previously appeared as the Preface to *The World System*, edited by Andre Gunder Frank and Barry Gills (1993). Copyright © International Thomas Publishing Services, Routledge, Andover, Hampshire, UK. Reprinted by permission.

understand whatever confronts us by fixing attention on whatever matters most. In this fashion, words quite literally blind us to irrelevant dimensions of reality and guide our action by turning the buzzing, blooming confusion that surrounds us into something intelligible. The whole trick is to exclude meaningless information from consciousness even, or especially, when it is readily accessible.

This characteristic of human intelligence makes historical study and writing possible. Each scale of history has an appropriate set of terms and concepts for excluding irrelevancies. As a result, world history is as feasible as national or local history—no more, no less—as long as appropriate terms and concepts for each scale of history are employed.

But do appropriate terms for writing world history exist? And how can would-be world-historians cope with the diversity of tongues and concepts that different human groups have used to guide their conduct and understanding of the world? This is not a trivial question, nor is it likely to be resolved unambiguously and to universal satisfaction. As long as different peoples use different languages and subscribe to different outlooks on the world, terms of historical discourse that seem appropriate to some will repel others. Intensified communication across linguistic and cultural boundaries will not alter this situation and is likely to reinforce conscious divergences.

Yet, the rich diversity of human behavior, guided by words of different languages, operates within the same natural world. This means that words and actions that come closest to matching consequences with expectation have positive survival value for those using them, whereas words and actions that lead to disappointment and confusion have a contrary effect, hampering collective action by dividing a community between those who want to adjust the old, ineffective words and actions and those who wish to reaffirm the ancient verities more strenuously than ever just because they seem to be faltering.

Over time, natural selection for terms more nearly adequate to reality certainly does occur in technology and the physical sciences. In the social sciences, however, the pattern of selection is more complex because words that generate enthusiastic agreement and inspire energetic adhesion to collective courses of action often prevail in ambiguous situations, whether or not the words in question match any external or natural reality. Indeed, a sufficiently energetic faith can often create its object. Modern nations have been created from local, peasant diversity by bands of zealots; and many other groups—youth gangs, religious sects, secret societies, and the like—also affect behavior solely because their members agree among themselves. Indeed, all human society is founded very largely on agreements, expressed in words and

ceremonies, that become ends in themselves and that are almost independent
of external reality.

Hence, the stubborn diversity of human society persists. Ever since Herodotus,
historians have noticed this fact. In modern times, a few historians, anthropologists, and other students of society have even attempted to pull away from
naive attachment to the pieties and practices of their own local community—
whatever it may be—seeking to understand what happened among the different peoples of the earth by using terms that try to take account of the
diversity of local outlooks and behavior without subscribing wholeheartedly
to any one of them. Whether the enterprise can be successful—and for whom—
remains problematic.

For many, the conception of "world system" derived from a Marxist
tradition and emphasized the economic exploitation of marginal peoples by a
capitalist core. But Marx's vision of the uniqueness of modern capitalism falls
to the ground if one affirms, with Gunder Frank and Barry Gills, that a
capital-accumulating core has existed (though not always in the same location) for some five thousand years. This constitutes revisionism, expected in
liberal discourse but repugnant to dogmatic upholders of Marxist Truth. Their
work will be judged accordingly. It may even signify, for the history of ideas,
the confluence of Marxist with more inchoate liberal ideas about world
history. Whether it will constitute such a landmark or not depends on the future
of Marxism on the one hand and of the literary and intellectual enterprise of
world history on the other.

That enterprise, in its inchoate, multiplex, and vaguely liberal form, seems
fully capable of absorbing and profiting from a Marxist (or ex-Marxist) stream.
It derives, like Marxism, from the West European civilizational tradition,
having absorbed data but no organizing concepts from encounters with the
other cultural traditions of the earth, whether great or small. Within the West
European tradition, two incompatible models of universal or world history
coexisted for many centuries. One was pagan and cyclical—a pattern of rise
and fall that repeated itself in essentials among different communities at
different times because human nature was everywhere the same. The other
was Christian and linear, beginning with Adam and ending with the second
coming of Christ as set forth in sacred scripture.

These models still lurk behind the scenes. The world system as described
by Frank and Gills is, after all, unique and linear, yet passes through a series
of repetitive cycles. Other recent efforts at world history also combine
linear and cyclical patterns, though where the emphasis is placed varies with
every author.

The first notable departure from the Christian unitary and linear vision of the human past took form in the 18th century, when Vico, Herder, and others started to speak of separate civilizations or cultures, each with a language and life cycle of its own. Their vision of the rise and fall of separate peoples and cultures was focused almost entirely within the bounds of the ancient Mediterranean and medieval and modern Europe. Only in the 20th century did the rest of the world enter seriously into the picture when Spengler first applied the notion of separate and equivalent civilizations to all of Eurasia and Toynbee then extended the scheme completely around the globe.

From the point of view of Spengler and Toynbee, differences among the peoples and languages of the classical Mediterranean lands and of medieval and modern Europe, which had loomed so large for Vico and Herder, became trivial. Instead, all the classical peoples belonged together in one civilization, and despite their differences, medieval and modern Europeans shared another. Thus, the civilizational building blocks for world history took on far larger proportions in their hands, and others, including myself, who came after, have continued to think and speak of multiple civilizations that embrace all of Western Europe, all of China, and comparably massive groupings in India, the Middle East, and pre-Columbian America.

The idea that humankind had developed a number of comparable civilizations, whose rise and fall followed approximately parallel lines, constituted a notable departure from the naively ethnocentric vision of the past that treated any departure from local norms as deplorable error and corruption of right and truth. But by treating a plurality of civilizations as separate entities, this vision of human reality minimized the importance of outside encounters and overlooked transcivilizational processes and relationships.

The historians represented in Frank and Gills's book seek to correct this defect, affirming that interactions among the principal civilizations of Eurasia-Africa in the centuries before 1500 constituted a world system. This enlargement of scale resembles the shift Spengler and Toynbee achieved in the first half of the 20th century, locating the most important entity of world history in a transcivilizational pattern of relationships that expanded geographically through time from an initial core in Mesopotamia.

It is undoubtedly true that some dimensions of human affairs transcended civilizational boundaries in ancient as well as in modern times. Traders, soldiers, and missionaries often operated among strangers of different linguistic and cultural traditions from themselves. Resulting contacts sometimes led one or both parties to alter their behavior by modifying old practices in the light of new information. Even in ancient and medieval times, a few really

useful innovations spread very rapidly within the circuit of Old World mercantile, military, and missionary contact. Thus, on the one hand, the stirrup
seems to appear simultaneously throughout Eurasia so that it is impossible to
tell for sure where it was first invented. On the other hand, we know that the
place value system of numerical notation originated in Indian mathematical
treatises, where it remained safely encapsulated for many centuries before its
sudden propagation throughout the Eurasian world for commercial calculations in the 11th century.

Mere logical superiority could also provoke widespread alteration of belief
and practice, though propagation of logically convincing ideas took longer.
Nonetheless, the seven-day week, invented in ancient Sumer, proved con-
tagious throughout Eurasia in very ancient times because it fitted obvious
heavenly phenomena (the phases of the moon, and the seven movable lights
of the firmament) so well. For similar reasons, Newtonian astronomy and the
Gregorian calendar met with worldwide success in far more recent times.

All the same, commonalities that ran across the entire civilized world in
ancient and medieval times remained exceptional. Differences of institutions,
ideas, customs, and techniques were far more apparent, within as well as
across civilizational lines. Is, then, the world system that Frank, Gills, and
others explicate really significant? Equally, is the term *civilization,* as used
by Spengler and Toynbee or by Vico and Herder, really meaningful in the light
of all the local variability it overlooks? These are capital questions for
world-historians and deserve the most careful consideration by anyone who
seeks to understand the human past as a whole because these are the key terms
currently available for the purpose.

To some degree, the choice between the rival concepts of "world system"
and "civilization" as building blocks for human history as a whole depends
on whether one reckons that material life is more important than ideas and
ideals. World-system thinkers are especially conscious of material exchanges
and assert (or perhaps rather assume) that the accumulation of wealth in
privileged centers through trade and the exercise of force conformed to a
common norm regardless of local cultural differences. Those who speak of
civilizations tend to emphasize religious and other ideas, arguing that actual
behavior in the pursuit of wealth and other human goals was subordinated
to, or at least affected by, the ideals professed by the ruling elites of each
civilization.

Even if one takes the view that pursuit of wealth was everywhere the same,
regardless of religious and other professed ideals, the question remains whether
long-distance trading and raiding were really massive enough to affect ancient

societies in more than superficial ways. No one doubts that most people lived as cultivators and consumed little or nothing that was not produced within the local community itself. But luxury and strategic goods mattered for politics and war; and such goods often came from afar, delivered by merchants who systematically weighed local variations in price against local variations in security for their goods and person.

Such calculations established a market that extended as far as merchants traveled and exchanged information about the potential gains and risks of their profession. And this, in turn, if we believe what Frank, Gills, and others have to tell us, established wealthy centers and dependent peripheries even in ancient times, when the physical volume of long-distance trade exchanges was comparatively small.

Incidentally, the term *world system* for such relationships is obviously a misnomer for ancient and medieval times inasmuch as large parts of the globe then remained outside the limits of the largest and most active transcivilizational market, which was based in Eurasia. Presumably, though the authors in Frank and Gills's book do not address the issue, smaller and less closely articulated world systems also existed in the Americas and elsewhere. A market that actually embraced the globe could only arise after 1500, when the opening of the world's oceans to regular shipping allowed the Eurasian world system to engulf all of humanity—a process that took some centuries but that is virtually complete today.

But this awkwardness of terminology does not really matter if the reality of human interrelatedness, which *world system* expresses, really shaped the human past. This is the critical question for the architecture and arguments of Frank and Gills's book, and it can only be answered individually and subjectively.

Across the past thirty years or so, my own view has been evolving away from *civilization* and toward *world system* as the best available framework for world history; but I have also concluded that both terms can best be understood as part of a far more inclusive spectrum of "communications nets," which are what really matter in defining human communities at every level of size, from biological family on up to the human race in its entirety.

Thus, I agree with the authors in Frank and Gills's book in thinking that the rise of specialized occupations producing goods for distant markets was a critical dimension of the deeper human past. Resulting alterations in everyday lives were among the most persistent and effective paths of innovation in ancient times, as well as more recently. Yet, markets and trade constituted only part of the communications network that crossed political, civilizational, and linguistic boundaries. Soldiers and missionaries, as well as refugees and wanderers, also linked alien populations together and carried information that sometimes altered local ways of life as profoundly as entry into market relationships did.

I conclude, therefore, that if the notion of a world system were tied more explicitly to a communications network and if more attention were paid to changes in that network as a new means of transport and communication came into use, the notion of a world system would gain greater clarity and power. Moreover, the polarity between the terms *civilization* and *world system* would disappear and the language of world-historians might gain greater precision if communications networks were to become the focus of attention. For what we commonly mean by a civilization is a population whose ruling elites, together with at least some segments of the people they govern, share norms of conduct, expressed through ceremonial and literary canons that are accepted in principle, however far actual conduct may fall short of the ideal prescriptions of the canon. Such agreement on norms of behavior is, of course, the result of communication across the generations, as well as among contemporaries. It resembles the communication merchants and artisans engage in when learning the skills of their trade and the state of the market.

Indeed, norms of conduct shared with others—whether superiors, equals, or subordinates—constitute an essential ingredient of all social life and are always established by communication. Communication is what makes us human; and if history were written with this simple notion in mind, networks of communication would become the center of attention and a more satisfactory history of the world (and of all the innumerable subordinate groupings of humankind) might emerge.

World system history, exemplified in Frank and Gills's book, is a step in that direction. At any rate, it seems so to me. But more explicit attention to communication networks and a serious effort to understand how human activity altered the natural environments of the earth throughout the past must be added to the conceptions explored in Frank's work before historians of the 21st century can be expected to produce a more nearly satisfactory world history.

REFERENCE

Frank, A. G., & Gills, B. K. (Eds.). (1993). *The world system: Five hundred years or five thousand?* London: Routledge.

12

The Continuity Thesis
in World Development

BARRY K. GILLS

It has been my privilege to work closely with Andre Gunder Frank during the past several years while jointly developing a new "world system" perspective (without the hyphen). In the course of this close collaboration, it has become clear to me that Frank has always been interested in world history, and particularly in world development—conceptualized as a set of interlinked historical processes. In fact, his interest in world history dates back to his early academic training at the University of Chicago, where he was influenced by, and likely influenced, his roommate Marshall Hodgson, who was in turn closely associated with William H. McNeill. I propose that, together, these three gentlemen constitute yet another "Chicago school," an important (and hitherto unrecognized?) school of world historians, or rather "world development" theorists.[1] As a "school," Frank, Hodgson, and McNeill share the magisterial scope that characterizes all of their work, as they do their mutual commitment to a history of humanity as a whole. The historical work of this other Chicago school can now be seen in a new light, given the recent rediscovery of Hodgson's work on Islam and especially on Eurasian and world history (Hodgson, 1974,

226

1993), Frank's recent departure into world system analysis, and the cumulative authority in the discipline of world history of the works of McNeill (McNeill graciously wrote the foreword to *The World System: Five Hundred Years or Five Thousand?* edited by Andre Gunder Frank and myself, which reproduces the first phase of the debate on the new world system approach and its larger social science implications). Indeed, Frank and I have found to our amazement how much of our own perspective was actually prefigured in the work of Hodgson and how much we have in common with McNeill's perspective.

Clearly, Andre Gunder Frank has always addressed the issue of world development: from his early work on dependency theory, to his pioneering work on world-system theory (with a hyphen), to his many works on world crisis and its political effects over the past twenty years, and finally to his recent work on social movements, and of course, our world system perspective (without a hyphen). Indeed, it is not possible to understand Frank's work unless one takes the view that it is all ultimately a contribution to a theory of world development. He is most insistent that no "part" of the world's development can be understood without adequate but appropriate reference to the "whole" dynamic of world development.

Obviously, I cannot address all the elements of Frank's work on world development theory, but I can at least address the ideas developed in his recent collaboration with me. This chapter, therefore, sets out to explain and extend the "continuity thesis" we developed in our world system approach. I begin by addressing the issue of what, in my view, is most distinctive about this approach to world historical development (WHD): its historical materialism, its unique structuralism, and its cosmopolitan humanocentrism.

HISTORICAL MATERIALISM

Sir Mortimer Wheeler once criticized, and meant to dismiss, the historical approach of Frederick J. Teggart (another early exponent of Eurasian history) by accusing him of viewing history simplistically "through a shop window."[2] This jibe was meant to dismiss Teggart's materialism as being inappropriate to the actual complexity of the subject. On the contrary, however, Teggart was right to emphasize the great importance in Eurasian history of the regular production of commodities for international exchange, the implied inseparability of economic and political systems, and above all, the systemic character of this transcontinental trade. Elegance should never be mistaken for mere simplification!

Following Teggart, we have argued (Frank & Gills, 1993; Gills & Frank, 1990/1991, 1992) that such a materialistic view is absolutely essential to understanding world historical development. We have argued that production of commodities, commerce, trade, (price setting) markets, private "enterprise," private capital, capital accumulation, and, yes, the "international" division of labor have all played much more important roles much further "back" in world history than has usually been recognized or accepted. It is precisely on this basis that we make the claim that "capital accumulation" has *always* been the driving force of world development, and not merely of the modern world political economy.

It is particularly important to clarify our controversial suggestion that "ceaseless accumulation," which according to Wallerstein is *the* differentia specifica of capitalism, is a feature of the world system throughout its development, and not unique to the modern period. Although there can be no doubt that industrialization of production played a crucial role in bringing about a qualitative change in the *rate* of ceaseless accumulation in the modern period, in our view, this change is essentially a matter of degree. Indeed, Wallerstein himself says, on a parallel tract, that the difference between so-called proto-capitalism and real, full-blown capitalism is really a matter of degree—in this case, the degree to which the capitalist mode of production (the capital-wage labor relation) is dominant in the entire socioeconomic system (Frank, 1994; Wallerstein, 1991). In our view, this debate is simply definitional and turns on the definition of *ceaseless* because Wallerstein also notes the existence and indeed even perhaps the prevalence of capital before the "modern" period.

In our view, following Marx (up to a point), "ceaseless" accumulation implies that capital is constantly reinvested into the circuits of production to sustain capital/accumulation. This ceaselessness is imperative, especially given the facts of competition. The historical evidence suggests to us (Gills & Frank, 1990/1991, 1992) that capital accumulation has normally been "competitive" and has been a process that involved a continuous reinvestment in the means of production and indeed in a whole social and political ensemble of sectors, including infrastructure. This investment process is carried out both by private capital and by the state, which is, of course, essentially the case even today in most modern economies.

I have argued (Gills, 1993) that there has been a fundamental misconception of the character of the "premodern" economy, particularly of Eurasia, based on the mistaken generalization of the "command economy," or as Anderson (1974) would have it, of the role of "coercion" and determination by the "political instance," rather than by "economics." Likewise, it is mistaken to generalize the notion of "feudalism" to the entire Eurasian economy. In my view, what Samir Amin (1976) calls the "tributary mode" is, more often than not, merely "taxation" by another name. The fact that all historical states have lived by some form of taxation is hardly a revelation to anyone, but it is not necessarily incompatible with the idea that, more often than not, these premodern states coexisted with a vibrant commercial sector in the economy, primarily directed by private merchants and bankers and conducted on international scale. This is also the argument made by Chaudhuri (1991), who says that

> even the great territorial empires drawing huge revenues from a productive agriculture could not turn that revenue into disposable state income without the intermediary of merchants and their role as bankers. If these empires were ruled by princes and warriors, they were also *financed* [italics added] in reality by merchants. (p. 431)

The sheer volume of evidence from each specialist history of the various parts of Eurasia corroborates the contention of the centrality of this world economic commerce and the role of private ("merchant") capital within it.

Then, as now, states lived partly on "rent" from this international commerce (through direct taxation on trade); partly from profits accumulated by their "national" merchants, manufacturers, and moneymen; and partly from taxing the national product or income of the general population. Imperialism has provided an additional source of revenue to powerful states throughout history, which often takes the form of "tribute" proper (either extortion or loot acquired through conquest).

The territorial logic of conquest often pursued control of the trade routes and the sources of raw materials and commodities that were central in the trade.

The debate over the character of the premodern economy is not new at all and has been conducted for generations between primitivists and modernists, formalists and substantivists. Our perspective has more in common with the modernists and formalists, though I do not regard market exchange as being totally exclusive to either "redistributive" or "reciprocal" forms of economic relations. Our perspective, however, is liberated from the narrow confines of argument based on any individual society, by virtue of being concerned with the character of the entire world system.

To further illustrate this question, let's take, for example, the classic contrast between Athens and Sparta. The substantivist/primitivist view of the ancient political economy takes the Spartan case and makes it into something akin to an ideal type: no economic law of value operating and no capital accumulation; rather, pure political coercion is seen as the means of surplus extraction. But Sparta was actually unique in its extremeness; indeed, it was something of a freak, or at least a historical oddity.

And why was Sparta, with its hereditary elites, "enserfed" and enslaved masses, and agrarian-dominated economy, afraid of the growth of Athenian power? Precisely because Athens was everything Sparta was not, especially in the "economic" sense. What can one say of the Athenian economy and its source of wealth and dynamism? It was an economy with many coexisting elements: a market economy, sophisticated credit mechanisms, widescale international commerce, industrial production and manufactured exports, agro-exports, tribute from the "allies" in the empire, profits from its rich silver mines, the "slave mode of production" in countryside and city, combined with free contract wage labor. This "mixed-modes" Athenian "ideal type," I would argue, is actually far more common, if not truly representative, of most premodern economies throughout Eurasia over a very long historical period. The Spartan model of excessive introversion and pure political determination is an anomaly. Thus, Thucydides can be reread not only as an inspiration for perennial realist philosophy in international relations but equally for a perennial philosophy in international political economy![3]

Above all, however, these narrow debates on the character of Athens, for instance, miss the larger point. Athens in the 5th or 4th century B.C.E. was not the whole world economy of the period. Indeed, it was still somewhat "peripheral" in character; the real center of economic gravity and the most "advanced" economies were located eastward of Hellas, as they had been already for millennia.

In my view, the macroeconomic reality of most of Eurasian history is rather close to what Abu-Lughod (1989) found in the 13th century: a world economy centered around highly commercialized cities linked to each other through systemic exchange networks and economically dominated, or at least "driven," by private merchants, albeit coexisting with bureaucratic or imperial state structures. But these states were often themselves a direct reflection of the location and ever-changing direction of this same international commerce.

The idea that empires have repeatedly tended to develop in key trading zones was reflected in the notion I developed that the "three corridors" (essentially, the Red Sea, Syria-Mesopotamia, and the "northern" Caucasus routes) were pivotal geopolitical ground in Eurasian political and economic development precisely because they were physically in the midst of the trading crossroads of Eurasia (Gills & Frank, 1990/1991). These same routes were in "competition" with each other. The rise and fall of empires and of major metropoles reflects the rivalry among the three corridors over a period of several millennia.

Because capital accumulation did occur in private hands on such a scale for most of Eurasian history and because what Abu-Lughod discovered about the 13th century would equally characterize the Eurasian economy over a much longer historical period, we can argue that capital accumulation has always been a driving force in world development and in the development of the world system.

We have argued that the first systemic appearance of the interlinking of city-centered exchange of surplus via international trade (à la Abu-Lughod) actually began from c. 2700-2500 B.C.E. between Mesopotamian cities, Levantine cities, and Egyptian cities, soon to be joined by Indus valley cities. Later, Chinese "cities" joined the nexus by perhaps as early as 1500 B.C.E. (according to new evidence found in Egypt of imported Chinese silk and to Chinese evidence of silk trade at this date) or perhaps by 1000 B.C.E. On this basis, we assume that the cities of Central Asia—for example, the Bactrian and Sogdian cities, and Taxila—also came into existence and flourished long before the Persians incorporated them into their empire, followed later by the "Westerner" Alexander. These pivotal Central Asian cities could have flourished on commodities other than silk (e.g., lapis and other precious stones) and therefore do not depend exclusively on the dating of the silk trade.

Precisely as Abu-Lughod argues for the Eurasian world economy/system of the 13th to 14th centuries (that the economic system of these interlinked cities does not "fall," so much as the ways in which it is organized change), the Eurasian world economy never truly "falls." Rather, it is continuous and is continuously rebuilt or reorganized, especially after each periodic "crisis." It is therefore not the world system that falls, but only temporary configurations *within* the same world economic system, to be inevitably replaced by new configurations on much the same foundation. This is essentially how we arrived at the formulation "the cumulation of accumulation" (Gills & Frank, 1990/1991), the title of our first joint publication on the new world system perspective.

Our historical materialist approach recognizes that private capital and private capital accumulation, though ever present in this world system history and ever central to its development dynamic, are not the sole aspects of the whole worthy of attention. We quickly realized that we must be political economists, as opposed to being either "economists" or "political scientists." This lesson was reinforced when we discovered a rhythm of the states that seemed to move in tandem to the rhythm of international trade—that is, to the production and exchange of commodities and the transfer of surplus. We posited the existence of a "world system cycle" stretching back some four thousand years from the present. Powerful "hegemonic" states or empires seemed to expand simultaneously in tandem with world economic expansion and the increase of international commerce, whereas a period of "decline" was often generalized to many states and empires and coincided with a general world economic crisis of a Eurasian scale (Gills & Frank, 1992). This finding is absolutely central to the continuity thesis in our world system analysis, as is the concept, discussed above, of the cumulation of accumulation.

Thus, we developed the perspective that the modes of production are not key to understanding the "transitions" in the history of world development (Frank, 1991; Frank & Gills, 1993). Rather, the developmental dynamic of the world system as a whole is far more important. Furthermore, real transitions seem to be more a consequence of larger competitive patterns in the world system than of changes in modes of production. Above all, real transitions seem to be a matter of the role and position a particular entity fills in the world accumulation process. Thus, we developed the concept of "super-accumulation" (Gills & Frank, 1992) to designate this process of "center-shift" as a cornerstone of our historical materialism. This is not simply an "economic" shift in the center of gravity. Rather, the underlying economic shift in the center(s) of accumulation in the world economy accompanies "simultaneous" political shifts in relative power. This also implies profound social change, sometimes even revolution.

I have argued, on this basis, that the concept of the "hegemonic transition" not only could be an alternative to traditional modes of production analysis but also could become a central concept of the analysis of all world history (Gills, 1993). From this perspective, hegemonic transitions have occurred throughout world history and not only entail a shift in the locus of the "concentration" of capital accumulation (within the framework of the world system among the centers/cores) but also necessarily entail profound changes in social, political, economic, cultural, and ideological aspects of the world system. These phenomena should be analyzed together, as aspects of one over-all historical process of change. This point brings me to the second distinctive feature of our world system theory: its structuralism.

STRUCTURALISM

World system theory's structuralism rests upon a rejection of the "unipolar" model of center-periphery relations, common in most approaches using this concept, in favor of a "multipolar" model of center-periphery relations on a world scale. Therefore, the world system is not viewed as having always been composed of a single core and single periphery, but rather of an interlinked set of center-periphery complexes (and also including a "hinterland" as dis-cussed in Gills and Frank, 1990/1991), joined together in an overall ensemble.

Thus, the world system, first in Eurasia before 1500 and then globally after 1500, has always been multicentric in structure. This includes even the period of supposed unipolar European or Western global hegemony in the modern world system. This approach to structuralist analysis allows greater flexibility because distinct regional, imperial, or market-mediated center-periphery com-plexes are accepted, yet are nevertheless seen as being part of a single whole, given their systemic links to one another.

This multicentricity is not a condition of "equality" between the various centers or between different center-periphery complexes in the world system. This multicentricity is hierarchically structured. There is a very complex "chain" of "metropole-satellite" relations of extraction and transfer of surplus throughout the whole world system. Frank discussed a similar schema in his early work on the world economy. For my part, I have defined hegemony in a way that embodies this notion of a hierarchical structure of surplus transfer. *Hegemony* is defined as a hierarchical structure of accumulation between classes and states, mediated by force (Gills, 1987, 1989a, 1989b; Gills & Frank, 1990/1991, 1992). In this sense, the center-periphery structure of the world system is simultaneously an economic hierarchy and a political hierarchy, as hegemony embodies both.

It follows, therefore, that hegemony at the scale of the entire world system, when conventionally defined as a unipolar hegemony, is extremely rare and perhaps nonexistent. Rather, the norm is a situation we have called "inter-linked hegemonies" (Gills, 1993; Gills & Frank, 1992). This notion is critical to our understanding of structure in the world system and to our notion of the centrality of shifts in the locus of capital accumulation as the key to "hegemonic transition." In this regard, we follow Abu-Lughod. We do not see hegemonic ascent and descent so much as a process of absolute rise and decline by particular states, but rather as a situation wherein some nations or groups of nations temporarily gain relative power vis-à-vis others. On this basis, they can set the terms of their interactions with subordinates as they ascend, but they gradually lose this capacity as they descend (Abu-Lughod, 1989).

This is how one arrives at the formulation that "global or world hegemony is always *shared* hegemony, exercised through a complex network composed of class coalitions, and also alliances and other forms of association between states, including competitive ones" (Gills, 1993, p. 210). Furthermore, the world system is "characterised by a number of coexisting core powers that via both conflictual and cooperative relations become increasingly integrated" (Gills, 1993, p. 210).

From our perspective, hegemonic rivalries of this complex, multilayered type are a continuous process accompanying the development of the world economy. In this sense, our view of political economy is that of a "perennial philosophy" (to use the phrase of Aldous Huxley), which has certain similarities to the perennial character of Robert Gilpin's version of the historical law of uneven development (Gilpin, 1987) but extends this perspective much farther back in the history of world development. Just as the world economy/system never entirely falls, but rather the ways in which it is constituted and the linkages through which it operates are changed, likewise hegemonic ascent and descent are usually quite gradual and do not occur in a unipolar framework, but rather in a multipolar one. This world historical process "favours some at a particular time while discriminating against others, and so on through time" (Gills, 1993, p. 211).

Indeed, it is integral to our structural theory of world development, though not unique to our position, that areas that were once peripheral may ascend to hegemonic or core status, whereas areas that have once been core may descend into the periphery. We particularly emphasize how economic rhythms common to the entire world economy/system, such as long cycles of expansion and contraction, affect the relative position of all parts of the system (Gills & Frank, 1992). The schema of the structure of the world system should perhaps be akin to a "truncated pyramid," at the apex of which there is not usually one sole hegemonic center of political power and capital accumulation, but rather several coexisting and interactive centers. Thus, if one descends from this truncated apex, there is not necessarily a "whole" there to be automatically filled by an entirely new ascending center. Thus, our position is distinguished by the argument that these ascents and declines occur *within* the same world economy/system.

To understand the distinctiveness of this argument, it is first important to clarify what we mean by the term *world system* and to clear up some misunderstandings.

MISPERCEPTIONS OF
THE "WORLD SYSTEM" THESIS

Since our joint work on the theory of world system development first appeared in print in 1990, a number of quite mistaken simplifications of it have been made by other scholars. Therefore, it is necessary to clarify these misperceptions so that the approach can be properly understood. We posit a definition of the world system in "The Cumulation of Accumulation" (Gills & Frank, 1990/1991) that rests upon the simple basis of regular exchange of surplus, but with a degree of regularity and significance that affects the "internal" character of each part of the world system. Some scholars, such as Wallerstein (1993), for instance, reject our definition because they do not believe that "mere" trade makes a "system." We do.

We not only believe that regular and significant trade is a sufficient ground for speaking of a system or of a real "world economy" (without the hyphen) but also that trade integrates social formations into something that should be called the international division of labor, even in the ancient Eurasian world economy. This takes place because trade and production are not (falsely) separated. The nature of trade directly affects the character of production, as the history of the early modern world system so clearly illustrates, but is also true much earlier. These effects are a consequence of specialization if nothing else, but we contend they are intimately related to the system of the regular transfer of surplus, as well as to specialization. Wallerstein sets very specific criteria for the level of integration in his international division of labor that, for him at least, precludes considering the pre-1500 international division of labor as being in the same formal category. We believe he has erected a false dichotomy, the aim of which is to preserve the distinctiveness of the "capitalist" world-economy, axiomatically.

Furthermore, we are not as concerned as some, particularly Wallerstein, with whether this trade is primarily composed of "necessities" or of so-called preciosities. Rather, we believe that the trade is significant and systemic not because of the specific character of the commodities concerned, but rather because the *transfer of surplus* between zones of the world economy/system that the trade embodies implies effects on the respective production structures.

This leads us to the most common misperception of our joint work to date: that of the term *world system* itself. First, it does not imply that there has only ever been one single world system throughout all of world history. This would be palpable nonsense, given the obvious separate development of the political economies of pre-Columbian America vis-à-vis those of Eurasia. Even in Eurasia, it would not be correct to conclude that there has only ever been one giant all-encompassing system. There have been many streams of regional development that, at some points in their development, certainly constituted some kind of separate "system." What we are saying is that one system, judged by the actual historical outcome and not all of the original "fountainheads," gradually came to "incorporate" (if only by "merger") all others—first in Eurasia and then over the entire globe after "1492." This particular overarching world economy we have called "the world system," which was perhaps, in hindsight, a somewhat unfortunate choice of words because it has given rise to misunderstandings of our theses on world development.

Perhaps if we simply said we posit a theory of the development of a very long-standing, indeed "ancient," *world economic system* or *world political economy,* this would not raise so many eyebrows. This is what we are indeed saying, simply the evidence suggests to us that we need a theory (or at least concepts and theses) for the development of a world economy on Eurasian scale, even back into ancient history, because such a world economy did actually exist. It not only existed, but it was very influential in terms of the development of the parts of the world economic system, which therefore cannot be properly understood if they are taken as separate developments.

This argument cuts against the grain of so much received theory and so many compartmentalized branches of knowledge and so many specialized histories (and historians) that it is still very controversial even when properly understood, as opposed to being grossly caricatured! Indeed, we are guilty of the sin Sir Mortimer Wheeler accused Teggart of: we are unashamedly (historical) materialist in our approach. That is, we define the world system on the basis of regular trade, which embodies a transfer of surplus and implies a division of labor and brings in its train systemic political, social, ideological, cultural, and even religious rhythms as well.

But we are not merely economic determinists either, precisely because we insist that the "economic" *is* "political." This is why, in our own defense, we chose the term *world system* for our concept of the world political economy. We argue that an integral aspect of the world system's development process is its "hegemonic" rhythm—that is, a "political" pattern. We have explicitly rejected what would have been an economistic position—that is, that the economic rhythms simply determine the hegemonic/political rhythms. Rather, we have insisted on an inseparable logic of political economic developments from the beginning. In our formulation of hegemony, economic and political power are inseparable, as are economic and political means to the desired end of hegemonic power and economic wealth. They are Siamese twins. We rejected any sterile debate about causality based on a false separation of the "infrastructural" from the "superstructural" or of the "economic" from the "political." In my mind, the true "original sin" was committed by those who, in the first place, saw fit to undo the elegance of political economy and falsely separate economics from politics and who pretended to de-politicize their "economics" to boot! (No names need be mentioned!)

Finally, as is the case with some critics of "world-system" theory (with a hyphen), our world system perspective has sometimes been misperceived as some kind of "totalizing notion." In fact, our world system approach is based on a *minimalist* definition of what a system is, rather than on a maximalist or totalizing one. By minimalist, I mean that the core processes of the system are simply the cycles of economic expansion and contraction and the accompanying hegemonic cycle. These systemwide patterns depend on the existence of a world economy, taking the form of extensive regularized trade (transfer of surplus). *This* constitutes a system, or an "international political economy." In our definition, it does not require a higher level of integration than this to constitute a real system. Nor does it imply some overarching iron logic of the system. I wish to avoid sweeping generalizations or any dogmatism while retaining a structuralist perspective on overall rhythms of change in world development.

For those who desire proof of the world system thesis, this large-scale Eurasian world economic system can be demonstrated to have existed precisely on the empirical basis that cycles of the "whole" existed, as we attempted to show in our 1992 article "World System Cycles, Crises, and Hegemonical Shifts, 1700 B.C. to A.D. 1700" (Gills & Frank, 1992). Second, it can be demonstrated to have existed on the basis of common, or at least sequential, crises periods empirically supported by data on the rise and decline of urban centers across Eurasia (Bosworth, 1992; Wilkinson, 1992). Third, it can be demonstrated to have existed from a reading of the many specialist histories of the many parts of Eurasia involved over millennia in long-distance and regularized trade.

In summary, our world system approach is based on the rejection of three conventional dichotomies: (a) between the premodern and the modern economies, or between the supposed "political determination" versus the (modern) "economic determination" of economies; (b) between the premodern and modern political cycles—that is, between a premodern "cycle of empires" versus a uniquely modern cycle of (single) hegemons; and (c) between a pre-capitalist world composed of several distinct world-economies and a unitary capitalist world system post-1500.

COSMOPOLITAN HUMANOCENTRISM

Our rejection of Eurocentrism has been made clear (Frank & Gills, 1992, 1993; Gills & Frank, 1992), but what has not yet been made clear enough is our equal rejection of *any* "centrism" in world history. Eurocentrism is not the only obstacle to a humanocentric world history. "Centrists" are found in Asian or African history circles and elsewhere. The fallacy in centrist approaches is not only that they privilege a particular people or civilization in the construction of their narrative of history, but equally or even more so, that they are confined by the methodological limitations imposed by viewing history as a set of separate regional compartments, each with its own unique importance and separate dynamic.

It is this latter methodological characteristic of centrist approaches we oppose the most. We oppose it because it seriously distorts understanding of world development. In our ongoing joint work, for instance, on the early modern world system, we have discovered that if one consults the Asianist historians, the perspective that Asia was by far the "weightier" part of the world economy even up to the end of the 18th century is extremely uncontroversial. In fact, the record also shows that Europeans knew this at the time and said so freely. Only in the 19th century, apparently, was the narrative of world history thoroughly reconstructed by a now "superior" Europe and projected back onto the distant past.

Now is the time to correct all such centrist deficiencies in the writing of genuine world history by doing so through a fully humanocentric approach. We have offered our own distinctive historical materialist/structuralist approach as one possible alternative. The reasons for doing so are not merely academic, but very practical and political as well.

I believe that such a humanocentric history of the world can form the intellectual basis for a new cosmopolitan praxis. Because we reject essentialist views on ethnicity and civilization in favor of our structuralist approach to ever-changing political economic configurations, our humanocentrism speaks directly to the present era of conflicting nationalisms, localisms, religious identities, and "fragmentation." From our perspective, humanity truly is *one,* having a true common heritage and sharing a common destiny. I do not propose to return us to the cause of universalism(s), and especially not of the Western-based universalism of "development" or "modernization," being sold in the guise of the equation of "democracy = free market" (Frank, 1993; Gills, Rocamora, & Wilson, 1993). This modern universalism has been inextricably linked with imperialism, and perhaps all universalism must be so to some extent. Modern European imperialism, it must be said, was not the first or only attempt to impose universal values. The career of the Mauryan emperor Asoka is proof enough of that.

However, one can, and I believe we should, propose a defense of a Kantian type of cosmopolitanism in the face of a growing chorus for particularism, methodological individualism, "fundamentalism," and emotive nationalism. A cosmopolitan praxis based on a humanocentric understanding of the common historical development of humanity (such as originally pioneered in McNeill, 1963) could serve to rechannel the impulses of rebellion so prevalent in the current world crisis in a more positive direction. The current situation breeds construction of new, separate historical narratives and emphasizes separation, distance, and otherness. Such "historiography," if that is what it can be called, can do little but encourage conflict and mutual suspicion, even hatred and contempt.

If humanity is to truly have a common future based on mutual trust, acceptance, and co-cooperation, it is imperative that the intellectual underpinnings of a new cosmopolitan praxis be established—and the sooner it is translated into practice, the better. Neither socialism nor capitalism can any longer flourish in a world divided against itself (Gills & Qadir, 1995). We must learn to accept our differences while recognizing our common history and working toward our common future. Those who have rejected our world system approach because they believed that it denied all practice in favor of some ahistorical view of unchanging world history have been totally mistaken. On the contrary, our perspective has been intended from the outset to rethink the fundamentals of both political economy and world history (and world development) precisely to try to find a new basis for progressive, cosmopolitan praxis.

CONCLUSIONS AND EXTENDED THESES

In the discussion above, I tried to explain the nature of our world system approach and thus the "continuity thesis" in world development, which is at the center of our work. By defining a world system in the materialist but minimalist sense, we are able to extend our analysis of cyclical patterns of development further back in world historical time than conventional world-system analysis or other conventional political economy approaches.

We do *not,* however, deny qualitative changes and secular trends in world development. Rather, we *emphasize* the essential continuity of fundamentally embedded patterns of overall systemic dynamics. Furthermore, this does not require a strict determinism whereby everything that happens "on the ground" at a "lower" level is simply a mechanical expression of overall patterns. Indeed, we think the specific characteristics of each area of the world system at any particular time should be taken into account in understanding the specific responses each makes to stimuli that come from the systemic rhythm as a whole.

This point leads me to extend our tentative initial theses and explore areas for further research. The first such issue is that already raised by some of our colleagues, such as David Wilkinson, concerning the need to clarify how, when, and why each region of Eurasia became integrated into the Eurasian world economy/system. In addition, it is necessary to investigate cases where there may have been "secessions" or "dropouts" from the world system, such as the case of India, which was "in" at an early point, but later apparently "out" for a few centuries, then "in" again.

Finally, there is the even more complex subject of refining the "calibration" of the overall world systemic cycles across all of the regions. The clearest working hypothesis seems to be that world systemic cycles are probably more "sequential" than "simultaneous," though there is a causal link in the sequentialization of course. In this regard, we should clarify the "unevenness" even of crisis periods—that even in a general world economic crisis, not all core areas are equally affected, nor all peripheral areas either. In addition, our project could be enriched by further specification of the existence of other regional "systems," coexisting with the Eurasian world economy/system or separate from it, thus also allowing comparative analyses along the lines proposed by Chase-Dunn and Hall (1991, 1993).

Most important, in my view, the world system approach must be extended by research into the causality of the cycles, both the economic and the hegemonic, and their mutual relations. As above, this statement invites research into how local conditions interact with systemic level impulses and stimuli. Specifically, further research should be conducted into how local responses affect ascent and decline in the "interlinked hegemonies" hierarchy. Furthermore, the role of technology and innovation, especially in "leading sectors," would be a most fruitful addition to our research agenda and has already become a central aspect of the work of Modelski and Thompson (1995).

In this regard, I propose the working hypothesis that "mercantilist" types of policy normally accompany a bid for ascent and that "openness" often accompanies already established core/hegemonic status (Gills, 1994). This hypothesis is general and is intended to refer to the entire development of the world economy/system, not merely to the modern period, where such a general hypothesis is fairly widely held.

On the matter of modes of production, it may be useful to further clarify the ways in which state and private spheres interact, also depending on the position in the world system of an entity and whether it is in an ascent or a decline phase. Moreover, on the issue of capitalism, I would propose that virtually all Eurasian core economies were already "capitalist," at least by the 15th century. However, if, as Braudel says, "capitalist cities" and indeed "capitalism" were already developed in 13th-century Italy, then the cities of the "Islamic world system" à la Abu-Lughod in the 13th century were equally (if not more so) "capitalist." If so, then really the entire Eurasian world economy/system of the 13th century was also "capitalist." If that is accepted, and given increasingly strong arguments for the commercial networks of 9th- to 10th-century Europe (Hodges, 1989) and Asia (Chaudhuri, 1991), then we ought to reconsider our view of the medieval economy, and we could further extend this hypothesis. China under the Sung was engaged in very extensive commerce at about the same time, as were India and the Arab domains. The evidence keeps leading us to extend our continuity thesis, even regarding "modes of production." Another similar reconsideration is prompted by new arguments on the "first millennium" political economy and the role of Europe and the Mediterranean within it (Randsborg, 1991), and we have already noted the recent reconsideration of the ancient economy and the role of market, credit, and capital (e.g., Millett, 1990). To undertake this exercise is not to do the ridiculous—that is, to contend that all of world history is "capitalist" in the *same* sense as capitalism as is conventionally understood after 1800 and industrialization. The point is simply to demolish false dichotomies and to allow new trains of thought on continuity in economic history. To say that we suggest the world economy was always "capitalist" is to distort our intentions and erect a straw man that any schoolboy could knock down. Indeed, McNeill has taken our approach as it was intended and has said that he believes he undervalued the importance of international commerce/trade, though he believes that the concept of "communications nets" is preferable to both his earlier and narrower "civilization" or our "world system." McNeill further amends our more materialist approach by adding that "markets and trade constituted only part of the communications network that crossed political, civilizational and linguistic boundaries" (McNeill, 1993, p. xii; also Chapter 11, this volume).

This, quite rightly, is the final area for further extension of our world system research agenda: to broaden the inquiry to really encompass the cultural and political patterns that form an integral part of the world systemic whole.

NOTES

1. For more detail on the genesis of the other Chicago school, see the preface by Andre Gunder Frank and Barry Gills to *The World System: Five Hundred Years or Five Thousand?* (1993, pp. xv-xxii).

2. Wheeler (1955) refers to Teggart's (1939) "brave attempt" to see in interruptions of international trade the cause of sequentialized wars across most of Eurasia in a chain reaction beginning in China and ending on the borders of the Roman empire between 58 B.C. and A.D. 107. Wheeler concludes that Teggart's thesis "by its very simplicity is suspect as an explanation of the complex workings of history" (p. 214). He adds,

> Other simple solutions of folk-disturbance have been sought from time to time in factors such as climatic fluctuation, evolving economy, overcrowding, personal or national ambition. These are facets of the problem, variously emphatic in varying circumstances; they are not its core, which is likely enough to lie embedded beyond the superficial view of history. Amongst them, trade-routes and commodities may be sufficiently stressed without the implication that history must be regarded persistently through a shop window. (p. 214)

3. The place of the Athenian economy in the debates over the character of the ancient or premodern political economy is very secure and well established, including in the arguments of M. I. Finley (e.g., 1973, 1981). Contra Finley, we follow Ekholm and Friedman (1982, 1993) in rejecting the primitivist perspective on the ancient economy. The Athenian economy continues to be the focus for ongoing debates on the character of the ancient economy. For instance, a lecture series at Cambridge University on the character of the ancient political economy opened with

Millett's argument for a political economy approach in which the "primacy of exchange" is central and the economy is "embedded in society." Millett's approach rests on an important criticism of Polanyi's formulation—that is, that Polanyi (Polanyi, Arensberg, & Pearson, 1957) unfortunately regarded the forms of exchange (e.g., redistributive, reciprocal, market) in an evolutionary way and thus as incompatible with one another (see Millett, 1983, 1990). Millett reviews the debate between the primitivist (minimizing the role of "credit" and capital in ancient economies) and modernist (viewing credit, capital, and markets in the ancient economy as being qualitatively similar to the "modern" forms) perspectives. The modernist position can be found in Boeckh (1817/1976); Glotz (1920/1926); Thompson (1978); and Davies (1981). The primitivists were headed by Karl Bücher (1979), and the modernists by Beloch, Busolt (1967), and Meyer (1910). The debate is summarized by Austin and Vidal-Naquet (1977). Millett cites Rostovzeff from his seminal *Social and Economic History of the Hellenistic World* (1941) that the difference between the (market) economy of the 4th century B.C. and the modern economy is "quantitative not qualitative." Millett throws doubt on Polanyi's thesis of the "invention" of the market economy in 4th-century Athens by pointing to recent work by anthropologists on the complexity of exchange in "noncapitalist" societies—that is, that the forms of exchange tend to blend together in real societies. Finally, Millett contends that the primitivist approach, which minimizes the role of "credit" (capital) in the ancient economy, is apparently contradicted by sheer volume of credit transactions in Athenian sources, and indeed credit was "everywhere" in antiquity. For evidence of the market/credit economy existing as far back as ancient Assyria, see, for example, Larsen (1967, 1976); Rowlands, Larsen, and Kristiansen (1987); and Silver (1985).

REFERENCES

Abu-Lughod, J. (1989). *Before European hegemony: The world system* A.D. 1250-1350. New York: Oxford University Press.

Amin, S. (1976). *Unequal development.* New York: Monthly Review Press.

Anderson, P. (1974). *Lineages of the absolutist state.* London: New Left Books.

Austin, M. M., & Vidal-Naquet, P. (1977). *Economic and social history of ancient Greece.* London: B. T. Batsford.

Boeckh, A. (1976). *The public economy of Athens: To which is added a dissertation on the silver mines of Laurion* (G. C. Lewis, Trans.). New York: Ayer. (Original work published 1817)

Bosworth, A. (1992, May). *World cities and world systems: A test of A. G. Frank and B. Gills' "A" and "B" cycles.* Paper presented at the Canadian Association of Geographers Conference, Vancouver.

Bücher, K. (1979). Ancient economic history. In M. I. Finley (Ed.), *The Bücher-Meyer controversy* (pp. 85-150, 1-97). New York: Arno.

Busolt, G. (1967). *Griechische geschichte bis zur schlacht bei chaeroneia.* Hildesheim: Verlag.

Chase-Dunn, C., & Hall, T. D. (Eds.). (1991). *Core/periphery relations in precapitalist worlds.* Boulder, CO: Westview.

Chase-Dunn, C., & Hall, T. D. (1993). Comparing world-systems: Concepts and working hypothesis. *Social Forces, 71*(4), 851-886.

Chaudhuri, K. N. (1991). *Asia before Europe: Economy and civilization of the Indian Ocean from the rise of Islam to 1750.* Cambridge, UK: Cambridge University Press.

Davies, J. K. (1981). *Wealth and the power of wealth in classical Athens.* New York: Ayer.

Ekholm, K., & Friedman, J. (1982). "Capital" imperialism and exploitation in ancient world systems. *Review, 4*(1), 87-109.

Ekholm, K., & Friedman, J. (1993). "Capital" imperialism and exploitation in ancient world systems (with postscript). In A. G. Frank & B. K. Gills (Eds.), *The world system: Five hundred years or five thousand?* (pp. 59-80). London: Routledge.

Finley, M. I. (1973). *The ancient economy.* Berkeley: University of California Press.

Finley, M. I. (1981). The Athenian empire: A balance sheet. In B. D. Shaw & R. Saller (Eds.), *Economy and society in ancient Greece* (pp. 41-61). London: Chatto & Windus.

Frank, A. G. (1991). Transitional ideological modes: Feudalism, capitalism, socialism. *Critique of Anthropology, 11*(2), 171-188.

Frank, A. G. (1993). Marketing democracy in an undemocratic market. In B. K. Gills, J. Rocamora, & R. Wilson (Eds.), *Low intensity democracy: Political power in the new world order* (pp. 35-58). London: Pluto.

Frank, A. G. (1994). The world economic system in Asia before European hegemony. *The Historian, 56*(4), 259-276.

Frank, A. G., & Gills, B. K. (1992). The five thousand year world system: An interdisciplinary introduction. *Humboldt Journal of Social Relations, 18*(1), 1-79.

Frank, A. G., & Gills, B. K. (Eds.). (1993). *The world system: Five hundred years or five thousand?* London: Routledge.

Gills, B. K. (1987). Historical materialism and international relations theory. *Millennium: Journal of International Studies, 16*(2), 265-272.

Gills, B. K. (1989a). International relations theory and the processes of world history: Three approaches. In H. C. Dyer & L. Mangasarian (Eds.), *International relations: The state of the art* (pp. 103-154). New York: Macmillan.

Gills, B. K. (1989b, April). *Synchronization, conjuncture, and center-shift in East Asian international history.* Paper presented at the Annual Meeting of the International Studies Association, London.

Gills, B. K. (1993). The hegemonic transition in East Asia: A historical perspective. In S. Gill (Ed.), *Gramsi and international relations* (pp. 186-211). Cambridge, UK: Cambridge University Press.

Gills, B. K. (1994). Hegemony and social change. *Mershon International Studies Review, 38* (Suppl. 2), 369-371.

Gills, B. K., & Frank, A. G. (1990/1991). The cumulation of accumulation: Theses and research agenda for five thousand years of world system history. *Dialectical Anthropology, 5*(1), 19-42.

Gills, B. K., & Frank, A. G. (1992). World system cycles, crises, and hegemonical shifts 1700 B.C. to A.D. 1700. *Review, 15*(4), 67-112.

Gills, B. K., & Qadir, S. (1995). *Regimes in crisis: The post-Soviet era and the prospects for development.* London: Zed.

Gills, B. K., Rocamora, J., & Wilson, R. (Eds.). (1993). *Low intensity democracy: Political power in the new world order.* London: Pluto.

Gilpin, R. (1987). *The political economy of international relations.* Princeton, NJ: Princeton University Press.

Glotz, G. (1926). *Ancient Greece at work* (M. R. Dobie, Trans.). New York: Knopf. (Original work published 1920)

Hodges, R. (1989). *Dark age economics: The origins of towns and trade* A.D. 600-1000. London: Duckworth.

Hodgson, M. (1974). *The venture of Islam.* Chicago: University of Chicago Press.

Hodgson, M. (1993). *Rethinking world history: Essays on Europe, Islam, and world history.* Cambridge, UK: Cambridge University Press.

Larsen, M. T. (1967). Old Assyrian caravan procedures. *Nederlands Historisch.* Arekaeologish Institut te Istanbul 22.

Larsen, M. T. (1976). *The old Assyrian city state and its colonies.* Copenhagen: Akademisk Forlag.

McNeill, W. H. (1963). *The rise of the West: A history of the human community.* Chicago: University of Chicago Press.

McNeill, W. H. (1993). Forward. In A. G. Frank & B. K. Gills (Eds.), *The world system: Five hundred years or five thousand?* (pp. vii-xiii). London: Routledge.

Meyer, E. (1910). *Klein Schriften.* Niemeyer: Halle.

Millett, P. (1983). Maritime loans and the structure of credit in fourth-century Athens. In P. Garnesey, K. Hopkins, & C. R. Whittaker (Eds.), *Trade in the ancient economy* (pp. 36-52). London: Hogarth.

Millet, P. (1990). Sale, credit, and exchange in Athenian law and society. In P. Cartledge, P. Millet, & S. Todd (Eds.), *NOMOS: Essays in Athenian law, politics, and society* (pp. 167-194). Cambridge, UK: Cambridge University Press.

Modelski, G., & Thompson, W. R. (1995). *Leading sectors and world powers: The coevolution of global politics and economics.* Columbia: University of South Carolina Press.

Polanyi, K., Arensberg, C., & Pearson, H. W. (Eds.). (1957). *Trade and markets in the early empires.* New York: Free Press.

Randsborg, K. (1991). *The first millennium* A.D. in Europe and the Mediterranean: An archeological essay. Cambridge, UK: Cambridge University Press.

Rostovzeff, M. I. (1941). *The social and economic history of the Hellenistic world.* Oxford, UK: Clarendon.

Rowlands, M. J., Larsen, M. T., & Kristiansen, K. (Eds.). (1987). *Center and periphery in the ancient world.* Cambridge, UK: Cambridge University Press.

Silver, M. (1985). *Economic structure of the ancient Near East.* London: Croom Helm.

Teggart, F. J. (1939). *Rome and China: A study of correlations in historical events.* Berkeley: University of California Press.

Thompson, W. E. (1978). *The Athenian investor.* Rivista di Studi Classici 36.

Wallerstein, I. (1991). World system versus world-systems: A critique. *Critique of Anthropology, 11*(2), 189-194.

Wallerstein, I. (1993). World system versus world-systems: A critique. In A. G. Frank & B. K. Gills (Eds.), *The world system: Five hundred years or five thousand?* (pp. 292-296). London: Routledge.

Wheeler, M. (1955). *Rome beyond the imperial frontiers.* Harmondsworth, UK: Pelican.

Wilkinson, D. (1992, April). *Decline phases in civilizations, regions, and Oikumens.* Paper presented at the Annual Meeting of the International Studies Association Convention, Atlanta.

13

World-Systems

Similarities and Differences

CHRISTOPHER CHASE-DUNN

All of our minds have cooked in the powerful juices of books and essays written by Andre Gunder Frank. His thought has shaped the global antisystemic consciousness of the last four decades. Rather than review the impact of his earlier work, I focus on his recent efforts to extend the world-system[1] perspective back in time to include the emergence of a regional, urbanized, state-based world system in Mesopotamia five thousand years ago. I am convinced that this is the most significant turn that Frank's thinking has ever taken. Although I disagree with some aspects of his approach (and some of his conclusions), I contend that the inclusion of a much greater time depth in world system analysis has the potential to generate a new and much more powerful theory of historical evolution and to provide us with important pointers about the possibilities for transforming the contemporary global world-system into a more humane and peaceful world society.

Several scholars working from a world systems perspective have extended that perspective back in time because they perceive important similarities in the processes and patterned phenomena operating in both modern and earlier periods of world system history. Andre Gunder Frank and his coauthor Barry

Gills (Frank & Gills, 1993) have stressed the continuities of systemic logic, cyclical waves of expansion and contraction, and the importance of hegemonic rivalry and exploitation of peripheral regions in a single state-based world system over the last five thousand years. They focus on the system that emerged out of Mesopotamia and incorporated all other regions. Following David Wilkinson (1991), this system may be labeled the "central world-system." Earlier work by Kasja Ekholm and Jonathan Friedman (1982) also stressed many of these same continuities. Ekholm and Friedman posited a "capital-imperialist" mode of production that emerged along with states in Lower Mesopotamia. This mode of accumulation oscillates back and forth between the use of state power and reliance on more family-based "private" forms of economic power to accumulate wealth. Frank and Gills (1993) make a similar argument.

THE WHEEL OF BEING

Frank (1993) adds that the whole discussion of transformations (or transitions) in modes of production is only an ideological smoke screen. According to Frank, there have been no qualitative transformations in the mode of production during the five-thousand-year history of this single world system. All of the "differentiae specificae" alleged by Immanuel Wallerstein (1993, pp. 292-293) to constitute the uniquenesses of the modern world-system are argued by Frank to have been features of a much larger and multicore Afroeurasian world system for millennia.

So, according to Frank, there was never a transformation to a uniquely capitalist world system in Europe in the 16th century. Europe did rise to hegemony after the 18th century, but it is alleged that this was similar in form and content to earlier emergences of new hegemonic regions. The Eurasian world system had experienced uneven development and the fall of old cores and the rise of new ones for millennia. Europe's rise was simply the most recent instance of successful "capital-imperialism." This claim is important not only for our understanding of the origins of the world we live in but also for understanding the possibilities for the future. Frank goes on to claim that, just as the transition from feudalism to capitalism was a myth, so is the Marxist hypothesis of a potential transition from capitalism to socialism or communism. The collapse of the Soviet Union and the current debate over the "transition from socialism to capitalism" in Russia, Eastern Europe, and China are cited as supporting the mythological nature of the transition hypotheses. Frank here breaks strongly with his own earlier endorsement of socialism as a real alternative for countries in the periphery and the semiperiphery.

This is heavy stuff. Frank is certainly right when he points to the totemic significance of the idea of transformation of modes of production for Marxists. In various guises and in different words, this idea is also important for all other radical critiques of the contemporary system. If nothing else is possible, then the system is a wheel that goes round and round. This is more than a recognition of certain cyclical phenomena. It is a wholesale move toward a timeless and endless model of historical repetition. Gunder Frank has become a Hindu. In such a worldview, evolutionary or revolutionary action is meaningless and one might as well tend to one's own garden. Never afraid of contradicting the shibboleths of his leftist friends, Frank has once again embraced a boldly skeptical conclusion. This particular turn may be welcomed by those idealogues who contend that the present system is the best possible, though they are not likely to listen to Frank no matter what he says. Greater enthusiasm may come from those disillusioned ex-leftists who were looking for a justification for cynicism or guiltless self-improvement. The grand debunking of progress as proclaimed by the celebrants of capitalism has led to the denial of not only its actuality but also its possibility.

If this is a dilemma, moralizing is not the way out. Rather, I propose an approach based on social science that uses many of the insights and conceptual leaps from Frank's recent work on the very long run history of the world system to generate new insights about the possibilities for qualitative transformation in the future.

COMPARING WORLD-SYSTEMS

Tom Hall and I, too, have been working on a "very long run" approach to understanding world-systems (Chase-Dunn & Hall, 1991, in press). Like Frank, we think it is important to compare empirically the contemporary system with itself at much earlier points in time. But we also argue that a comparative approach that looks at different world systems is important for understanding both the similarities and the differences. To do this, we have modified the Wallersteinian concepts of world-system and core/periphery relations to make them more useful for a very long run and comparative theoretical scope (Chase-Dunn & Hall, 1993). Our temporal and spatial framework includes all the small, medium-sized, and large world-systems on earth since the emergence of sedentary foragers in the Levant about ten thousand years ago. We argue that, though many world-systems include nomadic peoples, it is important to have at least some sedentary peoples exerting territoriality in a system for intersocietal relations to be understood as constituting a world-system. This requirement rules out the paleolithic nomads and begins with mesolithic hamlet-dwelling foragers. Our approach is designed to allow us to scientifically study structural and processual differences as well as similarities. This focus on the analysis of differences was provoked by the perceived overemphasis on similarities in the work of Ekholm and Friedman and of Frank and Gills.

One reason why Frank and Gills are able to point out great similarities across time in the central world-system is that states and classes have existed in this system during the whole period on which their analysis focuses. To look at a really different world-system, pick one in which there were no states or classes. We have closely examined a small world-system composed of sedentary foragers that existed in Northern California until the Gold Rush of 1849 (Chase-Dunn, Clewett, & Sundahl, 1992), and we are now studying the interchiefdom system that was in the Hawaiian archipelago before the arrival of Captain Cook (Chase-Dunn & Ermolaeva, 1994).

Northern California was really different. Not only were there no states or classes, but there also was very little hierarchy within groups and only mild core/periphery differentiation and hierarchy[2] between groups. The Hawaiian case, with its large, complex chiefdoms, was much more like the world-systems with which we are familiar. A radical class distinction between chiefs and commoners, and the rise and fall of chiefly polities, bear strong structural resemblances to classes and rise-and-fall processes in larger, state-based world-systems. But core/periphery relations were still rather unstable and mild.

Because of their emphasis on *the* world system that emerged in Mesopotamia, Frank and Gills have ignored the evolutionary histories of state-based systems in Mesoamerica and Peru. Our comparative approach avoids replacing Eurocentrism with Eurasiacentrism.

Although Frank and Gills acknowledge that the system that emerged in Mesopotamia five thousand years ago was not originally Eurasia-wide, they have yet to pay much attention to bounding the spatial extent of that system as it grew. They have gotten a lot of mileage out of arguing that interaction networks were larger much earlier than most area specialists imagine, but they have been quite vague about exactly when and in what way the central system expanded.

Our approach spatially bounds world-systems by focusing on interaction networks. We empirically determine the trade, political/military, and inter-marriage interaction nets in which people are involved. We observe that bulk goods (food and raw materials), political/military interaction networks (PMNs), and prestige goods trade networks often form nested systems with different spatial extents. Typically, bulk goods nets are small because of the transportation costs involved in carrying goods with a low ratio of value to weight. Political/military interaction networks are often somewhat larger because they are based on the logistics of moving armies and navies and the information flows that carry threats and alliances. Prestige goods nets are even larger because goods with a high value to weight ratio often travel very far by means of down-the-line (indirect) exchange.

Although we use the idea of modes of accumulation[3] (basic systemic logics) to organize our heuristic typology of world-systems (Chase-Dunn & Hall, 1993), we do not use mode of accumulation to spatially bound world-systems. We want to examine how modes of accumulation may have become transformed within world-systems. Spatially bounding world-systems in terms of modes of accumulation only confounds that task. Rejecting modes of accumulation as criteria for spatially bounding systems is not to throw them out entirely or to embrace Hinduism. Our comparative approach allows us to study how small, egalitarian, kin-based world-systems became transformed into larger, state-based, and tributary systems. If you exclude stateless systems, this important watershed cannot be considered.

RISE AND FALL

Frank and Gills build on the work of Ekholm and Friedman to conceptualize and study the sequences of political centralization and decentralization that have occurred in the Central World System during the last five thousand years. This sequence is well known to students of political history as the rise and fall of empires. The sequence of political centralization/decentralization is a prime example of a continuity between the modern world-system of the previous five hundred years and the earlier Central system. Indeed, even chiefdom-based world-systems exhibit a somewhat similar pattern. But these processes also exhibit important differences in different kinds of systems. Both chiefdom systems and state-based systems become centralized through military conquest, but the polities erected by chiefly conquerors must rely on kinship alliances to implement regional control, whereas states make use of specialized non-kin control institutions. This is why state-based empires usually were able to incorporate larger territories and populations than chiefdom-based polities did.

In the modern world-system, the pattern of political centralization/decentralization takes the form of the rise and fall of hegemonic core powers. This is analytically similar to the rise and fall of empires, but the differences are important. In the process of empire formation, a "rogue power"—most often a semiperipheral marcher state—conquers the other core states to form what David Wilkinson (1987) terms a "universal empire." Well-known examples are the Roman empire and the Han empire. This phenomenon approximately corresponds to what Immanuel Wallerstein calls a "world-empire." Wallerstein claims that the modern world-system is politically structured as an interstate system of competing states and that earlier world-systems frequently took the form of world-empires in which the economic division of labor came to be encompassed by a single state.

Rarely did the "universal states" encompass entire world economies, but they did often conquer an entire adjacent core region. This is the peak of political centralization in such systems. It is convenient to conceptualize centralization and decentralization as two ends of a continuum. Thus, although there have not been true "world-empires" in the sense that a single state comes to encompass an entire world-system, this idea may be understood to point to a relatively high concentration of control over a relatively great proportion of a world-system. The term I prefer, because it is more precise, is *core-wide empire*.[4] State-based world-systems prior to the modern one oscillated back and forth between core-wide empires and interstate systems. In some regions, the decentralization trend went so far as to break up into mini-states. Thus, feudalism may be understood as a very decentralized form of a state-based system.

Figure 13.1 illustrates the structural difference between a core-wide empire and a hegemonic core state. This may be understood as simply a difference in the degree of concentration of political/military power in a single state. In this sense, Wallerstein's distinction between world-empires and world-economies points to an important structural difference between the modern system and earlier state-based systems. But this is not only a systematic difference in the degree of peak political concentration. The whole nature of the process of rise and fall is different in the modern world-system. The rise and fall of hegemonies has occurred in a very different way from the rise and fall of empires. Empire

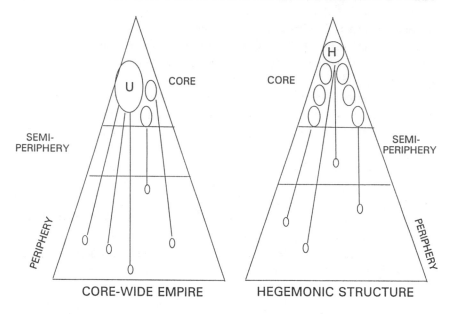

Figure 13.1 Core-Wide Empire (Universal State) Versus Hegemonic Structure
NOTE: U = universal state; H = hegemon.

formation was a matter of conquering adjacent core states. Modern hegemons did not conquer adjacent core states to extract taxes and tribute. Rather, they sought to control international trade, especially oceanic trade, that linked cores with peripheries.

This is why the modern world-system is resistant to empire-formation. The most powerful state in the system acts to block empire-formation and to preserve the interstate system. Thus, the cycle of political centralization/decentralization takes the form of the rise and fall of hegemonic core powers. This important difference is primarily because of the relatively great importance that capitalist accumulation has for the modern system.

THE LONG RISE OF CAPITALISM

Capitalist accumulation—the appropriation of surplus value from the production and sale of commodities—is not unique to the modern world-system. Frank is correct to note that this kind of activity existed well before the 16th century. But existence is not predominance. Commodified forms of wealth, land, goods, and labor existed *and became more important* during the five-thousand-year history of the central world system, but capitalism only began to *predominate* over the tributary modes of accumulation in the Europe-centered subregion after the 16th century.

The tributary modes of accumulation rely more directly on organized political power to extract surplus product. Taxation, tribute, and other forms of exploitation that rely directly on political coercion are the primary means by which ruling classes appropriate surplus product in societies based on the tributary modes. The early state-based world-systems were mixes of modes of accumulation in which tributary modes emerged over the top of kin-based modes.[5] But even in these early states, evidence suggests, some commodified forms existed. Thus, Diakonoff (1954) found documentary evidence of the sale of land in pre-Sargonic Sumer. But these commodified forms were rudimentary and did not play an important role in the dynamics of development of early state-based systems. As empires grew and trade networks expanded, commodified forms of wealth, goods, land, and even wage labor appeared within the commercializing empires. Both Rome and Han China had important market mechanisms, but these societies, now becoming linked to one another in a single Eurasian prestige goods network, remained predominantly governed by the logic of political/military conquest and the extraction of surplus product from peasant farmers.

Commodification in 10th-century Sung China was much more developed. Paper money, elaborate credit institutions, and perhaps Kondratiev waves were attributes of the Sung industrial revolution (Modelski & Thompson, in press), but the Chinese capitalists did not succeed in taking state power. Capitalist states had already existed for millennia, but these were always semiperipheral capitalist city-states (e.g., the Phoenician cities) that made a living in the interstices between the tributary empires. The first capitalist national state in a core region was the Dutch Republic of the 17th century, and this is the most important indication that capitalism was becoming more predominant in the European subsystem than in any other region.

The phenomenon of capitalist city-states was known to the ancient world at least as far back as the first Phoenician cities.[6] This phenomenon was by no means unique to Europe. Malacca was a semiperipheral capitalist city-state working the trade between Chinese, Siamese, Indian, and Javan tributary states. Semiperipheral capitalist city-states were agents of the spread of the institutions of commodification to the tributary empires and to peripheral regions. In Europe, the capitalist city-states that arose after the 11th century

(Venice, Genoa, the Hanseatic cities) were unusually densely concentrated in a region lacking strong central authority.

Frank and Gills (1994) are correct to point out that Eurasia was a single prestige goods system with three non-adjacent core regions (China, India, and the Near East) and that Europe was peripheral to this system. This argument was first made by Jane Schneider (1977). Frank (1994) is also right to point out that Europe remained peripheral or semiperipheral vis-à-vis Asia until at least the 18th century. Recent research on city populations in the central political/military network (PMN) demonstrates that the largest cities in the network of political/military interaction that included Europe were the capitals of large tributary states such as the Ottoman empire or the Mughal empire (Chase-Dunn & Willard, 1994). European cities such as Paris and London only became the largest cities in this PMN in 1750.

Yet, it would be wrong to ignore the unusual aspects of the core formation that was occurring in Europe from the 11th century on. True, this was yet another example of semiperipheral development, the rise of a formerly peripheral region, and the formation of a local core. This general phenomenon had occurred many times before. But the European semiperipheral development was different in several structural and processual ways. Market forces and state power in the hands of capitalists were stronger in Europe precisely because the tributary structures were weak and decentralized. European feudalism was important, not because of its cultural or organizational content, but because it was a very decentralized and weak form of the tributary mode of production. The institutions of capitalism, long developed in Rome and in China, took hold on European soil because tributary states were not able to prevent the rise of capitalists to political power. This occurred first in the unusually densely packed city-states and later in the national states.

CORE/PERIPHERY RELATIONS

Two other structural features of the Europe-centered subsystem indicate its uniqueness. I have already mentioned how the rise and fall of hegemons is different from the earlier pattern of the rise and fall of empires. The primary reason for the difference is that the hegemonic states in the modern world-system were capitalist states. Because they were pursuing wealth by means of commodity production, they did not seek to conquer adjacent core regions.

Rather, they used state power to set up a world order in which they could make profits from commodity production. All states were not as capitalist as the hegemonic states, however. Second-tier core states sometimes opted for versions of the marcher state strategy and tried to conquer the core. The Hapsburgs, Napoleonic France, and 20th-century Germany were all challengers of this type.

There is a second major structural difference between the modern world-system and the Central system before the rise of industrial capitalism. This is in the nature of the core/periphery hierarchy. Important core/periphery relations have existed in all state-based world-systems (but not in stateless world-systems). The ability to extract resources from peripheral areas has almost always been an important component of successful accumulation by using political coercion. Evolutionary change and the rise of newly powerful states have also been related to core/periphery relations because innovations and successful challengers to older core states have tended to come from the semiperiphery (Chase-Dunn, 1988).

But the operation of core/periphery relations is significantly different in the modern system from what it was before the coming of industrial capitalism. One important structural difference is indicated by the reversal of the location of relative intrasocietal inequalities. In premodern state-based world-systems (including the Central system, the Far Eastern system, the Mesoamerican system, and the Peruvian system), core societies had relatively greater internal inequalities than did peripheral societies. Typically, core states were urbanized and class-organized, whereas peripheral societies were nomadic pastoralists or horticulturalists or simply less densely concentrated peoples living in smaller towns or villages. These kinds of peripheral groups typically had less internal inequality than the core states with which they were linked.

In the modern world-system, this situation has reversed. Core societies typically have less (relative) internal inequality than peripheral societies. The kinds of jobs that are concentrated in the core, as well as the development of welfare states in the core, expand the size of the middle classes within core societies to produce a more-or-less diamond-shaped distribution of income that bulges in the middle. Typical peripheral societies, however, have pyramidal income distributions in which there is a small rich elite, rather a small middle class, and a very large mass of very poor people.

This reversal in the location of relative internal inequality between cores and peripheries was mainly a consequence of the development and concentration of complex economies needing skilled labor and the politics of democracy and the welfare state that have accompanied capitalist industrialization in the core. These processes have occurred in tandem with and are dependent on the development of peripheral capitalism, colonialism, and neocolonialism in the periphery, and these have produced the greater relative inequalities within peripheral societies.[7] Core capitalism is dependent on peripheral capitalism because exploitation of the periphery provides a good bit of the resources that core capital uses to pay higher incomes to core workers, and the reproduction of an underdeveloped periphery legitimates the national capital-labor alliances that provide relative harmony of class relations in the core and that undercut radical challenges to capitalist power (Chase-Dunn, 1989, chap. 11).

In premodern systems, core/periphery relations were also important for sustaining the social order of the core (e.g., the bread and circuses of Rome), but not to the same extent, because the system did not produce relatively more equal distributions of income and political power in the core than in the periphery. Thus, the core/periphery hierarchy has become an even more important structural feature of the modern world-system than it was in earlier state-based systems.

Frank's extension of the world-system perspective back in time can thus be used to tease out the real structural and processual *differences* as well as the similarities across time and across different systems. Perhaps it is natural that the similarities should be emphasized first because most social scientists are still in the habit of studying single societies, rather than world-systems. But to understand both social reproduction and social change, we need to apply the world-systems perspective to all intersocietal networks, not just those that are quite like the present one. And we need to compare carefully the structures of both the modern and premodern systems to observe both similarities and differences. This project is only in its first stages—concept formation, the development of comparative hypotheses, and the execution of case studies. Eventually, it will be desirable to gather systematic data on large numbers of world-systems to test hypotheses. And the mapping out of structural similarities will enable us to better understand how these systems have evolved and qualitatively transformed.

The possibilities for transforming the contemporary world-system into a more humane, just, and egalitarian world society will also become clearer from a very long run and comparative approach. The past processes of hierarchy formation (chiefdom formation, state formation, the rise and fall of hegemonic core states) certainly have important lessons about the possibilities (and probabilities) of global state formation. And the existence of early small-scale world-systems that did not have core/periphery hierarchies shows that inter-societal relations need not be hierarchical. Our new understanding of the rising predominance of capitalism in the Afroeurasian system has implications for how a new, more cooperative mode of accumulation might be arising in the modern world-system. For example, the theory of semiperipheral develop-ment mentioned above suggests that semiperipheral locations are fertile loci for innovations in many different kinds of world-systems, and this implies that the contemporary semiperiphery may be the weak link where transforma-tional action is most likely to occur (Chase-Dunn, 1990, 1992). What needs to be done now is to work out a theory of the historical evolution of world-systems and to test that theory against alternative formulations that take world-systems as the focal unit of analysis. The outcome of such a theoretical research program is likely to have important implications for understanding the cyclical and secular tendencies of the modern system and our collective future.

NOTES

1. Gunder Frank insists on using the term *world-system* without the hyphen to emphasize his theoretical differences with Immanuel Wallerstein. In this chapter, I follow Gunder's usage when referring to his concepts and conclusions, but I employ the hyphen when presenting my own perspective.

2. Chase-Dunn and Hall (1993) distinguish between core/periphery differentiation and core/periphery hierarchy. *Differentiation* means there are differences in the level of development (e.g., population density, intensity of production, internal hierarchy) between two societies that are interacting. *Hierarchy* means one of the societies is dominating and/or exploiting the other. These often go together, but not always.

3. We substitute "mode of accumulation" for "mode of production" to emphasize that we mean the whole system by which production, distribution, and accumulation are accomplished.

4. Wilkinson refers to the decentralization phase as constituting a "states system."

5. The kin-based modes of accumulation rely on normative integration, usually organized as kinship relations, to mobilize social labor and to organize collective accumulation.

6. And possibly much earlier. Assur may have been a capitalist trading city before it switched to the role of semiperipheral marcher state. And perhaps Dilmun (located on what is now Bahrain), specializing in the carrying trade between the old Lower Mesopotamian core and the developing cities of the Indus River valley, was the earliest semiperipheral capitalist city-state.

7. Another related consequence of capitalist development is the growing relative gap *between* the core and the periphery.

REFERENCES

Chase-Dunn, C. (1988, Fall). Comparing world-systems: Toward a theory of semiperipheral development. *Comparative Civilizations Review, 19,* 39-66.

Chase-Dunn, C. (1989). *Global formation.* Cambridge, MA: Blackwell.

Chase-Dunn, C. (1990). Resistance to imperialism: Semiperipheral actors. *Review, 13*(1), 1-31.

Chase-Dunn, C. (1992). The spiral of capitalism and socialism. In L. F. Kriesberg (Ed.), *Research in social movements, conflicts, and change* (Vol. 14, pp. 165-187). Greenwich, CT: JAI.

Chase-Dunn, C., Clewett, E., & Sundahl, E. (1992, April). *A very small world-system in Northern California: The Wintu and their neighbors. Paper presented at the Annual Meeting of the Society for American Archaeology, Pittsburgh.* [Also online. Available: csf.colorado. edu\wsystems\papers\pcid_working_papers\]

Chase-Dunn, C., & Ermolaeva, E. (1994, March). *The ancient Hawaiian world-system: Research in progress.* Paper presented at the Annual Meeting of the International Studies Association, Washington, DC.

Chase-Dunn, C., & Hall, T. D. (Eds.). (1991). *Core/periphery relations in precapitalist worlds.* Boulder, CO: Westview.

Chase-Dunn, C., & Hall, T. D. (1993, June). Comparing world-systems: Concepts and working hypotheses. *Social Forces, 71*(4), 851-886.

Chase-Dunn, C., & Hall, T. D. (in press). *Rise and demise: Comparing world-systems.* Boulder, CO: Westview.

Chase-Dunn, C., & Willard, A. (1994). Cities in the central world-system since C.E. 1200: Size hierarchy and domination. *Comparative Civilizations Review, 30,* 104-132.

Diakonoff, I. M. (1954). *Sale of land in pre-Sargonic Sumer.* Paper presented by the Soviet Delegation at the 23rd International Congress of Orientalists, Assyriology Section, U.S.S.R. Academy of Sciences, Moscow.

Ekholm, K., & Friedman, J. (1982). "Capital imperialism" and exploitation in the ancient world-systems. *Review, 6*(1), 87-110.

Frank, A. G. (1993). Transitional ideological modes: Feudalism, capitalism, socialism. In A. G. Frank & B. K. Gills (Eds.), *The world-system: Five hundred years or five thousand?* (pp. 200-220). London: Routledge.

Frank, A. G. (1994, Winter). The world economic system in Asia before European hegemony. *The Historian, 56*(2), 260-276.

Frank, A. G., & Gills, B. K. (Eds.). (1993). *The world-system: Five hundred years or five thousand?* London: Routledge.

Modelski, G., & Thompson, W. R. (1995). *Leading sectors and world powers: The co-evolution of global politics and economics.* Columbia: University of South Carolina Press.

Schneider, J. (1977). Was there a precapitalist world-system? *Peasant Studies, 6*(1), 20-29.

Wallerstein, I. (1993). World system versus world-system: A critique. In A. G. Frank & B. K. Gills (Eds.), *The world-system: Five hundred years or five thousand?* (pp. 292-296). London: Routledge.

Wilkinson, D. (1987). Central civilization. *Comparative Civilizations Review, 17,* 31-59.

Wilkinson, D. (1991). Cores, peripheries, and civilizations. In A. G. Frank & B. K. Gills (Eds.), *The world-system: Five hundred years or five thousand?* (pp. 113-166). London: Routledge.

14

The Art of Hegemony

ALBERT BERGESEN

THE DEVELOPMENT OF ART HISTORY

There has been a development, so to speak, of A. G. Frank's ideas about development. They have expanded in geographical scope and historical time. At first, the focus was on the underdevelopment of Latin America. Later his focus shifted to the development of the modern world-system. Regional development was becoming world development. His conceptualization, though, continued to expand. No sooner had he embraced the world-system idea than he began to find its 16th-century start date a somewhat arbitrary slice across a much longer historical continuity. Frank now believed the systematic interconnectedness of human life that made up world history, if not a world-system, went back some five thousand years. There may be more expansion to come. But at present, what is "developing" is world history. From Latin America to the modern world-system to five thousand years of world history, the breadth of human structuration has widened and widened in Frank's conception of what it is that's developing.

AUTHOR'S NOTE: This research was supported by the University of Arizona. I would like to thank A. G. Frank and Walter Goldfrank for comments on this paper.

In thinking this way, Frank helped open the intellectual door to theorizing social process at the distinctly world-systemic level. His thinking involved not just geopolitics that always had a worldwide reference, but more analytical dynamics such as development and, implicitly, the social evolutionary process itself. Because of Frank, we now conventionally conceive of the collective aspect of human life to be most fundamentally structured at the global, not the national level. Because of Frank, we further understand that this world-system expands and contracts in boom/bust economic cycles and hegemony/rivalry political cycles. We now theorize social process worldwide and over long periods of historical time. These global processes, though, have been most clearly articulated in the economic and political spheres, where cyclical rhythms, long-term trends, and structural constants are identified.

The understanding of world culture, though, remains underdeveloped. It is not for lack of discussion on world culture. There is much of this, but scant linkage has been made between systematic variation in world political economy and world culture. The global base and global superstructure have not been theoretically linked in any systematic way. In this chapter, though, I present a preliminary outline of the connection between world cycles of hegemony/rivalry and world cycles of culture, with a particular emphasis on art history since the 16th century.

The revolution in thought contained in Frank's notion of the "development of underdevelopment" involved turning away from theorizing economic development as mode after mode of production succeeding one another in a straightforward, linear, diachronic fashion. Interestingly, art history, in a way similar to pre-Frank development history, remains such a diachronic analysis, with art historical period after art historical period succeeding one another— from slavery to feudalism to capitalism in the economic sphere, and from the Gothic to the Renaissance to the Baroque in the art historical sphere. Like mode after mode in social theory, style following style is the predominate assumption of art theory.[1] Similar to the logic of the social sphere, transitions in art are often depicted as occurring through crisis and revolution, as in references to the revolution within the Parisian art world that was Impressionism, or the revolutionary nature of American Abstract Expressionism.

Frank challenged the sequential mode theory in two ways. The first challenge, with the interdependence of modes idea, involves the development of underdevelopment. Here the evolution of sequential stages within a social formation is interrupted in some parts of the world (the South) when other sectors reach certain levels of development (the predatory North). The development of one part of the world now inhibits the development of other areas. The second challenge involves the abandonment of stages and modes altogether with his more recent notion of one world history and, with that, one socio-economic mode of accumulation. The exact nature of this single system's inner logic is less well worked out and centers on suggestions that core-periphery hierarchies, hegemony/rivalry cycles, and expanding/contracting economic cycles have always been with us and have always characterized world history.

The conception of world art history advanced here is closest to this latter formulation: one world-system whose cyclical rhythms can not only be identified in art history but, most important, also exhibit the same cyclic periodicity as the hegemony/rivalry cycle, at least since the 16th century.

If we assume we have been in a singular world-system for at least the past five hundred years, then following established social psychological principles, we can assume this political/economic singularity has also produced a singular set of collective experiences.[2] Questions of mass psychology or collective consciousness, sociologically theorized to be the product of common class, caste, or national experience, should also exist globally if there is, in fact, a common world-system. We cannot argue for the existence of world-systemic political/economic structures without realizing there must also be world-systemic modes of consciousness. That is, if there is a group, there is group culture; if there is a class, there is class culture; if there is a nation, there is national culture; and if there is a world-system, then there must be world culture. And if this world-system has pulsated in long waves or cycles, then there should be a corresponding long wave in consciousness, such as in artistic forms of expression.[3]

Art history, then, should also exhibit cyclical rhythms of style and form. This is particularly the case for the most general styles because they are trans-societal, or world-systemic, in nature. Seventeenth-century Baroque forms, for instance, are identifiable not only in Italy and France but also in Peru and Brazil, and the Social Realism of the 1930s appeared in countries with very different political/economic systems, from the Mexican muralists of dependent capitalism to the Social Realists and Regionalists of American advanced capitalism to the socialist Realism of state communism and the Social Realism of Nazi Germany and Fascist Italy. The point here is that, independent of mode of production, state form, or core-periphery position, Social Realism was found worldwide in the 1930s. Style was a worldwide movement requiring, therefore, a worldwide or world-system explanation, which is exactly what is being proposed here. This correspondence between world-systemic cultural and political/economic rhythms is more than a Durk-heimian match of world order and world collective experience. Forms of expression also serve the power of the hegemon and partake in the legitima-tion of hegemonic domination.

FORM AND POWER

Power presents itself visually as form, and world hegemonic power presents itself as a particular form of world art. In general, the greater the concentration of hegemonic power, the more principles of form are important in structuring vision. The presence of hegemonic power is experienced as the presence of more abstract, idealized, and classicized forms of art, which emphasize order, balance, and symmetry. With hegemonic decline and a more competitive rivalrous world-system, modes of expression become more expressive and painterly, and subject matter more real and naturalistic. Wolfflin's (1929) theory of style that defines shape by line and arranged parallel to the picture plane with a closed sense of composition is art of the period of hegemony, whereas art that shapes form in a more painterly fashion, with more recessional depth to composition in a more open format, is present more often in periods of international rivalry.

For example, under the period of clear, uncontested American hegemony (1945-1970s), modern art was dominated by abstraction from Abstract Ex-pressionism in the 1940s and 1950s, through Minimalism in the 1960s, to conceptualism in the 1970s. Then, corresponding to American hegemonic decline in world production, world art turned toward more realism, with neorealist representations of figures and urban landscapes, and then into the 1980s and 1990s a multicultural realism emphasizing nationality, gender, ethnicity, race, and sexual preference. Gestural abstraction and the cool minimalist shapes of color fields came under postmodernist attack as suffocat-ing hegemonic tools of power used for—depending on the now grounded critique of modernism—patriarchal, white, male, heterosexual domination and control. The unity of abstraction was breaking up, and not only within nations. Within the world-system, the hegemony of American Abstraction was giving way to a realism that reflected the different countries in which it was produced, such as the German historical themes of Anselm Keifer. New York also felt the challenge of other centers of art, such as Cologne (Solomon, 1992).

A similar turn to everyday realism occurred during the second half of the 19th century (realism, Impressionism, Postimpressionism) with the decline of

Table 14.1 Styles of Art History and Phases of Hegemony/Rivalry Cycles

			Years			
Cycle Phase	1500	1600	1700	1800	1900	1950
Hegemony	Renaissance		•	Neoclassic/Romantic		Abstract
Transition	•	Mannerism	Rococo	Academic Art •	Art Deco	Concept Art
Rivalry	•	Baroque •	•	Realism	•	Multi-cultural Art
		•			•	•

British hegemony. Although art movements such as Impressionism are traditionally considered part of a fundamental break in art history—the rise of the modern—they in fact are a continuation of the non-idealized naturalistic expression that is produced by the post-hegemonic balkanization of the world-economy. Postimpressionism continues such realism, as does Cubism, which represents another means for getting at the true nature of reality. As the world-system further balkanizes, so does art, with the movements taking on more specific national coloration: Futurism from Italy; Dada and Surrealism from Zurich, Paris, and New York; Constructivism from Russia. Finally, the nationalistic 1930s is represented in the Social Realism of American art, the socialist realism of the Soviet Union, and the folk and nationalistic themes of Nazi and Fascist art. Then, following the Second World War, a new hegemon and a new center of world art—New York—saw a turn from Social Realism to generalized abstraction. Such abstraction is a negation of the social and national subject in favor of the transnational order and uniformity that is the hegemonic peace. Social and national imagery stay out of visual representation until the hegemon declines. Then, clearly seen in the 1980s, comes the return of the social subject, the particular, and the emergence of another period of realism.

Can this be generalized to earlier centuries? Does the world-system have long cycles of modes of visual representation in the same way it has economic and political cycles? The answer is yes. Forms of expression not only cyclically repeat but more interestingly co-vary with the hegemony/rivalry cycle (see Table 14.1). Further, these cycles of visual form partake in reproducing hegemonic domination and mobilizing state populations for interstate conflict.

For instance, in a world of hegemonic decline, such as the last quarter of the 19th century, the Impressionists purposely painted in open air, rather than using studio figures indoors. They painted light and reality as it is, not as it should be—reality as fact, not morals, ideals, principles, not therefore the cognitive and moral expression of power, constraint, and hierarchy. Vision without hegemony is naturalism. It is the eye without the overlay of a moral grid that not only structures and orders space but also tightens, controls, contours, shapes, and smoothes edges.

Between hegemonies, the eye is more uncontrolled. Following the Hapsburg hegemony came the conflictual 17th century and the swirls, twists, and jumbles of the Baroque. Following British hegemony in the late 19th century came the light of day, falling unstructured on people in the non-posed, relaxed, casual scenes of Impressionism. These are not the classically posed figures carrying out religious or historical themes of Neoclassicism under British hegemony, but the gritty images of lumped and ordinary bodies at work in Courbet and Millet's realism and the ordinary, nonclassical, nonidealized scenes of the fleeting snapshot like pictures of the Impressionists. Finally, following the American hegemony came the realism of the anti-abstract multicultural postmodernism of the late 20th century. With hegemonic decline, it is as if the artistic coat hanger of form, constant coloration, formal perspective, composition in ordered planes, and standardized fixed historical/mythical themes is now removed, allowing figures, scenes, buildings, and sculpture to drop, flop, and relax, moving in liberation from the hegemonic grid of formal composition.

During such periods of heightened international rivalry, there is a thaw in the orderliness of vision. The eye is now unconstrained and free to move, seeing in less formally ordered terms. During these rivalry phases of the hegemonic cycle, the socially particular reappears as church, state, aristocracy, and bourgeoisie and more recently as gender, race, ethnicity, and sexual preference. As hegemonic singularity lessens, non-hegemonic subjects reappear. If the one declines, the others grow, strengthen, and declare their interests, needs, wants, and desires, as the politically correct post-hegemonic 1990s Multicultural Art makes so clear. The social subjects, rather than the hegemonic subject of historical myth in formal classical modeling or modernist abstraction of a formality of line, shape, and color, are now empowered to express a socially situated voice. They visually exist, for a while at least, until the next winter of hegemony and the closing down of the code of expression, restricting the language of art to more minimalist expression and more classic poses.

HOW ART EXERCISES HEGEMONY

If art under rivalry emphasizes the specific and the many, art under hegemony emphasizes the general and the one. Art under hegemony acts hegemonic. General principles take precedence over particularities of region and nation, and in this way the interests of particular states, classes, or regions are suppressed. The unity of hegemonic order is visually manifest in the unity of formal compositional order. Hegemonic decline produces national competition, and art shifts to more naturalistic modes that allow the signaling of national difference and the mobilization of national populations around landscapes and folk traditions—that is, around the totemic structures of nationalism. Under hegemony, more classical, formal, idealized, and abstract figuration negates the national identity of other states that might resist the hegemon's intrusions. It is art in the service of power. Conversely, particularistic naturalism is a symbolic weapon in international struggle, aiding the mobilization of domestic populations, instilling loyalty, patriotism, and in highly politicized realism, conducting propaganda war against the foreigner. I am not talking just about the so-called political art of the 1930s. That is only the final stage and most explicit form of nationally political art.

Naturalism, then, is no more political than abstraction. Both serve power, but power at different levels of the world-system. Naturalism mobilizes populations *within* nations, accentuates *national* difference, and pits nation against nation. Classicism/Abstraction/idealism masks and suppresses national differences, thereby reducing national resistance to hegemonic domination and facilitates peaceful hegemonic penetration of not only world markets but also world consciousness. Cultural hegemony, then, is more than peripheral people's use of symbolic products of the core (e.g., music, art, dance, ideas). It is also the opening of global consciousness and a stripping or negation of national identity. What is known as *identity politics,* then, is a B-phase phenomenon when non-hegemonic groups within the hegemonic state (women, people of color, minorities) and other non-hegemonic states reclaim their identity through group-specific and nation-specific cultural expression.

As there is an opening and a closing of markets, opened with the power of a hegemon (free trade under hegemony), so there is an opening and closing of consciousness, opened under the general rules of hegemonic art, which does not allow a coagulation of consciousness around the nation and its national interest. Tariff barriers of B-phase rivalry close markets around national boundaries, and the more explicit time/space coordinates of realism/naturalism close visual consciousness around national imagery, preventing the cultural penetration of the hegemon. In the economic sphere, free trade is, in fact, a forced openness to the goods of the hegemon. It is eventually resisted when the hegemon declines and tariff barriers rise as national markets are protected during the crisis phase of downturn. In the cultural sphere, the emphasis on classical modeling and, more recently, pure abstraction act to similarly pry open national consciousness and are resisted only with hegemonic decline and national resistance in the form of time- and place-specific realism. Realism/naturalism, then, is resistance by the national society to the larger symbolic intrusions of the hegemon during the early phase of hegemonic decline. When decline turns to rivalry, competition, and overt conflict, then realism becomes a mobilization weapon for international conflict.

THE LONG WAVE OF ART HISTORY

The modern world-system of art has been through three hegemonies (Spanish/Hapsburg, British, United States), two between-hegemony periods of accelerated state rivalry (17th and mid-19th to mid-20th centuries), and is now beginning another rivalry period (1980s-   ). What follows is a brief outline of the different styles that appeared in these periods.

RENAISSANCE (1450-1550):
FIRST HEGEMONY AND CLASSIC FORM

The commencement of the modern world-system in the 16th century (1450-1550) is a period dominated by the Hapsburg hegemony in international politics and the Renaissance in art history. Political economy and cultural form are linked. Many of the key properties of Renaissance art will repeat during the later periods of British and then American hegemony. Although art historians have long noted the change from Renaissance emphasis on symmetry, balance, and order to the more painterly, twisting, swirling, emotion-filled images of the 17th-century Baroque, what has not been noted is that this change in art corresponds to the shift from the Hapsburg/Spanish hegemony of the 16th century to the plural world of state conflict of the 17th century. Because Renaissance and Baroque forms are international cultural movements they require a trans-societal or world-systemic explanation. The sociology of art must give way to a globology of art, the Durkheimian maxim that collective facts require collective explanations. Worldwide art movements require worldwide explanations.[4]

The High Renaissance emphasis on perspective and the use of line in ordering composition and its placement parallel with the picture plane (Panofsky, 1991; Wolfflin, 1929) represents the ascendancy of general principles of formal composition over naturally depicted content. Obvious differences are found between the Renaissance in the Netherlandish and German north—Hans Holbein, Albrecht Dürer, Matthias Grünewald, and Albrecht Altdorfer—and in the Italian south—da Vinci, Raphael, Michelangelo—but a common difference between earlier Gothic and later Baroque allows the Renaissance to be spoken of as a European-wide movement. Forms of art and conditions of hegemony are both collective properties of the world-system, and it is at this level that the logic of theoretical causation is being drawn. This mapping may seem crude, but the pattern is there. What is going on world-systemically in culture is the Renaissance. What is going on in political/economy is the first modern hegemony. And when hegemony turns to rivalry in the next century, art turns to the Baroque. When hegemony returns under Britain at the end of the 18th century, the Baroque/Rococo turns to another art of balance, symmetry, and classical form: Neoclassicism. Systematic variation in the world-system is empirically associated with systematic variation in style.

The Transition Period. During the height of hegemony, or rivalry, the coded forms, or languages, of art are in sync with the world-systemic distribution of power. But transition zones occur when the hegemon is both declining and ascending. Given the propensity for cultural forms to lag behind material social change, a lag in styles of art emerges. Specifically, when the hegemon begins to decline art is still in its more classic universal form, like the Renaissance, but also Neoclassicism under British and Abstraction under American hegemony. These forms are no longer in accord with the new reality of an ever more plural and rivalrous world. On the other side of the cycle, the upswing into hegemony when power is consolidating, art forms are also locked into the past, except this time it is particularistic naturalizing modes of the plural rivalrous phase, now out of sync when the world is moving toward another hegemony.

There are, then, two transition zones: one in the transition from hegemony to rivalry (post-hegemony), and the other the transition from rivalry to hegemony (pre-hegemony). The transition zone produces two opposite types of art: art codes without a material base (the older form when the system in moving on) and a material base without established art codes—that is, a desire to express the new material conditions when there is as yet no established art style.

A stable condition exists during the height of either hegemony or rivalry, as art form and world-system base are in sync, as the social forces of hegemony are expressed in the formal artistic universalism and the forces of rivalry expressed in naturalism, as the following diagram illustrates.

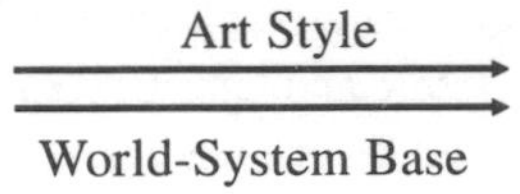

Art Style
_____>
_____>
World-System Base

Now, a change in the world-system, from hegemony to rivalry or from rivalry to hegemony, creates the cultural lag phenomenon as material conditions change more quickly than accepted, established, received forms of artistic expression. As diagramed below, the base moves more quickly than its collective representation. In Durkheimian terms, this creates totems without tribes (A) and tribes without totems (B).

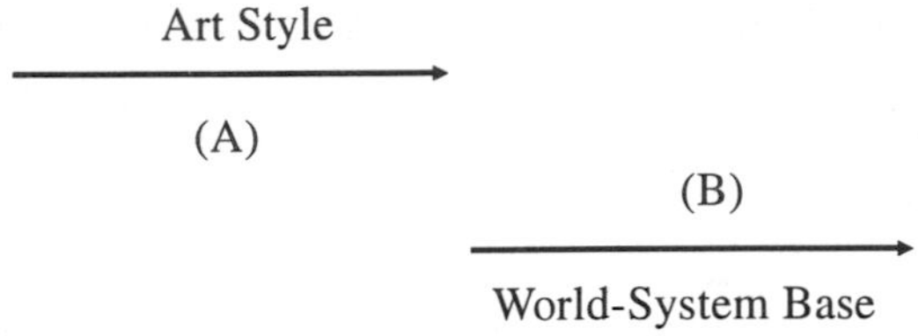

Art Style
_____>
(A)

                                            (B)
                                    _____>
                                    World-System Base

When the world-system is moving from hegemony to rivalry, art is heavy, pretentious, and overintellectualized. It is the older universal forms of hegemonic art in a world where hegemony is declining. It is a pretense without the power base to back it up. At the same time, the new situation of pluralism does not yet have sufficient form for its expression, and so this produces emergent forms of expression outside established channels, such as bohemias, avant-gardes, and revolutionary art movements (B above). Transition, then, produces both a stilted art from the past and a new avant-garde trying to capture the emerging social forces of the future. What this means for the sociology of art is that mannered Academic Art and bohemian avant-gardism are both produced by the cyclic rhythms of the larger world-system.

The same process operates at the other transition, from rivalry back to hegemony, except here the effect is different. The particularism of the rivalry phase is now out of sync with the concentration of power of the emerging hegemony, and the art form is insufficient to carry the gravity, weight, and universalism of the hegemonic era. The result is the appearance of styles that appear light and frivolous. Eventually, the new conditions give rise to new forms of expression that capture the new social forces, and the older forms recede. Style and world-system material base are again in sync, as diagramed below.

Art Style

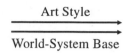

World-System Base

Four Stages of the World Art History Cycle. These transition zones represent identifiable stages of style. Elements of lag are found here, but artists do represent their historical period; it is just that their time is one of historical transition from hegemony to rivalry or rivalry back to hegemony. Artists represent the present, but the present is a combination of past and future social conditions. As listed below, the world art cycle has four stages: hegemony and rivalry, and the transitions to hegemony and to rivalry.

Stage 1: The art of hegemonic dominance
   High Renaissance (1500-1520)
   Neoclassicism/Romanticism (1750-1850)
   Abstract Expressionism/Minimalism (1950-1970)

Stage 2: The art of hegemonic decline
   Mannerism (1520-1600)
   Academic Art (mid-1800s)
   Conceptual Art (1970s)

Stage 3: The art of interstate rivalry
   Baroque (1600-1700)
   Realism to Social Realism (1850-1950)
   Multicultural Art (1980s-   )

Stage 4: The art of hegemonic ascent
   Rococo (1700-1750)
   Art Deco (1920s-1940s)

MANNERISM (1520-1600): THE FIRST ART OF HEGEMONIC DECLINE

The first such period between the hegemonic art of the mid-16th century and the rivalrous Baroque of the 17th is Mannerism (1520-1600). Here, the symmetry, balance, and proportional order of the Renaissance becomes more contrived, jumbled, and awkward, with fanciful gestures, distortions, exaggerations, and bizarre posturing. Such art can be best understood in the context of the hegemonic center declining, leaving the once symmetrical and balanced forms to sag, twist, and fall in on themselves and thus create the famed crowded and awkward effects of Pontormo, Rosso, Parmigianino, Tintoretto, El Greco, and other mannerist painters. Forms of expression will eventually catch up with the new international conditions of the 17th century, as art is moving toward the energized swirl of the Baroque. But it is still in Renaissance form, and this creates that halfway position of jumbled crowded composition that distinguishes Mannerism. As a declining hegemonic formalism, Mannerism could be called the first postmodernism—that is, a post-hegemonic praise of unstructured, jumbled, juxtaposed forms. This is the world of hegemonic decline where universal expression fades, but is not yet replaced by the national particularisms of the rivalrous phase. Modernism— the culture of universal form under American hegemony—is like Renaissance classicism, the universal form of the earlier Hapsburg hegemony. Post-hegemony produces the anticlassicism of Mannerism and the antiformalism of postmodernism. On the more general intellectual plane, both are periods of skepticism and doubt, a shiver of realization that the universals of Renaissance humanism or modernist theory from Marx to Freud are no longer valid and applicable to the problems of the day. The certainty of Renaissance and modernist ideals is in doubt in the Mannerist and Postmodern worlds of hegemonic decline.

BAROQUE (1600-1700): INTERSTATE
RIVALRY AND STATE EMOTIONALISM

From hegemony in the 16th century, the world-system swings to the rivalrous and crisis-prone 17th, which produces a more dramatic, pompous, elaborate, and ornate art that dramatizes the nation-state and its institutional infrastructure. The simple classical balance and symmetry of Raphael, da Vinci, and Michelangelo during the High Renaissance give way to the use of real-life models for religious figures in Caravaggio; ornate, emotion-filled turbulence of painterly flows and swirls of Rubens and Velazquez; the dynamic and explosive sculpture of Bernini; the lively portraits of Hals; the emotion-filled use of light and shadow in the figure modeling of Rembrandt; and the dramatic, emotion-filled architecture of ornate churches and palaces such as Versailles. Such heightened drama and emotion mobilize sentiment and political allegiance to the absolutist state for war, colonial expansion, and mercantile economics.

The Baroque is art serving national purpose. Fueled by social conflict and international rivalry, it is the cultural expression of the reorganization phase of the world-economy's long developmental swings. The decline of the Spanish/ Hapsburg hegemonic order manifests itself in the decline in the pictorial order of symmetry, balance, line, and plane as the predominant principles of art. The eye now coalesces around the nation and its people, in royal and aristocratic pose, and in bourgeois images of domestic life. Local scene and social circumstance replace the classic formalism that was the transnational grid of hegemonic art.

ROCOCO (1700-1750): HEGEMONIC
ASCENT AND LIGHT FORMS

Between the 17th-century Baroque and the art that appears under British hegemony lies another transitional zone between rivalry and hegemony. Whereas Mannerism was the art of hegemonic decline, Rococo is the art of hegemonic ascent. The underlying process is the same. Material conditions are once again changing more quickly than their cultural expression. The Baroque art of national particularism and international rivalry is now, going into the 18th century, the art of the past, as the world moves toward a new hegemony: Britain. With Mannerism, the world moved toward pluralism and thus made this post-hegemonic art heavy and cumbersome. Now, with the move toward hegemony, the experience is just the opposite. Power is concentrating, and Baroque forms, by their very nature, cannot represent the experiences produced by the consolidation of global power that is the emerging British hegemony in the 18th century. The new social situation begs larger, more general, more idealized modes of expression, and until the arrival of Neoclassicism around 1750, the existing forms become, in relation to their base, too light, thin, and frivolous. The changing base, combined with the cultural lag, transforms art from forceful expression (Baroque) to more surface decoration (Rococo). Without the competitive energy of absolutist state rivalry the particularism of the Baroque becomes lighter, just as Mannerism on the other side of the cycle became heavier. Rather than not being able to carry the new plural world experience, it is a plural art that cannot carry the social needs of an emerging concentration of world power.

The result is Rococo, a style that is light, airy, and dominated by pastel colors of light blue, yellow, and white, with twisted floral patterns that seem to float. Where the Baroque dramatized national interests through architectural space, Rococo is more of an interior design of surface decoration, floral pattern, and gold-gilded edges to white walls and door panels. It is the ornate drama of the Baroque without the national rivalries to drive it; hence, it is light, fluffy, and airy and gives the feel of frivolous indulgence, rather than firmly asserted national purpose. The once-public Baroque is now a private indulgence; the architectural massiveness of public statement is now, given the emerging hegemon's evaporation of rivalrous energy, indoor wall decoration, rather than an exterior facade projecting national power. British hegemony is coming with the defeat of their remaining rival, the French (the Treaty of Paris, 1763); the experience of the world is moving toward hegemonic seriousness and ordered, regulated, classic, formal experience, which will appear from 1750 onward in the rise of the Neoclassical style.

NEOCLASSICAL/ROMANTICISM (1750-1850):
THE ART OF BRITISH HEGEMONY

These cycles of art history do not really become apparent until the rise of another hegemon and the start of another cycle.[5] From hegemony in the 16th century to rivalry in the 17th century, the world-system moves back to hegemony at the end of the 18th century. With this is a second wave of hegemonic universalism in both art and thought—not the classicism of the first hegemony, but now a "Neoclassicism" of David, Ingres, West, and J. S. Copley in painting; Canova in sculpture; and Greco-Roman architectural imitation such as Thomas Jefferson's design for the University of Virginia. With the rise of Britain in the second half of the 18th century comes a notable turn away from the emotion-filled ostentatious drama of the Baroque/Rococo toward Winckelmann's ordered calm of classical style.

Mid-18th-century anti-Rococo sentiment is general, found in political and economic theory, as well as in art and architecture. The theory of the universal individual rises at the expense of theorizing corporate groups. The Enlightenment places great value on the universal rights of discrete individuals, as opposed to the rights of corporate bodies found in earlier mercantile theory. Similarly, Adam Smith's 1776 principle of the division of labor raises the absolute individual above the social collectivity in causal priority within economic theory. The collective regains priority in theory only with hegemonic decline after the middle of the 19th century; this can be seen in the rise of sociology and Marxism. Theoretical biases toward collectivism or individualism swing back and forth in theory, depending on the cyclical undulations of the world-system. Theory now socializes the subject as the Marx of class and mode rises to challenge the Smithian individual and utilitarian decision maker. Now, with the decline of transhistorical individualism, the historically situated group, class, and social formation recede and make possible the individual in theoretical logic.

The Romantic movement of the early 19th century is usually paired with Neoclassicism even though, on the surface, they seem quite different. Romanticism, though, concerns ultimates and eternals, in this case nature and all-powerful natural forces. These are general trans-social forces and raise the universalism of personal feeling above its shaped definition by the historically specific social factors of class, caste, region, or nationality. The key point is that Romantic sensibility is universal, not bound by class, caste, gender, or nation, and as such it is a manifestation of hegemonic culture.

ACADEMIC ART (MID-1800s): HEGEMONIC
DECLINE AND WEIGHTY FORMALISM

Around the middle of the 19th century, British hegemony peaks, to be followed by decline through the second half of the century. Mannerism in the latter part of the 16th century was Renaissance forms devoid of hegemonic energy; a similar cultural lag occurs in the middle of the 19th century. Here, the growing pluralization of the world-system reduces the hegemonic ability to inflate and energize the historical scenes and figures of Neoclassical art and results in more wooden and formalistic painting of mythology and historical scenes that is the Academic Art of the salons. In this transition zone emerge new forms of naturalism and particularism, the social face of art that is at first realism and later Impressionism/Postimpressionism.

REALISM TO SOCIAL REALISM (1850-1950):
ART BETWEEN HEGEMONIES

From the mid-19th to the mid-20th century, world art is in a particularizing realist mode as it falls between the universalizing tendencies produced by the bracketing British and American hegemonies. Abstract Expressionism under American hegemony is the universalizing form that is the analog to the

Neoclassicism/Romanticism of British hegemony and the Renaissance classicism of the 16th-century Spanish/Hapsburg hegemony. Between these three
hegemonies lies the particularizing art dramatizing the nationalism of hegemonic
succession struggles in the Baroque of 1600-1700, the realism to Social
Realism of 1850-1950, and multicultural realism since the 1980s. During the
period between British and American hegemony, art mobilizes and binds
national populations to their particular states. As the world-system degen-
erates into the conflict of the Second Thirty Years War (1914-1945), art is
more and more in the service of nationalism. Over this roughly one-hundred-
year period, art moves from a more neutral representation of people and place,
to filling in their surrounding social structure, customs, and manners, and,
finally, to bringing in the political with manifesto-accompanied art movements. By the 1930s, art comes to fully serve the nation in patriotic renditions
of a love of country. This sequential order of art styles between hegemonies
is one of ever-increasing socialization/nationalization of theme and content.
This overall politicization of art appears in four identifiable stages.

1. *Neutral realism: People and places.* First is the mid-19th-century realism
of Courbet and Millet, of ordinary figures, nonclassically posed, appearing in
ordinary light, performing ordinary tasks. It is the first step away from the
formal classicism of hegemonic Neoclassical/Romantic art and the mannerist
stage of academic salon art. The analog for American decline a century later
is the neorealism that stands in contrast to the formalism of Abstract modernism and the 20th-century Mannerism, 1970s Conceptual Art.

2. *Institutional realism: Painting in social space.* With hegemonic order
breaking down during the last quarter of the 19th century, art comes more and
more to the service of the nation and begins to visually represent national
social structure. Painting represents social and institutional space with Impressionism and its urban scenescapes and bourgeois social mannerisms of
people relaxed and at play. Class, status, and manners, the social, is increasingly the subject matter of art. The picture of the nation is taking shape in visual
consciousness as the world balkanizes into a plurality of competitive states.

3. *Manifesto realism: Adding a political program.* Into the 20th century,
Cubism, though seemingly abstract, in fact continues realism by focusing on
the deeper reality of underlying structures and compositional form. Whereas
realism, Impressionism, Postimpressionism, and to some extent Cubism represent more general styles, the art movements of the early 20th century
become increasingly associated with and limited to their national origin. The

growing balkanization of the world economy is reflected in a growing balkanization of modern art movements. In both the economy and the culture, things are turning inward. With growing protectionism and rising tariff barriers in a deteriorating world-economy, world art increasingly loses its transnational character and comes to reside in, reflect, and be used for the national interests of the polities in which it is produced. The politicization of art is also seen in the fact that art movements are increasingly accompanied by manifestoes and social programs for social transformation. Whereas 19th-century realism was something of a European-wide movement, into the 20th century, particularism in art predominates. From Italy comes Futurism; from Germany, Expressionism; from Russia, suprematism and Constructivism; from Zurich, Paris, and New York, Dadaism and Surrealism. These nationally specific movements in culture close off national boundaries of consciousness the way nationally specific tariffs close off national markets.

4. *Social Realism (1930s): Serving the nation.* Finally, by the 1930s, many art movements are explicitly nationalist and patriotic, and the turn is against avant-garde experimentation in favor of art that depicts politics—whether critical of system and class division as in the United States (Social Realists) or nostalgic folk nationalism found everywhere from capitalist to communist to fascist states. Love of country, people, and national traditions sweeps across the prewar balkanized world-system in the 1930s.

ART DECO (1920s-1940s):
20TH-CENTURY ROCOCO

Art Deco of the early 20th century is an instance of pre-hegemonic expression. Like Rococo, Art Deco is similarly more of a decorative style, with identifiable motifs, this time of the industrial age with geometric and Cubist influences and more stark colors. Rather than representing the interests of an indulgent aristocracy, now, centuries later, it reflects an indulgent bourgeoisie. Classes may rise and fall and elites may circulate, but the transitional stage of pre-hegemony still produces a light, decorative style.

ABSTRACT EXPRESSIONISM/
MINIMALISM (1950s-1970s): AMERICAN HEGEMONY

The center of the art world shifts from Paris to New York after 1945 with the ascendance of American hegemony. Another period of nongrounded generalized art emerges, this time as abstraction.[6] With the end of the Second World War and the decline of national rivalries among the capitalist powers, socially specific realism declines and is replaced by the transnational code of American-initiated abstraction. This hegemonic art negates national identities in favor of a purity and singularity of abstract splashes and dabs of pigment under Abstract Expressionism and then a further tightening of the hegemonic artistic code under the simple geometric hard-edged forms of 1960s Minimalism. The social and the national are banned from consciousness as pure form occupies the representational energies of advanced art.[7]

Abstract Expressionism is not the classicism of grand historical themes, religious imagery, or Greco-Roman architecture that characterized earlier hegemonies. But Abstract Expressionism is a similar rise in priority of form over any specific content and composition along the flat plane that Wolfflin identified with Renaissance art. The clean lines, symmetry, and balance of Renaissance architecture are also seen in the ascendance of the international style of the glass and steel office building[8] and the popularity of the slim, sparse, minimalist Danish modern style of 1950s furniture design. Like the concern with the essentialness of the human condition in the Renaissance or the universal power of natural forces in Romanticism, under the new hegemony the search for ultimate individual essence is expressed in the popularity of existentialism in philosophy, the Keynesian formalization of economic theory by Paul Samuelson, and the Abstract formalism in sociology of Talcott Parsons. With hegemonic decline comes a reassertion of the particular, the historic, and the social, as seen in the rise of a neo-Marxism, a turn against general Abstract theory in postmodernism, and an assertion of theoretical priority from the perspective of gender, race, ethnicity, and sexual preference.

CONCEPTUAL ART (1970s): 20TH-CENTURY
MANNERISM, HEGEMONIC DECLINE

The culture lag that produced Mannerism and Academic Art appears once again. In the 1970s, American hegemony is starting its decline while the universal cultural form, modernist abstraction, is still in place. This creates another gap between form and base and another period of strained, heavy, pompous, intellectualized art—1970s Conceptual Art, with all its weighty pseudophilosophical posturing. Mannerism was universal Renaissance form in a pluralizing world. Conceptual Art is universal modernism in a pluralizing

20th-century context. Overintellectualized art soon passes with the emergence in the later 1970s of a neorealism and in the 1980s a multicultural realism that once again puts the social subject back in artistic representation. The world at the end of the 20th century is strikingly similar to that at the end of the 16th and mid-19th centuries. Politically, hegemonies have peaked; culturally, there is a dissatisfaction with formalisms and a turn to realism/naturalism to represent social and political themes.

NEOREALISM/MULTICULTURALISM (1980s-   ):
TOWARD A RIVALROUS WORLD

Hegemonies do not last, and neither do their cultural forms. With American decline, formalism withered and realism once again appeared, just as it did with British decline a century earlier. Because this was a new realism, it was dubbed *neorealism.* This more neutral realism is increasingly socialized with the rise of the more Multicultural Art of gender, race, ethnicity, and sexual preference. Since the 1980s, the interests, struggles, and political concerns of social groups mattered more than issues of form, line, and shape—that is, more than formalistic modernism. It is now art for society's sake, or at least for the subgroups represented. The turn from the general and the universal in both the arts and social theory is considered "postmodern," which is another way of saying post-hegemony.

CONCLUSION

This outline is but a beginning. Much is left out, and much will no doubt be revised. But the world historical perspective on economic and political development, so well represented by Frank, is clearly applicable to cultural forms. As economic development is no longer thought of as a linear sequence of stage after stage and mode after mode, so too must we no longer think of art historical development as style after style. Cycles occur in the world economy, and cycles occur in world art. Further, these art historical and hegemony/rivalry cycles are synchronized. Hegemony produces one kind of art; rivalry another. Art fluctuates, yes, but in accord with fluctuations in the world-system.

NOTES

1. Cyclic theories of art do exist, such as the Archaic to Classic to Hellenistic (growth, maturity, decline) notion that is sometimes applied to the early Renaissance, High Renaissance, Baroque sequence; Sorokin's (1937) ideational versus sensate pulsations; Wolfflin's (1929) classic to Baroque cycle; and Kroeber's (1944) patterns of cultural growth. But such cycles and phases of cycles are not connected to phases of political/economic cycles. Art cycles, when discussed, are seen mostly as endogenous phenomena. They rise and fall on their own or as part of the "spirit of the age," which is still a cultural matter.

2. Frank believes that world history can be traced back five thousand years. That may very well be, and I am open on this issue. At this point, though, I simply wish to identify patterns of culture within the past five hundred years of world history without precluding the possibility of earlier movements.

3. There are also structural constants, such as the core-periphery hierarchy, and long-term trends, such as continued growth in production, trade, and severity of war; these should also be reflected in the structure and content of world culture. It is my task here, though, to principally deal with cyclic rhythms.

4. Unincorporated areas outside the world-system's structural parameters have the logic of the local social system of which they are a part.

5. There is sufficient debate over whether the Dutch in the middle of the 17th century may be considered hegemonic. This work accepts the position that they were not.

6. I am aware, of course, of earlier 20th-century instances of Abstract art (e.g., Piet Mondrian, Malevich) and that socialist realism continues within communist states. But if we are to speak of more general movements of world culture, if we are interested in central tendencies, as slippery as that seems to the descriptive specificity of the art historian, then it seems fair to assert that the postwar period was a major shift toward abstraction as the leading edge of modern art.

7. This movement can also be found in modern dance; see Bergesen and Jones (1991).

8. Although there are earlier origins of Bauhaus formalism, the 1950s-1960s is when the steel and glass skyscraper becomes a predominant form of architecture.

REFERENCES

Bergesen, A. (1995). Postmodernism and the world-system. *Protosoziologie, 7,* 54-59.

Bergesen, A., & Jones, A. (1991). Decoding modern dance. In R. Wuthnow (Ed.), *Vocabularies of public life* (pp. 169-181). New York: Routledge.

Kroeber, A. L. (1944). *Configurations of cultural growth.* Berkeley: University of California Press.

Panofsky, E. (1991). *Perspective as symbolic form* (C. S. Wood, Trans.). New York: Zone Books.

Solomon, D. (1992, September 6). The Cologne challenge: Is New York's art monopoly kaput? *New York Times Magazine,* p. 22.

Sorokin, P. A. (1937). *Social and cultural dynamics.* New York: American Book.

Wolfflin, H. (1929). *Principles of art history: The problem of the development of style in later art* (M. D. Hottinger, Trans.). New York: Dover.

PART IV

On Social Movements and Social Justice

15

Social Movements
in the Underdevelopment
of Development Dialectic

A View From Below

GERRIT HUIZER

Andre Frank's gradual discovery of the underdevelopment of development started with the top "Chicago Boys," who did not play with these terms but rather intended to "develop," if not manipulate, global policies and projects. My own process of the same discovery started, also in the 1950s and early 1960s, at the opposite side of the social scale: among peasants and women who suffered the consequences of those policies and projects in the interplay or dialectic of "community development" and "social movements" in many parts of the Third World.

In the mid-1960s, when Frank was briefly working for the United Nations Economic Commission for Latin America (ECLA), to which I was also attached, we discovered that our experiences and findings, though coming from different sides, seemed to confirm one another. He was finalizing his for ECLA circles' controversial paper that became known as "The Indian Problem" (Frank,

1967). This paper, originally circulated in mimeo form, showed, with many quotations from Eric Wolf and Rodolfo Stavenhagen, that the problem of the Indian peoples in Mexico and other Latin American countries was not that they lacked economic integration or acculturation, as many mainstream anthropologists, like Redfield, thought. The problem was that they had been integrated into the capitalist system for several hundred years through (class) exploitation or as a labor reserve. At that time, I was also trying to show, in a debate with Benno Galjart in *America Latina,* that "class-struggle" did exist in the rural areas of Latin America and elsewhere where I had been a development worker and organizer (Galjart, 1964; Huizer, 1965b).

Although Frank and I had few differences of opinion on such facts and their contexts, we used different ways to present our findings. Whereas Frank bluntly attacked the established mainstream opinions, I "cepalized" (CEPAL is Spanish for ECLA) my language and tried to influence and contribute to the radicalization of UN-sponsored policies in the field of rural development. This worked to some extent. Social movements (peasant organizations) became, in the mid-1960s in UN circles, an important factor to be supported as a precondition for measures such as land reform that were then considered essential for any feasible rural development policy (see United Nations, 1968, of which I drafted some parts).

During the following years, I could experience from within and from below how these more or less radical reformist developments in UN-sponsored policies were systematically blocked and underdeveloped, particularly through overt and covert, direct and indirect Western, particularly U.S., influence as an old UN colleague, Riad El Ghonemy (1990), later demonstrated. I highlight some elements of this influence but should mention that the U.S. policy interventions were themselves a reaction to social movements that had taken place before, during, and shortly after the Second World War, particularly in China. In that country, the usefulness of land reform as a starting point for overall rural and industrial development had been clearly shown (see World Bank, 1983, for an overview). And as Frank (1991) observes, "The Chinese Communist peasant victory among one quarter of the world's population in 1949 put the fear of God in many minds; they feared its extension or indigenous repetition in newly independent India, self-liberated Korea, and elsewhere" (p.21).

Currently, the literature in the social sciences about social movements is extensive, and many definitions have proliferated. I am aware that, by not presenting any precise definition, I could provoke the same criticism of "conceptual imprecision" that Dhanagare and John (1988, p. 1090) gave to the "nine theses on social movements" by Frank and Fuentes (1987). I do not even pretend, however, to give any theses or hypotheses or to enter into theoretical issues regarding social movements; I merely review some grassroots experiences in the dialectical relationship of development and underdevelopment and raise some practical questions particularly relevant to those involved with the "agenda" for "antisystemic" social movements as proposed by Wallerstein (1990, pp. 48-53), I suppose in connivance with Frank and Fuentes (1990a). As Wallerstein recommended, I will try to emphasize the common elements between the variety of antisystemic social movements and their possible convergences, rather than differences. The questions I deal with mainly concern the role of voluntarism and leadership in social movements and the probably as crucial role of leading figures in the power groupings to which antisystemic movements are opposed.

Frank and Fuentes (1987, pp. 1503-1510) stated that social movements, particularly of the type commonly called "new" (to distinguish them from "classical" social movements, such as labor union movements), have existed since time immemorial. Among these are ethnic, peasant, slave, women's, religious, and other broad movements that have influenced social transformation or even taken over state power. Such movements continue to play crucial roles, though they may take new forms, such as indigenous, the green, and the peace movements. This certainly is confirmed by my own experience with a great variety of movements in Third World countries, as well as in the West. I thus also have noticed a growing relationship, though often indirect, between movements there and here: a kind of globalization. This indeed seems also to have gone on for many centuries.

It could be interesting to discuss the many movements that have played a role in the history of globalization, the emergence of the world system, probably indeed for about five thousand years as Frank (Frank & Gills, 1993) tries to prove with considerable evidence. Most of these movements seem to have religious/ideological/cultural implications that too often have been ignored by those concerned with the world system. Some of them started one to three millennia ago and have continued, as more or less institutionalized ideological currents or world religions, to be influential in present-day globalization processes. These include Confucianism, Daoism, Buddhism, Christianity, and Islam. However, in view of our concern with the underdevelopment of present development ideology and the continuous underdevelopment of large sectors of the Third World's population, recently joined in this fate by many from the Second World, if not the First, I deal mainly with social movements taking place during the current century and, I hope, the beginning of the next one too.

Some generalizing (but not really defining) statements could be made on such movements in the past. They were mostly initiated by charismatic personalities, and after gaining considerable following became institutionalized, structured, or routinized, often in a very hierarchical manner that sometimes provoked new, heretical movements that competed successfully or not with the original ones (see Mühlmann, 1962; Weber, 1956). The sociology of religion/ideology has observed relationships, mostly not very clear, between such movements and the political-economic circumstances (often in flux) under which they emerged. Often, they were initially antisystemic but almost as often transformed themselves to become part of the system or to create a new one. Frank and Fuentes's (1990a) hypothesis that social movements follow certain cycles or waves, comparable to or even parallel with the Kondratieff cycles, appears to make sense. The question remains to what extent they are determined by economic trends, if they are, and to what extent they themselves influence those trends.

Samir Amin, Giovanni Arrighi, Andre Gunder Frank, and Immanuel Wallerstein (1990) tried to come to grips with the role of antisystemic movements during the previous 150 to 200 years. Frank and Fuentes (1990a) give evidence that, in the areas where the world economic trends were most strongly felt—in Western Europe and the United States and those Third World areas most strongly dominated by or integrated into the Western capitalist economy—social movements of peasants or workers and those for anticolonial or environmental protest were strong. They observed considerable "coincidences" in the emergence and decline of a variety of social movements in different countries and continents, perhaps reacting more or less simultaneously to changing historical circumstances. Both authors openly recognized, however, that they have a different opinion regarding the cyclical nature of movements, Fuentes arguing that this idea implies too much economic determinism that leaves too little room for "voluntarism."

From my own observations and experience, I would say that the voluntarist element is visible in the roles of social actors—powerholders on the one hand, and opposing leading personalities capable of mobilizing a following on the other hand. To avoid too strong an emphasis on the role of persons as actors, the concept of "strategic groups," introduced by Hans-Dieter Evers (Evers & Schiel, 1988), can be useful. The powerholders, as well as their opponents, are not purely individual actors; they operate in some kind of grouping. Evers (Evers & Schiel, 1988, pp. 92-98), when discussing the bourgeoisie (capitalists), landowners, and wage laborers as classes, proposed the concept of strategic group as possibly corresponding to what Marx was developing when he elaborated the conceptualization of different classes in his unfinished last chapter of *Capital.*

Marx himself, in his life and works, implied a good measure of "voluntarism" in what he said about the working class as well as the "bourgeoisie," the force behind the creation of the world market and the growing of what he called "universal intercourse, of all-round interdependence of the nations":

> That which characterizes the bourgeois epoch in contradistinction to all others is a continuous transformation of production, a perpetual disturbance of social conditions, everlasting insecurity and movement. All stable and stereotyped relations with their attendant train of ancient and venerable prejudices and opinions, are swept away, and the newly formed becomes obsolete before it can petrify. All that has been regarded as solid crumbles into fragments; all that was looked upon as holy, is profaned; at long last, people are compelled to gaze open-eyed at their position in life and their social relations. (Marx, 1848/1962, pp. 48-49)

The role of voluntarism is a difficult one in social research because it implies some measure of subjectivity, the role of the subject(s), including perhaps the researchers themselves and their stand in certain cases. On the one hand, there is no doubt that certain trends in macro- or microsocioeconomic conditions (e.g., the Kondratieff cycles, forms of underdevelopment) are related to the emergence of social movements. On the other hand, one has to take into account the level of consciousness about the effects of such trends and the willingness and ability of people or strategic groups of the elites to react to such trends or not.

In their effort to come to grips with the emergence and decline (or repression) of social movements in a more or less cyclical manner, Frank and Fuentes mostly overlooked the variety of strategies used by the "enemies" against whom most social movements have felt the need to move. One of the most successful social movement organizers, the Chinese peasant leader Mao Ze-dong, pointed out in his strategic writings that the peasant movement had to be developed by taking into account many contradictions of interests. To achieve an effective mobilization, it was necessary to study in each different local grassroots situation the composition of the prevailing contradictions and to distinguish between those that were fundamental and those that were of secondary importance. Mobilization could often be achieved along the lines of the most fundamental contradiction (e.g., against the "enemy" that provokes most widespread or acute opposition). Such strategic study-cum-action regarding the locally, nationally, and internationally operating contradictions made the successful advance of the Chinese peasant movements possible and, depending on local circumstances and broader world-economic and political contexts, that of many others (for examples, see Huizer, 1980).

SOCIAL MOVEMENTS AS A BASIS
FOR DEVELOPMENT THROUGH RADICAL REFORM

During the decades up to the 1920s, China had been seriously underdeveloped by Western economic interests and internal corruption. More than half of the peasantry was landless or semi-landless, and prevailing exploitative relationships had become more blatant because of the regional power struggles among the so-called warlords. Thus, Mao encountered rural unrest and social movements on a large scale on his return to his province of origin (Hunan) after his efforts to rally the Shanghai working class for a communist revolutionary movement had been ruthlessly crushed by the Kwomintang government in 1926. Mao's *Report on an Investigation of the Peasant Movements in Hunan* (1927/1971) shows the strength of the movements and also the surprise of its author to find peasants organizing on their own behalf. Given his theoretical Marxist conception, only the urban proletariat should be capable of doing this. Learning by trial and error from and with the local people, Mao followed the age-old folk tradition of (mostly Daoist inspired) people's rebellions in Hunan when he helped the peasants there organize against overwhelming odds. In his strategic writings about organization and guerrilla war, he later used Daoist and folkloric texts as much as those of Marx and Lenin (Freiberg, 1977). One of the greatest feats of the more than twenty years of struggle of the Chinese peasant guerrilla armies was a kind of modern Exodus, the Long March in 1934-1935 in which they escaped total annihilation by the far superior armies of Chiang Kai-shek by withdrawing through outlying inhospitable parts of China to isolated Yenan province. Here, the numerically weakened but spiritually and morally strengthened peasant rebels could establish their base, distribute the land to the tillers, and build a society based on "rural egalitarianism," which served as a base for the conquest of all China in the late 1940s.

It is not accidental that Mao was aware that if the rebellion he guided had to become a revolution, he had to ensure the participation of women, to whom he gave great importance. In China's past, women sometimes played a considerable role in rebellious or revolutionary movements. As Wolf (1969, p. 112) noted about the secret societies that opposed Confucianism during the past centuries in China: "Most of them were strongly feminist, contrary to Confucian thinking which asserted the male yang over the female yin: the secret societies tended to accord equal status to women." These societies facilitated the entrance and orientation of the Communist Party considerably.

The social movements of the Chinese peasants increasingly became a militant political organization, not merely struggling for concrete benefits and abandonment of unjust practices, but with the objective of taking over the power of the state to achieve those original purposes. Thus, a social movement resisting state power for more than two decades finally came to take up state power itself and so could bring about the reforms the peasants and women had been agitating for. Most important were the land redistribution, which enabled all tillers access to land, and the mobilization, initiated from above, for the formation of cooperatives and collectives in the rural areas to the benefit of rapid industrialization, as even the World Bank (1983, p. 28) observed. This report further observed that, despite disastrous mistakes that were made in the process, the establishment of cooperatives and later communes not only enabled more efficient use of land resources but also created conditions for collective efforts in the field of soil conservation and flood control, in which great advancements were made. In the World Bank's 1991 *Development Report,* it was noted that, starting in 1780, the United Kingdom took fifty-eight years to double its per capita output while Japan took thirty-four years. China, however, doubled its living standards in only a decade. Does the "bourgeoisie," declaring Deng Xiaoping the *Financial Times* 1992 man of the year, finally find a match?

Too much trust in voluntarism has, however, great risks. In China, the idea that bureaucratization and routinization of the cadres of the Communist Party and the state bureaucracy could be halted and simply reversed by mobilizing students and teenagers in a "cultural revolution" turned out to be the most dramatic mistake, if not crime, committed by Mao and Lin Piao. It destroyed the lives of millions of people. History can be made by social movements and revolutionary upsurges guided by charismatic leaders, but overconfidence in the malleability of society by voluntary effort can create disaster.

China's socialist social movement of the 1920s and its aftermath prepared the way for the spectacular economic development we now observe in East Asia. Does this fact confirm Frank's preliminary hypothesis that the first waves of the world system began in China several thousands of years ago and that, in the course of centuries, moved westward, apparently ending up in their place of origin after bringing the whole globe into turmoil through waves or cycles of development and—following—underdevelopment (Frank & Fuentes, 1990b, p. 126)? Can we even suppose that these waves sometimes apparently originate from below, as social movements, and now even seem to accelerate? The Chinese revolution also helped indirectly with the rapid development of a few neighboring countries. Already before the triumph of the Chinese peasant movements, the land reform implemented in the areas under their control had a strong radiating influence.

In Japan, semi-landless peasants, mainly tenants, had been organizing since the First World War to achieve better tenancy conditions. This movement was growing rapidly under charismatic leadership but was seriously hindered by the Japanese military when they came to power after the Manchuria Incident in 1931 (Huizer, 1980, pp. 31-34). After the defeat of the Japanese Army in 1945, the peasant movement proved still viable, though many leaders had spent years in jail, and it was quickly reactivated and able to agitate for reforms in the land tenure situation as had been tried in China. The supreme commander for the Allied forces exercised strong pressure on the postwar Japanese government to implement land reform. Between 1946 and 1949, almost all land property in excess of one hectare was redistributed among the tillers mainly through purchase and resale. In this process, the organized peasants played a crucial role, together with the rich farmers and landlords, whose tight grip on rural social life was broken (Huizer, 1980, pp. 38-44; also Dore, 1959). This happened with close supervision and advice by the technicians of the occupation authorities, so the opposition of the landlords was largely overcome by giving them institutionalized forms of expression and a stake in industrialization. A broad internal market for industrial goods was created by giving the peasantry access to the means of production and by helping them further improve their situation by officially sponsored farmers' associations.

A few years later, a similar land reform was implemented in Taiwan, strongly backed by the Joint Commission on Rural Reconstruction (JCRR), created by a former Kwomingtang top official, James Yen, with U.S. support and guidance. The Taiwanese government was then dominated by Chinese who had fled from mainland China and had no landed interests to defend in Taiwan (for an overview, see Huizer, 1980, pp. 46-63). The government was determined to carry out reforms and found ways to deal with the landlords' opposition. One technique to dispel such opposition was the wide dissemination of information on drastic reform measures taken in China. The moderate forms of the reform program in Japan were also pointed out in comparison. This form of publicity was reported to be highly successful. In addition, the reforms were introduced in a "gradually progressive" manner. Later, the Syngman Rhee government in South Korea initiated a radical land reform under pressure from the U.S. occupation forces. They sought to counter the growing rural unrest and movements sympathetic to the communist government in North Korea that had carried out reforms similar to those in China. These land reforms carried out in reaction to radical social movements in the area made it possible for the NICs to emerge and later become a challenge to the "development of underdevelopment" highlighted—in most cases, rightly so—by Frank and the *dependentistas*.

Land reform, or better land redistribution to formerly dispossessed peasants, had already been part of state policies in Mexico during the first part of this century and had been carefully studied by many U.S. experts. This reform occurred because of the strength of revolutionary social movements but did not bring about a complete overhaul of the country's power structure. Although the social movements had strong and charismatic leadership, they had no clear idea of ways to bring about an overall change in control over the economy, as did Mao Ze-dong.

In 1910, the most outstanding peasant leader in Mexico was Emiliano Zapata, who at the age of thirty was elected president of the committee of his native Anenequilco in the state of Morelos, which was attempting recovery of lands lost to the aggressive expansion of sugar estates (for an extensive study, see Huizer, 1972, chap. 4). Zapata had returned from a period of forced military service imposed on him as a kind of punishment for his rebellious attitude, and thus he had gained experience and insight that served him later as a peasant leader. Because of his charismatic leadership, three other villages with similar problems formed a joint committee and hired a lawyer to defend their rights in court against the large sugar haciendas. After legal means proved time and again ineffective, the peasants, who thought they had the right to take the law into their own hands, occupied the lost lands and, when threatened by the army, joined the national revolutionary movement begun in

1910 by middle-class intellectuals who opposed the dictatorship of Porfirio Diaz. This insurrection was supported by the peasants in the hope that the revolutionary forces, once they were in power, would do justice to the peasant cause as had been promised. When the new government gave only lip service to the agrarian reform question, Zapata formulated, with the support of some sympathetic lawyers and a local priest, a program for radical land recovery. In accordance with this program, Zapata distributed land to the peasants in the areas that fell under the control of his guerrilla forces. Also in this movement, women and traditional culture played crucial roles. The movement's banner carried the Virgin of Guadalupe, a saintly symbol that embodies the Virgin Mary as she appeared to an Indian peasant in 1531 at the place where traditionally the fertility goddess Tonatzin was honored.

Thanks partly to this continuous pressure, the ideas of the local reform program were integrated into the Mexican Constitution (Article 27) in 1917. Despite this official acceptance, however, effective redistribution of land took place only in those areas where peasant movements were well organized or armed for protection against the violent opposition of the landlords. For years, Zapata resisted many attempts to frighten or bribe him. He was finally assassinated in 1919 by a man who was bribed by the government and the landlords. State power remained in the hands of the urban-based middle-class elites who opposed radical reform of the country's economic structure. As a consequence, the dialectical relationship between development (for some) and underdevelopment (for many others) remained largely intact in Mexico. This justified the critical analysis of the "Indian problem" by Frank (1967) as part of internal colonialism and the reemergence of Zapatistas at the beginning of 1994 (which I predicted in Huizer, 1972; see *La Jornada,* 6/1/94). The Zapatistas confirm earlier findings that, at the local level, the underdevelopment of development, such as the NAFTA magic, is well understood despite official verbiage.

Mexico was one of the few countries where community development as a strategy was debated and tested long before it became part of the global strategy of Western (and international) agencies (Huizer, 1969). Community development emerged as an internationally sponsored strategy in the early 1950s mainly as a reaction to the Chinese revolution. In India, the community development program was initiated in 1952 with support from the Ford Foundation and the Indo-American Technical Cooperation Fund. This approach was soon adopted on a large scale and in a few years became a nationwide program that was then widely propagated inside and outside India (Bowles,

1954, pp. 195-214). As the U.S. ambassador to India at that time, Chester Bowles (1954, p. 2) indicated:

> With China now Communist, Asia and the whole underdeveloped world would be looking to India to see if another way were possible. The Kremlin, too, would be looking to India; for long ago Lenin has said, "The road to Paris lies through Peking and Calcutta." Although the Marshall Plan and related policies for European reconstruction and defense had blocked the direct path to Paris, at least for the present, even a firmly democratic Western Europe might eventually be undermined if all of Asia with its billion or more people should go the way of Communist China. The debacle in China, which aroused such partisan argument and confusion, had virtually paralyzed American policy making in Asia. It seemed to me that India was a place to start afresh.

Bowles was clearly in line with President Harry Truman's 1949 inaugural address's Point Four, the Bold New Program, which propagated development of what were for the first time called "underdeveloped countries" as a "containment policy" to halt the advance of communism. During my involvement in such "community development from above" in the 1950s, it could soon be found that peasants were often aware that this was designed as a palliative to keep them from achieving the radical changes they really wanted. They remained highly distrustful or openly showed their passive resistance (Huizer, 1965a, 1972). It became also clear in this context that the simplest rural development efforts were part of a global confrontation, the cold war, capitalism versus communism.

The context of global confrontation became even more obvious at that time through the emergence of so-called modernization theory, designed in U.S. power-elite think tanks. Walt W. Rostow (1984) shows in an autobiographical article how, during the 1950s, he contributed to "the collective effort mobilized in the 1950's at the Center for International Studies (CENIS) at MIT." As an alternative to the Communist Chinese model, his group of "development crusaders" (his words), partly funded by the CIA as Rostow (1984, p. 241) himself points out, laid the basis for his *Stages of Economic Growth: A Non-Communist Manifesto* (1960). This modernization theory, as it is known, has served the establishment well; its idea of gradual stages of economic growth up to the U.S. consumerist society model has been implicitly guiding much policy making in the development cooperation ministries and agencies of the West, including the International Monetary Fund (IMF) and World Bank. While Frank attacked this "theory" through macroeconomic analysis,

I was confronted with its adverse developments (underdevelopment) at the practical grassroots level.

COMMUNITY DEVELOPMENT
FROM WITHIN AND FROM BELOW

Although Frank demonstrated that studying the dialectic of development and underdevelopment from above (academia), where theories about these subjects emerged, can be highly fruitful, a look at this dialectic from within and from below can also be useful and complement the first approach. From 1954 onward, I was lucky to be able to learn about such phenomena through participation in the struggle for survival and justice of the people I became involved with as a community development worker for the UN in various countries and through careful reflection on the experiential knowledge thus acquired. This form of research can be called "research-through-action" (see Huizer, 1979). In many cases, the people I worked with shared in this reflective process, making it "participatory action research."

From the start of my twenty years of more or less intensive work with peasants, I often experienced the distrustful and seemingly apathetic or fatalistic peasant response when faced with "modernizing" agents or processes. This was a highly rational attitude (Huizer, 1972, chap. 2). My first real experience with the rationality of peasant distrust occurred in 1955 when I lived as a UNESCO-sponsored voluntary community development worker in a village in El Salvador. This was after a well-intentioned and badly needed drinking water project our agency tried to introduce there failed because the peasants did not show up to work with us. Thus, I experienced the first crisis in my then still "developmentalist" ideology.

I discovered the reason for the peasants' apparent apathy only after I had actually lived in their village for some time, not really knowing what to do but simply sharing their life without asking too many questions (see Huizer, 1965a). The peasants gradually taught me how projects, especially those for which people had to contribute voluntary labor, usually benefited the better-off, particularly landlords, rather than themselves. Peasant "apathy" and nonparticipation in "development" projects initiated from above proved, in this and many other cases, to be justified as a rationally and consciously adopted strategy of not letting themselves be exploited more than they already were. I also experienced that, under more encouraging conditions, their apathy could easily transform itself into enthusiastic support and considerable effort (Huizer, 1965a, 1972, chap. 3). On the whole, peasants, and particularly the women, took their position much less for granted than outsiders (e.g., development workers like myself initially) thought. Moreover, peasants, as well as the local elites, appeared to have a good deal of awareness that development (coffee, sugar, banana productivity) had to do with historical trends toward land alienation and gradual erosion of the soil. Those "from above," however, were also quite aware of potential peasant rebelliousness and felt the need to maintain a strong military police force to keep people "in their place."

During all such village experiences in Latin America, Sicily, and North Africa, it often struck me that certain men and women had a special capacity to express clearly what their peers were feeling about exploitative situations (Huizer, 1972, pp. 153-160). I learned to recognize such people as persons with "charisma." When crisis situations became acute and confrontation with the powerful could no longer be avoided, those with charisma were the crucial motivators of their peers to act against the physical and psychological power landlords and rich farmers have over "their" peasants. (This includes patronage as a covert form of the exercise of power.) In this confrontation, those with established power had most of the advantages, particularly the backing of heavily armed police, the army, or private gunmen.

In trying to answer the question of what kept peasants going under such circumstances, I gradually came to the conclusion that two aspects were crucial (see Huizer, 1985, 1991):

1. A certain clearness in people's minds about who constitutes the main cause of their plight: those "from above." This kind of class consciousness was combined with a historical perspective, bridging generations, that gave them the (mostly unspoken) conviction that, because their society had been more just and egalitarian in the past, it might or should be so in the future.
2. A continuous spiritual revitalization grounded in a (holistic) religious awareness, particularly strong among women, which takes the continuity of one-ness of life and afterlife, good and evil, natural and supernatural, more for granted than is the case for Western middle-class Christian-educated people like myself. Such spiritual or traditional cultural roots of people's resistance, appealed to by leaders like Zapata and Mao Ze-dong, have unfortunately been ignored. It also took me a long time to appreciate their importance.

These two aspects of poor people's worldview often appeared to have enough coherence to give them the strength to endure what to Western eyes were virtually unbearable crisis situations. It sometimes prompted them to resist or rebel. This latter approach, however, was not the purpose of most "community development" as promoted worldwide in those years, as I also gradually learned.

During the mid-1960s, I had a revealing look at the dialectic between development and underdevelopment in the establishment of a UN-sponsored regional community development program in the Punitaqui Valley in the north of Chile (see Huizer, 1972, chap. 2 for details). The initial nonparticipation of the peasant communities was transformed into an active reform movement. The reason for the original distrust and nonparticipation was the typical state of underdevelopment of the area where the woods as well as the small gold mines had in the recent past been depleted by Chilean entrepreneurs. The community development projects to be introduced were, on closer scrutiny, clearly and expressedly resented by the local population as palliatives. It was relatively easy to discover through a participatory approach that the people really wanted the recovery of the fertile valley lands from those entrepreneurs and landlords who had dislodged their communities and pushed them up the deforested mountain slopes during the past decades. With a new land reform law just passed in 1965 in the Chilean parliament, petitions, a few peaceful rallies, and demonstrations could be organized in the nearby town and the land reform process put in motion against the then rather passive opposition of the local elites.

During the emergence of this social movement, I learned a great deal from a number of charismatic peasant leaders who carefully guided their peers into increasingly broadly organized actions on their own behalf. They only raised demands that were strongly felt and pursued cases where justice was so clearly on their side that even the local elites were somewhat embarrassed by the publicity. In this case, the state (police as well as the local development agency employees) was hesitantly backing the new legislation that favored reforms and that just had been promulgated by a Christian-Democratic government. Fear of a spreading impact of the communist and socialist trade-union influence that years before had entered the area because of the mining industry may have been a reason to appease the movement and keep it localized. In September 1973, eight years later, some of the outstanding leaders from this valley were summarily executed without trial as "Communist agitators." The Chilean state then had radically changed its character because of the direct intervention of the army supported by the CIA and a number of multinational corporations.

Modernization theory and its derivative of gradual development at the local level produced underdevelopment and thus confirmed the critique of Frank and other *dependentistas*. It also, ironically, led to social movements for real development. Particularly, community development trying to foster gradual trickle-down improvement to consolidate harmony in the villages (not explicitly: among different classes) often proved to have a contrary effect. Studies on the vastly extended national community development program in India, as well as my own experiences in Latin America and Southeast Asia, clearly showed that the better-off benefited proportionally much more, often at the cost of the majority, and that disharmony and conflict resulted from this effort. As in the world economy, local level development for one category implied remaining behind or underdevelopment for other categories, often the majority. This was already observed for India by Rene Dumont in a United Nations report in 1959 (see Huizer, 1980, for details). The Indian Ministry of Home Affairs concluded in 1969 that, in areas where community development and the following Green Revolution (promoted by Western foundations such as Rockefeller) were most successful, rural contradictions and violent conflicts emerged most frequently and strongly and destabilized the countryside. Landlessness rapidly increased to more than half the population, a level that compared with that of China in the 1920s. In fact, this implied that, in the long-term view, "development" theories promoting gradual changes crumbled (underdeveloped?) under the weight of their own effects, though they might foster in the short run local, national, and international elite interests.

Thus, during the early 1960s, a combination of Frank's and others' *dependentista* macroeconomic findings and feedback from rural practice, like my own, enhanced the discussion of the need for radical structural reforms (e.g., land reform) as proposed by Raul Prebisch and other UN officials. This reform included the need for supporting social movements (e.g., those of peasants) to bargain for such reforms (see United Nations, 1968). In those same years, many militant resistance and peasant movements proliferated in all continents and culminated in the late 1960s and early 1970s.

A main question related to the UN's increasing interest in structural reforms, one that became part of my work during the late 1960s, was why social movements emerge in some places and become large-scale and effective (e.g., in China in 1949) and not in others? An even more pragmatic and important question was, How exactly do social movements emerge, and what can be done to stimulate or support them?

Generalizations about the emergence of peasant movements based on experiences in Latin America (Huizer, 1967, 1969) were confirmed by observation and experiences with similar movements in several Southeast Asian countries (Huizer, 1980, pp. 161-184). Important preconditions for the emergence of peasant movements in almost all instances include the following:

1. The occurrence of a blatant and strongly felt case or situation of injustice or disadvantage (e.g., a deterioration of the actual situation or the raising of false hopes or improvement or redress), mostly related to the dialectic of development and underdevelopment
2. The availability locally of able, mostly charismatic leaders who could clearly voice the discontent, indicate steps for the correction of grievances, and inspire their peers to action
3. Some measure of tolerance by the state or active support from urban allies (politicians, intellectuals, development workers) in coping with the effects of the state's monopoly of force
4. A strategy of gradual escalation of the struggle in reaction to the degree of opposition or oppression the movements encounter

The actual emergence of a movement depends on its strategy. Chances of success are greater if it is not explicitly directed against the state, but rather begins with demands that correspond to the most strongly felt concrete grievances and needs. When the elites and/or the state respond to the demands by trying to block the growing movement, it could well become more radical and, if violently oppressed, become revolutionary. The state loses its legitimacy by violently oppressing movements that are clearly viewed as representing justified demands. Such a process of growing revolutionary struggle may take months, years, or decades to come about. The struggle itself helps the peasants involved develop from a "class-in-itself" to a "class-for-itself" (Huizer, 1965b). The Chinese peasant movement gradually, and in reaction to opposing forces, transformed itself into a strongly organized party and army.

Being nonhierarchical is considered by Frank and Fuentes (1987) an important characteristic of social movements. I could observe that most of these social movements were initially not very hierarchical (but hierarchical to some extent, depending on the qualities of the mostly charismatic leadership) and were often considerably influenced and backed by women (though not often in leading roles). They were purposely nonviolent and just held to correct strongly felt injustices. When movements gained attention and were then violently oppressed, often by the state, they would become more militant and prepared to use violence to counter state violence that was viewed as illegitimate. The movements then often became or had to become more hierarchical. They lost the character of a movement and sometimes became a revolutionary organization or party. In some cases, this was the objective of certain urban supporters, who joined and guided emerging peasant movements. Generally, peasants follow revolutionary political leaders only after all other alternatives of peaceful and gradual achievement of a more just and sustainable livelihood have been ruthlessly blocked.

ELITE COUNTERSTRATEGIES

Considerable evidence suggests that, in the dialectical relationships between important social movements and the state, international elite actors (e.g., the CIA) are playing crucial roles. The CIA used a variety of approaches as diverse as outright oppression (finding out who the leaders were and then literally or figuratively "decapitating" the movement) and the creation of "parallel" social movements to co-opt existing or competing movements with big funding (Agee, 1975; Blum, 1986; Kumar, 1981). In not a few cases, well-intentioned existing, small grassroots movements (e.g., Christian peasant-unions) were heavily subsidized to compete with more radical Socialist or Communist unions. In some cases, such parallel movements radicalized on their own because of the opposition they encountered from the power elites whenever they made demands on behalf of their following. People's movements are not merely spontaneous forces that occur when there is a need to confront an issue. They can be manipulated by leaders and strategic groups of elites for purposes that the participants do not envisage.

The escalation during the 1960s of the confrontation in Latin America between popular social movements and the states and international "strategic groups" behind them went somewhat parallel to the escalation in the U.S.-supported war against peasant guerrillas in Vietnam. An increasing number of people's movements were facing oppression and began to consider the need for armed self-defense. Those that did take up arms were even more violently oppressed, whereas those that did not were branded and persecuted as "subversive" or "Communist." On the one hand, leaders like Che Guevera tried to start violent revolutionary movements in the expectation of creating "several Vietnams" in Latin America. On the other hand, the Colombian sociologist-priest Camilo Torres tried for years to create nonviolent popular reform movements in his country until he was so vehemently persecuted that he had practically no other way than to escape and join the guerrillas. Both Guevera and Torres were killed in violent encounters in 1966-67.

Their lives and later their deaths, together with the growing anti-Vietnam war campaign, however, had a considerable influence on the emergence in the United States and Europe of certain "new" social movements. They were the heroes of "the Movement" that culminated in Paris 1968 and similar happenings elsewhere. The movement in the United States led Richard Nixon to not pursue an escalation of the Vietnam War in November 1969 (Kissinger had secretly delivered a nuclear threat to Hanoi that same month).

Thus, the hard lessons learned by people's movements and their leaders and supporters in Third World countries were taken up by the new social movements in the West. A process of "conscientization" started about social confrontation with global power elites among Western middle-class people who were not themselves suffering oppression. A solidarity movement with the oppressed emerged that was not based on direct class interests, but rather on sympathy with those of other classes and in other parts of the world.

Middle-class solidarity movements that later transformed themselves into grassroots movements also emerged in Latin America in the late 1960s. As more and more people became involved with social movements and increasingly felt the ruthless oppression of the state and foreign elements, certain circles in the Catholic Church, traditionally strongly related to the ruling elites in most countries, began to reconsider their role. The Church had frequently been involved in the creation of parallel organizations. But these had little effect or, if they were effective, were later opposed by the local elites and were attracted to some of the more radical social movements with which they became active allies. From these initiatives gradually emerged a new social movement within the church called "liberation theology" or "the people's church." Its precursor was the priest-sociologist Camilo Torres, who became a martyr in 1967, and its first main spokesperson was Gustavo Gutierrez (1972), a priest working in slum areas in Lima. The thinking and action of these priests were strongly influenced by the *dependentistas*.

Although the Roman Catholic hierarchy initially reacted with considerable reservation about this growing movement, more and more bishops became attracted and involved, partly in response to the way the military in many countries persecuted the activist clergy at the grass roots. Thanks to room for renovation created by the Second Vatican Concilium in the early 1960s, the "option for the poor" was endorsed in 1968 by the Second General Conference of the Latin American Roman Catholic Episcopate in Medellin. It could be expected that (some strategic groups of) the "bourgeoisie" would react. The *Rockefeller Report* on the Americas stated:

> Actually, the church may be somewhat in the same situation as the young with a profound idealism, but as a result, in some cases, vulnerable to subversive penetration; ready to undertake a revolution if necessary to end injustice, but not clear either as to the ultimate nature of the revolution itself or as to the governmental system by which the justice it seeks can be realized. (Rockefeller, 1969, p. 31)

The *Rockefeller Report* strongly recommended increased military assistance and spending for the sake of "Western Hemisphere Security," concluding that "the people of the United States do not recognize that as a whole, the other American nations spend a smaller percentage of their gross national product on defense than any other area except Africa south of the Sahara" (p. 62).

As Lernoux (1982) pointed out, during the 1960s "national security," promoted by the military and supported and coached by the United States, became in Latin America and other continents the main opponent to almost all kinds of people's movements, including those sponsored by the Church. Such movements were "demonized," declared to be part of "devilish communism" in all kinds of official statements, and ruthlessly persecuted or even destroyed. A most crucial learning experience in this respect was Chile and the fate of the Allende regime.

During a period of work with Food and Agriculture Organization (FAO) in Chile in early 1973, it became clear to many of us that the radically but democratically reformist policies promoted by the Allende government in Chile were being boycotted and might also be ruthlessly blocked by the international power elites. Multinational corporations, mostly from the United States but including the Dutch-British Unilever Company (Induslever, a joint enterprise of Unilever and the Chilean Edwards clan interests of *El Mercurio* and the Edwards Bank), were not going to let their profit making be limited by the reformist socialization or nationalization efforts of the Chilean government.

The turmoil created in Chile in 1972-73, months before the September 11th murder of President Allende and the discussion with Andre and Marta Frank and other friends and colleagues in Santiago, facilitated my decision to shift attention and activity from supporting peasant organization and land reform (with which I had also been involved in Chile) toward studying the increasingly obvious opponents of reform. These were strategic groups of local and

Western power elites, particularly multinational corporations. This shift of attention coincided with my nomination in 1973 as professor of development studies at the Catholic University of Nijmegen, where since 1968, students had been agitating for the establishment of this chair and the simultaneously created Third World Center.

From working with social movements in many contexts and from seeing their oppression, I had come to realize the crucial importance of dealing with the (counter)movements from above and the activities and (under)development policies of the power elites. Frank's radical *dependencia* theory was here a great help. This theory had, among other factors such as the Vietnam War and Che Guevara's death, been an inspiration to the 1968 student movement. Thus, social movements in the Third World influenced the emergence of new social movements in the metropolis—the beginning of what could be called a globalization from below, in a dialectical relationship with the globalization movement(s) of the world's power elites, the "bourgeoisie" or "international capital" as some would more abstractly call it. The social movements (and the reactions from above they provoked) had dialectically also a considerable influence on the way social scientists were dealing with the realities of development and underdevelopment.

.

THE NEED FOR STUDY OF ELITE STRATEGIES

Do social movements influence scientific breakthroughs or even "revolutions" as Frank and Fuentes (1990a, p. 153) seem to suggest? In several countries during the 1950s and 1960s, activist scholars were persecuted or had difficulties being academically recognized as serious scholars. Frank was one of them and came up with the term *liberation anthropology* (Frank, 1969, chap. 2), to be followed soon by the *sociology of liberation* (Fals Borda, 1973) and the *theology of liberation* (Gutierrez, 1972). Moreover, an acute crisis in the social sciences had already become evident through the Vietnam controversy and the discovery of the Camelot project in Chile, where millions of dollars (supplied by the U.S. Department of Defense) were made available to social scientists (Horowitz, 1967). The official *Inquiry into the Ethics and Responsibilities of Social Scientists* contained the conclusion that the social scientists involved had been "extra-ordinarily naive" (Beals, 1969, p. 6). As a result, a few social scientists were beginning to recognize that their profession had to be "decolonized" (Stavenhagen, 1971) or "reinvented" (Hymes,

1972). As a consequence, in Hymes's (1972) pioneering reader, both Eric Wolf (1972) and particularly Laura Nader (1972) argued for the need to come to grips with the powers that be through what was called "studying-up": researching the power-elite strategies that determine, to a large extent, both the life and crises of Third World peoples and, to some extent, the nature of anthropology. In sociology, the pathbreaking work of C. Wright Mills (1956) had inspired some studying-up in the United States. Now this had to become global.

During the 1973 Conference of the International Union of Anthropological and Ethnological Sciences at Chicago, this topic was dealt with in an ad hoc, improvised, special symposium on multinational corporations (see Idris-Soven, Idris-Soven, & Vaughan, 1978). It was also treated in a few contributions to the symposium on the ideology and education of anthropologists brought together in Huizer and Mannheim (1979), particularly the articles by June Nash, Alex Mamak, and Al Gedicks. Despite protests from many participants, Frank did not get a visa for entrance to the United States to attend this conference to present his paper *Anthropology = Ideology, Applied Anthropology = Politics,* which was nonetheless published in Huizer and Mannheim (1979, see also Frank, 1984).

A burning and related question arose: Was it useful to study peasant and other social movements, given the risk that research results would be used by the powers that be against the peasantry? If one is in solidarity with peasants and other oppressed groups, is it not more useful to study their enemies and the strategies they develop? Although presented at this conference for the first time were a considerable number of papers dealing with social movements and feminist issues, one important topic that remained in the shadow was the mentality of those who have shown the capacity to become rich and powerful at the cost of others—that is, colonizers, entrepreneurs, corporate managers, merchants, and the military. Many such "big men" had considerable charisma and skills and have, through the trends or movements they unleashed, made important contributions to the rise (and fall) of civilizations. Why have anthropologists, some of whom are experts in the study of "big men" in some of the most remote areas in the world, paid so little attention to the big entrepreneurs and their strategic groups that play a crucial role in the development and underdevelopment and who are found in much more accessible places? (For a notable exception, see June Nash's excellent 1979 study of corporate managers in New York.)

When theorizing about development and underdevelopment, Frank shows how in his own development he reacted to those who in the 1950s and 1960s dominated important discussions. Those against whom he at times fulminated were well aware of their own role and sometimes explicitly said so. Thus, it was no great surprise to grassroots representatives that the economic crisis around 1973 brought another strategic group into the picture that soon became a topic for analysis (Assmann, 1978; Huizer, 1980; Sklar, 1980).

In 1973, at a critical moment for the world economy, leaders of the world's largest multinational corporations (David Rockefeller—Exxon, Chase Manhattan; John Loudon—Royal Dutch Shell; and others, with help from intellectuals such as Zbigniew Brzezinsky) created the Trilateral Commission, uniting most of the corporate elites and statesmen who had already been meeting for years in a less formal way at the Bilderberg Conferences. More sophisticated ways of dealing with Third World issues were outlined in one of the Trilateral Commission's first reports, which pointed out: "A world which has reached current levels of interdependence and is condemned by technological and economic progress to still more complex relationships in the future, must devise new forms of common management" (1974, p. 35). The policies designed at that time by the IMF, headed by Johannes Witteveen, and the World Bank, headed by Robert McNamara, were explicitly part of these proposals. There appears to be a considerable element of voluntarism in the way strategic groups of the power elite design strategies to cope with antisystemic movements, which, dialectically, are taken seriously into account by (some of) their opponents.

Within the "bourgeoisie" and its strategic groups, as well as in social movements, some actors are playing more or less recognized leading roles; others, the majority, follow. In most studies of social movements, scant attention has been given to the types of leadership or to leading personalities of strategic groups within the bourgeoisie(s). As Van der Pijl's (1984) dissertation has shown, considerable differentiation or even polarization exists between "fractions" of the "bourgeoisie(s)." It appears crucial for social movements and their leaders or sympathizers to carefully study and assess contradictions within (and between) sectors of the "bourgeoisie(s)" (e.g., between U.S. and West European interests as Van der Pijl shows). The role of leadership in the dialectical relationship between the state, power elite strategic groups, and grassroots social movements is a crucial issue for research.

THE STUDY OF THE CHARISMA OF CAPITALISTS

Although historians have, at times, overemphasized the role of "person-alities" in history making, social scientists have probably underemphasized their influence within the social forces and structures under consideration. Tentatively, it can be observed that most renovating movements are led by charismatic personalities (e.g., Mao, Zapata) who can either empower their followers toward taking their fate into their own hands or who can become authoritarian power-holders not much different from their original enemies. Combinations or intermediate positions of these two "ideal types" are the most frequent in peasant movements, as I have observed in many instances (Huizer, 1972, 1980).

The economist Marglin (1990), in a provocative study on knowledge and power, indicated that, in Western society, the power to make people follow and believe is a crucial element in determining behavior, even modern economic behavior:

> It would be a mistake to think that the power of belief is a characteristic of traditional society from which we are liberated by modernization. One cannot, I have argued, understand the workings of modern capitalist society without understanding the power of belief. Indeed, the most enduring contribution of John Maynard Keynes to 20th-century economics may turn out to be his insight into the social construction of reality, particularly as to the way in which belief mediates between profit and investment. In the Keynesian view, the key to prosperity is the "animal spirits" (his phrase) of the capitalist class. If business-men are optimistic and believe profits will be high, they will invest in new plants and equipment to take advantage of the high level of profits. In this case, production and employment will be high, and growth will be rapid. In a word: prosperity. (p. 14)

Charisma is one concept used in Western sociology, as well as in theology, that appears as hard to define as "animal spirits." Max Weber (1968) gave a classic description of charisma when he tried to make a typology of different kinds of authority and leadership:

> The term "charisma" will be applied to a certain quality of an individual personality by virtue of which he is set apart from ordinary men and treated as endowed with supernatural, super-human, or at least specifically exceptional powers or qualities. These as such are not accessible to the ordinary person, but are regarded as of divine origin or as exemplary, and on the basis of them the individual

concerned is treated as a leader. In primitive circumstances this peculiar kind of deference is paid to prophets, to people with a reputation for therapeutic or legal wisdom, to leaders in the hunt, and heroes in war. It is very often thought of as resting on magical powers. (p. 48)

C. Wright Mills (1956, pp. 95-96) also highlighted "something demonic," "personal acumen and supernormal efforts," "native intelligence or the magical luck," "fanaticism" to the tycoons who developed capitalism in the United States in its initial stages. This is further elaborated in the little-known but highly interesting study of American millionaires and their strategic groups by the Russian economist Stanislaw Menshikov (1969).

An outstanding example of the voluntarism of the more recent managers' approach is ITT General Manager Harold Geneen (whose company offered $1,000,000 to the CIA to help overthrow the Allende regime), who noted with regard to his management approach:

> I wanted to create the kind of an invigorating, challenging, creative atmosphere at ITT. I wanted to get the people there to reach for goals that they might think were beyond them. I wanted them to accomplish more than they thought was possible. And I wanted them to do it not only for the company and their careers but also for the fun of it. (Geneen, 1984, p. 129)

The main objective of this management effort was "a steady stable growth of 10 to 15 percent increase in earnings per share for each and every year. Together we set out to double our earnings in five years" (Geneen, 1984, p. 131). This motivation was apparently enough to overcome moral qualms about killing thousands of Chileans and overthrowing a democratically elected government. To what extent is such economic "belief," as Marglin (1990) called it, part of the "abstract heartless philosophy" that, according to two experts in management studies, Peters and Waterman (1982, p. 45), predominates among the top managers who reach "excellence" in their field? These experts observed,

> Professionalism in management is regularly equated with hardheaded rationality. We saw it surface at ITT in Harold Geneen's search for the "unshakable facts." It flourished in Vietnam where success was counted by body counts. Its wizards were Ford Motor Company's whiz kids and its grand panjandrum was Robert McNamara. The numerative, rationalist approach to management dominates the business schools. (Peters & Waterman, 1982, p. 45)

When facing escalating confrontation with social movements such as the peasant rebellion in Vietnam, this "hardheaded" management approach, an "affliction," as it was called (Peters & Waterman, 1982, p. 45), can lead to catastrophe:

> Our obsession with body counts in Vietnam and our failure to understand the persistence and long-time horizon of the Eastern mind culminated in one of America's most catastrophic misallocations of resources—human, moral and material. (Peters & Waterman, 1982, p. 45)

Regarding the leading figures of the "bourgeoisie" and their philosophies, "beliefs," and "obsessions," one should make a distinction between those who can be considered trendsetters for a certain style and those who, though very powerful in their own direct environment, do not strongly influence or modify corporate culture as such. The trendsetters have an impact far beyond their companies through their influence in strategic groups. Harold Geneen and Robert McNamara are examples.

In the postindustrial phase as it first developed in the United States and later spread to Western Europe, the growing influence of "mind managers" shows new aspects of strategic voluntarism as observed by Herbert Schiller (1973):

> Where manipulation is the principal means of social control, as it is in the United States, the articulation and refinement of manipulative techniques take precedence over other intellectual activities. In accordance with market principles, therefore, manipulative work attracts the keenest talent because it offers the system's richest incentives. Talented Ph.D.'s in English literature wind up as advertising copywriters. Madison Avenue pays a lot more than do college English departments. (p. 4)

Schiller (1973, pp. 8-24) describes and analyzes some of the "myths" that form part of this manipulation of consciousness, among which are the myth of individualism and personal choice, the myth of the "end of ideology," and the myth of unchanging human nature and a pessimistic appraisal of human potential. Among the techniques to mold consciousness are the fragmentation and immediacy of information and entertainment. This strategy has now been effectively globalized and brought under power elite control (Hamelink, 1993; Petras, 1993).

The varieties of brainwashing and "hidden persuasion" as already observed by Vance Packard (1953, presently rediscovered and reprinted in Germany) that worked to mold people's minds globally into following the "American dream" have provoked a growing resistance that even worries the managers in that type of "communication" business. Some of the more sophisticated global business managers have thought about ecological limitations to free-market profit making since the 1972 Club of Rome *Limits to Growth* report. Although the report of the Business Council for Sustainable Development (Schmidheiny, 1992) that was presented to the United Nations Conference on Ecology and Development mainly reflects the interests of many multinational concerns, it indicates that certain doubts about future developments are emerging. In contemporary business circles, there is an increasing call for creative and even charismatic leaders, which probably has to do with the crises and trends of an increasingly complicated and unpredictable global economy. It seems that these crises and complications are no longer to be faced with rationality and the development of a total view on how and where the world economy (not to speak of ecology) is going in the long term, but rather with irrationalities or "IMFundamentalist" dogmas. Moreover, Tom Peters (1988, p. 8), in his latest work on excellence in management, speaks of "facing up to the need for revolution" and "thriving on chaos": "Mergers and de-mergers are just one part of the madness. Strategies change daily, and the names of firms, a clear indicator of strategic intent, change with them." Such recent management literature is full of movement language on creative and "revolutionary" leadership.

The "economic ironies in world politics," highlighted by Frank (1991), are worrying the global power elites, but apparently no significant strategic groups have yet emerged among them to creatively work toward a New Deal or a new world order that means more than U.S. hegemony continued. Frank's (1983) appeal for a "European challenge" is still to the point, it seems, particularly since much of Eastern Europe has virtually become part of the Third World.

A FUTURE FOR SOCIAL MOVEMENTS

As one can learn from Third World peasant farmers in oppressed conditions, it is necessary to look at the reasons and interests behind certain official projects and policy statements. This is good practical class-struggle wisdom from people who themselves generally never heard of Marx. How carefully have concerned intellectuals analyzed the power elites, not merely as an abstract economic power block to be opposed, but rather as a complicated network of internally contradicting and/or allying interests and strategic groups? Gill's (1991) study of power elite groups within and at the margin of the Trilateral Commission provides interesting examples of such contradictions. In the early years of the Trilateral Commission, the common threat of the socialist bloc could serve as one rallying point to help the bourgeoisie(s) of the United States, Western Europe, and Japan more or less agree on a common global strategy for the "management of interdependence." Now this threat has disappeared, but already in the years that preceded *perestroika,* the differences, if not contradictions of interests, within trilateralism became apparent. Reagan's conservative and militaristic policies contributed significantly to this. The ongoing recession, if it is not a depression as Frank suggests, contributed to an even further deterioration of trilateral unity. Is it surprising that, in some of the more conservative U.S. elite circles, reflected by Huntington's (1993) "The Clash of Civilizations?" the search for a new "common enemy" has emerged? As conflict-sociologist Lewis Coser pointed out in his classic book *The Functions of Social Conflict* (1968), to have a "negative reference group" is the best incentive for unity.

During the next few decades, the various kinds of contradictions pertaining to the dialectics of development and underdevelopment outlined above will probably become more acute. It appears crucial to assess the influence of these contradictions on local situations where they are active, as well as on the long-term global trends that form the context of local development. Following Petras's (1993) analysis of the way Western bourgeoisies (particularly the United States) are trying to manage globalization processes to their advantage, one could say that class contradictions have not diminished, but rather have been globalized and thus become more complicated. In many Third World countries, the urbanization of the past decades has undercut the potential social influence of the rural areas. We now note a predominance of the urban marginalized, the so-called informal sector, that will have a considerable bearing on the future development of social movements. Hernando de Soto's (1986) widely publicized effort to mobilize the informal sector for the free-market ideology in Peru is strongly supported by strategic groups of the global power elites. It appears doubtful whether this "magic" will be able to solve the problems of increasing pauperization of large sectors of the population. But this and similar forms of elite crisis management should also be carefully scrutinized.

Learning from the global strategic analyses of spokespersons for the bourgeoisie (e.g., Huntington, 1993), we should also take more into account civilizational, cultural, and religious aspects. People's movements (e.g., workers, women, peasants, indigenous, environmental, civic) that try to face the manipulations of the global power elite(s) should be able to find common ground, rather than be tempted to fight among each other on the civilizational or ethnic fault lines suggested by Huntington. As shown by Tim Allen (1992), the cultural and religious implications of global developments (e.g., the Islamic revolution in Iran) have not been well studied or understood by radical scholars, including Marxists, too much inclined as they were toward materialist political-economic explanations.

It is crucial, in such efforts and investigations, to take the view of "globalization from below," of linking people's movements rooted in their own local cultures. Grassroots movements can "regenerate people's space" by forming "hammocks." This idea, elaborated on by Gustavo Esteva (1987), looks like a fruitful initiative. Learning from concrete experiences in the São Paolo Forum is another way. As described by Robinson (1992), in Latin America a New Left appears to be emerging through the São Paolo Forum since the first meeting in 1990 of a number of socialist parties from various countries at the invitation of the Workers Party of Brazil (PT). The recent radical changes in South Africa that followed decades of struggle by a variety of social movements, and the emerging policies of transformation, can become an example of reversing the underdevelopment of development. In addition to the Sandinistas from Nicaragua and the Farabundo Marti Liberation Front of El Salvador, there were representatives of leftist parties from Mexico, Peru, Bolivia, and others. Delegates at that meeting concluded that, contrary to what happened in Eastern Europe, socialism should be democratic and participatory and strongly rooted in a pluralist civil society. The "fetishism of armed struggle" should be abandoned, and the emphasis on "ideology" make way for politics rooted in specific local realities. The transformation of society as a one-class project, vanguardism, and verticalism are of the past. Indigenous communities, women, peasants, trade unions, and ecological and religious movements are all working for a new social order. Interesting is the strong influence of radical Christians in several of the groups and parties participating in this ongoing forum.

Global theorizing should emerge from, or at least be closely related to, local efforts and learning experiences as Frank and Fuentes have done. Among radical Christians in Latin America is a renewed interest in elements of Marxist analysis and praxis. The same interest may be discovered among progressive sectors of Buddhism, Gandhian Hinduism, and Islam (e.g., see Aliran, 1991). It is most probable that the process of "globalization from below" will generally not be initiated, promoted, and guided by Westerners. Since the fall of the Berlin Wall, leftist scholars in Western countries appear to be in disarray, if not in crisis. The realities in most Third World countries, as noted above, are harsh enough, if not deteriorating, that taking a radical or even Marxist point of view remains an appropriate approach. In addition to the São Paolo Forum, many other initiatives are taking up undogmatic and critically spiritual or ecological positions. The Consumer Association of Penang's 1986 seminar "The Crisis in Modern Science" is an initiative that came to a useful critical assessment of global modernity and a search for new paradigms (Sardar, 1988).

Frank and Fuentes (1990a) rightly point out at the end of their essay on civil democracy and the cyclical influence of social movements that numerous local initiatives are emerging in all corners of the world. They are related to the informal sector, and particularly to the increasing influence of self-emancipation for women. Women suffer the worst effects of the present globalization from above, as shown most recently by eco-feminists Mies and Shiva (1993). More or less simultaneous with the Zapatista rebellion against NAFTA's free-market globalization, which gained wide publicity, there occurred in Karnataka in India a peaceful peasant mobilization of some 500,000 against GATT and the Cargill Corporation's benefiting from the new regulations patenting local seed varieties for commercial use. This rally was ignored in the Western media (Shiva, 1995). Let's hope that violent resistance is not the only way to bring international power elites to a serious consideration of alternatives.

Elite divide-and-rule strategies are widely practiced by using local cultural and ethical contradictions (e.g., see Blum, 1986; Kumar, 1981). As Frank rightly pointed out, some social movements reacting from below to the underdevelopment that the global economy is enhancing locally can have a reactionary character in their struggle against Western-style modernization. His emphasis on taking such movements seriously is borne out by grassroots experiences with some of these movements or even cults, such as the partly spirit-medium guided liberation struggle in Zimbabwe or the role of Independent Christian Churches in South Africa (Huizer, 1991). There is considerable debate about such pre- (or possibly post-?) modern expressions of dissent with globalization from above (see also Huizer, 1985). Is the kind of spirituality or magic still cherished and apparently at times effectively practiced by local people's movements for their own benefit any less adept for overcoming underdevelopment than (the "belief" in) the "magic of the market"?

Frank (in Amin et al., 1990, p. 183) may be right that it is uncertain whether "the dominant forces of the capitalist world economy will have exhausted their ingenuity and therefore their ability to keep the system operating." But the real ingenuity of some strategic groups among the dominant forces would probably bring them into serious dialogue (perhaps confrontational in the beginning) with strategic groups emerging from below to ensure that development will not be further underdeveloped, but turned again into what the first enlightenment philosophers at the beginning of modernity (and many other visionaries in other cultures and societies) had envisaged for the future of humanity and the globe as a whole.

REFERENCES

Agee, P. (1975). *Inside the company: CIA diary.* New York: Penguin.

Aliran. (1991). *The human being: Perspectives from different spiritual traditions.* Penang: Consumers Association of Penang.

Allen, T. (1992). Taking culture seriously. In T. Allen & A. Thomas (Eds.), *Poverty and development in the 1990s* (pp. 331-346). Oxford, UK: Oxford University Press.

Amin, S., Arrighi, G., Frank, A. G., & Wallerstein, I. (1990). *Transforming the revolution: Social movements and the world-system.* New York: Monthly Review Press.

Assmann, H. (Ed.). (1978). *Carter y la logica del imperialismo, tomo I y II.* San José, Costa Rica: Editorial Universitaria Centroamericana (EDUCA).

Beals, R. (1969). *Politics of research: An inquiry into the ethics and responsibilities of social scientists.* Hawthorne, NY: Aldine.

Blum, W. (1986). *The CIA: A forgotten history. U.S. global interventions since World War II.* London: Zed.

Bowles, C. (1954). *Ambassador's report.* New York: Harper & Brothers.

Club of Rome. (1972). *The limits to growth: A report for the Club of Rome's Project on the Predicament of Mankind.* New York: Universe Books.

Coser, L. A. (1968). *The functions of social conflict.* New York: Free Press.

de Soto, H. (1986). *El otro sendero* [The other path]. Lima, Peru: El Barranco.

Dhanagare, D., & John, J. (1988). Cyclical movements toward the eternal. *Economic and Political Weekly, 23*(21), 1089-1092.

Dore, R. P. (1959). *Land reform in Japan.* Oxford, UK: Oxford University Press.

Esteva, G. (1987). Regenerating people's space. In S. N. Mendlowitz & R. B. J. Walker (Eds.), *Toward a just world peace: Perspectives from social movements* (pp. 5-48). London: Butterworth.

Evers, H-D., & Schiel, T. (1988). *Strategische Gruppen; Vergleichende Studien zu Staat, Bürokratie und Klassenbildung in der Dritten Welt.* Berlin: Verlag.

Fals Borda, O. (1973). *Ciencia propia y colonialismo intelectual.* Mexico: Ed. Nuestro Tiempo.

Frank, A. G. (1967). *Capitalism and underdevelopment in Latin America.* New York: Monthly Review Press.

Frank, A. G. (1969). *Latin America: Underdevelopment or revolution.* New York: Monthly Review Press.

Frank, A. G. (1983). *The European challenge.* Nottingham, UK: Spokesman Press.

Frank, A. G. (1984). *Critique and anti-critique: Essays on dependence and reformism.* New York: Macmillan.

Frank, A. G. (1991). Economic ironies in world politics; A sequel to political ironies in world economy. *Far Eastern Economic Review, 26*(30), 93-102.

Frank, A. G., & Fuentes, M. (1987, August 29). Nine theses on social movements. *Economic and Political Weekly, 22*(35), 1503-1510.

Frank, A. G., & Fuentes, M. (1990a). Civil democracy: Social movements in recent world history. In S. Amin, G. Arrighi, & I. Wallerstein (Eds.), *Transforming the revolution: Social movements and the world system* (pp. 139-180). New York: Monthly Review Press.

Frank, A. G., & Fuentes, M. (1990b). *Widerstand im weltsystem.* Wien: Promedia.

Frank, A. G., & Gills, B. K. (1993). *The world system: Five hundred years or five thousand?* London: Routledge.

Freiberg, J. W. (1977). The dialectics in China: Maoist and Daoist. *Bulletin of Concerned Asian Scholars, 9,* 1.

Galjart, B. (1964). Class and "following" in rural Brazil. *America Latina, 7*(3), 3-24.

Geneen, H. (1984). *Managing.* Garden City, NY: Doubleday.

Gill, S. (1991). *American hegemony and the Trilateral Commission.* Cambridge, UK: Cambridge University Press.

Gutierrez, G. (1972). *Teología de la liberacion: Perspectivas.* Salamanca: Sigueme.

Hamelink, C. (1993). Our common information future: Does it matter? In M. Reuver, F. Solms, & G. Huizer (Eds.), *The ecumenical movement tomorrow* (pp. 57-67). Kampen/Geneva: Kok/World Council of Churches.

Horowitz, I-L. (Ed.). (1967). *The rise and fall of Project Camelot.* Cambridge: Massachusetts Institute of Technology Press.

Huizer, G. (1965a). Evaluating community development at the grassroots: Observations on methodology. *America Indigena, 25,* 3.

Huizer, G. (1965b). Some notes on community development and rural social research. *America Latina, 8,* 3.

Huizer, G. (1967). *On peasant unrest in Latin America.* Washington, DC: ILO-Comite Interamericano de Desarrollo Agricola.

Huizer, G. (1969). Community development, land reform, and political participation. *American Journal of Economics and Sociology, 28*(2), 159-178.

Huizer, G. (1972). *The revolutionary potential of peasants in Latin America.* Lexington, MA: Lexington Books.

Huizer, G. (1979). Research-through-action: Experiences with peasant organizations. In G. Huizer & B. Mannheim (Eds.), *The politics of anthropology: From colonialism and sexism toward a view from below* (pp. 395-420). The Hague, The Netherlands: Mouton.

Huizer, G. (1980). *Peasant movements and their counterforces in Southeast Asia.* New Delhi, India: Marwah.

Huizer, G. (1985). Spirituality against oppression: Strength or weakness of the poor? *Third World Book Review, 1,* 4-5.

Huizer, G. (1991). *Folk spirituality and liberation in Southern Africa.* Bordeaux, France: Centre d'Etude d'Afrique Noire.

Huizer, G., & Mannheim, B. (Eds.). (1979). *The politics of anthropology: From colonialism and sexism toward a view from below.* The Hague, The Netherlands: Mouton.

Huntington, S. P. (1993, Summer). The clash of civilizations? *Foreign Affairs, 72,* 3.

Hymes, D. (Ed.). (1972). *Reinventing anthropology.* New York: Vintage.

Idris-Soven, A., Idris-Soven, E., & Vaughan, M. K. (Eds.). (1978). *The world as a company town: Multinational corporations and the social sciences.* The Hague, The Netherlands: Mouton.

Kumar, S. (1981). *CIA and the Third World: A study in crypto-democracy.* New Delhi, India: Vikas.

Lernoux, P. (1982). *Cry of the people: The struggle for human rights in Latin America—The Catholic Church in conflict with U.S. policy.* New York: Penguin.

Mao Ze-dong. (Ed.). (1971). Report on an investigation of the peasant movements in Hunan. In *Selected readings from the works of Mao Ze-dong.* Beijing, China: Foreign Language Press.

Marglin, S. A. (1990). Toward the decolonization of the mind. In F. A. Marglin & S. A. Marglin (Eds.), *Dominating knowledge: Development, culture, and resistance* (pp. 25-38). Oxford, UK: Clarendon.

Marx, K. (1962). Manifesto of the Communist Party. In C. W. Mills (Ed.), *The Marxists* (pp. 46-67). New York: Dell. (Original work published 1848)

Menshikov, S. (1969). *Millionaires and managers.* Moscow: Progress Publishers.

Mies, M., & Shiva, V. (1993). *Ecofeminism.* Halifax, Nova Scotia: Fernwood.

Mills, C. W. (1956). *The power elite.* Oxford, UK: Oxford University Press.

Mühlmann, W. E. (1972). *Chiliasmus and nativismus.* Berlin: Verlag.

Nader, L. (1972). Up the anthropologist: Perspectives gained from studying up. In D. Hymes (Ed.), *Reinventing anthropology* (pp. 284-311). New York: Vintage.

Nash, J. (1979). Anthropology of the multinational corporation. In G. Huizer & B. Mannheim (Eds.), *The politics of anthropology* (pp. 421-446). The Hague, The Netherlands: Mouton.

Packard, V. (1953). *The hidden persuaders.* New York: Cardinal.

Peters, T. (1988). *Thriving on chaos: Handbook for a management revolution.* New York: Macmillan.

Peters, T. J., & Waterman, R. H. (1982). *In search of excellence: Lessons from America's best run companies.* New York: Harper & Row.

Petras, J. (1993). Cultural imperialism in the late 20th century. *Journal of Contemporary Asia, 23,* 2.

Riad El Ghonemy, M. (1990). *The political economy of rural poverty: The case for land reform.* London: Routledge.

Robinson, W. I. (1992). The São Paulo Forum: Is there a new Latin American left? *Monthly Review, 44,* 7.

Rockefeller, N. A. (1969). *The Rockefeller Report on the Americas: The official report of a United States Presidential Mission for the Western Hemisphere.* Chicago: Quadrangle.

Rostow, W. (1960). *The stages of economic growth: A non-communist manifesto.* Cambridge, UK: Cambridge University Press.

Rostow, W. W. (1984). Development: The political economy of the Marshallian long period. In G. M. Meier & D. Seers (Eds.), *Pioneers in development* (pp. 227-261). Washington, DC: World Bank.

Sardar, Z. (1988). *The revenge of Athena: Science, exploitation, and the Third World.* London: Manshell.

Schiller, H. (1973). *Mind managers.* Boston: Beacon.

Schmidheiny, S. (with the Business Council for Sustainable Development). (1992). *Changing course: A global business perspective on development and the environment.* Cambridge: Massachusetts Institute of Technology Press.

Shiva, V. (1995). Nature, creativity, and the arrogance of patenting life-forms. In G. Huizer (Ed.), *Agriculture and spirituality.* Utrecht, The Netherlands: International Books.

Sklar, H. (Ed.). (1980). *Trilateralism: The Trilateral Commission and elite planning for world management.* Boston: South End.

Stavenhagen, R. (1971). Decolonializing applied social sciences. *Human Organization, 30,* 4.

Trilateral Commission. (1974). *A turning point in North-South relations* (prepared by R. N. Gardner, S. Okita, & B. J. Udink). New York: New York University Press.

United Nations. (1968). *Report of the World Land Reform Conference* (E/4298/Rev.1). New York: Author.

Van der Pijl, K. (1984). *The making of an Atlantic ruling class.* London: Verso.

Wallerstein, I. (1990). Antisystemic movements: History and dilemmas. In S. Amin, G. Arrighi, & I. Wallerstein (Eds.), *Transforming the revolution: Social movements and the world system* (pp. 13-53). New York: Monthly Review Press.

Weber, M. (1956). *Wirtschaft und Gesellschaft: Grundrisse der Verstehende Soziologie.* Tübingen: Mohr (Sieberk).

Weber, M. (1968). *On charisma and institution building: Selected papers* (S. N. Eisenstadt, Ed.). Chicago: University of Chicago Press.

Wolf, E. (1969). *Peasant wars of the twentieth century.* New York: Harper & Row.

Wolf, E. (1972). American anthropologists and American society. In D. Hymes (Ed.), *Reinventing anthropology* (pp. 251-263). New York: Vintage.

World Bank. (1983). *China: Socialist economic development.* Washington, DC: Author.

16

Frank Justice Rather Than Frankenstein Injustice

Homogenous Development as Deviance in the Diverse World

PAT LAUDERDALE

Because my intentions in this chapter are to reflect on Andre Gunder Frank's impact on justice, rather than the usual just-us philosophy of ostensible Western culture, let me begin at the personal level. After having returned from working in Costa Rica for a year and attending a national sociological meeting, I met Gunder Frank. In a large, anomic room the size of an aircraft carrier, at a reception organized for intimate revivals of alumni of graduate programs, I found myself unable to join in the celebrations and moved alone to the edge of the room, trying to make sense of my work in Costa Rica.

AUTHOR'S NOTE: I would like to thank Ken Kyle, Victor Perez, David Theo Goldberg, and Annamarie Oliverio for their thoughtful comments on an earlier draft of this chapter. Oliverio also provided crucial insights into liberation theology and revolution from her work on spirituality and social movements. I presented some of the ideas in this chapter during the Distinguished Scholar session of the International Political Economy Section of the International Studies Association meeting in London, March 1989. Andre Gunder Frank was honored as the first Distinguished Scholar.

I had gone to Costa Rica to study and write about land reform, welfare, peasant movements, law, and how disputes were managed, rather than resolved. Frank introduced himself, and we discussed my work, or, more aptly, I lamented about the problems of all Costa Ricans, but particularly of the peasants and indigenous peoples. I complained about the intrusion of the world system and its homogenous development schemes on the peaceful and community-oriented people of Costa Rica and the country's struggle to maintain its self-determination in the midst of severe austerity measures and exploding inflation. I noted that my proposed research had taken a backseat to writing about the attempted militarization of Costa Rica. I said that as best as I could ascertain, other countries, often through their security councils or organizations, were violating the Costa Rican Constitution by playing a major role in establishing military bases and recruiting local forces in Costa Rica to continue attacks against the Sandinistas in Nicaragua. I mentioned the *dependencia* process and how nonmilitary aid from those countries would increase and technological development would be subsidized further if Costa Rica simply kept silent about the violation.[1] I mumbled something about the interests of countries that wanted to control Costa Rica for economic, political, and geographical reasons under the thin veil of developing the nation. Realizing that I was rambling, being imprecise, and too simplistic, I asked: Do you understand? What do you think? What should be done?

First, Frank spoke at a personal level, explaining why such concerns were about justice, not about just the two of us or some glad to be rad(ical) prattle. Second, in a passionate manner, he expressed his interest in pursuing justice. His comments suggested to me that he pursued science with compassion without falling into the false dichotomy of subjective versus objective analysis. It seemed to me that his science was a very old science, the indigenous science of accuracy, rather than the often pretentious claims of objectivity by normal science or the pompous social science fiction of subjectivity. Third, he spoke of the larger, structural factors that have led and lead to similar events throughout the world, and he explained his reaction to injustice. It became clear that the real place where our paths crossed was in the study of injustice because justice as an academic and policy concept was, unfortunately, a chimera.

Let me therefore discuss the relevance of some of Frank's work for eliminating or reducing injustice. Of course, this discussion includes Frank's explicit as well as implicit objections to facades of justice. Justice not informed by spiritual and material conditions and social relations that are historically specific is often nothing other than injustice or ethnocentric prescriptions for fairness—justice for just-us, rather than for all. Frank objects to attempts to develop all people, nations, states, and even nature under the same homogenous model, the model that can tolerate no deviation. His objections to the dynamics of dependency and marginalization and to the capital over-accumulation of core nations also are examples of his concerns with injustice. In philosophical and legal words, he protests against the unjust distribution of benefits and burdens, including rights, responsibilities, deserts, and needs.

Here, I present (a) some suggestions about the importance of his work for understanding the relationship between his objections as a form of protest, and deviance as a form of diversity; (b) how his work serves as a profound and timely critique of many dominant theories of justice via its relationship to liberation theology; (c) the relevance of his and Marta Fuentes's analysis of social movements for the study of indigenous peoples in their native nations, not states; and (d) the usefulness of their work for future research agendas. I begin with the terms *deviants* and *political deviants* and a brief examination of their relationship to fighting injustice (Lauderdale, 1980).

FRANK THE POLITICAL DEVIANT

The social sciences have a long tradition of studying deviants as bad people (e.g., work following Freud, Skinner, Wilson). The dominant approach is to figure out why they become bad and how to put them on the road to normal development to develop personal conformity. This development is seen as creating justice, because deviants are viewed as a relatively homogenous group of people who infringe disproportionately on the rights of others while they shirk their responsibilities. Responsibilities are defined in narrow terms, focusing on conformity usually without reference to diversity. From this view, the political aspects of deviance are obscured. A less popular perspective on deviants, however, views their behavior as simply a departure from current, dominant norms (Matza, 1969). From this view, a deviant can be a genius such as Galileo or a moral entrepreneur such as Gandhi by following a path that leads to positive consequences. These deviants depart from or challenge the existing order for a higher moral good, such as pointing to or working against injustice (Gamson, 1975; Lauderdale, 1980). They appear in many places throughout time, from Socrates to Mother Teresa and Rigoberta Menchu. These "deviants" are often labeled political deviants as a means of separating them from those who ostensibly need to be developed or normalized.

Why has Andre Gunder Frank been viewed as a deviant—sometimes as a devil, or at least stigmatized for much of his adult life—rather than as a political deviant? Why are individuals such as Frank, countries such as those in the "underdeveloped" periphery, and native nations (the nations of indigenous peoples) defined by the developers as deviant or demonic? Has Frank been labeled a deviant or devil because he notes that development became equated with economic growth that was measured by the growth of GNP per capita with the residual ostensible social aspects then defined as modernization and the political aspects as freedom?

THE SOCIAL CONSTRUCTION OF THE DEVIL

Is it ironic that any similarity exists between the lives of Andre Gunder Frank and Salman Rushdie? Frank was born in Berlin in 1929 and is listed as living in Amsterdam, although he continues to be found working in numerous places throughout the world. His books and articles have been translated into more than twenty languages. Rushdie was born in Bombay in 1947 and is listed as living in London, although he went into hiding in 1989. His books have been translated into more than twenty languages.

At the beginning of his book *The Satanic Verses* (1989), Rushdie quotes Daniel Defoe:

Satan, being thus confined to a vagabond, wandering, unsettled condition, is without any certain abode; for though he has, in consequence of his angelic nature, a kind of empire in the liquid waste or air, yet this is certainly part of his punishment, that he is . . . without any fixed place, or space, allowed him to rest the sole of his foot upon. (p. 1)

Rushdie's two main characters, Saladin and Gibreel, fight the eternal battle between good and evil. Throughout the match, Rushdie asks us whether angels can be demonic or whether the devil can be an angel in disguise. Under what conditions could Frank be defined as a devil or an angel?

Societies continually try to answer such questions. Is, for example, the leader of a loosely knit band of hit-and-run killers of British soldiers a "crazed cult killer" or a "bandit"? Or should George Washington be labeled a revolutionary hero? The answer depends on the cultural location of the person or society, as well as a determination of actors' intentions and the consequences of their actions. The social negotiation of intent and consequences is a contest that includes political, economic, and cultural factors often emphasized or de-emphasized at convenient times. Unfortunately, most analyses of intent are confined to the study of psychology or criminal law, and analyses of consequences are found primarily in sociology or philosophy. Interdisciplinary, theoretical work on both intent and consequences would, at least, help crack those hegemonic facades that support misguided politics and policy (cf. Christenson's research on political trials, 1986, 1991). The definition or characterization of political deviance that dominates during any given historical period can have a critical impact on politics, policy, and research. The relationship between politics and deviance can be explicated, for example, when Socrates was accused of being a threat to the postwar construction in Athens, when Joan of Arc faced the Inquisition, when Galileo stood before the Vatican, and when Leonard Peltier was tried for being a leader of the American Indian movement.

Some of the demonic characterization of Frank and his work stems from a letter he wrote from Chile to friends and former colleagues in the United States on July 1, 1964. Most of the letter focuses on his concern with creating a more adequate analysis and interpretation of underdevelopment and development in an attempt to provide a theory of "capitalist reality." The letter also serves as a rallying cry to friends to oppose injustice through a critical analysis of development policies and analyses. On page two of his letter, Frank states,

> I reject as contrary to fact the more commonly held supposition that underdevelopment is somehow original or traditional, or that developed countries were once underdeveloped as the underdeveloped ones are now; and I try to suggest how internationally, nationally, and regionally underdevelopment developed no less than "development," each in a close causative relation with the other, as a result of capitalist development itself. I suggest, moreover, that the development of underdevelopment no less than that of development itself is a necessary consequence of capitalism and that under capitalism this process continues today essentially as it did in the past. I suggest, finally that insofar as this thesis is well taken, a whole set of theses about development that are widely accepted in the social sciences as points of departure and arrival for research and policy formation are very far off the mark of reality.

And, in commenting on his research on Brazilian agriculture, Frank continues,

> Here, I criticise as factually erroneous and theoretically inadequate the widely accepted "dual society" thesis and its related or sub thesis which attributes the ills of agriculture and often of everything in Latin America (and elsewhere also) to the survival of an isolated, feudal, non-market, or folk society or sector.

Examining the same reality that is usually interpreted along the above lines, I seek to derive them and underdevelopment itself from the development, structure, and functioning of the capitalist system and monopolized market of the economy and society as a whole, rather than falling back on the supposed feudality or folkness of part of the supposedly "dual" society.

And he criticizes the strikingly similar policies and analyses of the Alliance for Progress and the Communist Parties in Latin America. He argues that policymakers base their analyses on an inappropriate concept of dualism and an incorrect view of feudalism. He demonstrates how their policies have had disastrous results for Latin America both in terms of retarding development and increasing underdevelopment (cf. Hirschman, 1961).

On page three of his letter, Frank stridently challenges the claims and implications of liberal positivism:

My thus emerging research, teaching, pamphleteering, and maybe one day fighting orientation has several personal, political, intellectual, and professional implications that I would like to consider with you now. I can no longer distinguish political from professional aspects and maybe also from personal relations in my life and work. I have long thought that the liberal positivist creed or ideology of trying to separate one's politics from one's social science is not only politically and morally but also scientifically objectionable in that the supposed political and moral dispassion, far from permitting objectivity, condemns to scientific failure.

In the remaining pages of his letter, Frank reviews many of his debunking perspectives, including a scathing critique of Milton Friedman's *Capitalism and Freedom* (1962), and presents more of his analysis of capitalism. In the concluding paragraph, Frank emphasizes that because of its structure, the developed world, especially the metropolis, cannot help the underdeveloped world develop and that he is willing to struggle for the liberation of capitalism's underdeveloped periphery.

In essence, Frank presents a timely analysis of the relevance of political-intellectual climates and their impact on the researcher; a passionate plea for an overdue critique of ideology, social science, policy, and politics in relation to the development thrust; and a call for "a more holistic structural and historical analysis and interpretation of underdevelopment and development" from a theoretical perspective on capitalism (cf. Bergesen, 1993). Nonetheless, Frank's intent and actions were renegotiated, redefined. He and his letter of 1964 were viewed as dangerous to the best interests of the U.S. government.

Frank notes in his autobiographical chapter in this book that the 1964 letter and an article on the mechanism of imperialism were "subsequently cited in a letter to me by the U.S. government as the ideological reasons and supposedly legal grounds for which I was then, and for fifteen years more after that, inadmissible to the United States."

Clearly, the reactions to and reconstructions of the letter are only part of the story. Part of the redefinition of Frank and his work is a result of his attack on sacred hegemonic concepts in the West and elsewhere, such as modernization and development. Who dare oppose modernization? To oppose becoming modern, in the United States, for example, is often equated with opposing freedom, democracy, and therefore justice, as well as a technologically advanced and efficient style of life (cf. Inkeles & Smith, 1974; Lauderdale & Cruit, 1993; Mies, 1986; von Werlhof, 1991). Similarly, to attack development is to attack individual rights and progress. Development has become part of the Western project of progress, and only a madman or demon could oppose such a development (cf. Thomas, Meyer, Ramirez, & Boli, 1987). Moreover, Frank's critics quickly noted that he is well known for his antimodern development of underdevelopment theme (also see Frank's *Capitalism and Underdevelopment in Latin America,* 1967). Having relocated to Chile, Frank based his theme partially on his test of Western economic theory, which teleologically claimed the success of the development scheme for economically "underdeveloped" nations. Frank found no empirical support for the theory.

Certainly, another part of the degradation ritual focusing on Frank is easily traced to politicians, policymakers, and academics who found their interests to be threatened or compromised by Frank's work. Despite his scholarly attempt, for example, to establish the concept of dialectical rather than dual society, the attacks on him have been personal and often scandalous. As Frank (1989, p. 18) notes: "One of my honorable academic critics went so far as to say in a public lecture in Poland that I had been in charge of exterminating Jews in a Nazi concentration camp there during World War II (during which [time] I was in high school in the United States and at whose end I was 16 years old)." Another attack, couched in the reductionist psychology of deviance, implied that Frank's critique of development stemmed from a desire to kill his academic father figure, Bert Hoselitz, to which Frank (1989, p. 4) replied, ". . . (but then it was also said that Fidel Castro made a revolution against the Yankees because they would not accept him as a major league baseball pitcher)."

Frank's development of underdevelopment theme intended to expose capital accumulation as the force that was underdeveloping the periphery. His explications suggest that developmental programs such as Kennedy's Alliance for Progress were, at best, suspect, and cast serious doubts on the potential of the U.S. Agency for International Development.

In *Crisis: In the World Economy* (1980), Frank extends his analysis from *World Accumulation 1492-1789* (1978) and makes it abundantly clear that the massive unemployment and poverty in the "underdeveloped" periphery stems from the return-on-investment needs of Western capitalists. Frank's focus on the modern processes and contradictions of capital accumulation is clear and unwavering (Wolf, 1982). Capital overaccumulation is identified as the source of numerous crises and reactions. Efficiency has not led to equality, but rather to more inequality, to greater injustice (Amin, 1974; Chase-Dunn, 1989). And his unambiguous analysis in *Crisis: In the Third World* (1981) contrasts sharply with the price fetishism of neoclassicism and quantitative analyses using econometric techniques in which social relations of power, dependency, and marginalization are deliberately abstracted by the creation of models that produce fatuous answers to trivial questions (Clairmont, 1982).

Opponents of Frank, nonetheless, typically construct a view of him as they perceive the Third World, a dualistic view. Both Frank and the Third World are viewed (and defined) as negative, even dangerous, with the potential for unruly or even revolutionary consequences. Those same politicians, policymakers, and turgid academicians, however, usually see the actions of researchers who tout homogenous development and the core countries as safe and secure, leading to a calm and predictable environment.

Policymakers in particular are defensive when faced with Frank's encompassing analysis because they continue to (a) focus on "paste pot" measures of change, (b) address agendas after basic items have been ignored or removed, and/or (c) expend their resources on implementing the existing but inadequate policies from each "new" agenda. In the 1980s, for example, mainstream policy analysts predicted that deflation would create a major crisis for the core countries where people were already dangerously in debt. They predicted that politicians in the United States would blame Mikhail Gorbachev for the deflation, basing their prediction on the observation that Gorbachev needed foreign money to implement the *perestroika* initiatives. These policy analysts reasoned that Gorbachev would make concessions to Germany and Japan, the U.S.S.R.'s largest trading partners, to obtain the billions needed in foreign credit. Ostensibly, this arrangement would lead to deflation in the core. Being unable to understand more encompassing events because their speculations were based on apt and isolated variables, however, politicians and policy-makers ignored the crisis of confidence with transnational corporations. Chevron's economic losses from the overthrow of the Sudan government, Occidental's losses from the increase in guerrilla warfare in Columbia, and international banking's swoons from Garcia's declaration of a debt mora-torium on assuming the presidency of Peru are classic examples of the inability of mainstream analyses to offer timely and insightful predictions.

Ex post facto analyses from the mainstream also are often a conundrum. The analysis that claimed Mexico was on the edge of defaulting on its huge debt was wrong, and the ex post facto explanation was that the chairperson of the U.S. Federal Reserve secretly diffused the crisis. Of course, such inter-pretations often miss the mark (see McGowan & Kegley, 1983, for foreign policy implications, in particular their presentation of world system theorists, e.g., Wallerstein, Modelski). Compare the mainstream interpretations with the following analysis of part of the 1980s by Frank and Fuentes (1992):

> Export-led growth had failed in Latin America and self-reliance instead in Africa. Socialist national product and income had also fallen 25 percent during four years in Poland. Economic and political crisis went from bad to worse in Stalinist Rumania (lights out), worker-management Yugoslavia (threat of army interven-tion), and even in reformist showcase Hungary (1989 average real wages falling back to the 1970 level and recent revelations of 25 percent of the population living in poverty) and not to mention liberated Vietnam (chaos and reprivatiza-tion). In the Soviet Union the Brezhnev period was rebaptised one of "stagna-tion," although in reality many economic sectors (heavy industry) and social indices (infant mortality rates) had in fact slid backwards. (p. 342)

Analyses such as this one, with an emphasis on accuracy rather than simply ideology, have turned, for example, many politicians who wanted to embrace Frank into those defining him as a deviant. And sometimes political ideologists/ apologists from all sides have joined in the ritual. As is evident from his comments in this book, he even has been defined as the extreme form of the deviant, the devil, when he was called an "ideologist of terrorism in Latin America" or "the cat's paw of the CIA" (Frank, 1989). He suffered a similar fate when he (a) characterized Western Europe and the United States as having a top-down economic democracy and Eastern Europe as having a top-down political democracy; (b) refused to accept the claims of democracy by political modernizers who defended right-wing authoritarianism as a necessary condition against left-wing totalitarianism; (c) pointed to U.S. counterrevolutionary actions in Guatemala, El Salvador, and Lebanon; (d) complained about a U.S. university that was training "police" forces in South Vietnam; (e) supported Muhammad Ali for changing his name from Cassius Clay for religious reasons; (f) noted his exile from Hitler's Germany and Pinochet's Chile (when Allende was killed, friends hid him in their home until he could gain asylum and leave Chile under Pinochet); and (g) explained that some Third World countries often paid their debt many times over and yet still owed double the original amount. From Frank's analysis, we also can see that the term *Third World* has been traditionally employed as another concept for the "underdeveloped" periphery, and in related research it also includes the economically and technologically disadvantaged populations in the core, especially those in large urban centers and isolated rural "development" areas (cf. Lauderdale, 1980).

Frank's refusal to be an apologist for various forms of state power or to restrict his discussions to narrow nations of disadvantaged people has led to unusual characterizations. Benjamin Higgins claims that Frank had to return to Chile with his family after refusing a professorship offer at the University of Havana in Cuba because they wanted him to lecture critically on bourgeois economics (Higgins, 1992, p. 240). And in the United States, the American Enterprise Institute, for example, which had close connections with the Reagan and Bush administrations, publishes works such as *Toward a Theology of the Corporation,* which views Frank as the devil, allowing only people such as Oliver North to be considered as a political deviant or, more correctly from their overdeveloped stance, as a hero. If nothing else, books that combine theology with corporations raise interesting questions about the contribution of Frank to the interface between theology and justice.

In his quest to uncover the fundamental underpinnings of injustice through his theoretical and empirical work, it comes as no surprise to find that Frank often is identified according to the political agenda of his critics. Despite depictions, for example, by politicians, corporations, and their client administrations, a dramatically different view is presented by people concerned with justice, ethics, and theology.

JUSTICE, ETHICS, AND LIBERATION THEOLOGY

The urgent cry for justice continues today while the more frequent accusation of injustice permeates history (Frank, 1992; Goldberg, 1993). The formulas for justice in the West primarily are contained in philosophical approaches: Mill's (1907) utilitarianism, the social contract of Rawls (1972) via Kant, or Nozick's (1974) entitlement/libertarian view. On the basis of Frank's more recent analysis of who is the majority in the world system, it might be tempting to present him as a utilitarian under Western philosophical traditions because he reveals that the majority of the world's population consists of minorities. Justice under utilitarianism typically calls for a scheme that provides the greatest utility or happiness for the majority; however, such a scheme, when it has been put into action, redefines who is the majority. From Aristotle's exclusion of slaves to modern nation-states' exclusion of indigenous peoples in their native nations, the majority is defined within the parameters of those who support implicitly or explicitly the narrow meanings of the rational human or technological development (cf. Goldberg, 1993).

Frank also does not conform to either justice under the social contract or justice from entitlement (or libertarian formulations). Although the Rawlsian social contract's use of the veil of ignorance under which people make fair decisions about resource allocation obviously appeals to his sensibilities, the inability of "developed" people to understand or confront underlying inequalities would not. And, more important, the role of conventional planning and policy making in implementing the contract and their consistent allegiance to development with efficiency before equality would not serve justice from a Frankian perspective. Although Frank usually talks about inequity and inequality rather than justice, he consistently suggests that planning and planners do not serve the interests of justice because the planners (and/or their political bosses) serve their own interests at the expense of others, despite Rawls's argument that development for some would be justified only if it benefited everyone. Frank also reminds us of the serious mistakes of modern planners who miscalculated the role of non-economic factors when the Ayatollah Khomeini defeated the modernizing Shah of Iran without military force and rejected the goals of Western development.

Entitlement theory, which emphasizes private property and individual freedom, fares even worse as a model because its assumptions about fairness in acquisition and transfer not only have proved unworkable but also are a central part of the allegiance or entitlement to commodities for the privileged and few or none for the rest. Entitlement theory suffers most from Frank's concern about efficiency before equity. The efficient system never arrives because inequity continues to dominate and expand.

The connection between dominant Western philosophy and theology, though often contentious, is striking. The manner in which some religions respond to philosophical arguments or formulas for justice is quite varied, as is the style in which some philosophical schools of thought react to theological formulas for justice (Gottwald, 1983; Lebacqz, 1986; Niebuhr, 1935/1979; West, 1982). The most unexpected event for most religious scholars and philosophers, however, has been a religious response to Frank justice, rather than the standard philosophies of justice. That response, partly based on Frank's analysis, is now coined *liberation theology*.

Liberation theology emerged in the 1940s and 1950s in Latin America, where it appeared as a religious social movement in reaction to (a) the growing ties between the elites and the Catholic Church and (b) increasing inequities, especially those of land use and ownership. The roots of such movements, in which religion plays a powerful revolutionary role, have been traced to attempts to develop new areas or areas with temporary absences of stable international diplomatic and monetary order (see Engels, 1926; Oliverio & Desjardins, in press; Sorel, 1950, on revolution; Wuthnow, 1980, on social movements and religion). By the 1970s, the movement received world attention primarily through the publication in 1972 of Gustavo Gutierrez's *Teología de la Liberación* (*Theology of Liberation*). The theology begins, not with theory, but with the realities of injustice experienced by the peasants and indigenous peoples of Latin America.[2] The theology emphasizes that justice is to be understood as a structural phenomenon and that injustice is traced to private ownership, with the market system portrayed as violent. The commandment following the interpretations of the work of Jesus is to fight against poverty and oppression, to liberate the poor and oppressed here and now, rather than wait for heavenly justice.

Gutierrez cited some of Frank's analysis blaming part of Latin American underdevelopment on development in the North. Gutierrez's discussion details the affluence and technological development of the Northern Hemisphere and its relationship to the impoverishment and marginalization of the dependent and underdeveloped nations of Latin America. His discussion also included some qualifications by Cardoso about dependency theory, and numerous books have attempted to either confirm Frank's contributions to the liberation theology of justice or reduce them to simplistic slogans (compare Anderson & Dawsey, 1992; Ellis & Maduro, 1990; and Goizueta, 1988; with Novak, 1987, 1991; Rubenstein & Roth, 1988; Smith, 1991). Voices from other countries also entered the debate. In commenting on the Canadian Conference of Catholic Bishops and their discussion of ethical reflections on economic crisis, Lind (1983) notes,

> For Frank, surplus value is the basic building block of developmental life. When surplus value is expropriated through staples export, the centre or metropolis can develop beyond its normal capacity and the margin or satellite is permanently restricted to the underdeveloped role allowed for it in that relationship. (p. 159)

The Canadian Catholic Churches actively supported the Dene Indian Nation in their resistance to various development plans. They referred to Frank's insistence that development is a relational and qualitative term:

> One of the resources they were able to draw on was the experience of the Catholic missionaries with indigenous peoples in Latin America. Andre Gunder Frank was an obvious ally in that regard. Pursuing the phenomenon of the repeating satellitic structure, Frank was able to show how the Native people of Latin America, rather than having had development pass them by, have suffered the butt-end of capitalist development. They have been marginalized not because they occupy remote areas of the country but because they occupy the final hinterland of the last metropolis and they therefore bear the weight of all the other satellites upon their heads. (Lind, 1983, p. 159)

Lind points out that Frank's work is only one way to explain the relationship, but it was the most attractive to the bishops because the parts of his analysis that political economists most criticize are the ones that attract them most. The bishops were most concerned with the development of peoples, not economies. Dependency works against community determination and autonomy. In essence, "the argument is about whether certain kinds of growth could really solve the problems at hand. . . . This ethical dimension to Frank's conception of underdevelopment and dependency is what attracts the attention of the Catholic Bishops" (Lind, 1983, p. 161). Referring to Gutierrez's position that sacredness is found in the relationship between the land and the people who work it, the bishops argue that the dominance of capital as the developing principle contradicts the ethical principle that labor must be given priority in development of an economy based on justice. There must be an ethics of means as well as ends. Maybe Harvey Perloff's perception that Frank was "the most philosophical person" he had ever met makes some sense if we consider Frank's view of injustice from the theology of liberation (see Chapter 2, this volume).

Frank's contribution to the study of justice also questions the dominant perspective that focuses on what justice should be. The turgid scholasticism found in many ethnocentric theories of justice based on Western philosophy can profit from analyses of where perceptions of justice emerge (Frank, 1992; Inverarity, Lauderdale, & Feld, 1983; Lauderdale & Cavender, 1986). Philosophical formulas become hollow without systematic explorations of the sources of injustice. These examinations include, at least, (a) the continued exposure of exploitation in labor relations, (b) the exclusion of participants in decision-making and policy agendas, (c) the erosion of community solidarity and identity and the right to sovereignty, and (d) the long-term cost to nature when it is defined in indigenous terms—that is, both humans and the environment as nature, rather the modern notion of nature as separate and subservient to humans. The relevance of Frank's work for understanding indigenous peoples in their native nations is imminent.

INDIGENOUS JUSTICE

More than 100 military conflicts are taking place in the world, and approximately 75% consist of indigenous peoples trying to resist or free themselves from political centralization and homogenous development (cf. Nietschmann, 1987). These indigenous peoples living within the current 192 or so nation-states comprise, at the least, three thousand native nations—people with a common culture, heritage, language, geography, political system, and a desire for common interaction (e.g., the Basques of Spain and France; the Kurds of Syria, Turkey, Iran, and Iraq; the Sami of Scandinavia; the Karens of Burma; the Miskito of Nicaragua; the Mayans of Guatemala and Mexico, along with hundreds of other native nations of the Americas, Asia, Africa, and the Pacific). Yet, most of the nations are invisible to the developers until their resources are "discovered"; then, attempts usually are made to make them invisible if they resist top-down development. Nietschmann (1987), for example, identifies eleven separate native nations in Burma, fifty-five in China, and three hundred in Indonesia (also see Mander, 1992). The people of these native nations who resist control usually are defined as deviants by the states that control their lands (Deloria, 1992). The deviant labels include such terms as *terrorists, insurgents,* and *extremists,* or *separatists, tribal dissidents,* and *ethnic groups.* Although native peoples typically resist state-centered development because it destroys their culture and therefore nature, these varying labels of deviance are imposed by the larger states (Riding In, 1992). Nietschmann suggests that larger states understand the commonalty of their interests, because changing the labels from *deviants* to *diverse people,* confirming rights of sovereignty, and granting independence to the native nations would subvert the worldwide development plan, including the plans and functions of the International Monetary Fund (IMF) and the World Bank.

People in the native nations are confronted with problems that developers take for granted, including free expression of language and religion, the right to live within indigenous cultures and traditions, and basic sustenance, such as clean water, clean air, and land. Many of the nations are approached increasingly by developers who want to modernize them by establishing economic incentives via waste disposal sites, mining corporations, energy producers, and other development schemes that have proved in the past to be polluting. Yet, non-indigenous communities increasingly reject similar proposals to develop as they refuse to pollute their own backyards.[3]

Frank and Fuentes note that indigenous peoples' conceptions of equity, efficiency, and economy in development are a world apart from those measured by GNP growth rates (cf. J. Riding In, 1992). The development plan includes the domination of nature for economic profit. The European tradition, especially the philosophical justifications of Kant, Hobbes, and Locke, emphasize "the state of nature" from which humans must separate themselves in order to dominate it (cf. von Werlhof, 1988). Under the melting pot banner of development, people were instructed to ignore diversity or to homogenize it when possible. Most indigenous peoples valued and encouraged diversity and personal expression for the good of the collective, including nature. Nature and people were viewed as one entity from the indigenous perspective (Deloria, 1973). Deloria suggests that

> if all things are related the unity of creation demands that each life form contribute its intended contribution. . . . Any violation of another entity's right to existence in and of itself is a violation of the nature of creation and a degradation of religious reality itself. (p. 299)

The care for and examination of nature provided the lessons that demonstrated the relevance and importance of diversity (Lauderdale, 1992).

Indigenous cultures following the traditional lessons typically embody ideas and methods of practicing social diversity and responsibility. Social responsibility, rather than the modern imposed notion of individual rights by the state, serves as the cornerstone of justice (cf. Deloria, 1992; Monture-OKanee, 1993; Thomas & Lauderdale, 1987, 1988). Law emerging from this jurisprudence contrasts with contemporary Western law, which tries to achieve order through hierarchical structures, privilege, and conformity. Under the arm of homogenous development, social and political stability are viewed as a result of "law and order." This claim that law and order creates justice ignores the inequitable use of punishment much in the same fashion that Frank notes how economic development claims to create freedom but ignores equality while creating inequity as a form of punishment in all areas of life.[4]

The expansion of inequality and punitive sanctions is largely a consequence of the development and growth of the centralized state's emphasis on efficiency and control (Foucault, 1977; Inverarity et al., 1983). The developed state continues to legitimate its control and expand its jurisdiction by deconstructing indigenous solidarity, experiential education, and family and community welfare for people as it constructs national citizenship, formal education, and limited forms of government welfare for individuals, including ostensible protection via nuclear armaments. Communal solidarity, education from experience, family welfare, and real diversity are defined as "underdeveloped." Often, indigenous values are eroded; for example, family welfare is sacrificed to economic development as the home increasingly loses its hearth with parents or guardians absent and as diverse people increasingly lose their land and culture (Lauderdale, McLaughlin, & Oliverio, 1990; Thomas & Lauderdale, 1987). Indigenous people are instructed by various agents of the state to view the nation-state and the concept of citizen as major sources of solidarity and identity with an emphasis on abstract conceptions of nationalism. Formal education, especially higher education, with rigid hierarchical organization, unbridled competition, and conceptions of good versus bad students, is presented as superior to experiential learning. Modern forms of welfare often have created varying levels of stigma for recipients as new constructions of deviant people are created.

The label of deviance is created by reductionist logic, rather than by a focus on the structural inequities explicated by Frank. Whereas protesters in the street, for example, become the focus during an economic crisis, price gougers in the suite are defined as only playing the market. Moreover, the state has created new and disproportionate forms of repressive punishment. The emphasis on the punitive powers of the developers at the expense of the restitutive rights of victims provides an exploitative device to maintain political power and derive pecuniary benefits (Oliverio & Lauderdale, 1991). In the modern legal system, the state has become the principal claimant regarding criminal action. The expansion of the process of rationalization in production—couched in formal, predictable procedures and rules—for example, has spread beyond the workplace and influenced the direction of legal change where indigenous rights are eroded or dismissed as primitive. Foucault (1977, p. 49) observed that "the ceremony of punishment, then, is an exercise in 'terror' "—a policy aimed at reflecting the "unrestrained presence" of the developed state.

Pushed into the corners of the developing world, indigenous peoples resist through patience, protest, spirituality, and persistence, often with persistent humor. Many readers overlook the relevance of Frank's sense of humor and its direct relation to the everyday humor of indigenous peoples. He often displays this sense in his scholarly titles, some of which are quite blunt—for example, "Equating Economic Forecasting With Astrology Is an Insult—to Astrologers." He also uses a play on words to alert the reader to the importance of reassessing traditional concepts and analyses—for example, "The Economics of Crisis and the Crisis of Economics," "Development of Underdevelopment or Underdevelopment in China," "Crisis of Ideology and the Ideology of Crisis," "Sociology of Development and Underdevelopment of Sociology." The analyses following these amusing titles are serious, displaying Frank's overarching concern with accuracy. Social scientists claiming to be objective and normative scholars who give their allegiance to subjectivity ignore the modest role of accuracy and Frank's implicit connection with indigenous knowledge (science). And his critique of planners and policymakers reflects the indigenous skepticism of homogenous ideas:

> These true believers in the power of social/political ideology and of individual faith not only believe that they can move mountains (and put them down where they want instead of where the advancing glacier does), but that their social ideology and individual faith is *the* active ingredient (the motor force as Marx put it) in defining the course of history. They take any denial of this view to be treasonous consorting with the forces of evil, which they consider to be as voluntarist as themselves. Populist incarnation of any of these forces through the charisma of a leader who is a great communicator will of course generate a force to contend with even if the leader is better at creating the illusion of being able to move mountains than at moving them or the course of history. (Frank, 1984, p. 148)

And in his disagreements in public, such as the one with Ben Higgins, Higgins (1992) claims that Frank begins with a story about lending his car to Higgins during a visit in Texas:

> I let Ben drive it one day from the University to his house at Bull Creek Ranch. He drove with great speed, flair, and skill. Then when he drove the car into his garage he left the brake off and the door open, so that the car rolled back and took off the door on the entrance to the garage. Ben does economic analysis the same way he drives a car. It is brilliant up to the very end, but the end is a disaster. (p. 240)

Frank's personal history also suggests that persistence and patience within the context of an understanding of the relevance of timing are essential for scholars, young and old alike. In commenting on his early research on the development of underdevelopment as the result of dependence, he observes (Frank, 1991, p. 24), "All of these ideas and terms were in *the original 1963 manuscript, which was not published until 1975* by Oxford University Press in India under the title *On Capitalist Underdevelopment*." Is it ironic that Big Mac has been celebrating the 25th year of its development while Frank's persistent humor reappears with his comment about McWorld in Chapter 2 in this volume? Frank also now persists with his analysis of the problems of "delinking" from the worldwide development project. This analysis is captured in everyday terms by an author who refers to her- or himself under the alias of P.M., a gimmick that privileges her or his ideas over her or his status:

> We are all parts of the Planetary Work-Machine—we are the machine. We represent it against each other. Whether we're developed or not, waged or not, whether we work alone or as employees—we serve its purpose. Where there is no industry, we "produce" virtual workers to export to industrial zones. Africa has produced slaves for the Americas, Turkey produces workers for Germany, Pakistan, for Kuwait, Ghana for Nigeria, Morocco for France, Mexico for the U.S. Untouched areas can be used as scenery for the international tourist business: Indians on reservations, Polynesians, Balinese, aborigines. Those who try to get out of the Machine fulfill the function of picturesque "outsiders" (bums, hippies, yogis). As long as the Machine exists, we're inside it. It has destroyed or mutilated almost all traditional societies or driven them into demoralizing defensive situations. If you try to retreat to a "deserted" valley in order to live quietly on a bit of subsistence farming, you can be sure you'll be found by a tax collector, somebody working for the local draft board, or by the police. (P.M., 1985, p. 9)

AN AGENDA FOR FUTURE RESEARCH

In the light of broad human concerns with injustice, it is not surprising to find references to Frank in religion and philosophy, or even the varied reaction to his work in human biology and archaeology. In archaeology, for example, he contributes to the understanding of how development forced indigenous peoples from their traditional use of the land and its preservation via their cultivation of maize (Street-Perrott, Perrott, & Harkness, 1989). In the near future, we may see a similar contribution regarding the cultivation of coffee in Chiapas. But there are new objections to his dependency theory in human biology (Lewis, 1990). While researchers debate the usefulness of his original dependency theory, however, Frank continues to revise or extend his earlier work (cf. Corbridge, 1986, 1993).[5]

Frank's project, for example, created in conjunction with the late Marta Fuentes, focuses on social movements and emphasizes their lifelong concern with equality before efficiency. They examine the sense of morality and injustice that mobilizes social movement participants. These social movements include cultures that did not and do not want to dominate other cultures or seek power and position over people within the culture. Moreover, Frank and the late Fuentes point to the misguided ahistorical and non-empirical interpretations of the causes and consequences of worldwide social movements and stress that "the strength and importance of social movements are cyclical and related to long political economic and (perhaps associated) ideological cycles" (1990, p. 127).

They explore social movements that have appeared, disappeared, and reappeared for centuries and, in some cases, for millennia throughout the world. Their comparative, historical framework should prove useful for current indigenous and anticolonial movements recognized in the West because of varied media coverage, such as the indigenous and peasant movements in the Americas, including various North American Indian Nations, the struggle in Chiapas, the seemingly non-ending resistance and mobilizations by peasants and indigenous peoples in Guatemala, as well as movements in South Africa or, in other words, for those throughout the world, especially those social movements that receive scant, if any, media coverage.

Their analysis is important particularly because it provides a clearer background for viewing and understanding ostensible new movements:

Yet many of these are now commonly called "new," although European history records countless social movements like the Spartacist slave revolts in Rome, countless religious wars, the peasant movements, or wars, of sixteenth century Germany, historical ethnic and nationalist conflict throughout the continent, and women's movements that unleashed backlashes of witch hunts and more recent forms of repression. In Asia, the Arab world and the expansion of Islam, Africa and Latin America, of course, multiple forms of social movements have been the agents of social resistance and transformation throughout history. (Frank & Fuentes, 1990, p. 128)

Their discussion also notes the importance of recognizing that the majority of large-scale movements in core countries are middle class, whereas those in the Third World are primarily popular or working class. Frank and the late Fuentes note that Third World movements emerge from world economic crises and that Third World participants are struggling for sheer physical and economic survival and cultural identity while experts talk about crisis or dispute resolution or similar Band-Aid tactics. Crisis management, rather than development or dispute resolution, is prevalent because the disputes or crises usually are not resolved and often reappear in the same or similar forms after they have festered because of the lack of structural solutions (cf. Lauderdale & Cruit, 1993).

The success of worldwide movements is compromised by competition among the movements (cf. Lauderdale, 1988; Ramirez, 1981). Focusing on the women's movement, they remark, "In particular, virtually all religious, ethnic and nationalist movements—like working class and Marxist oriented movements and political parties as well—negate and sacrifice women's interest" (Frank & Fuentes, 1990, p. 140). Policies or practices of movements that employ hierarchical and dualistic means to their ends are enemies of most women's movements, particularly in the Third World.

Here, as in the capitalist countries, the free wage-labourer, the proletarian, the hero from whom the Marxists expected the revolutionary transformation, is, as Claudia von Werlhof has put it, far too expensive, he works far too little, is not flexible enough and cannot easily be "squeezed" for the generation of more surplus because he is better organized than peasants, and particularly women who, as we saw, are the ones who provide the bulk of the labour force in the "subsidiary" sector. (Mies, 1986, p. 197)

Frank and Fuentes (1992) emphasize,

> [I]t has belatedly been statistically confirmed (as women knew all along in their
> bones if not in their minds) that women do most of the work in the world. They
> also do much of the productive work: most agricultural work in Africa and many
> other parts of the world, including the socialist countries, and much low paid
> industrial and service work everywhere. Adding in the other minorities, probably
> almost all of the . . . [hard] work is done by minorities. (p. 364)

Public policies have not changed this workload, access to work, or fair
payment for work. Affirmative action increasingly is rejected for giving too
much to minorities or for creating new problems in the attempt to counteract
original inequities (von Werlhof, 1991). As Frank and Fuentes (1992, p. 347)
emphasize, "And, equal competitive market treatment of unequals, not to
mention monopolistic treatment of those who have neither property or power,
further increases both inequality and inequity."

Furthermore, policies that tout efficiency through planning typically are
bankrupt:

> Planning . . . gives the planners or their political bosses inequitous and unequal
> power to serve their own interests at the expense of others; and it produces more
> red tape than economic welfare besides. . . . Efficiency may be individual or
> group means to their respective ends, but equity between individuals or groups
> is hardly considered. For world development, which still seems to follow a macro
> historical course largely beyond intentional human micro controls, policy (making)
> is hardly even relevant at all. (Frank & Fuentes, 1992, p. 347)[6]

Accordingly, Frank has revised his earlier proposal about delinking from
the hegemonic development scheme to entertain the notion of different kinds
of links to economy and society. He suggests that these new and different links
may be created by some social movements. Frank and Fuentes (1990) note
that the problems and prospects of transition to socialism must be reinterpreted because the current form of socialism has not been able to delink from
the world capitalist economy. Yet, they warn us,

> So many economic slogans and "solutions" like "economic growth," "economic
> development, economic ends, economic means, economic necessities and eco-
> nomic austerity," do not satisfy people's needs for community, identity, spirituality,
> or often even material welfare. (p. 135)[7]

Frank and Fuentes also stress recognition of the unique relationship between
economic development policies, life-threatening implications of unchecked

"progress," and social movements. Frank and Fuentes (1992) explicate the disastrous consequences of development policies from a few years ago that sound strangely familiar today:

> Although strong peace movements are more visible in the North, the real problem of war is, of course, particularly important in and for the South. For during the past four decades of accelerated Third World "development," every war in the World has taken place in the South, and every year there have been several wars going on there simultaneously. Any break out of peace there, such as in 1988, is therefore a real (contribution to) development. Similarly, although environmental degradation may be more (locally visible in the North including the East), the globally most serious environmental anti-development is now probably taking place in the South, as in the deforestation of Amazonia, Indonesia, the Himalayan slopes, etc. and the desertification in Africa and Asia. (p. 367)

CONCLUDING REMARKS

I close with a comment on the environmental crisis and the development of law where law narrowly construed is touted as the vehicle for the preservation of the environment, just-wars, and justice. For most indigenous peoples, law was (and in some cases, is) carried around as an integral part of their existence, rather than confined to intimidating law books, schools, courts, and legal experts who largely control the language as well as the cost of using the law (Deloria & Lytle, 1983; Monture-OKanee, 1993). Oral tradition as an institution in indigenous life stimulates, develops, protects, and delivers knowledge in a systemic manner and has qualities different from those of the written word. Burning or banning books does not destroy law based on oral tradition, and revisionist machinations have not altered completely the diversity and respect for all life embedded in the cultures of many native nations (cf. Monture-OKanee, 1993).[8] Studying, rather than rejecting or romanticizing, indigenous cultures will provide a better understanding of why injustice persists. Rejecting the knowledge of indigenous cultures or defining them as deviant is a misguided technique used to transform identities and maintain or increase social solidarity while promoting the social status of people who misunderstand the advantages of diversity. Despite claims of acting in the name of collective responsibility, this technique of defining others as deviant, rather than as diverse, often is only part of the struggle over social identity, status, and mobility.

The recent call for cultural diversity in North American universities being implemented, in part, through law is, in fact, a rediscovery, if not a conundrum. The modern states' attempts to control and dominate nature and to define this process as progress stands in stark contrast to most indigenous ideas of "progress" and nature. The lessons of nature are diverse and require respect, rather than simply tolerance, especially in the sense that nature does not stand outside or alongside the human animal. Progress for one part of nature may well be regress for another. Modern linear, univariate plans for controlling and dominating nature—whether rainforests, animals, the human animal, or natural technologies—has not been a lesson plan taken from indigenous peoples.[9] Merchant (1989) notes,

> The colonial revolution extracted native species from their ecological contexts and shipped them overseas as commodities. It was legitimated by a set of symbols that placed cultured European humans above wild nature, other animals, and "beastlike savages." It substituted a visual for an oral consciousness and an image of nature as female and subservient to a transcendent male God for the Indians' animistic fabric of symbolic exchanges between people and nature. (p. 2)

In recent work, Frank discredits Eurocentrism and moves toward a "humanocentric" view of history, carrying with it implicit notions of the benefits arising from understanding that the world system has existed, at least, for five thousand years (Frank & Gills, 1993). Currently, Frank is considering the relevance of an ecocentric perspective.

Frank notes the prediction of others that indigenous peoples will disappear. From his long-view of history and analysis of the persistent struggle by indigenous peoples, however, he is not convinced of their demise. It appears that part of the prediction of indigenous demise can be attributed to the fear of going backward, of losing ground, coupled with the denial of abundance, which characterizes much of the world history of indigenous life (cf. Deloria, 1992; Mander, 1992; Merchant, 1989). From the long-view of history, we may come to realize that indigenous life is not backward. Ostensible civilizations are known for their various forms of slavery and for turning time into money; civil indigenous peoples are known for their tolerance and for putting place before time. Indigenous life is known for its expansion of time; modern life, with its exploding technology to save time, results in less and less time, including the hegemonic facade of quality time. Quality time born through authoritarian, homogenous development? The U.S. experience, for example, where homogeneity has been enforced through the melting pot plans of development, reveals incredibly high levels of violence inside and outside the country. Moreover, "developed" people have been trying to deny the death of the earth much as they try to deny their own physical death.

Denial and guilt are products of homogenous development. We all come from indigenous roots, roots that created respect, not simply tolerance for the diversity of life. Our existence is, in part, due to the old time accuracy of indigenous science, not the claims of the modern times. Linear time has led to short-term efficiency and profound inequity. The study of spiral time may be the path of diversity and equality. Real cultural diversity, the heterogeneous "cultivation" of all living things, is not only a viable path but also may prove to be the only path to survival, the survival of future generations. As Frank emphasizes—the struggle continues!

NOTES

1. In 1995, ten years after my first conversation with Gunder Frank, the boundary between military and nonmilitary aid remains ambiguous because nonmilitary aid has often included assistance from the U.S. Army Corps of Engineers and components of the U.S. National Guard (Lauderdale, 1986). Debates rage over the activities of these outsiders with disclaimers from groups inside and outside Costa Rica that point to new bridges, roads, and communication systems, whereas their opponents suggest that these developments are part of the construction of a growing infrastructure for waging war. Social protests also appeared from various groups in Costa Rica reacting to severe austerity measures imposed by international lending organizations, unpredictable changes in work location and policy by transnational corporations operating in the country, and an increasing number of attempts by other nations to impose their strategies of international security. Yet, 30% of the annual budget of Costa Rica is devoted to education and there is a 90% literacy rate. The budget dedicated to education and health in Costa Rica is over twenty times larger than that of the Ministry of Public Security (Lauderdale, 1989). The creation of an effective democratic system and the constitutional abolition of the army in 1949 are important elements contributing to Costa Rica's uniqueness in the region (see Schlesinger & Kinzer, 1982, for a comparison with Guatemala). The external aid has helped Costa Rica pay its enormous debt-service demands and continue to enjoy the highest standard of living in Central America. Many Costa Ricans are also well aware of their economic dependency on transnational corporations. Throughout most of the history of the United Fruit Company, for example, which is known as the "Octopus" in many rural regions, profound debates have taken place over the advantages and disadvantages of dependency relationships. These debates have included discussions of the advantages of modernization via the transportation systems built by the transnational corporations and the disadvantages of such "progress" resulting in the related deterioration of the ecosystem. More general discussions still continue over the short-term versus long-term effects of economic dependency on workers, natural resources, and political development (cf. Bornschier & Chase-Dunn, 1985; Bunster & Chaney, 1985; von Werlhof, 1986). In recent years, Costa Ricans have also become concerned with the precarious position of being heavily dependent on the export of such items as beef, coffee, bananas, and some fabrics and the ensuing problems with terms of trade with other countries.

2. Scott (1986) presents convincing evidence that peasants maintain, first and foremost, the norms of reciprocity and the right to subsistence, rather than profit or accumulation, even in the face of major obstacles. When these norms are constantly violated, peasant movements often emerge.

3. Efforts to resolve disputes that result from resistance to such pollution have been inadequate. The efforts emphasize development and efficiency, rather than justice. Modern attempts to resolve disputes under the rubric of alternative dispute resolution are exemplified by alternative dispute resolution centers or dispute processing programs. These ostensible alternatives offer little in the way of change for at least three reasons. First, they typically resolve only those few disputes that would have been resolved without the intrusion of professional or experts in dispute resolution or processing. Second, they usually work with relatively homogenous populations, ignoring people and groups who are marginalized because of economics, gender, race, or age. Third, even those centers and programs employ homogenous means to address the problems, and more fundamentally, they ignore or minimize the fact that most of the resolutions are short term and usually reappear after they have festered to the point they reproduce or increase the underlying inequalities. The programs seem unable to respond systematically to indigenous peoples throughout the world who are still experiencing the absence of dispute resolution in the form of poverty, landlessness, dispossession, political and religious oppression, and genocide. In essence, experts at dispute resolution or processing often create the illusion of being able to resolve disputes, rather than actually resolving them or the underlying structural problems.

4. The incarceration rate in the United States is approximately 500 per 100,000. The closest incarceration rate of comparable countries is South Africa, with 311. Hungary is third, with 117 per 100,000. And the vast majority of prisoners in the United States are from the economically poor, with a disproportionate number of minorities in U.S. prisons; for example, in 1990, over 50% of the state and federal prisoners were classified as "black." In the United States the police increasingly are turned, at great expense, into paramilitary agents who are asked to control deviant citizens and to prepare them for repressive punishment.

5. Frank's future agenda includes, at least, two provocative areas. One is work on the world system prior to 1500. The other examines the role of worldwide social movements in the world system. In the first project, Frank (1989, 1993) and Frank and Gills (1993) are developing an alternative analysis of world history, beginning with the proposition that a single world system has existed for thousands of years with historical continuity and unity (Wallerstein, 1974, 1980). Frank emphasizes the cyclical nature of hegemonic relationships:

> [T]he post 1500 world system did not rise in Europe out of the transition from feudalism a la Wallerstein, but . . . it represents a shift of hegemonic core to Europe from the Middle East, and possibly to there from farther East before (and now of course continuing on its observed westward shift around the globe in the direction of where it may have started millennia ago), back via Japan towards China. (Frank, 1989, p. 23)

Frank suggests that a single world system has historical continuity for five thousand years, emerging from its core in West Asia and Egypt and spreading to Afro-Eurasia. Frank's image of human relations in this five-thousand-year history of the world system is usually a Hobbesian one and often is quite deterministic. His view of the Hobbesian world and his deterministic comments in this project seem to leave little hope for movement, less social movements that attempt to oppose domineering humans who seek only power and position over others. In a provocative manner, this project and one on social movements are disparate because the social movement evidence reveals numerous cases where human relations are contingent and more complex because some seek autonomy rather than domination.

6. Frank and Fuentes (1990) maintain that,

as long as the social movements have to write their own scripts as they go along, they cannot use and can only reject as counterproductive, any prescriptions from on high or outside as to where they should go or how they should get there. (p. 139)

Despite this appropriate warning, it is clear that many scholars study these movements and often write about their origin, their activities, and their potential impact on the world without the sensitivity of Frank and Fuentes. In so doing, theories of the role of these movements appear in print (cf. Alexandrov, 1974; Bouchier, 1986). In fact, these ostensible nonparticipants become participants (cf. Mies, Bennholdt-Thomsen, & von Werlhof, 1988; Rupp & Taylor, 1987). Although their values may not be directly imposed, they often become part of the script of the movements, either through productive or counterproductive statements. Project Camelot, wherein the role of the intellectual became direct and quite obvious in blocking local social change, should remind us of the numerous ways in which values can be imposed.

7. Concepts of a sacred society persist in diverse forms from the past (Celtic society) to the present (Tibetan society). What Charles Krautheimer calls the "new tribalism" (the worldwide interest in ethnic or indigenous roots) suggests the importance of understanding the return to spirituality and ritual. Diverse forms of spirituality and ritual appear to provide a more meaningful sense of identity than that of "modern individual" imposed by the state, as well as a different sense of subsistence and security. What type of knowledge helps us understand the reemergence of the American Indian movement, the protests of the Amazonian Indians or the Basques in Spain, and conflicts in general—Shiite and Sunni Muslims, Protestant and Catholic Irish, Sikhs and the Indian state, Xhosas and Zulus in South Africa, Southern and Northern Italians, French and English-speaking Canadians, China and Tibet, Turks and Greeks in Cyprus, Palestinians and Israelis, and Iraq and the United States (Oliverio & Lauderdale, 1991)?

8. The written history of North American Indian cultures, for example, continues to be embroiled in controversy.

The Hurons, for example, have been described consistently as a culture which did not have social classes, a government independent from their kinship system, or private property. The Zunis were noted for their political structure based on "a council of the oldest men" (papas) rather than a chief (Weatherford, 1988). The Comanches, at present, disagree over the historical interpretation of "chief" with some arguing that the concept was adopted or affixed only in the past two hundred years. (Lauderdale, 1992, p. 9; see also Thornton, 1987, 1990)

9. Attempts to modernize or develop indigenous peoples, peasants, and, in general, the rural poor have usually resulted in more inequality.

What has been the response of the rural poor who have all along been at the losing end of such a developmental process? . . . Agrarian radicalism and peasant militancy are only sequels to the growing contradictions in rural India. Naxalism, whether in West Bengal, or in Srikakulam or Tanjore districts in South India, is just the warning signal. Even then, prospects of this mobilization process developing into a transformative movement on the pan-Indian scale are obliterated by a number of factors. The chief among them is the structural dependence of the rural poor on the rural rich who not only control the economic resources but also largely determine political policies and programmes. (Dhanagare, 1984, p. 198; also see the discussion of the Chipko women's protest in India).

REFERENCES

Alexandrov, Y. (1974). The peasant movements of developing countries in Asia and North Africa after the Second World War. In H. Landsberger (Ed.), *Rural protest: Peasant movements and social change* (pp. 351-377). New York: Macmillan.

Amin, S. (1974). *Accumulation on a world scale* (Vol. 1). New York: Monthly Review Press.

Anderson, R. V., & Dawsey, J. M. (1992). *From wasteland to promised land: Liberation theology for a post-Marxist world.* Maryknoll, NY: Orbis.

Bergesen, A. (1993). The rise of semiotic Marxism. *Sociological Perspectives, 36,* 1-22.

Bornschier, V., & Chase-Dunn, C. (1985). *Transnational corporations and underdevelopment.* New York: Praeger.

Bouchier, D. (1986). The sociologist as anti-partisan: A dilemma of knowledge and academic power. In K. Lang & G. Lang (Eds.), *Research in social movements, conflicts, and change* (pp. 1-24). Greenwich, CT: JAI.

Bunster, X., & Chaney, E. M. (1985). *Sellers and servants: Working women in Lima, Peru.* New York: Praeger.

Chase-Dunn, C. (1989). *Global formation: Structures of the world-economy.* Cambridge, MA: Blackwell.

Christenson, R. (1986). *Political trials.* New Brunswick, NJ: Transaction Books.

Christenson, R. (1991). *Political trials in history from antiquity to the present.* New Brunswick, NJ: Transaction Books.

Clairmont, F. (1982). *Review of* Crisis: In the Third World *by Andre Gunder Frank.* Geneva, Switzerland: UNCTAD.

Corbridge, S. (1986). *Capitalist world development: A critique of radical development geography.* New York: Macmillan.

Corbridge, S. (1993). *Debt and development.* Cambridge, MA: Blackwell.

Deloria, V., Jr. (1973). *God is red.* New York: Grosset & Dunlap.

Deloria, V., Jr. (1992). *God is red* (2nd rev. ed.). Golden, CO: North American Press.

Deloria, V,. Jr., & Lytle, C. (1983). *American Indians, American justice.* Austin: University of Texas Press.

Dhanagare, D. N. (1984). Agrarian reforms and rural development in India: Some observations. In L. Kriesberg (Ed.), *Research in social movements, conflicts, and change* (pp. 177-201). Greenwich, CT: JAI.

Ellis, M. H., & Maduro, O. (Eds.). (1990). *Expanding the view: Gustavo Gutierrez and the future of liberation theology.* Maryknoll, NY: Orbis.

Engels, F. (1926). *The peasant war in Germany.* New York: International Publishers.

Foucault, M. (1977). *Discipline and punish: The birth of the prison* (A. Sheridan, Trans.). New York: Pantheon.

Frank, A. G. (1967). *Capitalism and underdevelopment in Latin America.* New York: Monthly Review Press.

Frank, A. G. (1975). *On capitalist underdevelopment.* Bombay, India: Oxford University Press.

Frank, A. G. (1978). *World accumulation 1492-1789.* New York: Monthly Review Press.

Frank, A. G. (1980). *Crisis: In the world economy.* New York: Holmes & Meier.

Frank, A. G. (1981). *Crisis: In the Third World.* New York: Holmes & Meier.

Frank, A. G. (1984). Political ironies in the world economy. *Studies in Political Economy, 15,* 119-149.

Frank, A. G. (1989). *A world system history before 1500.* Unpublished manuscript, University of Amsterdam, ISMOG.

Frank, A. G. (191). The underdevelopment of development. *Scandinavian Journal of Development Alternatives, X*(3), 24.

Frank, A. G. (1992). Nothing new in the East: No new world order. *Social Justice, 19,* 34-61.

Frank, A. G. (1993). Bronze age world system cycles. *Current Anthropology, 34,* 383-429.

Frank, A. G., & Fuentes, M. (1990). Social movements. In School of Justice Studies, Arizona State University (Ed.), *New directions in the study of justice, law, and social control* (pp. 127-141). New York: Plenum.

Frank, A. G., & Fuentes, M. (1992). The underdevelopment of development. In D. J. Savoie (Ed.), *Equity and efficiency in economic development: Essays in honor of Benjamin Higgins* (pp. 341-393). Montreal: McGill Queen's University Press.

Frank, A. G., & Gills, B. K. (Eds.). (1993). *The world system: Five hundred years or five thousand?* London: Routledge.

Friedman, M. (1962). *Capitalism and freedom.* Chicago: University of Chicago Press.

Gamson, W. A. (1975). *The strategy of social protest.* Belmont, CA: Dorsey.

Goizueta, R. S. (1988). *Liberation, method, and dialogue: Enrique Dussel and North American theological discourse.* Atlanta, GA: Scholar Press.

Goldberg, D. T. (1993). *Racist culture.* Cambridge, MA: Blackwell.

Gottwald, N. K. (Ed.). (1983). *The Bible and liberation.* New York: Orbis.

Gutierrez, G. (1972). *Teología de la liberación.* Salamanca, Spain: Ediciones Sígueme.

Higgins, B. (1992). *All the difference: A development economist's quest.* Montreal: McGill Queen's University Press.

Hirschman, A. O. (1961). *Latin American issues: Essays and comments.* New York: Twentieth Century Fund.

Inkeles, A., & Smith, D. H. (1974). *Becoming modern.* Cambridge, MA: Harvard University Press.

Inverarity, J., Lauderdale, P., & Feld, B. (1983). *Law and society.* Boston: Little, Brown.

Lauderdale, P. (Ed.). (1980). *A political analysis of deviance.* Minneapolis: University of Minnesota Press.

Lauderdale, P. (1986). Social and economic instability in Costa Rica: Pre-conditions for militarization? *Policy Studies Review, 6,* 220-232.

Lauderdale, P. (1988). Domination, social movements, and change. In C. von Werlhof & M. Mies (Eds.), *The subsistence perspective* (pp. 59-79). Bad Boll, Federal Republic of Germany: Evangelische Akademe.

Lauderdale, P. (1989). Rationalization of law in Costa Rica. *Judicial Review of the Supreme Court of Justice of Costa Rica, 44,* 9-17.

Lauderdale, P. (1992). Alternativas al castigo: Una percepcion indigena del derecho [Alternatives to castigation: An indigenous perception of law]. *Opciones, 20,* 9-17.

Lauderdale, P., & Cavender, G. (1986). The study of justice. *Legal Studies Forum, 10,* 87-101.

Lauderdale, P., & Cruit, M. (1993). *The struggle for control: A study of law, disputes, and deviance.* Albany: State University of New York Press.

Lauderdale, P., McLaughlin, S., & Oliverio, A. (1990). Levels of analysis, theoretical orientations, and degrees of abstraction. *American Sociologist, 21,* 29-40.

Lebacqz, K. (1986). *Six theories of justice.* Minneapolis, MN: Augsburg House.

Lewis, D. E., Jr. (1990). Stress, migration, and blood pressure in Kiribati. *American Journal of Human Biology, 2,* 139-151.

Lind, C. (1983). Ethics, economics, and Canada's Catholic bishops. *Canadian Journal of Political and Social Theory/Revue, 7,* 150-166.

Mander, J. (1992). *In the absence of the sacred.* San Francisco: Sierra Club Books.

Matza, D. (1969). *Becoming deviant.* Englewood Cliffs, NJ: Prentice Hall.

McGowan, P., & Kegley, C., Jr. (Eds.). (1983). *Foreign policy and the modern world system.* Beverly Hills, CA: Sage.

Merchant, C. (1989). *Ecological revolutions.* Chapel Hill: University of North Carolina Press.

Mies, M. (1986). *Patriarchy and accumulation on a world scale.* London: Zed.

Mies, M., Bennholdt-Thomsen, V., & von Werlhof, C. (1988). *Women, the last colony.* London: Zed.

Mill, J. S. (1907). *Utilitarianism.* New York: Longmans, Green.

Monture-OKanee, P. A. (1993). Ka-Nin-Geh-Heh-Gah-E-Sa-Nonh-Yah-Gah. *Canadian Journal of Women and the Law, 6,* 119-131.

Niebuhr, R. (1979). *An interpretation of Christian ethics.* New York: Seabury. (Original work published 1935)

Nietschmann, B. (1987). The third war world. *Cultural Survival Quarterly, 2,* 1-19.

Novak, M. (Ed.). (1987). *Liberation theology and the liberal society.* Washington, DC: American Enterprise Institute for Public Policy Research.

Novak, M. (1991). *Will it liberate: Questions about liberation theology* (2nd ed.). New York: Madison Books.

Nozick, R. (1974). *Anarchy, state, and utopia.* New York: Basic Books.

Oliverio, A., & Desjardins, C. (in press). Women's leadership and spirituality: A different choice. *Fifth International Interdisciplinary Congress on Women Proceedings.*

Oliverio, A., & Lauderdale, P. (1991). Indigenous jurisprudence. In F. Tabakthe (Ed.), *Implementation of equal rights for men and women* (pp. 59-78). Onati: Onati International Institute for the Sociology of Law.

P. M. (1985). *Bolo'Bolo.* New York: Columbia University Semiotext(e).

Ramirez, F. O. (1981). Comparative social movements. *International Journal of Comparative Sociology, 22,* 3-21.

Rawls, J. (1972). *A theory of justice.* Oxford, UK: Clarendon.

Riding In, J. (1992). Without ethics and morality: A historical overview of imperial archeology and American Indians. *Arizona State Law Journal, 24,* 11-34.

Rubenstein, R. L., & Roth, J. K. (Eds.). (1988). *The politics of Latin American liberation theology: Understanding the challenge to U.S. public policy.* Washington, DC: Washington Institute Press.

Rupp, L. J., & Taylor, V. (1987). *Survival in the doldrums: The American women's rights movement.* New York: Oxford University Press.

Rushdie, S. (1989). *The satanic verses.* New York: Viking.

Schlesinger, S., & Kinzer, S. (1982). *Bitter fruit: The untold story of the American coup in Guatemala.* Garden City, NY: Doubleday.

Scott, J. C. (1986). *Weapons of the weak: Everyday forms of peasant resistance.* New Haven, CT: Yale University Press.

Smith, C. (1991). *The emergence of liberation theology: Radical religion and social movement theory.* Chicago: University of Chicago Press.

Sorel, G. (1950). *Reflections on violence.* New York: Free Press.

Street-Perrott, F. A., Perrott, R. A., & Harkness, D. D. (1989). Anthropogenic soil erosion around Lake Patzcuaro, Michoacan, Mexico, during the preclassic and late postclassic-Hispanic periods. *American Antiquity, 54,* 759-765.

Thomas, G., & Lauderdale, P. (1987). World polity sources of national welfare and land reform. In G. Thomas, J. W. Meyer, F. O. Ramirez, & J. Boli (Eds.), *Institutional structure* (pp. 198-214). Newbury Park, CA: Sage.

Thomas, G., & Lauderdale, P. (1988). State authority and social welfare in the world system context. *Sociological Forum, 3,* 383-399.

Thomas, G., Meyer, J. W., Ramirez, F. O., & Boli, J. (1987). *Institutional structure.* Newbury Park, CA: Sage.

Thornton, R. (1987). *American Indian holocaust and survival.* Norman: University of Oklahoma Press.

Thornton, R. (1990). *The Cherokees.* Lincoln: University of Nebraska Press.

von Werlhof, C. (1986, February). Por que los campesions y las amas de casa no desaparecen en el sistema capitalista mundial? *El Gallo Ilustrado, 9,* 1-11.

von Werlhof, C. (1988). The concept of nature and society in capitalism. In M. Mies, V. Bennholdt, & C. von Werlhof (Eds.), *Women: The last colony* (pp. 96-112). London: Zed.

von Werlhof, C. (1991). *Was haben die Huhner mit dem Dollar zu tun?* [What do the chickens have to do with the dollar?]. In *Women and economy?* Munich, Germany: Frauenoffensive.

Wallerstein, I. M. (1974). *The modern world-system: Capitalist agriculture and the origins of the European world economy in the sixteenth century.* San Diego: Academic Press.

Wallerstein, I. M. (1980). *The modern world system* (Vol. 2). San Diego: Academic Press.

Weatherford, J. (1988). *Indian givers.* New York: Fawcett Columbine.

West, C. (1982). *Prophesy deliverance.* Philadelphia: Westminster.

Wolf, E. (1982). *Europe and the people without history.* Berkeley: University of California Press.

Wuthnow, R. (1980). World order and religious movements. In A. Bergesen (Ed.), *Studies of the modern world system* (pp. 19-29). San Diego: Academic Press.

17

⊞

Women's Interests and
Emancipatory Processes

VIRGINIA VARGAS

Cristian Harris, Translator

To discuss women's interests in the light of programs, approaches, and strategies of development is a difficult enterprise. It implies a great deal of criticism of the strategies, approaches, and programs of the concept of development itself.

It is, however, an urgent enterprise. I am interested in analyzing women's interests as they are constructed in specific historical contexts and in processes of confrontation, negotiation, alliances with men, with the community, with the state, and with the "same-other-women"—in other words, women's interests relative to society and its powers. In this chapter, I analyze this process par excellence where the interests, always flexible and changing, never predetermined, begin to unfold, are selected, and are turned into proposals in the women's movement in Latin America. In its different perspectives, this rich movement draws us closer to other processes fundamental to the discovery, selection, display, and negotiation of women's interests: the processes of autonomy and corresponding empowerment. I conclude with a criticism of development, not just because it has not considered women's interests (or it

344

has considered them according to its own interests), but because recent experience proves that human society cannot be viewed as a process of homogenization that provides universal patterns or rules for its "homogeneous entities" (Nederveen Pieterse, 1991).

THE WOMEN'S MOVEMENT IN
LATIN AMERICA: A CHALLENGE TO HOMOGENEITY

The women's movement in Latin America is vast, heterogenous, multicultural, and multiethnic, just like the stories, experiences, and lives of women. Each of these contexts is expressed in a form in which women understand, connect, and act on their subordinate situation. Three basic perspectives can nonetheless be distinguished within these many contexts that express the specific and different forms in which women construct their identities, interests, and proposals: a feminist perspective, a popular perspective, and that perspective of women acting inside formal-traditional spaces of organization and political action.

The feminist perspective explicitly aims at identifying and denouncing the existence of a gender hierarchy that is articulated into the different contexts and systems of oppression (e.g., race, class, ethnicity, generation, sexual orientation). Women are absorbed by this system and subordinated. Acting on this reality, the feminist perspective seeks the breakup and transformation of gender relations in the continent.

The second perspective is composed mainly of women who seek to satisfy interests and needs that emerge from their "traditional" roles by using abilities and skills acquired in the socialization process. By doing this, they have given a more public meaning to their roles. They have made of their fragmented, individual activities the basis of their collective action. This perspective, which is basically urban, is composed mostly of women living in marginal areas and is known as the *popular perspective*.

The third perspective emerges from formal public spaces (e.g., political parties, trade unions, peasants' and workers' federations). Women in these spaces begin to experience the first clear signs of their subordination. They attempt to modify and/or open new spaces to achieve greater participation in decision making at the local and national levels and to modify the traditional relations in which they are involved both inside and outside the political parties, trade unions, federations, public institutions, and so forth.

These perspectives have their own objectives, interrelational dynamics, and contradictions. They promote diverse interests and generate important intersections. They are flexible as well, in the sense that they continuously cut and intersect. Some women may feel identified with and/or represented by more than one perspective. Some women from political parties or marginal areas have also seen themselves as feminists; others from the feminist perspective have identified and become involved in party politics. But the perspectives also develop their own actions and aggregate different objectives. They may even clash or contradict with expressions and/or interests of other perspectives in the movement. In short, the perspectives are spaces in which women are discovering in their own specific settings a different way of being women and of being in society, thus laying the foundations for their new identities.

Each perspective has developed, and continues to develop, its own mechanisms of interaction and solidarity. Each promotes its own interests: sometimes coincident, sometimes contradictory or simply different. Their differences reflect the way women construct the movement in relation to their own contexts, experiences, individualities, and deficiencies. These processes are not simple. Once these different realities, experiences, and influences mix, a new, rich interaction among the different contexts, contradictions, and individualities develops. The relations between perspectives are complex. At times, they are tense; at times, they are full of solidarity and creativity. Class, racial, ethnic, and regional differences are all present in these relations.

Perhaps it is for this reason that these processes reflect, more than any other, the richness and innovative quality of the movement. They cast light on the differences among women and express a new practical and vital form of recognizing and transforming them into a driving force. The social, cultural, ethnic, and geographical plurality of the movement takes shape in all perspectives influencing the development of and profile adopted by female social actors.

This diversity may explain why the women's struggle can have so many different starting points (e.g., food, health, political organization, explicit gender issues) from which to question subordination and to construct the movement. These initiatives open the possibility to answer to perceived needs and organize around them, thus socializing their experiences, perceptions, and emotions. They also provide fertile ground to promote interests, make explicit latent ones, and articulate them in collective enterprises (Connell, 1991). Women can thus crystallize their capacity to be individuals with specific demands and interests. The perspectives are concrete, geographical, and symbolic spaces in which individualization can be expressed collectively.

These experiences have been outlining an increasingly autonomous and important social and political presence of different expressions of the women's movement.

THEORETICAL CONSIDERATIONS

FROM GENDER IDENTITY
TO WOMEN'S MULTIPLE IDENTITIES

One of the most relevant aspects in the development of the women's movement in recent years has been the elucidation of the numerous paths women open to confront their gender subordination by way of their social practices, struggles, and collective proposals and dynamics. It has implied recognizing that gender relations are neither experienced in the same way nor have a single manifestation. Thus, if gender relations cannot be abstracted from other social relations because they are included and implied in them (and vice versa), women then cannot be reduced to their gender condition (although this has enormous significance in their development as social actors) or have their individualities and identities outlined exclusively by their experience as a subordinated gender. Their interests will not follow automatically from their subordinated situation. According to Mouffe (1992), each social actor engages in a multiplicity of social relations—for example, production, race, nationality, ethnicity, gender, sex—and these specific relations can neither be reduced nor added to the others. Each of them determines different individualities and interests, creating and accepting different discourses, also understood as social practices.

In other words, women may be able to see their gender specificity and their political, social, and personal interests through their many other social contexts—for example, class, racial, ethnic, regional, national, age, sexual orientation—not only because all of these social relationships are informed by gender but also because some of their other identities may contain, at certain moments, more flexibility and energy to stimulate processes of questioning and mobilization around some aspects of their subordination.

It is then necessary to overcome the restricted vision of the gender identity of women anchored and constructed primarily around their experiences as a subordinated gender. Instead, it is possible that each subjective position promotes specific identities in the same person. These identities are not introspective, but relational, both in asserting similarities and differences. Neither are they fixed in the sense that people redefine themselves through their lives. On the contrary, identities selectively mobilize in response to specific economic, social, political, and cultural processes (Cchacchi and Pittin, 1991). They are thus multiple identities that open the possibility of multiple interests—multiple strategies not just as different modes of action by collectivities or the perspectives of the women's movement, but multiple strategies related to multiple interests of the same social actor and/or the same social collectivity.

AUTONOMY AND WOMEN'S INTERESTS

I mentioned at the beginning of this article that women's interests are not implicit facts. Women's different identities promote these interests in each historical moment or specific situation. It is necessary not only to avoid "essentialist" notions of women's interests but also to distance ourselves from the popularized application of Maxine Molineux's interesting distinction between practical and strategic interests. This distinction opened an interesting space for reflection in its time. Currently, however, the paradigm of "interests converted into practical and strategic gender needs" has been transformed into a vacuum (*ausencia*), into a void that politics could come to fill by stressing a biased vision of rationality and voluntarism where each individual's independent interests are carefully separated, categorized, and put in their place (Anderson, 1992), thus failing to grasp the diverse, changing, and conflicting nature of the experiences and representations of the human subject (Pringle & Watson, 1992). More than affecting or defining women's specific interests in a universally valid way, we must analyze how these interests are constructed and/or constituted through different articulations in specific historical situations and different contexts.

The process of selecting, promoting, and negotiating interests at any given time is parallel to another personal and collective process: the process of autonomy. In other words, the more the process of women's autonomy advances, the more women's interests are promoted and prioritized and the more sure they are of what they want and what they are willing to negotiate.

I pause for a moment to analyze the political implications of autonomy. Accepting autonomy as a valid concept entails negating some of the most common and traditional conceptions about the dynamics of societies. We negate the existence of only one contradiction (traditionally, class has been the primary contradiction, but this negation also applies to any other reductionist explanations—for example, gender reductionism), represented as the "universal interest" encompassing all other interests. Consequently, it also presupposes negating the existence of only one privileged subject who struggles to achieve the final revolution in the name of all the oppressed. Autonomy acquires its political meaning in opposition to all these assumptions by pointing out the right of the people to defend their interests and to control their lives and circumstances. Thus, the concept of autonomy refers to the existence of a multiplicity of subjects and social actors outlining their own interests, demanding their own space and voice in society, and pressing to satisfy their own demands. Autonomy is the concept that best speaks to the recognition of diversity, differences, and plurality.

These elements lead me to suggest that a fundamental dimension of autonomy is to outline the processes of individuation and the construction and articulation of identities and interests. Such autonomy implies the possibility of conflicts and contradictions among women's identities, and their interests as members of other groups, sectors, and movements that have basic identities as well. Autonomy is a right, not only of women or any particular group, but also of all people in their individual and collective dimensions. (If my identity is not coterminous with that of others, how can we decide where my autonomy ends and that of others' begins? What are the social limits to my personal and collective autonomy?). There is a permanent struggle among social actors to prevent one's autonomy from coming at the expense of another's.

Likewise, the struggle for autonomy is also a space in which people learn how and when to consider other interests, how and what to negotiate, when and with whom to make alliances, and on what basis to seek a dialogue with society. It is also a privileged space within which to exercise democratic practices. One's autonomy becomes relative as multiple interests and demands compel us to negotiate, to accept others' rights and demands if we want ours to be respected and heard. And this is the basic core of democratic politics: negotiation of the plurality and diversity of interests. Democracy is the process of negotiating conflicting interests, not the imposition of specific interests that negate and/or destroy others' (Lechner, 1989).

AUTONOMY AS A PERSONAL AND
POLITICAL PROCESS: AMBIVALENT INTERESTS

Autonomy contains personal and collective processes. Autonomy involves heterogeneous and seemingly contradictory practices. It is neither a permanent condition nor a linear process ranging from the lack of autonomy to full autonomy. It is, instead, a complex process of advances and retreats that could even be simultaneous. Autonomy is a process that does not take place in a vacuum, but rather in specific contexts of power relations that those social actors involved want to modify or maintain. Therefore, it is a vital process involving not only ideals but also basically "flesh and blood" people who traverse the difficult path from dependency to freedom. Being a vital process, autonomy also entails contradictory and ambivalent practices. These practices express the affective and subjective pursuit and fracturing that collectivities and people experience in the process of becoming social actors.

This contradiction has a special significance in the case of women because their social practices are marked with a continuous process of opposition between submission and rebellion. Indeed, women do not acquire self-confidence and a sense of their rights as social actors through a linear process, but rather through a subjective process with advances and retreats, where at the same time that new identities are defined and old identities are strengthened and/or re-created, new interests are discovered and outlined. These interests are not always coherently articulated; some of them may be based on more autonomous conceptions women have of themselves; others may be anchored in more "traditional" conceptions and practices. This is neither good nor bad in and of itself. It is part of the difficult process of growing as individuals and as collectivities. It is also a way of avoiding uncertainty and paralysis in the face of the new, the unknown, and sometimes the threatening.

> The path from dependency to freedom is a complex, painful, and constant process for anyone. For women it includes risking to lose social legitimacy guaranteed by others, and learning to find strength in our own legitimacy. Assuming new responsibilities, being receptive to new ideas, and recognizing the consequences of our acts is not something that "falls from heaven" or just an act of will or intelligence but it is—in each women—a fresh process emotionally charged with insecurity, guilt, fear of rejection . . . [however] . . . the advances and retreats are part of the dynamics of social movements and—I will add—its most human expression. (Vargas, 1992, pp. 54-55)

Moreover, women's social practices also include two important characteristics: (a) Generally, they are anti-heroic practices (different from the all-or-nothing proposal or total revolution that the Latin American left has made us used to), and (b) they have also developed some intuitive political understanding. That is, women perceive that it is not possible to win all the battles at the same time, that it is not possible to modify centuries of subordination in the short term. The perception that it is preferable to maintain and secure what has been gained before thrusting into another struggle or demand for which they do not believe they have enough personal and/or collective force has prevailed many times. That is why we can use traditional arguments and/or behaviors (e.g., avoiding the struggle to modify the sexual division of domestic labor and instead waking up earlier and/or letting our daughters take care of these tasks) to secure more valuable objectives and interests, such as active participation in organizations.

PROCESSES OF DEVELOPMENT:
FAILING TO KEEP UP WITH WOMEN'S INTERESTS

Which strategy or development approach best responds to the multiple, flexible, and changing interests of women? Perhaps the question should be the other way around: Which strategies let women start to define their own agenda and enhance their power? That is, which strategies facilitate and enrich women's autonomy? This rapprochement recognizes that the exercise of autonomy cannot be reduced to just one space, type of organization, particular condition, privileged type of project, or be subscribed to a specific development approach. It is, instead, a strategy of empowerment. It involves developing a space for maneuver for women (and for subordinated sectors in general). It involves a process of personal and collective growth that guarantees the challenging of the different forms of subordination, as well as the capacity to develop control of their lives, their organizations, and their specific contexts from any position and/or from any of the multiple personal and social relationships in which women participate.

To discuss autonomy and development requires further reflection. The prevailing conceptions of development have failed dramatically to consider the interests of all subordinated sectors and all regions. The "processes of development" of the previous decades have been unable to address "basic" women's and men's interests, such as minimum standards of living. They have been unable to develop long-term strategies to confront and modify the existing power structures in our societies.

Indeed, there is a growing consensus about the crisis of development. After so many "Northern" projects and programs, 80% of the world's resources are still consumed by 20% of the world's population, which is largely located in the North. "Development" is basically supported by a totalizing discourse

whose central premise is the conception of social change according to prees-
tablished patterns, according to a predictable logic and direction (Nederveen
Pieterse, 1991). Development asserts one "truth" from what has been and
continues to be the fundamental core of power in Western society that turns
its own pattern of development into an ideology:

> In the South, the crisis of development takes multiple forms. . . . Development
> discourse in its ahistoric and apolitical character is incapable of coming into
> terms with the realities of world power and global interests, as evidenced in the
> question of Third World debt. . . . The resistance to development in the South is
> also an affirmation of autonomy and an expression of cultural resistance to
> western ethnocentrism. (Nederveen Pieterse, 1991, p. 18)

But the resistance to development in the South does not stand a chance of
being proposed if political will from countries and governments is lacking. In
this period of increasing globalization, people in the countries of the South
have to deal primarily with the effects of structural adjustment instead of the
effects of real integration, not just with the world but more urgently within
Latin America.

This process of interrelationship should also entail the possibility of
developing equitable economic, social, and political relations at the international level. This is not the case. And definitions of development, cooperation,
and global interdependence become empty words when we face what they
really entail: the inhuman deterioration of standards of living, the increasing
marginalization of even larger sectors of the population (among them, women,
undoubtedly), and the alarming increase of social and political violence. In
each of these dramatic situations, women continue to be the poorest of the
poor and to enjoy the least space for action to confront them. This precarious,
diminished, devaluated, and painful space for displaying their interests as
women, as mothers, and as citizens is also part of the reality of women's
interests. The future seems uncertain and alarming.

In the face of such a danger, the support of democratic men and women in
the North, the South, and the East for changing the rules of the game is
fundamental. And in this sense, it would be better to search for more adequate
terms to speak of the processes of struggle and transformation that Latin
American peoples are promoting through their women and men, through their
social movements, and through their organizations. Perhaps a more adequate
concept would be that of "emancipatory processes" (Waterman, 1992). It is
plural, not singular, because I believe it is essential to overcome the idea of a

single unifying process (as is claimed with the concept of "development") in order to open ourselves up to multiple processes and ethical/political projects reflecting the vast diversity of the continent. According to Giddens (1991), we can define *emancipatory politics* as a perspective attempting above all to liberate individuals and groups from constraints adversely affecting their life's possibilities.

According to Giddens, emancipatory politics implies liberation of social life from the shackles of the past; the reduction or elimination of exploitation, inequality, and oppression; and correspondingly the redistribution of power and resources. The ethical imperatives that inform it are those of justice, freedom, and participation. In this political perspective, autonomy processes find the adequate space to develop in their full dimensions:

> If there is a mobilising principle of behaviour behind most versions of emancipatory politics it could be called the principle of autonomy. Emancipation means that collective life is organised in such a way that the individual is capable—in some sense or another—of free and independent action in the environments of her social life. Freedom and responsibility here stand in some kind of balance. The individual is liberated from constraints placed on her behaviour as a result of exploitative, unequal or oppressive conditions; but she is not thereby rendered free in any absolute sense. Freedom presumes acting responsibly in relation to others and recognising that collective obligations are involved. (Giddens, 1991, p. 213)

I believe this quote gives a better account of the processes of empowerment, autonomy, and decolonization in which social movements and democratic forces both in the South and in the North are involved. Undoubtedly, it is not just a problem of new concepts. In a period of transition, such as ours, perhaps we can only give new meaning to old concepts. We must think about our future in an interconnected and interdependent world in which the highest value will not be dominion and power, but rather interconnection, interdependence, and respect for the diversity of ideas, options, struggles, and transformative democratic projects.

REFERENCES

Anderson, J. (1992). ¿Intereses o justicia? ¿A dónde va la discusión sobre la mujer y el desarrollo? *Cuadernos de Trabajo. Red Entre Mujeres: Un Diálogo Sur-Norte.* Lima, Perú.

Cchacchi, A., & Pittin, R. (in press). *Multiple identities, multiple sites of struggle.* The Hague, The Netherlands: Institute of Social Studies.

Connell, R. W. (1991). *Gender and power.* Cambridge, MA: Polity.

Giddens, A. (1991). *Modernity and self-identity: Self and society in the late modern age.* Cambridge, MA: Polity.

Lechner, N. (1989). *Los patios interiores de la democracia.* Santiago, Chile: FLACSO.

Mouffe, C. (1992). *Dimensions of radical democracy.* London: Verso.

Nederveen Pieterse, J. (1991). Dilemmas of development discourse: The crisis of developmentalism and the comparative method. *Development and Change, 21,* 1.

Pringle, R., & Watson, S. (1992). Women's interests and the post-structuralist state. In M. Barrett & A. Phillips (Eds.), *Destabilizing theory: Contemporary feminist debate* (pp. 53-73). Cambridge, MA: Polity.

Vargas, V. (1992). *Como cambiar el mundo sin perdernos.* Lima, Perú: Ediciones Flora Tristán.

Waterman, P. (1992). El suceso Olvidado de Rosa de Luxemburgo. *Cuadernos de Trabajo. Red Entre Mujeres: Un Diálogo Sur-Norte.* Lima, Perú.

18

Underdevelopment and Its Remedies

IMMANUEL WALLERSTEIN

The dominant political/intellectual question of the post-1945 period has been how to develop. At least, this was true in what came to be called the Third World, but in fact it is probably a statement equally true of the rest of the world. What most people really meant by "developing" was how they might become prosperous and live as well as people lived in the United States, or at least as well as how they thought people lived in the United States (as reflected in Hollywood movies, where even supposedly poor people seemed to live in ten-room houses with lots of furniture, clothes, and food). Furthermore, almost everyone seemed to think that becoming individually prosperous depended, at least in large part, on his or her country becoming prosperous.

The hegemonic power of this period, the United States, made "development"—everywhere, for everyone—its official rhetorical objective, beginning with President Truman's Point Four. The counterrhetoric of the U.S.S.R. was that economic development could only be achieved if it was "socialist development." In addition, all the nationalist and national liberation movements joined in the chorus, asserting that, once victorious, they would be able to achieve the development of their countries, their peoples.

To be sure, the formulas proposed to achieve this universally accepted objective of development were quite diverse. The more "conservative" or "establishment" versions emphasized the importance of private enterprise and participation in the world market. The more "radical" versions emphasized the importance of collective ownership, or at least of national ownership, of the means of production and a restructuring of the world market. But in the Keynesian world of the Kondratieff A-phase (1945-1967/73)—"We are all Keynesians now," said Richard M. Nixon—both conservatives and radicals, both the United States and the U.S.S.R., indeed virtually everyone agreed that development required state action of some sort. This was, after all, the logic of Point Four and of all subsequent "aid" programs by the "more" developed countries to the "less" developed ones.

The intellectual/political contribution of ECLA and Raúl Prebisch was to insist that the problem derived from the different roles different countries played in the world-economy. They popularized the concept of core/periphery. Fifteen years later, the *dependentistas* gave this analysis a more radical rhetoric, talking as they did of imperialism, but their originality for the time —now it seems banal—was the discovery that the program of the Latin American Communist Parties (and behind them, of the U.S.S.R.) was not the opposite, but rather a variant, of the program of the "bourgeois" parties (and therefore of the United States and its Alliance for Progress). This discovery came in the wake of Khrushchev's Report to the Twentieth Party Congress, the Cuban Revolution, Guevarism/*focoismo,* and, of course, the world revolution of 1968.

The *dependentistas* were very radical politically. When one looked at the *economic* program recommended by the *dependentistas,* however, it was disappointing; it was simply one more proposal for state action, with perhaps a greater insistence on "delinking" than in other variants. As of 1970, the *dependentistas* were as optimistic as anyone else. They looked forward to significant change in a relatively short run, one that could truly achieve the prosperous world for everyone. In that sense, the *dependentistas* were as surprised as anyone else by the pessimistic turn world events began to take in the 1970s, becoming worse in the 1980s.

By the 1990s, it became hard to remember that anyone was ever optimistic. No one today seems to think there will be significant change in a relatively short run, a prosperous world for everyone. And everyone, or almost everyone, it seems, has given up on state action as the remedy. "We were all Keynesians once," I suppose, is the new slogan. Now, bless our souls, most of us, even most of us who were most radical in our politics a short time ago, are "free marketeers." I doubt, personally, that the faith in the slogan of a free market is very deep or will be widely professed for too much more time. It seems more a cynical ploy on the part of those who hold world economic power, because they wish to apply free-market principles to everyone except themselves. And it seems a desperate ploy, a sort of mantra, on the part of most governments. Maybe Jeffrey Sachs truly believes it is a collective remedy; most advocates really mean it is a personal road to wealth for those who are streetwise and unscrupulous.

For those of us who have and have had a basic commitment to struggling against the injustices and inequalities of the world-system in which we are living and who also have believed it is possible to construct an alternative and better world-system, the dilemma we face in the 1990s is quite simple. The fundamental political strategy that we (our forbears) had evolved in the 19th century to achieve this objective—political conquest of state power, state by state—has failed, and we all more or less recognize that it has failed. This, of course, reflects on the strategy for change, and not on the objective of a basically egalitarian and democratic world.

Still, strategies for change are not all that readily available. It took a great deal of collective effort to think through and implement the previous strategy for change. The fact is that its collapse has led to confusion and to a void, and our primary political task now is to construct an alternative strategy for change. Lucidity is the prerequisite. What is it that needs change? What can change that which needs change? What can we do in practice to speed up that change? And, of course, it is important to think not only about change *from* what but change *to* what?

In the CNN television coverage of the 1994 South African elections, in which Africans voted for the first time, a reporter interviewed a wizened, elderly African, an ordinary voter, and asked him what he wanted for the future. He replied, "Things better than they were before." There lies the nub of the question. There are three possible chronosophies to apply to this statement. First is the view of those who think *that this is an impossible dream,* that hierarchy in human social structures is permanent and inevitable, and that any effort to change this is futile. This is, in fact, a larger group than we sometimes credit. Second is the view of those (on the right and on the left) who think that things have been getting better all the time and will continue to do so. Third is the view of those who think that things have not, on the whole, been getting better but that it is possible (possible, not certain) that they could do so. I count myself among the third group, and I address these words to those who also do.

What is it that needs changing? It seems very clear to me that it is our existing world-system, which is a capitalist world-economy, which is hierarchical and polarizing, racist and sexist, and fundamentally undemocratic. I think it is quite clear we have not always lived in such a historical system. This is not the place to analyze the limited and varying merits of earlier forms of historical systems. I certainly do not advocate returning to any of these forms. But I do think the capitalist form is distinctive and pernicious and that if we do not concentrate on its particularities and peculiarities, we shall not understand its resilience and strength, nor shall we identify well its weak points, nor shall we be in a position to struggle for a better replacement when it collapses (as it surely must, as all historical systems have always collapsed) of its internal contradictions. If we take our eyes off the main target of change and its specificities, we are in no position to be useful politically.

What is able to change that which needs change? The first thing to say is that any change comes within a process of internal evolution of the system that is self-propelling. This system, like all other historical systems, combines cyclical rhythms and secular trends. Or to be more precise, its cyclical rhythms generate secular trends that, in turn, over a long run, create impossible dilemmas (contradictions) that cannot be surmounted and that must lead to the disintegration of the system. Or to put it a third way, and not paradoxically at all, it is the successes of the system that guarantee its eventual collapse.

Is it then a matter of sitting back and watching the beneficiaries of the system dig their own grave? Shall we just patiently await the automatic installation of the good society? Not at all! Quite the opposite. The problem we face is that the beneficiaries of the system are at least as aware as its victims of this process. They will struggle to maintain the status quo as long as that is feasible. But as the ship sinks, they will seek to construct new ships, new historical systems that, though different in form, are the same in essence—that is, are hierarchical and exploitative and therefore can guarantee to a minority a privileged position.

Because the powerful will thus organize, and organize well, to control the process of transition from our current system to some other one, the rest of us have to organize as well, or else we shall lose, as we have lost in all previous transitions from one historical system to another. A political strategy for change must thus start from two premises: (a) What needs changing is the capitalist world-system, a system that has not been eternal, but is delimited temporally and spatially and (b) this system will change in any case in the sense that it will disintegrate; the question is whether the system or systems that replace it will be better or worse.

Because we are still living in this system and because any transition is still a matter of fifty years or more, we need a strategy for change that can rally support, combined with clarifying alternatives. We thus need a strategy with three time components: immediate, middle run, and long run. The *immediate* involves the struggles that go on now at the local level (and, of course, local includes state level) that impinge on how lives are led immediately. It is not that any changes achieved at this level are wide ranging. It is rather that people want and need the immediate ameliorations now and that the struggle to achieve them is not only mobilizing but also disconcerting for the forces of the status quo. These struggles all involve the immediate hurts of the system: a bit of racism here, a bit of sexism there, a squeeze on workers' income in a third place. No one needs instruction in how to fight these battles; we are all now well experienced. What we need to remember is only the two lessons we can draw from the long history of such immediate struggles. First, they are useful insofar as they improve lives immediately, but they can never be allowed to become ends in themselves because, as soon as they do, they become instruments of our own co-optation. Second, because all such struggles are local and therefore reflect the hurts of some particular group, it is important to remember that there are many hurts of many groups and that, therefore, alliances are essential if these struggles are not to become modes of division. These seem homely truths, and I only repeat them because, in this period of disillusionment with all the old lefts (for good reasons), we risk forgetting their wisdoms.

The middle and long run are more controversial. I advocate overloading the system for the middle run and utopistics for the long run (the long run here defined as just fifty years or so). Overloading the system is a very simple idea. The discourse of the powerful of the modern world is a discourse of freedom: free markets, free elections, free choice. This is by and large a false discourse in the sense that those who preach it usually do not mean it. They mean free markets to sell U.S. computers in Brazil, not Brazilian computers in the U.S. They mean no or little government redistribution to the weak, but lots of government redistribution to the strong. They mean free elections when they will win, or at least not lose anything very much, but not when the elections may bring to power the groups they fear. They mean free choice of schools, if that means that middle-class whites can escape from schools in which too many lower-class blacks are enrolled, but not when it means the reverse. And so forth. One can easily expand the examples.

There are two ways to overload the system. The first is to take the rhetoric of freedom literally. A free market? Why not end all subsidies, open or hidden, to all private enterprises? What subsidies? Guaranteed government markets at cost overruns. Tax write-offs. Rescue of corporations facing closure. Privatization of results of government expenditures on research. The externalization of costs whereby industries do not have to pay the full costs of damage to the environment. Freedom to move? Campaigns to permit dissident intellectuals the right to leave countries? Of course. And why not campaigns to permit boat people to enter countries? What more elementary freedom than the abolition of frontier controls? It is not that each of these proposals is necessarily a good idea in the short run. It is that each underlines the hollowness of the rhetoric, or rather its deeply unequal application to real issues. Taking the rhetoric seriously overloads the system in that it forces the powerful either to drop the rhetoric (and thereby lose the political advantage of manipulating it) or suffer the consequences of the rhetoric (and thereby lose immediate material and political advantage).

The second way to overload the system is to take economic self-interest seriously. The capitalist world-system has been marvelous in its ability to preach the importance of allowing the entrepreneurial classes to pursue their economic interests as they wish on the ground that this provides the necessary incentive to make the system work while simultaneously preaching to the working classes the necessity to restrain their economic self-interest on the ground that this is what provides the necessary profit margin in a competitive world market to allow the continuance of productive activities. But of course, this does not hold up logically. If tomorrow the workers in every enterprise everywhere in the world were to receive a 10% increase in real wages, this would not affect competitivity at all; it would only affect the margin to profit, and therefore the ability to accumulate capital.

But have not workers been struggling for at least several centuries to increase their real wages? Well, yes, but not as systematically and intensively as one might think. Workers have been constantly responsive to demands they should be responsible, show self-restraint, *and not jeopardize their jobs.* A little less self-restraint might work wonders in overloading the system. The point about overloading the system is only in small part that it will accelerate the disintegration of the system. It will do that, to be sure, but because the system is crumbling in any case, this is a relatively minor advantage. The point is that overloading the system serves the same function for opponents of the system as offering minor privileges to particular oppressed groups plays for supporters of the system. It divides the opposition. Those who stand for a more equal, more egalitarian world need to worry that pursuing their immediate needs can lead to divisions among them. When the oppressed overload the system, however, it is its defenders who become divided between those who are ready to scrap the rhetoric and those who believe (tactically or sincerely) it is necessary to preserve the rhetoric. Such division will weaken this group as it tries to control the direction of the transition from our present historical system to its successor(s).

This discussion brings us to the transition and therefore to the long run, for which I recommend utopistics. What can that possibly mean? It means we have to engage seriously in the project of inventing the future system—not by a philosopher-king, but collectively. We need to debate priorities and the nature of institutions that could implement them. If we want equality, that means equality in what, and when, and exactly how? It is not that these issues have never been discussed, but that they have never been collectively and widely debated. If we wish to maximize participation in every level of decision making, there is, of course, a role for electoral processes. But the issues of democratization of everyday life go far beyond electoral processes. They have to do with distribution of information, with timely possibilities for collective processes, with creating a balance between our right to a decision and our right to be left alone.

We have been historically constrained not to engage in utopistics: first, by arguments of authority (traditional authority, the authority of experts); then, by arguments of impossibility (what works in a town meeting cannot apply to large-scale structures). Nonetheless, those who have power engage in utopistics all the time. That is how they conceive the new structures that emerge out of historical transitions, structures that maintain the hierarchical world. In a sense, I am not calling for the launching of some new activity called utopistics, but for the democratization of a very old activity.

Will such a strategy work? Is a combination of immediate mobilizations plus middle-run overloading of the system plus long-run utopistics enough to ensure that the transition from our present historical system to its successor(s) will be one we find good? It is not sure, but it gives us a fighting chance, provided we keep our eye on the ball: We are living in a capitalist world-system; this system is in structural crisis and therefore in inevitable transition; the key political battle is the direction of this transition. These are the waters into which we entered in the previous forty to fifty years in our debates about underdevelopment and its remedies.

Andre Gunder Frank

Bibliography of Publications 1955-1995

This bibliography is organized in three categories: books, collections, and periodical articles. Publications in pamphlets have been assigned to one of the three categories. The bibliography contains 880 items published in 27 languages. The bibliography avoids listing the same item a dozen or more times in different languages and in various versions of the same item in one language. If the 126 different editions of the 36 books and the about 600 versions of over 350 articles in periodicals, as well as the 158 chapters in 134 collections, were each listed with the title under which they were published, the bibliography would be almost twice as long and take up nearly double the space below. Therefore, the bibliography is organized as follows:

Books. Each title is listed only once, in English or Spanish. For instance, *Capitalism and Underdevelopment in Latin America* was published in eleven language editions, but the book title is listed only once with its different editions listed below it. *Lumpenbourgeoisie: Lumpendevelopment* was published in fourteen editions, which include eight Spanish-language editions in as many countries. Only these editions, but not titles, are listed separately. The number of printings of each edition is indicated where known. The Spanish *2a edicion* is listed as the same edition because it means and is counted as a second printing. The books are listed in chronological order by first publication in English or Spanish. The English or Spanish title of each book is followed by the publishers, places, and dates of publication in different languages without mentioning their translated titles. A book is also listed under the same title when its content is essentially, even if not entirely, the same. For instance, parts of *Capitalism and Underdevelopment in Latin America* and of *Latin America: Underdevelopment and Revolution* were combined into a single book in Japanese. It is listed only once under the first title. Books that were coauthored and/or coedited by Frank are listed as books. Chapters by Frank in the coedited, but not in the coauthored, books are listed again under collections.

Collections. These are also called anthologies, readers, or volumes edited by others. Each collection is listed separately. It is listed in the language in which it appears, unless it is transliterated from a non-Roman script (e.g., Arabic) or translated from a non-Indo-European or a Slavic language. In each case, the chapter title(s) by Frank are listed first, then the collection/book title, its editors when known, the place of publication, publisher, date of publication, and the page numbers of the contribution by Frank. The same item, for instance "The Development of Underdevelopment," appears in many collections, each of which is listed separately. New editions of the same collection are not listed again unless their contents have changed significantly. In some collections, a particular item by Frank that may have appeared in a shortened form nonetheless appears with the same title. The collections are listed in chronological order by date of publication.

Periodicals. These include academic journals, magazines, newspapers, and some other periodical series, such as proceedings or some pamphlet series. In most cases, especially for the 1960s and 1970s, the title of a particular article, such as "The Development of Underdevelopment," is listed only once, by preference in English, if it was published in that language, and by second preference in Spanish if the item was not published in English. If an article was only published in some other language, such as German, the title appears in that language. The list is in more or less chronological order by year of first publication in English or Spanish. The periodicals, places, and dates of other publications of the same article are then listed under the article title even though in some cases the publication may have appeared many years later. In translation, of course, the title of each article is different, and sometimes very different. Nonetheless, the article is listed under the same title if its contents are the same or essentially so. Sometimes, essentially the same article was published in versions of different length and somewhat different content. Even so, the different versions are mostly listed under one title as the same article. For more recent years, however, articles are sometimes listed separately as published. Therefore, the same article is sometimes listed again in different languages or versions. Page numbers are indicated where easily available. If not, they are omitted. Where some information, such as volume number or precise date of publication, is not readily available, the item is listed with the information that is available. The principle here is, better some incomplete information than none at all.

Efforts were made to make this bibliography as accurate as possible. Errors of commission and omission, typing, and typesetting, however, are bound to creep in, particularly regarding numbers (e.g., in dates, volume or page numbers) and languages, which are difficult to check by proofreading. An effort has been made to achieve some uniformity of notational style for the listings within each of the three categories of publications. (The lists were compiled by using copies of the original publications and many earlier lists with very different styles of notation) Mostly, the simplest style, using the fewest punctuation marks, was preferred. Months of publication are usually given in English, and often in abbreviated form (e.g., Jan. for January). When a publication in another language itself mentions *enero* or *janiero,* however, that wording is sometimes retained. Volume numbers are usually given as Vol. 21 or Vol. XXI, and for reasons of space sometimes only as XXI. For various reasons of convenience, some differences in notational style were retained between the three categories of books, collections, and periodicals. Even so, the bibliography is incomplete. Recent visits to large libraries with computerized catalogs, such as the Library of Congress and the University of California Libraries in the United States, have revealed published versions of the author's writings in book or pamphlet form, of whose existence he was not previously aware. If the author's writings are published as books or pamphlets without his knowledge, the same happens all the more so in periodical publications. These are not usually catalogued, and many are not indexed. Even those that are may not be known or accessible. Therefore, trying to make this bibliography complete would be impossible—and a Sisyphean task as new publications continue to appear.

BOOKS

Capitalism and Underdevelopment in Latin America
New York: Monthly Review Press 1967; revised ed., 1969, 12 printings
Revised Edition 1969, 12 printings
London: Penguin Books 1971
Paris: Maspero Editeur 1972, 3 printings
Torino: Einaudi Editore 1971, 4 printings
Frankfurt: Europäische Verlagsanstalt 1968, 2 printings
Stockholm: Bo Caferfors 1970
Helsinki: Tammi 1971
La Habana: Instituto del Libro 1970
Buenos Aires: Ediciones Signos 1970
Buenos Aires & Mexico: Siglo XXI, Enlarged Edition, 10 printings
Tokyo: Tsuge Shobo, 3 printings
Latin America: Underdevelopment or Revolution
New York: Monthly Review Press 1969, 7 printings
Paris: Maspero Editeur 1972, 3 printings
Torino: Einaudi Editore 1971
Stockholm: A. B. Rabenm & Sjorgren Bokforlag
Mexico: Ediciones ERA 1972, 2 printings
Frankfurt: Raubdruck 1971
Lumpenbourgeoisie: Lumpendevelopment. Dependence, Class and Politics in Latin America
New York: Monthly Review Press 1972
Caracas: Editorial Nueva Izquierda 1970
Bogotá: Ediciones Oveja Negra 1970
Montevideo: Ediciones La Banda Oriental 1970
Santiago: Prensa Latinoamericana 1971
La Habana: Referencias 1970
Mexico: Ediciones ERA 1971, 4 printings
Buenos Aires: Ediciones Periferia
Barcelona: Ediciones Laia 1972, 2 printings
Paris: Maspero Editeur 1971, 2 printings
Milano: Gabriele Mazotta 1971
Oporto: Editora Portocalense 1973
Amsterdam: Van Gennep 1974
Tokyo: Iwanami Shoten 1977
Sociology of Development and Underdevelopment of Sociology
London: Pluto Press 1971
Stockholm: Zenit 1969
Barcelona: Ediciones Anagrama 1971
Mexico: Escuela Nacional de Antropologia e Historia 1970, 2 printings
Montevideo: Aportes 1969

Milano: Lampugnani Nigri Editore 1970
Coimbra: Editora Centelha 1976
Teheran: Progressive Publishers n.d.
Indonesia: Putaska Pusar 1984 [in Bahasa Indonesia]
Malaysia: Penerbit Universiti Kebangsaan 1989 [in Bahasa Malaysia]
Ibadan, Oyo State, Nigeria: Afrografika

Dependence and Underdevelopment: Latin America's Political Economy (with
J. Cockcroft & D. Johnson)
New York: Doubleday Anchor Books 1972
Buenos Aires: Ediciones Signos 1970

Dependencia (with P. Sweezy, T. Dos Santos, & J. O'Connor)
Santiago: Cuadernos Universitarios 1972

America Latina: Feudalismo o Capitalismo? (with E. Laclau & R. Puiggros)
Bogotá: Ediciones Oveja Negra

Aspectos de la Realidad Latinoamericana (with O. Caputo, R. Pizarro, & A. Quijano)
Santiago: Quimantu Editora 1973

Quien es el Enemigo Immediato?
Buenos Aires: Editorial Centro de Estudios Politicos 1974
La Molina, Peru: Universidad Agraria. Centro de Estuduantes en Ciencias
Sociales 1968

Carta Abierta en el Aniversario del Golpe Militar en Chile
Madrid: Alberto Corazón Editor 1974

Polémica Sobre los modos de Produccíon en Iberoáerica (with R. Puiggros and
Jorge Aberlardo Ramos)
Buenos Aires: Agrupación Universitaria Nacional 1974

Chile: El Desarrollo el Subdessarrollo
Montevideo, Fundación de Cultura Universitaria 1969

On Capitalist Underdevelopment
Bombay: Oxford University Press, 1975, 4 printings
Milano: Edizione Jaca Book 1971
Barcelona: Editorial Anagrama 1977
Lisboa: Edicioes 70, 1981

Raices del Desarrollo y del Subdesarrollo en el Nuevo Mundo
Caracas: Universidad Central de Venezuela. Facultad de Ciencias Económicas y
Sociales 1975

Development of Underdevelopment in Brazil
Theran: Progressive Publishers n.d.

Economic Genocide in Chile
Nottingham: Spokesman Books 1976
Madrid: Ediciones Zero 1976
Coimbra: Editora Centelha 1976
Freiburg: Iz3W 1977

No Esperar a 1984. Quale 1984? (with S. Amin & H. Jaffe)
Madrid: Ediciones Zero 1976
Milano: Edizione Jaca Book 1976

Reflexiones Sobre la Crisis Economica
Lisboa: Iniciativas Editoriais 1976
Barcelona: Editorial Anagrama 1977
Paris: Maspero Editeur 1978
Hamburg: Rowohlt Verlag 1978
Oslo: Gyldendal Norsk Bokforlag 1979
Catania: Pelicani Libri 1979
Mexican Agriculture 1521-1630: Transformation of the Mode of Production
Cambridge: Cambridge University Press 1979
Mexico: Escuela Nacional de Antropología e Historia 1976
Mexico: Ediciones ERA 1981
Crítica y Anti-Crítica
Madrid: Ediciones Zero 1978
World Accumulation: 1492-1789
New York: Monthly Review Press 1978
London: Macmillan Press 1978
Paris: Calmann-Levy Editeur 1977
Rio de Janeiro: Zahar Editor 1977
Lisboa: Editora Estampa 1979
Madrid: Siglo XXI Editores 1979
Dependent Accumulation and Underdevelopment
London: Macmillan Press 1978
New York: Monthly Review Press 1979
Paris: Edicions Anthropos 1978
Mexico: Ediciones ERA 1980
Frankfurt: Suhrkamp Verlag 1980
Sao Paulo: Editora Brasiliense 1980
Tokyo: Iwanami Shoten 1980
Crisis: In the World Economy
New York: Holmes & Meier 1980
London: Heinemann 1980
Barcelona: Bruguera 1979
Crisis: In the Third World
New York: Holmes & Meier 1980
London: Heinemann 1981
Barcelona: Bruguera 1980
Reflections on the World Economic Crisis (Revised)
New York: Monthly Review Press 1981
London: Hutchinson 1981
Rio de Janeiro: Zahar Editora 1983
Tokyo: TBS Books '80 1981
Dynamics of Global Crisis (Crise, Quelle Crise?) (with S. Amin, G. Arrighi, & I. Wallerstein)
New York: Monthly Review Press 1982
London: Macmillan Press 1982

Paris: Maspero Editeur 1982
Mexico: Siglo XXI Editores 1983, 2 printings
Opladen: Westdeutscher Verlag 1986
Beograd: Radnicka Stampa 1985
Istanbul: Pirate Edition 1985
Critique and Anti-Critique: Essays on Dependence and Reformism
New York: Praeger Publishers 1984
London: Macmillan Press 1984
Paris: Editiones Anthropos 1985
Chile onder Pinochet: Een Latijnamerikaans Volk in Gejzeling (edited with
O. Catalan)
Amsterdam: SUA/Novib 1984
**The European Challenge: From Atlantic Alliance to Pan-European Entente for
Peace and Jobs**
Nottingham: Spokesman Books 1983
Westport USA: Lawrence Hill Publishers 1984 (rev. ed.)
Stuttgart: Alektor Verlag 1983
Madrid: Editorial Pablo Iglesias 1983
Athens: Economic Chamber of Greece 1988 (with new Foreword)
El Desafio de la Crisis
Madrid: IEPALA Editorial 1988
Caracas: Editorial Nueva Sociedad 1988
**Wiederstand im Weltsystem: Zum Verhältnis von kapitalistischer Akkumula-
tion, staatlicher Politik und sozialem Protest** (with M. Fuentes, H. Hofbauer,
& A. Komlosy, eds.)
Wien: Promedia Verlag 1990
**Transforming the Revolution: Social Movements and the World System Le
Grande Tumulte? Les Mouvements Sociaux dans l'Economie-Monde** (with
S. Amin, G. Arrighi, & I. Wallerstein)
New York: Monthly Review Press 1990
Paris: La Dècouverte 1990
**The Underdevelopment of Development (El Subdesarrollo del Desarrollo: Un
Ensayo Autobiográfico)**
Stockholm: Bethany Books 1991
Caracas: Editorial Nueva Sociedad 1991
Madrid: Editorial IEPALA 1992
Athens: Gordios Publishers 1993
The Centrality of Central Asia
Amsterdam: VU University Press, Center for Asian Studies, Amsterdam Com-
parative Asian Studies (CAS) No. 8, Feb. 1992
The World System: Five Hundred Years or Five Thousand? (editor/contributor
with B. K. Gills)
London and New York: Routledge 1993
El Sistema Mundial Tras la Guerra del Golfo with S. Brucan, J. Galtung, &
I. Wallerstein
Alicante: Instituto de Cultura Juan Gil-Albert 1993

CHAPTERS IN COLLECTIONS,
EDITED BOOKS, AND ANTHOLOGIES

"The Economy"
Aspects of Contemporary Ukraine, A. Hurwicz, ed. New Haven, Human
Relations Area Files 1955, pp. 340-490

"The Economy"
Aspects of Contemporary Belorussia, A. Hurwicz, ed. New Haven, Human
Relations Area Files 1955, pp. 270-380

"Introduction to Social Structure and Organization"
Social Science Readings, Sally Cassidy, A. G. Frank, et al. Detroit, Monteith
College, Wayne University 1959

"Mexico: The Janus Faces of Twentieth-Century Bourgeois Revolution" and "Varieties
of Land Reform"
Whither Latin America? P. Sweezy & L. Huberman, eds. New York, Monthly
Review Press 1963, pp. 57-63 and 72-90

"Mexico: Les Faces Janus de la Révolution Bourgeoise de 20ème siècle" et "Les
Variétés de la Reforme Agrarie"
Ou Va L'Amerique Latine? P. Sweezy & L. Huberman, eds. Paris, François
Maspero Editeur 1964

"Brazil: Aid or Exploitation?"
The Anatomy of Foreign Aid, Foreword by Lord Boyd Orr. London, *Peace
News* 1964, pp. 13-22

"Estructura social rural"
Realidad Social de America Latina, Manual para Institutos de Lideres, Montevideo, Iglesia Sociedad en América Latina 1965, pp. 55-68

"Tipos de Reforma Agraria"
Reformas Agrarias en America Latina, O. Delgado, ed. Mexico, Fondo de
Cultura Económica 1965, pp. 184-188

"Class, Politics, and Debray" (with S. Shah)
Regis Debray and the Latin American Revolution, L. Huberman & P. Sweezy,
eds. New York, Monthly Review Press 1968, pp. 12-17

"El desarrollo del subdesarrollo"
Lecturas de Filosofía. La Habana, Instituto del Libro 1968, pp. 421-430

"Desenvolvimento do subdesenvolvimento Latino-Americano"
Urbanização e Subdesenvolvimento, L. Pereira, comp. Rio de Janeiro, Zahar
Editores 1969, pp. 25-39

"Die Entwicklung der Unterentwicklung" und "Lateinamerika: Kapitalistische Un-
terentwicklung oder sozialistische Revolution"
Kritik des Bürgerlichen Anti-Imperialismus, B. Echeverria & H. Kurnizky.
Berlin, Klaus Wagenbach, Rotbuch 15, 1969, pp. 30-44, 91-132

"Science and Underdevelopment in the Third World"
Scientific Research and Politics, L. Dencik, ed. Lund, Studentliteratur 1969,
pp. 152-190

"Taloudellinen riippuvuus, yhteiskintarakenne ja alikehitys Latinalisessa Amerikassa"
Latinalaisen Amerikan Haaste, O. Alho, ed. Helsinki, Werner Soderstom Osakeyhtio 1969, pp. 62-111

"Development of Underdevelopment" and "On the Mechanisms of Imperialism: The Case of Brazil"
Imperialism and Underdevelopment. A Reader, R. I. Rhodes, ed. New York, Monthly Review Press 1970, pp. 4-17 and 89-100

"The Development of Underdevelopment" and "Capitalism and Underdevelopment in Latin America"
Human Nature: A Sourcebook in Anthropology, D. G. Epstein, ed. New York, Simon & Schuster 1970, n.p.

"Klasse, Politik, und Debray" (with S. Shah)
Focus und Freiraum: Debray, Brasilien, Linke in den Metropolen, L. Huberman & P. Sweezy, eds. Berlin, Wagenbach, 1970, Rotbuch 16, pp. 18-22

"Lo sviluppo del sottosviluppo" and "Chi e il nemico immediato?
Il Nuovo Marxismo Latinoamericano, G. Santerelli, ed. Milano, Feltrinelli Editore 1970, pp. 141-155 and 310-351

"Walt Whitman Rostow: Ode zur Unterenwicklung"
Tricontinental 1967-1970 Eine Auswahl, K. D. Wolf, ed. Frankfurt, Märzerverlag 1970, pp. 282-299

"Urban Poverty in Latin America"
Masses in Latin America, I. L. Horowitz, ed. New York, Oxford University Press 1970, pp. 215-234

"El Siglo XX: Amarga Cosecha del Subdesarrollo"
América Latina Documentos e Información, La Habana, ICAIC, n.d., pp. 225-248

"On the Mechanisms of Imperialism: The Case of Brazil"
Readings in U.S. Imperialism, K. T. Fann & D. C. Hodges, eds. Boston, Porter Sargent Publisher 1971, pp. 237-248

"W Kwestii Indianskiej"
Ameryka Indianska? R. Romano, ed. Warszawa, Panstwowe Wydarnictwo Naukowe 1971, pp. 399-430

"Administrative Role Definition and Social Change"
Studies in Managerial Process and Organizational Behavior, J. H. Turner, A. C. Folley, & R. J. House, eds. Glenview, IL, Scott, Foresman and Co. 1972. pp. 172-176

"Latin America: Capitalism Underdevelopment or Social Revolution?"
Latin America Theory and Dynamics of Social Change, S. A. Halper & J. R. Sterling, eds. London, Allison & Busby 1972, pp. 119-156

"Kapitalistische Onderentwikkeling of Sozialistische Revolutie?"
Wat is Imperialisme? Nijmegen, Sunschrift 1972, pp. 88-128

"Capitalism and Underdevelopment in Latin America"

Problems of Industrial Society, W. Chambliss, ed. Reading, MA, Addison-Wesley 1972, pp. 125-129

"The Development of Underdevelopment"
The Political Economy of Development and Underdevelopment, C. K. Wilber, ed. New York, Random House, 1st ed. 1973, pp. 94-104, 3rd ed. pp. 99-108

"Die Entwicklung der Unterentwicklung"
Internationale Beziehungen, E. Krippendorf, ed. Köln, Kippenheur & Witsch 1973, pp. 91-103

"El Desarrolo del Subdesarrollo"
La Formación del Subdesarrollo, A. Redondo, ed. Barcelona, 1973, pp. 5-26

"Functionalism and Dialectics" and "Latin America Economic Integration"
Sociological Readings in the Conflict Perspective, W. J. Chambliss, ed. Reading, MA, Addison-Wesley 1973, pp. 62-73 and 406-410

"Funcionalism and Dialectics"
Theories and Paradigms in Contemporary Sociology, S. Denisoff, O. Callahan, & M. H. Levine, eds. Itasca, IL, F. E. Peacock Publishers 1974, pp. 342-352

"Underutviklings utvikling"
Underutvikling, T. L. Eriksen, ed. Oslo, Gyldendal Norsk Forlag 1974, pp. 211-224

"The Development of Underdevelopment"
Colonialism and Development Part II: On the Roots of Backwardness, Colombo, Marga Institut 1975, pp. 31-44

"The Development of Underdevelopment"
Readings in Development, R. D. H. Sallery, M. L. McDonald, & P. G. Duchesne, eds. Ottawa, CUSO, n.d.

"Desenvolvimento do subdesenvolvimento Latino-Americano"
Urbanização e subdesenvolvimento, L. Pereira, ed. Rio de Janeiro, Zahar 1975, pp. 25-38

"Die Entwicklung der Unterentwicklung"
Theorie der Internationalen Politik, H. Haftenhorn, ed. Hamburg, Hoffman, und Campe Verlag 1975, pp. 171-182

"The Lessons of Chile"
The Lessons of Chile, J. Gittings, ed. Nottingham, Spokesman Press 1974

"Sociologia do Desenvolvimento e Subdesenvolvimento da Sociologia"
Sociologia do Desenvolvimento II. J, G. Durand & L. Pihhero Machado, eds. Rio de Janeiro, Zahar 1975, pp. 109-182

"Über die Begrenzung des Binnenmarks durch die Internationale Arbeitsteilung und die Produktionsverhältnisse"
Herrschaft und Befreiung der Weltgesellschaft, K. J. Gäntzel, ed. Frankfurt, Campus Verlag 1975, pp. 161-211

"World Crisis, Class Struggle and 1984"
Radical Perspectives on the Economic Crisis of Monopoly Capitalism, New York, Union for Radical Political Economics 1975, pp. 82-87

"Zur Krise des Kapitalismus und die Zukunft Lateinamerikas"
Handbuch II—Unterentwicklung, V. Brandes & B. Tibi, eds. Köln, Europäische Verlagsantalt 1975, pp. 264-270

"On World Capital Accumulation, International Exchange, and the Diversity of Modes of Production in the New World"
Actes du XLIIe Congress Internationale des Americanistes, Paris, Sept. 1976, v. 1 pp. 187-207

"Weltkrise, Klassenkampf und 1984"
Die Zukunf der Wirtschaft, A. Reif, ed. München, Paul List Verlag 1976, pp. 235-245

"Friedmanism in Chile, Equilibrium on the Point of a Bayonet" (with T. Wheelright)
Political Economy of Development, Sydney, Australian Broadcasting Commission 1977, pp. 71-85

"Eine Krise der Kapitalakkumulation"
Lateinamerika, Kirche Zwischen Diktatur und Wiederstand, Essen, Evangelische Studentengemeinschaft 1977, pp. 9-15

"Crisi Mondiale e Sottosviluppo"
La Crisis Contemporanea, Annual Register of Political Economy, Milan, Jaca Book 1978, v. 1 pp. 170-181

"Anthropology = Ideology, Applied Anthropology = Politics"
The Politics of Anthropology, G. Huizer & B. Manheim, eds. The Hague, Mouton & Co. 1979

"El Desarrollo del Subdesarrollo," "Las Raices de Desarrollo y del Subdesarrollo en el Nuevo Mundo," and "La Inversión Extranjera en el Subdesarrollo Latinoamericano"
Las Causas del Subdesarrollo, J. Consuegra, ed. Bogota, Ediciones Tercer Mundo 1979, pp. 129 266

"Le radici dello sviluppo e del sottosviluppo nel Nuovo Mundo"
Il Sottosviluppo Latinoamericano, J. C. Scapini, ed. Milano, Franco Angeli Editore 1979, pp. 51-69

"Über die sogenannte ursprüngliche Akkumulation"
Kapitalische Weltökonomie, Kontroversen über Ihren Ursprung und Ihre Entwicklungsdynamik, D. Senghaas, ed. Frankfurt, Suhrkamp Verlag 1979, pp. 68-102

"Development of Underdevelopment or Underdevelopment of Development in China"
The Development of Underdevelopment in China: A Symposium of China's Economic History, P. C. C. Huang, ed. Armonk, NY, M. E. Sharpe Publishers 1980, pp. 90-99

"L'Ennemi inmédiat" and "Capitalisme et question indigène"
Le Marxisme en Amerique Latine de 1909 a nous Jours: Antologie, M. Lowy, ed. Paris, Maspero Editeur 1980, pp. 423-433

"Los Mecanismos del Imperialismo: El Caso de Brasil"
Economía Internacional II Teorías del Imperialismo, la Dependencia y su Evidencia Histórica, R. Villareal, ed. Mexico, Fróndo de Cultura Económica 1980, pp. 346-357

"Az ugynevezett eredeti felhalmozasrol"
Periferikus Nemzetek es Nemzetek Feletti Kozpontok, B. Laszlo & M. Ferenc, eds. Budapest, Fejlodes-Tanulmanyok 1980, v. 4 pp. 41-92

"Weltsystem in der Krise"
Krisen in der Kapitalistischen Weltökonomie, F. Fröbel, J. Heinrichs, & O. Kreye, Hamburg, Rowohlt 1980, pp. 19-34
"Wirtschafts Krise und der Staat in der Dritten Welt"
Struktuveränderungen in der Kapitalistischen Weltwirtschaft, Max-Planck Institute, ed. Frankfurt, Suhrkamp Verlag 1980, pp. 225-268
"Az elmaradottsaq fejlodese. Ki a kozvetlen ellenseg"
Az Elmelet es a Fegyverek Kritikaja Ideologusolk es Filozofusok a Harmadik Vilagrol, B. Laszlo & M. Ferenc, eds. Budapest, Fejlodes-Tanulmanyok 1980, v. 3 pp. 1-50
"Crisis, Transition, Delinking, and Destabilization with Special Reference to Greece"
Transition to Socialism, Athens, Center for Mediterranean Studies 1980, pp. 191-207 (in Greek)
"Economic Crisis, Third World and 1984"
Contemporary Peace Research, G. Pardesi, ed. New Delhi, Radiant Publishers 1982, pp. 273-290
"Crisis and Transformation of Dependence in the World System"
Theories of Development: Mode of Production or Dependency? R. H. Chilcolte & D. Johnson, eds. Beverly Hills, Sage Publications 1983, pp. 181-200
"The Crisis, What Crisis?"
What Is the Future? Ruschlikon, Switzerland, Gottlieb Duttweiler Institut 1983, pp. 12-28
"Die Gegenwertige Krise und die Perspektive des Weltsystems"
Perspektiven des Weltsystems, J. Blaschke, ed. Frankfurt, Campus Verlag 1983, pp. 23-255
"Nord-Süd und Ost-West Keynesianische Paradoxe im Brandt Report"
Unfähig zum Überleben? Reaktionen auf den Brandt Report, Friedrich Ebert Stiftung. Frankfurt, Ullstein Sachbuch 1983, pp. 269-284
"Norte-Sür y Este-Oeste Paradojas Keynesianas en el Informe Brandt"
Balance Crítico y Perspectivas: Dialogo Norte-Sur, Friedrich Ebert Stiftung, ed. Mexico, Editorial Nueva Imagen 1983, pp. 349-362
"World System in Crisis"
Contending Approaches to World System Analysis, W. R. Thompson, ed. Beverly Hills, Sage Publications 1983, pp. 27-42
"De Derde Wereld en Latijns-Amerika en de huidige ekonomische wereldkrisis" and "Ekonomisch evengewicht op de punt van een bajonet. Milton Friedman in Chile" (with T. Wheelwright)
Chile Onder Pinochet, Een Latijnsamerikaans Volk in Gijzeling, O. Catalan & A. G. Frank, eds. Amsterdam, SUA/Novib 1984, pp. 31-42
"Kapitalizam i nerezvijenost u Latinoskoj Americi"
Latinska Amerika, Nerazvijenost i Revolucija, L. Paligoric, ed. Belgrad, Prosveta Publishers 1984, pp. 63-120
"Lumpenburzoaxia, Lumpenfejlodes"

Torz Osztalytarsadalmak es Formalodo Tarsadalmi Osztalyok, M. Fernec, ed. Budapest, Fejlodes-Tanulmanyok 1984, v. 6 pp. 335-355

"Rhetoric and Reality of the New International Economic Order"
Transforming the World-Economy? Nine Critical Essays on the New International Order, H. Addo, ed. London, Hodder & Staughton Publishers in collaboration with United Nations University 1984, pp. 165-230

"Transformacion y Crisis Global"
Adonde Vamos? Cuatro Visiones de la Crisis Mundial, O. Nudler, ed. Bariloche, Fundación Bariloche, Editorial de la Patagonia 1985, pp. 187-222

"Cuba: A Revolution of the People (Nov. 23, 1960)"
Cuba: Twenty-Five Years of Revolution, 1959-1984, S. Halebsky & J. M. Kirk, eds. New York, Praeger Publishers 1985, pp. 413-419

"From Atlantic Alliance to Pan-European Entente: Political Economic Alternatives"
Development as Social Transformations: Reflection on the Global Problematique, ed. H. Addo, London, Hodder & Staughton Publishers in association with the United Nations University 1985, pp. 125-182

"A Marx, Keynes, Schumpeter Centenary and the Editors of Monthly Review"
Rethinking Marxism: Struggles in Marxist Theory, Essays for Harry Magdoff and Paul Sweezy, S. Resnick & R. Wolff, eds. New York, Autonomedia with Praeger Publishers 1985, pp. 119-130

"Politica ad hoc: Disoccupazione e Crisi Mondiale della Formazione della Politica Economica"
La Disoccupaziones su Scala Mondiale, H. Jaffe, ed. Milano, Jaca Book 1985, pp. 123-137

"The Political Challenge to Socialism and Social Movements"
Socialism on the Threshold of the Twenty-First Century, London, New Left Verso Books 1985, pp. 58-71

"Die Weltwirtschaftskrise als Herausforderung an den Sozialismus und die sozialen Bewegungen"
Sozialismus im 21 Jahrhundert, M. Nicolic, ed. Berlin, Argument Verlag 1985, v. 1, pp. 26-36

"The World Crisis and Economic Policy Formation"
Canada and the New International Division of Labour, D. Cameron & F. Houle, eds. Ottawa, University of Ottawa Press 1985, pp. 13-26

"The Development of Underdevelopment"
Promises of Development: Theories of Change in Latin America, P. S. Klaren & T. J. Bossert, eds. Boulder, Westview 1986, pp. 111-123

"The Political Challenges of Socialism and Social Movements in the World Economic Crisis"
Socialism on the Threshold of the Twenty-First Century, Tunis, Bourac Publishers 1986, pp. 77-92 (in Arabic)

"Global Crisis and Transformation"
International Capitalism and Industrial Restructuring, R. Peet, ed. Boston, Allen & Unwin Publishers 1987, pp. 293-312

"Political Ironies in the World Economy"
America's Changing Role in the World-System, T. Boswell & A. Bergesen, eds. New York, Praeger Publishers 1987, pp. 25-55

"World Economic Crisis and Policy Perspectives in the Mid-1980s"
Economic Theory and New World Order, H. W. Singer, R. Tandon, & N. Hatti, eds. New Delhi, Ashish Publishers, New World Order Series, v. 1, 1987, pp. 507-530

"La Ripresa di Reagan E'Reale, o E'La Calma Prima della Tempesta?
L'Europa e L'Economia Politica del Sistema-Mondo, R. Parboni & I. Wallerstein, eds. Milano, Francoangeli Editore 1987, pp. 237-267

"The Perils of Economic Ramboism: The Next Recession Threatens Deflation and Depression"
The Imperiled Economy: Left Perspectives on Macroeconomics, New York, Union of Radical Political Economics 1987, pp. 277-287

"Illusions of Recovery and Threat of Depression in the World Economy: Interplay Between Real and Financial Factors"
Economic Development and the World Debt Problem, v. 4 pp. 1-31. International Conference of Economists, Faculty of Economics, University of Zagreb, Sept. 8-11, 1987

"The World Economy, International Relations, and the European Challenge"
Europe: Dimensions of Peace, B. Hettne, ed. London and New Jersey, United Nations University Zed Books 1988, pp. 249-265

"Low Profit Invention and High Profit Innovation in Technological Change"
Technology Transfer by Multinationals, H. W. Singer, N. Hatti, & R. Tandon, eds. New Delhi, Ashish Publishing House, New World Order Series: Three, 1988, Part I, pp.183-202

"Internationale Ökonomische Beziehungen"
Frieden. Ein Handwörterbuch, E. Lippert & G. Wachtler, eds. Opladen, Westdeutscher Verlag, Studienbücher zur Sozialwissenschaft 47, 1988, pp. 192-206

"A Debt Bomb Primed for the Next Recession"
The Guardian Third World Review. Voices From the South, V. Brittain & M. Simmons, eds. London, Hodder and Stoughton Publishers 1987, pp. 244-247

"A Step in the Right Direction"
Perestroika: Global Challenge. Our Common Future, K. Coates, ed. Nottingham, Spokesman Press 1988, pp. 110-114

"East-West-South Relations in the World Economy"
New Perspectives in North-South Dialogue: Essays in Honour of Olof Palme, K. Buenor Hadjor, ed. London, I. B. Tauris Publishers & Third World Communications 1988, pp. 77-101

"Defuse the Debt Bomb? When Apparent Solutions Become Real Problems"
Resource Transfer and Debt Trap, H. W. Singer, N. Hatti, & R. Tandon, eds. New Delhi, Ashish Publishing House, New World Order Series: Five, 1988, Part II, pp. 550-585

"East-West Versus North-South Relations"
Challenges of South-South Co-Operation, H. W. Singer, N. Hatti, & R. Tandon, eds. New Delhi, Ashish Publishing House, New World Order Series: Six, Part I, pp. 92-101

"The Development of Underdevelopment"
The Political Economy of Development and Underdevelopment, C. K. Wilber, ed. New York, Random House 1988, 4th rev. ed. pp. 109-120

"American Roulette in the Globonomic Casino: Retrospect and Prospect on the World Economic Crisis Today"
Research in Political Economy, P. Zarembka, ed. Greenwich, CT, USA, JAI Press 1988, v. 11, pp. 3-43

"The Socialist Countries in the World Economy: The East-South Dimension"
Theory and Practice of Liberation at the End of the XXth Century. Lelio Basso International Foundation, ed. Bruxelles, Bruylant Editor 1988, pp. 307-328

"Sociology of Development and Underdevelopment of Sociology"
Modernization and Social Change, R. Pandey, ed. New Delhi, Criterion Publications 1988, pp. 212-283

"Hearing Fragestellungen"
Geld für Wenige oder Leben für alle? Ökumenisches Hearing zum Internationalen Finanzsystem, Berlin, 21-24 Aug. 1988. Oberursel, Publik-Forum Dokumentation, 6 pp. passim

"Debt Where Credit Is Due"
Economic Development and World Debt, H. W. Singer & S. Sharma, eds. London, Macmillan Press 1989, pp. 33-38

"Causes and Consequences of the World Debt Crisis" and "Legal Logic for Taxation Without Representation"
Las Transformaciones del Sistema Financiero Internacional, Madrid, Universidad Complutense, Cursos de Verano El Escorial 1988, 1989, pp. 19-34

"Liberty, Equality, and Fraternity/Solidarity: From Transitory Revolution to Transformatory Social Movements"
Revolutions in the World-System, T. Boswell, ed. Westport, CT, USA, Greenwood Press 1989, pp. 33-40

"The Socialist Countries in the World Economy: The East-South Dimension"
The Soviet Bloc and the Third World: The Political Economy of East-South Relations, B. H. Schulz & W. H. Hansen, eds. Boulder, Westview Press 1989, pp. 9-26

"Diez Tesis Acerca de los Movimientos Sociales" (with M. Fuentes)
El Jucio al Sujeto, R. Guidos Bejar y O. Fernández, Coordinadores. Cuadernos de Ciencias Sociales 25, San José, Costa Rica, Secretaría General Facultad Latinoamericana de Ciencias Sociales (FLACSO), Sept. 1989, pp. 19-42

"Social Movements" (with M. Fuentes)
New Directions in the Study of Law, Justice, and Social Control, School of Justice Studies, Arizona State University, ed. New York, Plenum Publishers 1990, pp. 127-141

"On 'Feudal' Modes, Models, and Methods of Escaping Capitalist Reality"
Agrarian Relations and Accumulation: The 'Mode of Production' Debate in India, U. Patnaik, ed. Bombay, Sameeksha Trust & Oxford University Press 1990, pp. 107-110

"Rumbo a la quiebra: El casino globonómico y la ruleta americana"
Américá Latina Continente de Mañana, M. Chavarría, ed. San José, Costa Rica, Cátedra de Historia de la Cultura, Escuela de Estudios Generales, Universidad de Costa Rica 1990, pp. 141-152

"Riccardo Parboni's World" and "Europe from Helsinki to Finnlandization"
Riccardo Parboni (1945-1988) In Memoria, Modena, Studie e Ricerche del Dipartimento di Economia Politica-55, Universita degli Studi di Modena 1990, pp. 12-13, 20-24

"Revolution in Eastern Europe: Lessons for Democratic Social Movements (and Socialists?)"
The Future of Socialism, W. Tabb, ed. New York, Monthly Review Press 1990

"5000 Years of World System History: The Cumulation of Accumulation" (with B. K. Gills)
Precapitalist Core-Periphery Relations, C. Chase-Dunn & T. Hall, eds. Boulder, Westview Press 1991, pp. 67-111

"Der Krieg der Scheinheiligen"
Krieg für Frieden? Startschüsse für eine neue Weltordnung, K. D. Bredthauer, ed. Berlin, Elefanten Press 1991, pp. 10-27

"American Roulette in the Globonomic Casino: Retrospect and Prospect on the World Economic Crisis Today"
Adjustment and Liberalization in the Third World, New World Order Series v. 12, H. Singer, N. Hatti, & R. Tandon, eds. New Delhi, Ashish Publishing House 1991, pp. 191-240

"World Economy and Social Movements" (with M. Fuentes)
The Legacy of Karl Polanyi: Market, State, and Society at the End of the Twentieth Century, M. Mendell & D. Salee, eds. New York, St. Martin's Press 1991, pp. 155-176

"Mas Sagrado que Vosotros en el Golfo: Una Maldición sobre las Casas de Ambos"
Golfo Pérsico. Visiones y Reflexiones, E. Cabrera & J. L. Camacho, eds. Mexico, El Día en Libros 1991, pp. 179-210

"La Guerre Tiersmondiale: Economie Politique de la Guerre du Golfe et du Nouveau Ordre Mondial"
Bush Imperator: Guerre du Golfe et Nouvel Ordre Mondial, S. Jaber, ed. Paris, Editions la Breche 1991, pp. 11-81

"Gorbachev's United Nations Initiatives: Steps in the Right Direction"
Building a More Democratic United Nations, Proceedings of CAMDUN-1. F. Barnaby, ed. London, Frank Cass 1991, pp. 146-151

"Andre Gunder Frank" (autobiographical entry)
A Biographical Dictionary of Dissenting Economists, P. Arestis & M. C. Sawyer, eds., London, Edward Elgar Publishers 1991, pp. 154-163

"1492 e America Latina o marxe da historia do sistema mundial: 492-992-1492-1992 es os cambios de hexemonia Leste-Oeste"
America Latina: Entre a Realidade e a utopia, A. C. de Filosofia, ed. Vigo, Edicions Xerais de Galicia 1992, pp. 171-211

"The Underdevelopment of Development" (with M. Fuentes Frank)
Equity and Efficiency in Economic Development: Essays in Honor of Benjamin Higgins, D. J. Savoie, ed. Montreal, McGill Queens University Press 1992, pp. 341-393

"The Development of Underdevelopment" and "Revolution in Eastern Europe: Lessons for Democratic Socialist Movements (and Socialists)"
The Political Economy of Development and Underdevelopment, C. K. Wilber & K. P. Jameson, eds. New York, McGraw-Hill, 5th ed. 1992, pp. 107-118 and pp. 209-225

"Third World War: A Political Economy of the Persian Gulf War and the New World Order"
Triumph of the Image: The Media's War in the Persian Gulf. A Global Perspective, H. Mowlana, G. Gerbner, & H. Schiller, eds. Boulder, Westview Press 1992, pp. 3-21

"Fourteen Ninety-Two Once Again"
1492: The Debate on Colonialism, Eurocentrism, and History, J. M. Blaut with contributions by A. G. Frank, S. Amin, R. A. Dodgshon, R. Palan, & R. Taylor. Trenton, NJ, Africa World Press 1992, pp. 65-80

"No End to History! History to No End?"
Beyond National Sovereignty: International Communication in the 1990s, K. Nordenstreng & H. I. Schiller, eds. New Jersey, Ablex Publishers 1993, pp. 3-28.

"Marketing Democracy in an Undemocratic Market"
Low Intensity Democracy: Elite Democracy in the Third World, B. K. Gills, J. Rocamora, & R. Wilson, eds. London, Pluto Press 1993, pp. 35-58

"Economic Ironies in World Politics"
The Ecumenical Movement Tomorrow, M. Reuver, F. Solms, & G. Huizer, eds. Kampen, The Netherlands, Kok Publishers 1993

"A World Economic Interpretation of East-West European Politics"
Transcending the State-Global Divide: A Neostructuralist Agenda in International Relations, R. Palan & B. K. Gills, eds. Boulder, Lynne Rienner Publisher 1994, pp. 145-168

"The Development of Underdevelopment"
Paradigms in Economic Development. Classic Perspectives, Critiques, and Reflections, R. Kanth, ed. Armonk, NY, M. E. Sharpe 1994, pp. 149-160

"The 'Thirdworldization' of Russia and Eastern Europe"
Russia and the Third World in the Post-Soviet Era, M. Mesbahi, ed. Gainesville, University Press of Florida 1994, pp. 45-72

"Soviet and East European 'Socialism': A World Economic Interpretation of What Went Wrong"

Regimes in Crisis: The Post-Soviet Era and the Implications for Development, S. Qadir & B. K. Gills, eds. London, Zed 1994

"On Studying the Cycles in Social Movements" (with M. Fuentes)
Research in Social Movements, Conflict, and Change, L. Kriesberg, M. Dobowski, & I. Walliman, eds. Greenwich, CT, USA, JAI Press, v. 17, 1994.

"The World Is Round and Wavy: Demographic Cycles and Structural Analysis in the World System"
Debating Revolutions, N. Keddie, ed. New York, New York University Press 1995

"The Modern World System Revisited: Re-reading Braudel and Wallerstein"
Civilizations and World Systems: Two Approaches to the Study of World-Historical Change, S. Sanderson, Ed., Walnut Creek, CA, Altamira Press, 1995.

"The Thirdworldization of Russia and Eastren Europe"
The Aftermath of "Real Existine Socialism"—East Europe Between Western Europe and East Asia, Jacques Hersch & Johannes Schmidt, Eds., London, Macmillian 1995/1996

"The Five Thousand Year World System: An Interdisciplinary Introduction"
The Historical Evolution of International Political Economy, C. Chase-Dunn, ed. London, Edward Elgar 1995/1996

PERIODICALS

Comments on Problems of Economic Development
Canadian Journal of Economics and Political Science, Toronto, XXI, 2, May 1955, pp. 237-241

The Economic Development of Nicaragua
Inter American Economic Affairs, Washington, VIII, 4, Spring 1955, pp. 559-568

Policy Decision and the Economic Development of Ceylon
Economia Internazionale, Milano, VIII, 4, Nov. 1957, pp. 797-809

Organization of Economic Activity in the Soviet Union
Weltwirtschaftliches Archiv, Kiel, v. 75, 1, March 1957, pp. 104-156

Review of Custom and Conflict in Africa, by M. Gluckman
American Journal of Sociology, Chicago, LXII, June 1957

General Productivity in Soviet Agriculture and Industry: The Ukraine 1928-1955
Journal of Political Economy, Chicago, LXVI, Dec. 1958, pp. 498-515

Industrial Capital Stocks and Energy Consumption
Economic Journal, London, LXIX, March 1959, pp. 170-174

Escalator Wage Contracts and Real Income
Southern Economic Journal, Southern Economic Assoc., XXV, 4, April 1959, pp. 474-477

Labor Requirements in Soviet Agriculture
   Review of Economics and Statistics, Cambridge, MA, LXI, 2, May 1959,
   pp. 188-192
Goal Ambiguity and Conflicting Standards: An Approach to the Study of Organization
   Human Organization, Ithaca, v. 17, 1, Winter 1958-59, pp. 8-13
Industrial Organization in the Soviet Union
   Business Topics, East Lansing, V, March 1958, 10 p.
   Mercurio, Milano, No. 6, Sept. 1958
Soviet and American Economic Organization: A Comparison
   Economic Weekly, Bombay, Special Number, XI, Jan. 1959, 15 p.
Human Capital and Economic Growth
   Economic Development and Cultural Change, Chicago, VIII, 2, Jan. 1960,
   pp. 170-173
Summary of a Workshop in Economic Anthropology
   Current Anthropology, Chicago, 1, 2, March 1960
Built in Destabilization: A. O. Hirschman's Strategy of Economic Development
   Economic Development and Cultural Change, Chicago, VIII, 4, July 1960,
   pp. 433-440
The Michigan Economy: More Eggs in Our Manufacturing Basket?
   Michigan Economic Record, East Lansing, II, 4, April 1960
Amerikanischer Nazionalkarakter
   Deutsche Woche, München, July 19, 1960, 10 p.
History Will Absolve Me. The Promise and Record of Fidel Castro
   Economic Weekly, Bombay, Special Number, XIII, July 1961, pp. 1101-1112
Kennedy and Khrushchev in the World Revolution
   Economic Weekly, Bombay, Aug. 19, 1961, pp. 1335-1337
The Cuban Revolution: Some Whys and Wherefores
   Economic Weekly, Bombay, Special Number, July 1961
Mexico: The Janus Faces of Twentieth-Century Bourgeois Revolution
Mexico: Las Dos Caras de una Revolución Burguesa del Siglo XX
   Economic Weekly, Bombay, Oct. 13, 1962, 15 p.
   Monthly Review, New York, v. 14, 7, Nov. 1962
   Política, México, IV, No. 74, May 15, 1963
   Monthly Review Selecciones en Castellano, Buenos Aires, 2, Aug. 1963
The Varieties of Land Reform
Tipos de Reforma Agraria
   Monthly Review, New York, v. 51, 12, April 1963
   Panorama Económico, Santiago, No. 237, July 1963
   Monthly Review Selecciones en Castellano, Buenos Aires, No. 1, July 1963
   O Semanario, Rio de Janeiro, No. 347, Aug. 22-28, 1963
Brazil: Aid or Exploitation?
As Relaçoes Economicas entre o Brasil e os Estados Unidos
Las Relaciones Económicas entre los Estados Unidos y América Latina
   Jornal do Brasil, Rio de Janeiro, March 17, 1963

Marcha, Montevideo, Año XXIV, 1153, April 26, 1963
Economic Weekly, Bombay, XV, Nos. 28, 29, & 30, Special Number, July 1963
Economía y Agricultura, Lima, I, 1, Sept.-Nov. 1963
The Nation, New York, v. 197, 16, Nov. 16, 1963
Peace News, London, Jan. 17, 1964
Arauco, Santiago, No. 51, April 1964
Latin American Economic Integration
    Monthly Review, New York, v. 15, No. 5, Sept. 1963, 10 p.
    Revista Brasiliense, Sao Paulo, No. 48, July-Aug. 1963
    Monthly Review Selecciones en Castellano, Buenos Aires, No. 3, Oct. 1963
A Pre-Revoluçao de Celso Furtado
A Contrarevoluçao de Celso Furtado
    Movimento, Rio de Janeiro, No. 11, May 1963
    O Semanario, Rio de Janeiro, No. 342, July 18-24, 1963
The Underdeveloped Countries and the Problem of Peace
Os Paises Subdesenvolvidos e o Problema da Paz
    A Liga, Rio de Janeiro, No. 52, Oct. 30, 1963
    Revolution, Paris, No. 8, Dec. 1963
Not Feudalism: Capitalism
Feudalismo no: Capitalismo
    Monthly Review, New York, v. 15, 8, Dec. 1963
    Monthly Review Selecciones en Castellano, Buenos Aires, No. 2, Aug. 1964
    Economía y Administración, Universidad de Zulia, Maracaibo, IV, 1, Jan. 1966
Administrative Role Definition and Social Change
    Human Organization, Ithaca, v. 22, 4, Winter 1963-64, pp. 238-242
A Agricultura Brasileira: Capitalismo e o Mito do Feudalismo (Part 1)
    Revista Brasiliense, Sao Paulo, No. 51, Jan.-Feb. 1964, pp. 45-70
Brazil in Perspective: The Goulart Ouster
Brésil: l'Arrière-Plan d'un Coup d'Etat
    The Nation, New York, v. 198, 18, April 27, 1964
    El Día, México, May 20, 1964
    Révolution, Paris, No. 13, Dec. 1964-Jan. 1965
Positive Aspects of the Sino-Soviet Dispute
    Monthly Review, New York, v. 16, 1, May 1964
On the Mechanisms of Imperialism: The Case of Brazil
Los Mecanismos del Imperialismo
    Monthly Review, New York, v. 16, 5, Sept. 1964
    Monthly Review Selecciones en Castellano, Buenos Aires, 2, 14, Oct. 1964
    Economía y Administración, Maracaibo, III, 3, July 1964
    Nuestra Industria, Revista Económica, La Habana, No. 13, June 1965
Triple Delusion
    Monthly Review, New York, v. 16, No. 9, Jan. 1965, pp. 569-572
Statement to the Memory of Paul Alexander Baran
    Monthly Review, v. 16, 11, March 1965, pp. 99-101

Brazil: One Year From Guerillas to Gorillas
The Minority of One, Passiac, New Jersey, USA, VII, No. 7 (68) July 1965
El Día, Mexico, Oct. 8, 1965
El Nuevo Confusionismo del Precapitalismo Dual en América Latina (con "Ni 'Tercer Mundo' ni 'Sociedad Dual': Solo Capitalismo o Socialismo & La Contrarevolucion de Celso Furtado")
Economía, Mexico, No. 4, mayo-junio 1965
The Imperialist Humanitarianism of Mr. Johnson
Challenge/Desafío, New York, Aug. 10, 1965
Con que Modo de Producción Convierte la Gallina Maiz en Huevos de Oro?
El Gallo Ilustrado. Suplemento de El Día, Mexico, No. 175, Octubre 31, 1965
Izquierda Nacional, Buenos Aires, No. 3, Octubre 1966
Modesta Respuesta
El Gallo Ilustrado. Suplemento de El Día, Mexico, No. 179, Nov. 28, 1965
Izquierda Nacional, Buenos Aires, No. 3, Octubre 1963
La Democracia en México
Historia y Sociedad, Mexico, No. 3, otoño 1965, pp. 122-132
Services Rendered
Servicio Extranjero o Desarrollo Nacional?
Monthly Review, New York, v. 17, No. 2, June 1965
Monthly Review Selecciones en Castellaño, Buenos Aires, II, 24, Aug. 1965
Presente Económico, Mexico, No. 1, Julio 1965
Comercio Exterior, Mexico, v. XVI, No. 2, Febrero 1966, pp. 105-107
Un Aula, Medellin, 2, Nos. 5-6. 1er semestre 1969
The Strategic Weakness of the Johnson Doctrine
Progressive Labor, New York, v. 5, No. 2, Dec. 1965
Unstable Urban Latin America
Studies in Comparative International Development, St. Louis, II, No. 5, 1966
Cuadernos Americanos, Mexico, Año XXV, No. 1, Enero-Feb. 1965
Necesidad de Nuevos Enfoques en la Enseñanza e Investigación de la Ciencia Económica en América Latina (con A. Bonilla, J. Consuegra, y G. Parra)
Revista de la Facultad de Ciencias Sociales y Económicas, Universidad de Zulia, Maracaibo, Año IV, No. 4, Oct.-Dic. 1965
Desarrollo Indoamericano, Barranquilla, No. 1, Enero 1966
Encuentro con Andre G. Frank (entrevista por Hiber Conteris)
Marcha, Montevideo, Febrero 19, 1965
La Política de Sustitución de Importaciones: Callejón sin Salida en Brasil
Investigación Económica, Mexico, No. 97, 1er trimestre 1965
Politica Externa Independente, Rio de Janiero, 1, No. 3, Janeiro 1966
Partisans, Paris, No. 26/27, Feb. 1968, pp. 29-40
Black Nationalism Is the Correct Strategy
Progressive Labor, New York, v. 4, No. 3, March 1965
Prensa Latina, La Habana, No. 284, Diciembre 15, 1967
Vodka and Conversation
The Illinois Political, Champaign-Urbana, v. 1, No. 2-3, May-June 1966

Colonialismo Interno en Brasil
Investigación Económica, Mexico, No. 101, 1966
Functionalism and Dialectics
Science & Society, New York, XXX, No. 2, Spring 1966
Cahiers Vilfredo Pareto, Genève, No. 16-17, 1968
L'Homme et la Societé, Paris, No. 12, Mai-Juin 1969
Revista del Centro de Alumnos del Departmento de Sociología, Universidad de Chile, Santiago, Marzo-Abril 1969
The Development of Underdevelopment
El Desarrollo del Subdesarrollo
Monthly Review, New York, v. 18, No. 4, Sept. 1966
Monthly Review Selecciones en Castellano, Santiago, v. 4, No. 36, Marzo 1967
Desarrollo Indoamericano, Barranquilla, v. 1, No. 2, Marzo 1966
Pensamiento Crítico, La Habana, No. 7, Agosto 1967
Economía y Administración, Maracaibo, V, Abril-Junio 1966
Publicaciones de la Bilbioteca Universidad Nacional de Colombia, Bogotá, No. 1, 1967
Coleção Universitaria Edicoes Sinal, São Paulo, No. 2, 1968
Liberation, Calcutta 1967
Cahiers Vilfredo Pareto, Genève, No. 16-17, 1968
Critiques de l'Economie Politique, Paris, No. 3, avril-juin 1971, pp. 4-16
Izquierda, Escuela de Economía, Santiago, No. 2, 1968
Bobbs-Merrill Reprint Series in Anthropology, Indianapolis, IN, USA, A 524, 1969
Le Point, Bruxelles, Septembre 1969
Información Comercial Española, Madrid, No. 460, Dec. 1971, pp. 81-85
Critiques de l'Economie Politique, Paris, No. 3, avril-juin 1971
Colección Lee y Discute, Editorial Zero, Madrid, Serie V, Editorial Zero, Madrid, Serie V, No. 45, 1974, pp. 5-52
Estudio de América Latina, Kobe, No. 3, June 1974, pp. 136 (Japanese)
La Inversión Extranjera en el subdesarrollo Latinoamericano desde la Conquista hasta la Integración Neo-Imperialista
Desarrollo Indoamericano, Barranquilla, No. 5, Jan. 1967
Pensamiento Crítico, La Habana, No. 27, Abril 1969
Chile: El Desarrollo del Subdesarrollo
Monthly Review Selecciones en Castellano, Santiago, Edicion especial de 168 paginas, 1967, 2 ediciones.
Sociology of Development and Underdevelopment of Sociology
Catalyst, Buffalo, No. 3, June 1967
Pensamiento Crítico, La Habana, Nos. 22 y 23, 1968
Desarrollo Indoamericano, Barranquilla, Año 3, No. 10, 1969
Cahiers Vilfredo Pareto, Genève, No. 15, 1968
Cahiers Internationaux de Sociologie, Paris, v. XLII, Jan.-June 1967
Aportes, Montevideo, 1969

Introduction to "Industrialization vs Colonialization"
    Edge, Montreal, No. 6, Spring 1967
Hugo Blanco Must Not Die
    Free Hugo Blanco, R. Mc Carthy, ed. Toronto 1967, pp. 7-16
On Responsibility in Anthropology
    Current Anthropology, Chicago, v. 9, No. 5, Dec. 1968, pp. 412-414
Sur le Probleme Indien
    Partisans, Paris, No. 26/27, Feb. 1968, pp. 15-28
Integración Económica de América Latina
    Un Aula, Medellin, Año 1, No. 3-4, Septiembre 1968
The Roots of Hunger
    Canadian Dimension, Winnipeg, v. 5, No. 8, Feb. 1969
    The Radical Education Project, Ann Arbor, pp. 1-7
    Presente Económico, Mexico, No. 2, Julio 1965
Class, Politics, and Debray (with S. A. Shah)
    Monthly Review, New York, v. 20, No. 3, July-Aug. 1968, pp. 12-17
    Monthly Review Selecciones en Castellano, Santiago, Año 5, No. 55, pp. 30-36
    Unidad Rebelde, Caracas, No. 3, Mayo-Junio 1970
Walt Whitman Rostow: Ode to Underdevelopment
    Tricontinental, La Habana, No. 7, 1968, pp. 30-42
    Tricontinental Edition Française, Paris, No. 4, IV trimestre 1968, pp. 40-51
    Tricontinental, La Habana, No. 7, July-Aug. 1968 (in Spanish)
Rostow's Stages of Economic Growth Through Escalation to Nuclear Destruction
    Radical Education Project, Ann Arbor, 1968, pp. 1-10
Quien es el Enemigo Inmediato? Latinoamerica: Subdesarrollo Capitalista o Revo-
    lución Socialista
    Cuadernos de Ruedo Ibérico, Paris, No. 15, 1968, pp. 1-28
    Pensamiento Crítico, La Habana, No. 13, 1968, pp. 3-41
    Hora Zero, Mexico, No. 4, 1968, pp. 105-143
    Les Temps Modernes, Paris, No. 2, May 1969, pp. 1963-2008
    SC Libre Trimestre Ideológico, Caracas No. 3, 1970, pp. 19-26
    3er Mundo, Santiago, No. 1, 1970, pp. 45-81
    Casa de las Américas, La Habana, No. 57, 1969
    Persian Journal for Science and Society, Alexandria, VA 1980
The Underdevelopment Policy of the United Nations in Latin America
    NACLA Newsletter, New York, v. III, No. 8, Dec. 1969, pp. 1-9
    Pensamiento Crítico, La Habana, No. 33, Oct. 1969, pp. 184-21
    PEL Panorama Económico Latinoamericano, La Habana, 10, No. 317,
        Diciembre 1969, pp. 7-21
    Punto Final, Santiago, Suplemento de la Edición No. 89, Oct. 14, 1969,
        pp. 1-12.
Visión marxista de la historia chilena (reseña)
    Punto Final, Santiago, 1969, 3, No. 79, Mayo 20, 1969, pp. 20-21

Importancia del estudio científico de los problemas del desarrollo y del sub-desarrollo
Problemas del Desarrollo, Mexico, Año 1, No. 1, Oct.-Dic. 1969
Terzo Mondo, Milano, Anno 11, No. 7-8, March-June 1970
El socialismo es la unica via para salir del subdesarrollo (entrevista por Fidel Vascos)
Verde Olivo, La Habana, Año XI, No. 29, Julio 19, 1970
Qué desenlace tendrá la crisis?
Punto Final, Santiago 1972
On "Feudal" Modes, Models, and Methods of Escaping Capitalist Reality
Economic and Political Weekly, Bombay, VIII, No. 1, Jan. 6, 1973, pp. 36-37
Reflections on Green, Red, and White Revolution in India
Economic and Political Weekly, Bombay, VII, No. 3, Jan. 20, 1973, pp. 119-124
Comercio Exterior, Mexico, Marzo 1973, pp. 367-371
Dependencia Económica, Estructura de Clases y Política del Subdesarrollo en Latinoamerica
Revista Mexicana de Sociologia, Mexico, XXXII, No. 2, Mar.-Apr. 1970, pp. 229-282
Even Heretics Remain Bound by Traditional Thought in Formulating Their Heresies
Economic and Political Weekly, Bombay, July 1970, V, 29-31, pp. 1171-1186
ECO, Bogotá, Sept. 1970, XXI, N. 5, pp. 439-465
Hacia una Teoria Historica del Subdesarrollo Capitalista en Asia, Africa y America Latina
UN, Universidad Nacional, Bogotá, 1970
Importancia de estudiar los problemas del desarrollo
Terzo Mondo, Milano, v. II, No. 7-8, marzo-giuno 1970, pp. 72-73
Problemas del Desarrollo, Mexico, No. 1, Oct.-Dec. 1969, pp. 12-13
On Dalton's "Theoretical Issues in Economic Anthropology"
Current Anthropology, Chicago, v. 11, No. 1, Feb. 1970, pp. 67-71
Riformismo e sottosviluppo negli anni '60
Problemi del Socialismo, Roma, v. X, May-Aug. 1970, pp. 377-404
El Socialismo es la Unica Via Para Salir del Sub-Desarrollo (Interview)
Verde Olivo, La Habana, XI, No. 29, 19 Julio 1970, pp. 15-17
Debate sobre el Peru (con V. Bambirra, M. Lajo, T. Dos Santos, R. M. Marini, & T. Vasconi)
Sayari, Arequipa, Agosto 1971, 14 pp.
El Cobre: Los Ladrones quieren Indemnización (con G. Diaz)
Punto Final, Santiago, Supl. 135, 20 Julio 1971, pp. 1-14
Imperialisti, Socialisti, Subimperialisti, Sfruttati nel Meccanismo della Crisi que Desenlace Tendra la Crisis?
Il Manifesto, Roma, 21 di settembre 1972, p. 4
Punto Final, Santiago, VII, No. 175, 16 enero 1973, pp. 12-14
Imperialism, Nationalism, and Class Struggle in Latin America
Socialist Digest, Bombay 1972, pp. 26-46

Acerca de las Ventajas Comparativas y el Intercambio Desigual
  Economia y Ciencias Sociales, Caracas, v. XV, Nos. 1-4, Numero extraordinario, enero-diciembre 1973
On Chile and Imperialism: Answer to José Rodríguez Elizondo
  Monthly Review, New York, v. 24, No. 7, Dec. 1972, pp. 61-62
  Economic and Political Weekly, Bombay, March 31, 1973, pp. 621-622
  Punto Final, Santiago, 1972
La Política Económica en Chile: Del Frente Popular a la Unidad Popular
  Punto Final, Santiago, 14 de Marzo 1972, Supp. No. 153, pp. 1-23
Dependence is Dead. Long Live Dependence and the Class Struggle—An Answer to Critics
  Problemas del Desarrollo, Mexico, No. 13, 1972, pp. 19-44
  Problemi del Socialismo, Roma, XIV, No. 10, luglio-agosto 1972, pp. 536-558
  Partisans, Paris, No. 68, 1972, pp. 52-70
  SC Libre Trimestre Ideólogico, Caracas, No. 13, Oct.-Dic. 1972
  Desarrollo Económico, Buenos Aires, v. 13, No. 49, Abril-Junio 1973, pp. 199-220
  Marcha, Montevideo 19 y 26 Enero, 2 Feb. 1973, n.p.
  Latin American Perspectives, Riverside, I, No. 1, Spring 1975, pp. 87-106
  World Development, Oxford, v. 5, No. 4, 1977
Politics and Bias: A Critical Review of Rostow and Hirschman
  Economic and Political Weekly, Bombay, VII, No. 38, Sept. 16, 1972, pp. 1917-1920
  Zona Abierta, Madrid, No. 2, Invierno 1974-75, pp. 141-147
  Desarrollo Indoamericano, Barranquilla
Reflexiones Sobre la Crisis Económica Mundial
  Marxismo y Revolución, Santiago, No. 1, 1973, pp. 153-160
On Sathyamurthy's Political Study of New Nations
  Current Anthropology, Chicago, v. 14, No. 5, Dec. 1973
Como la ampliación del mercado interno esta limitado por la división internacional del trabajo y las relaciones de produccion
  Ciencias Económicas y Sociales, Caracas, XV, Nos. 1-4, Numero Extraordinario 1973
Reseña critica de la historia del capitalismo en México de Enrique Semo
  Problemas del Desarrollo, Mexico, No. 17, Feb.-Abril 1974, pp. 147-151
World Crisis and Latina America's International Options
  Economic and Political Weekly, Bombay, IX, No. 27, July 6, 1974
  Holiday, Dacca, July-Aug. 1974
  Cuadernos Políticos, Mexico, No. 1, Julio-Sept. 1974, pp. 14-17
Discusion sobre la crisis actual del capitalismo. No esperar a 1984 (with S. Amin)
  Il Manifesto, Roma, Feb. 10, 1974
  Cuadernos Políticos, Mexico, No. 2, Oct.-Dec. 1974, pp. 101-126
  Neues Forum, Wien, Heft 253/254, Jan.-Feb. 1975, pp. 15-18
  Pontos de Vista, Lisboa, No. 26, Jan. 1976, pp. 3-49

Cuadernos de la Sociedad Venezolana de Planificación, Caracas, No. 122-123, n.d., pp. 81-92

Problemas del Desarrollo, Mexico, No. 20, Nov. 1974-enero 1975, pp. 150-165
La Lezione del Cile
  Terzo Mondo, Milano, VII, No. 23, Marzo 1974, pp. 73-75
Open Letter About Chile to Arnold Harberger and Milton Friedman (I)
  Desarrollo Indoamericano, Barranquilla, No. 26, Oct. 1974, pp. 59-71
  El Expresso, Roma, Nov. 1974
  De Groene Amsterdammer, Amsterdam, 21 Aug. 1974, p. 8
  Holiday, Dacca, Nov. 1974
  Neues Forum, Wien, Heft 251 Nov. 1974, pp. 13-24
  Politique Aujourd'hui, Paris, Aug.-Sept. 1974, pp. 1-14
  SC Trimestre Ideologico, Caracas, No. 16, Oct.-Dec. 1974, pp. 52-79
  Bulletin of the Conference of Socialist Economists, London, VI, 3, Oct. 1975
  Review of Radical Political Economics, New York, v. 7, No. 2, Summer 1975, pp. 61-76
  Les Temps Modernes, Paris, No. 342, Jan. 1975, pp. 817-846
  El Cronista, Lima, 2 Oct. 1975, p. 19
  Materiales, Hunancayo, No. 3, 1976, pp. 1-15
  Ideologia y Sociedad, Bogotá, No. 20, Enero-Marzo 1977, pp. 61-90
On the Roots of Development and Underdevelopment in the New World: Smith and Marx vs. the Weberians
  International Review of Sociology, Rome, II, No. 2-3, Aug.-Dec. 1974, pp. 109- 155
  Theory and Society, Amsterdam, II, 1975, pp. 431-466
  L'Homme et la Société, Paris, No. 35-36, Jan.-June 1975, pp. 53-69
  Desarrollo Indoamericano, Barranquilla, No. 27, Jan. 1975, pp. 53-69
  Terzo Mondo, Milano, No. 31-32, Jan.-June 1976, pp. 3-36
Ook in West-Europa kan allen en socialistische revolutie het fascisme tegen gaan (Interview at Chile Conference)
  De Groene Amsterdammer, Maart 20, 1974, pp. 5 & 8
Economic Crisis, Class Struggle and 1984
  Economic and Political Weekly, Bombay, Dec. 14, 1974, pp. 2055-2058
  Zona Abierta, Madrid, No. 2, Invierno 1974/1975, pp. 3-14
  Cuadernos de la Sociedad Venezolana de Planificación, Caracas, No. 122-123, Marzo-Abril 1975, pp. 73-80
  Holiday, Dacca, Oct.-Nov. 1975
  Leviatan, Frankfurt, v. 3, No. 2, Juni 1975, pp. 285-291
  Revolutionäre Bewegung und Marxismus, Frankfurt, No. 1, Dec. 1975, pp. 5-7
  Sekai, Tokyo, No. 361 (12), Dec. 1975
  Socialist Revolution, San Francisco, v. 5, No. 3 (25), July-Sept. 1975
  Den Ny Venden, Copenhagen, v. 11, No. 2, pp. 20-36
  World Development, Oxford, v. 4, No. 10 & 11, Oct.-Nov. 1976, pp. 853-862
Anthropology = Ideology, Applied Anthropology = Politics
  Race and Class, London, v. XVII, No. 1, Summer 1975

Uno y Multiple, Caracas, No. 2, 1976
L'Homme et la Société, Paris, No. 31-32, Jan.-June 1974, pp. 185-194
La Inversión Extranjera en el Subdesarrollo Latino-Americano
    Cuadernos Causachun, Serie Ideología y Política, Lima, No. 1, 1976, pp. 5-44
Friedmanism in Chile: Equilibrium on the Point of a Bayonet (Interview by
    T. Wheelwright)
    **Transcripts on the Political Economy of Development from the ABC Radio
    Programs Lateline and Investigations.** Sydney, Australian Broadcasting
    Commission, April 5, 1976
On Some Questionable Questions About Marxist Theory and International Capital
    Flows
    Review of Political Economics, New York, Summer 1976
What Is Underdevelopment
    The Ripening of Time, Dublin, No. 1, 1976
Economic Crisis, Class Struggle, and 1984
    World Development, Oxford, v. 4, Nos. 10/11, 1976
Adam Smith y el Tercer Mundo
    Problemas del Desarrollo, Mexico, VII, No. 28, Nov. 1976
That the Extent of the Market Is Limited by the International Division of Labor and
    the Relations of Production
    Economic and Political Weekly, Bombay, Annual Number, Feb. 1976
    Ciencias Económicas y Sociales, Caracas, Año XV, Nos. 1-4, Numero Extraor-
    dinario, 1973-74
Trade Balances and the Third World: A Commentary on Paul Bairoch
    Journal of European Economic History, Rome, v. 5, No. 2, Fall 1976
On Al Szymanski's Questionable Question About Marxist Theory and International
    Capital Flows
    Review of Radical Political Economics, New York, v. 8, No. 2, Summer 1976
Akkumulationskrise des Kapitalismus
    Frankfurter Rundschau, 24 Marz 1976
Multilateral Merchandise Trade Imbalances and Uneven Economic Development
    Journal of European Economic History, Rome, v. 5, No. 2, Fall 1976
Nuestra Batalla Contra el Mercantilismo en el Siglo XIX
    Pensamiento Político, Mexico, v. XXII, No. 86, June 1976
Nieuwe Depressie Dwingt de Politiek Rechts
    Dagblad, Eindhoven, Oct. 29, 1976
On So-Called Primitive Accumulation
    Dialectical Anthropology, New York/Amsterdam, No. 2, 1976
    L'Homme et la Société, Paris, No. 39-40, Jan.-June 1976
    Zona Abierta, Madrid, No. 14-15, 1977
    Desarrollo Indoamericano, Barranquilla, No. 30, Aug. 1977
Economic Genocide in Chile: Second Open Letter to Milton Friedman and Arnold
    Harberger
    Economic and Political Weekly, Bombay, June 12, 1976

Comercio Exterior, Mexico, No. 26, No. 12, Dec. 1976
Punto Crítico, Mexico, No. 67, Nov. 22, 1976
Neues Forum, Wien, No. 171-172, July/Aug. 1976
Blätter des Iz3W, Freiburg, No. 58, Dec. 1976
Links, Offenbach, No. 81, Oct. 1976
Ideología y Sociedad, Bogota, No. 20, Jan.-March 1977
Chile América, Roma, No. 19-20-21, June-July 1976
Emergence of Permanent Emergency in India
    Economic and Political Weekly, Bombay, March 12, 1977
    Holiday, Dacca, Feb.-March 1977
    Les Temps Modernes, Paris, Aug.-Sept. 1977
Economic Crisis and Underdevelopment
    Contemporary Crisis, Amsterdam, No. 3, 1977
    IAB, Köln, May 1977
Exploitation and Imbalance: A Reply to Sidney Pollard
    Journal of European Economic History, Rome, v. 5, No. 3, Winter 1977
Adam Smith y el Tercer Mundo
    Problemas del Desarrollo, Mexico, v. VII, No. 28, Enero 1977
Anskuelseundervisining I "Berufsverbot"
    Gyldendals Aktuele Magasin, Oslo, No. 1, 1977
Vansterekonom omm Konjukturkrisen: Okad Utsugning I U-Landerna
    Dagens Nyheter, Stockholm, Sept. 15, 1977
Long Live Transideological Enterprise! The Socialist Countries in the Capitalist
    International Division of Labor
    Economic and Political Weekly, Bombay, Annual Number, Feb. 1977
    Review, Binghamton, USA, v. 1, No. 1, Summer 1977
    L'Homme et la Société, Paris, Nos. 45-47, 1978-1979
    Zona Abierta, Madrid, Nos. 16-17, 1978
New International Division of Labour?
    Economic and Political Weekly, Bombay, Dec. 27, 1977
    Neues Forum, Wien, May/June 1978
    Frankfurter Rundschau, Dec. 24, 25, 26, 1977
    Comercio Exterior, Mexico, May 1979
    Synthesis, San Francisco, v. 3, No. 1, Fall 1979
Dependence Is Dead, Long Live Dependence and the Class Struggle: An Answer to
    Critics
    World Development, Oxford, v. 5, No. 4, April 1977
The Economics of Crisis and the Crisis of Economics
    Critique, Glasgow, No. 9, 1978
    Zona Abierta, Madrid, No. 13, 1977
    Cuadernos Políticos, Mexico, No. 12, 1977
La Crisis Mundial y el Tercer Mundo
    Monthly Review, en Espñol, Barcelona, v. 1, No. 5, 1977
Genocidio económico en América Latina (entrevista por R. Vasquez)
    Triunfo, Madrid, Año XXXII, No. 774, Nov. 1977

Imperialismus (Interview by Y. Broyles)
  Blätter des Iz3W, Freiburg, Juni 1977, No. 62
Warum Arbeitslosigkeit schwer zu beheben ist
  Frankfurter Rundschau, Weihnachten, No. 299, 1977
El cautiverio de la Deuda y la explotación del Tercer Mundo
  Desarrollo Indoamericano, Barranquillla, Año 13, No. 44, Sept. 1978
Die neue Kolonisierung
  Neues Forum, Wien, Mai/Juni 1978
"Entrevista con A. G. Frank" (por P. Subiros)
  Transición, Barcelona, Año I, No. 2, Nov. 1978
Super-Exploitation in the Third World
  Two Thirds, Toronto, No. 2, 1978
  Human Futures, New Delhi, Spring 1978
Dynamics of Capitalist Domination in Latin America
  Nase Teme, Zagreb, v. XXII, Nos. 7-8, 1978 (in Serbo-Croatian)
The Postwar Boom: Boom for the West, Bust for the South
  Millennium: Journal of International Studies, London, v. 7, No. 2, 1978
Development of Underdevelopment or Underdevelopment of Development in China,
  Comments on Victor D. Lippit
  Modern China, Beverly Hills, v. 4, No. 3, July 1978
Is Left-Wing Eurocommunism Possible?
  New Left Review, London, No. 108, 1978
  Cuadernos para el Diálogo, Madrid, Jan. 21, 1978
  Kritik, Berlin, v. 16, No. 17, 1978
  Ideología y Sociedad, Bogota, No. 23-24, Nov. 1978
Equating Economic Forecasting with Astrology Is an Insult—to Astrologers
  Contemporary Crisis, Amsterdam, v. 4, No. 4, 1978, pp. 97-102
  Il Manifesto, Roma, 1978
  Der Gewerkschafter, Frankfurt, v. 26, 1978
  Transición, Barcelona, v. 1, No. 1, Oct. 1978
Rhetoric and Reality of the New International Economic Order
  Human Futures, New Delhi, v. 2, No. 2, Summer 1979
  Desarrollo Indoamericano, Barranquilla, No. 51, 1979
Unequal Accumulation: Intermediate, Semi-Peripheral, Sub-Imperialist Economies
  Review, Binghamton, USA, v. II, No. 3, Winter 1979
Causes of Inflation
  Financial Times, London, July 25, 1980
The Arms Economy and Warfare in the Third World
  Current Crisis, Amsterdam, v. 4, No. 2, 1980
  Third World Quarterly, London, v. II, No. 2, 1980
Economic Crisis and the State in the Third World
  Desarrollo Indoamericano, Barranquilla, No. 55, 1980
  Perspectives Latino-Américaines, Paris, No. 1, 1980
Another Recession and Its Forecasting Confusion Worse Confounded
  Inprecor, Paris, No. 67-68, 1980

Third World Manufacturing Export Production
  The South East Asian Economic Review, Singapore, v. 1, No. 2, Aug. 1980
Development of Crisis and Crisis of Development: Living in the Real World
  Economic and Political Weekly, Annual Number, Bombay, Feb. 1980
  Transición, Barcelona, No. 15, Dec. 1979 & No. 16, Jan. 1980
  Comercio Exterior, Mexico, March 1980
Keynesian North-South and East-West Paradoxes in the Brandt Report
  Economic and Political Weekly, Bombay, v. XV, No. 31, Aug. 1981
  Third World Quarterly, London, v. II, No. 4
  Transición, Barcelona, No. 28, 1981
  Inprecor, Paris 1981, pp. 96-97
World System in Crisis
  Journal of Social Studies, Dacca, No. 10, 1980
  Contemporary Marxism, San Francisco, No. 2, 1981
  Zona Abierta, Madrid, No. 23, 1980
Kampuchea, Vietnam, China: Observations and Reflections
  AMPO, Tokyo, v. 13, No. 1, Spring 1981
  Social Praxis, Amsterdam, March 1980
  Viejo Topo, Barcelona, No. 46, July 1980
  Alternatives, New York & New Delhi, VII, No. 2, Fall 1981
World Crisis Theory and Ideology
  Alternatives, New Delhi & New York, VII, No. 1, Spring 1981
The New Economic Crisis in the West
  Journal of Social Studies, Dacca, Nos. 12/13, Apr.-June 1981
Crisis of Ideology and Ideology of Crisis
  Contemporary Crisis, Tokyo, No. 9, 1981 (in Japanese)
  The Seventies, Hong Kong, No. 5, 1981 (in Chinese)
After Reaganomics and Thatcherism, What? From Keynesian Demand Management via Supply-Side Economics to Corporate State Planning and 1984
  Contemporary Marxism, San Francisco, No. 4, Winter 1981-82
  El Viejo Topo, Barcelona, No. 63, Dec. 1981
  El Diario/Marka, Lima, No. 16, April 5, 1982
  Cuadernos Políticos, Mexico, No. 31, Jan.-March 1982
  Moderne Zeiten, Hanover, Feb. 1982
  Thesis Eleven, Australia, Summer 1982
World Economic History of Capital Accumulation
  Economic Review, Tokyo, No.4, April 1981 (in Japanese)
Scrambling for a Place at an Austere Table
  Guardian Third World Review, London, Jan. 8, 1982
Economic Crisis, Export Promotion, and Political Repression in the Third World
  Amerique Latine, Paris, No. 9, Jan.-March 1982
  Investigación Económica, Mexico, No. 157, July-Sept. 1981
Political Economic Crisis and the Shift to the Right
  Crime and Social Justice, San Francisco, No. 17, Summer 1982

Armoede Waarom? (Interview)
Onze Wereld, The Hague, No. 3, March 1982
Asia's Exclusive Models
Far Eastern Economic Review, Hong Kong, June 25-July 1, 1982
Global Crisis
Third World First: North-South Links, Oxford and London, Summer 1982
The Atlantic Alliance in Disarray
Marxism Today, London, Oct. 1982
Our Socialism, San Francisco, v. I, No. 1, March 1983
Socialistisk Debatt, Stockholm, v. 17, No. 1, 1983
The Old Order Changeth Not
Far Eastern Economic Review, Hong Kong, Sept. 3, 1982
Crisis and Transformation of Dependency in the World System
Scandinavian Journal of Developing Countries, Stockholm, 4, Dec. 1982
Some Limitations of NIC's Export-Led Growth From a World Perspective
IFDA Dossier, 33, Jan.-Feb. 1983
Moonshine Growth Models
The Patriot, India, Feb. 24, 1983
La guerra e il solo sbocco possibile alla crisi del sistema-mondo?
Pace e Guerra, Roma, No. 7, Jan. 13, 1983
Policy Ad Hockery: Unemployment and World Economic Crisis of Policy Formation
Economic and Political Weekly, Bombay 1983
Volkskrant, Amsterdam, June 18, 1983
Global Crisis and Transformation
Development and Change, Den Haag, v. 14, No. 3, July 1983, pp. 323-346
Crisis y Transformación de la Dependencia en el sistema Mundial
Desarollo Indoamericano, Barranquilla, Colombia, v. XVII, No. 76, April 1983, pp. 11-18
What Is to Be Done With Artificial Straw Men?
Development and Change, Den Haag, v. 14, No. 4, Oct. 1983, pp. 625-626
From Atlantic Alliance to Pan-European Entente: Political Economic Alternatives
Alternatives, A Journal of World Policy, New York & New Delhi, v. VIII, No. 4, Spring 1983, pp. 423-482
Socialism in the World, Belgrad, Year 7, No. 37, 1983, pp. 57-105
Socijalizam u Svetu, Beogard, Godima 7, No. 37, 1983, pp. 52-100 (in Serbo-Croatian)
Real Marxism is Marxist Realism
Viertel Jahres Berichte, Bonn, No. 93, Sept. 1983, pp. 209-226
Socialism in the World, Belgrad, Year 7, Special Issue, 1983, pp. 70-80
St. Mark's Review, Australia, No. 13, March 1983, pp. 15-21
Shiso, Tokyo, No. 705, March 1983 (in Japanese)
Nueva Sociedad, Caracas, No. 66, May-June 1983, pp. 72-80
Naar een verenigd Europa
Rostra, No. 102, Feb. 1983, pp. 5-6

The Latin American Left and Democracy: Discussion
Marski Stika Misao, Belgrad, No. 4, 1983 (in Serbo-Croatian)
Discussion on Political Economy
Socialism in the World, Belgrad, Year 7, No. 36, 1983, pp. 162-163, 170, 172
Crisis del Marxismo en América Latina (with C. Franco, J. Arico, & E. Gomariz)
Leviatán, Madrid, No. 11, Spring 1983
El Método Marxista en los países del Este
El Socialista, Madrid, No. 302, 23-29, March 1983, p. 57
On Losing Sight of the Forest for Looking at the Trees
Development & Change, Den Haag, v. 15, No. 3, July 1984, pp. 457-463
World Economic Crisis and the Third World in the Mid-1980s
Economic and Political Weekly, Bombay, May 12, 1984, pp. 799-804
Economia e Socialismo, Lisboa, No. 62, July-Sept. 1984, pp. 3-14
Espaces et Sociétés, Paris, No. 4, Jan.-June 1984, pp. 15-32
Political Ironies in the World Economy
Studies in Political Economy, Ottawa, No. 15, Fall 1984, pp. 119-150
Democrazia Proletaria, Milano, v. III, No. 6, June 1985, pp. 39-44
De groei naar wederzijdse afahandelijhkeid
De Waarheid, Amsterdam, Oct. 12, 16, 19, 1984
Is There a Crisis of Marxism?
Socialism in the World, Belgrad, No. 41, 1984, p. 199
Defuse the Debt Bomb? When Apparent Solutions Become Real Problems
Can the Debt Bomb Be Defused? (Revision of above)
Economic and Political Weekly, Bombay, July 7, 1984, pp. 1036-1046.
World Policy Journal, New York, I, 4, Summer, pp. 723-740
Revue Tiers Monde, Paris, v. XXV, No. 99, July-Sept. 1984, pp. 586-600
Development and Peace, Budapest, v. 5, No. 2, Autumn 1984, pp. 5-25
On the Debt Bomb
De Volkskrant, Amsterdam, Aug. 18, 1984
Folha de São Paulo, Brasil, Aug. 25, 1984
El País, Madrid, Sept. 30, 1984
The Guardian, London, Oct. 12, 1984
Der Überblick, Hamburg, No. 4/84, Dec. 1984
Boletín Económico, Buenos Aires, Oct. 1984
Development and Contradictions of Socialist Societies
Socialism in the World, Belgrad, No. 45, 1984, p. 199
The Unequal and Uneven Historical Development of the World Economy
Contemporary Marxism, San Francisco, No. 9, Fall 1984, pp. 71-95
Can the Debt (and Nuclear) Bomb(s) Be Defused?
IFDA Dossier, Nyon Switzerland, No. 46, March/April 1985, pp. 67-72
O Desafio Europeu para a Paz e o Progresso
Economia e Socialismo, Lisboa, Nos. 64/65, Jan.-June 1985, pp. 49-59
La Crisis Económica Mundial y las Perspectivas Políticas
Desarrollo Indoamericano, Barranquilla, No. 82, May 1985, pp. 9-18
Es posible desactivar la bomba de la deuda?
Nueva Sociedad, Caracas, No. 79, Sept. 1985

Kriza u Svjetskoj Privredi i Socializam
  Kumrovecki Zapisi, Jugoslavia, No. 3, 1985, pp. 41-51, 176-178
Crise de la Economia Mundial y Perspectivas Politicas a Meados da Decada 1980
  Terra Firme, Rio de Janeiro, v. I, No. 1, 1985
The European Challenge for Peace and Progress
  Socialism in the World, Belgrad, No. 51, 1985, pp. 3-14
Armament and Disarmament
  Socialism in the World, Belgrad, No. 49, 1985, pp. 168-169, 185-186
Gaeldskrisen er en Tidistillet Bombe
  Information, Oslo, Feb. 12, 1985
De Menseoffers van het Niewuwe Kapitalisme: Een Debat tussen Crisisbestrijders
  (met E. Hefkens, L. Emmerij, E. Izboud, L. van Ulden, J. Breman, & A. Meier)
  De Waarheid, Amsterdam, March 2, 1985
Der Ost-West Konflikt-Ein Deckmantel (with I. Wallerstein)
  MOZ Grün-Alternative Monatszeitung, Wien, No. 9, July-Aug. 1985
  Blatter des Iz3W, Freiburg, No. 127, Aug. 1985, pp. 53-56
Can the Crash Be Averted?
  Washington Report on the Americas, Sept. 24, 1985, p. 2
Gunder Frank Sees Economic Crash, Populist Wave
  Latin America Index, Washington, DC, Nov. 1, 1985, pp. 78-79
Is the Reagan Recovery Real or the Calm Before the Storm?
  Economic and Political Weekly, Bombay, v. XXI, No. 21, May 24, 1986 & No.
  22, May 31, 1986
Appropriate Marxism is Marxist Realism (in Serbo-Croatian)
  Praska, Belgrad, No. 2, 1986, pp. 261-274
The Blocs in Disarray: New Hope for Europe
  ENDpapers, Nottingham, No. 11, Winter 1985-86, pp. 18-27
Taxation That Stirs Revolt
  South, London, No. 71, Sept. 1986, pp. 64-65
Kampuchea, Vietnam, China: Observations and Reflections With 1985 Postdate
  Contemporary Marxism, San Francisco, Nos. 12-13, Spring 1986, pp. 107-119
The European Challenge (in Greek)
  Estrinon, Athens, Dec. 7, 1986, pp. 12-13
Coping With the Debt Crisis: When the Solution Becomes the Problem
  CALC Report, New York, v. 12, No. 1, Jan.-Feb. 1986, pp. 3-9
Est-il Possible de Désarmer la Bombe de la Dette?
  Cahiers du CRAL, Paris, Cahier 4, 1986, 25 pp.
La Recuperación Reagan
  Leviatán, Madrid, II Epoca No. 25, Otoño 1986, pp. 47-62
Third World Agriculture and Agribusiness (in Chinese)
  Social Science Journal of Hainan University, Hainan Dao, No. 3, 1986, pp. 43-48
Is the Reagan Recovery Real or the Calm Before a Storm?
  Socialism in the World, Belgrad, v. 11, No. 58, 1987, pp. 102-118
The World Economic Crisis: Retrospect and Prospect
  Development and Peace, Institute for World Economy, Budapest, v. 8, No. 1,
  Spring 1987, pp. 5-28

Debt Where Credit Is Due
  Economic and Political Weekly, Bombay, XXII, 42 & 43, Oct. 17-24, 1987,
    pp. 1795-1798
  Journal für Entwicklungspolitik, Wien, III, 3, 1987, pp. 87-92
Nine Theses on Social Movements (with M. Fuentes)
  Economic and Political Weekly, Bombay, XXII, 35, Aug. 29, 1987, pp. 1503-1510
  Newsletter of International Labour Studies, The Hague, No. 34, July 1987
  IFDA Dossier, Nyon/Geneva, No. 63, Jan./Feb. 1988, pp. 27-44
  Thesis Eleven, Australia, Nr. 18/19, 1987/1988, pp. 143-165
  Socialism in the World, Belgrad, No. 66, 1988, pp. 62-81
  Transnational Associations, Bruxelles, 40, No. 1, 1988, pp. 24-32
Crash Course
  Economic and Political Weekly, Bombay, XXII, 46, Nov. 14, 1987, pp. 1942-1946
The Next Recession Threatens Deflationary Depression
  Razvoij/Development International, Institute for Developing Countries,
    Zagreb, II, No. 2, Dec. 1987, pp. 219-239
Comment on Janet Abu-Luhod's "The Shape of the World System in the Thirteenth
  Century"
  Studies in Comparative International Development, New Brunswick,
    USA, v. 22, No. 4, 1987, pp. 35-37
La Crisi Economica Mondiale: Esame Retrospettivo e Prospettive
  Marx Centuno Revista Internationale di Dibattit Teorico, Milano, No. 6,
    Dec. 1987, pp. 67-77
Problems of Marxist Economic Theory (Discussion)
  Socialism in the World, Belgrad, v. 11, No. 59, 1987, pp. 154-155, 156, 158,
    177-178
Socialism, Capitalism, and the World System of Capitalism
  Socialism in the World, Belgrad, 11, No. 63, 1987, pp. 178, 185, 187, 193-194
Il crollo finanziaro di Wall Street previsto da Gunder Frank. Il '29 diertro l'angolo
  Il Manifesto, Roma, Oct. 31, 1987, p. 8
La deuda en aquellos paises merecedores de credito
  El País, Madrid, Sept. 29 & 30, 1987, pp. 58 & 60
Nieuwe wet moet schuld arme landen beter regelen
  Volkskrant, Amsterdam, Sept. 26, 1987, p. 21
Arms and the Poor Man
  The Guardian, London, Oct. 2, 1987, p. 22
Bankrott als Zuflucht
  Wirtschaftswoche, Düsseldorf, v. 48, No. 20, Nov. 1987, pp. 90-99
Lógica Legal para la Deuda del Tercer Mundo
  Le Monde Diplomatique en Español, Mexico, v. 9, No. 105, Nov. 1987, p. 28
Amerikanse Roulette
  Intermediare, Amsterdam, v. 23, No. 49, Dec. 4, 1987, pp. 19-23
Schnellkurs: Amerikanisches Roulette und das Globonomische Kasino
  International, Wien, No. 6, Dec. 1987

Interview
  Socialist Theory and Practice, Athens, No. 2, Mar.-Apr. 1987, pp. 41-55 (in Greek)
The World According to Frank (Interview)
  Discorsi, Amsterdam, v. 21, No. 1, Oct. 1987, pp. 8-9 (in Dutch)
World Crisis: The Next Recession Will Be a Depression (Interview)
  Privredivjesnik, Zagreb, XXXV, No. 2516, June 21, 1987 (in Croatian)
Andre Gunder Frank: Practical Strategies for Social and Economic Development
  (Interview by T. Simmons)
  Aurora, Athabasca University, Alberta, Canada, v. 11, No. 2, Winter 1987-88,
    pp. 26-29
Para una Nueva Lectura de los Movimientos Sociales (with M. Fuentes)
  Nueva Sociedad, Caracas, No. 93, Enero-Feb. 1988, pp. 18-29
A Modest Proposal
  Economic and Political Weekly, Bombay, XXIII, 6, Feb. 6, 1988, pp. 246-247
Itinerario del Colapso
  Desarrollo Indoamericano, Barranquilla, XXII, 87, Jan. 1987, pp. 19-24
Nueve Tesis Acerca de los Movimientos Sociales (with M. Fuentes)
  David y Goliath, Buenos Aires, XVIII, 53, Aug.-Sept. 1988, pp. 44-54
The World Economic Crisis Today: Retrospect and Prospect
  Scandinavian Journal of Development Alternatives, Stockholm, v. VII,
    Nos. 2 & 3, June-Sept. 1988, pp. 181-215
Gorbachev's United Nations and Peace Initiatives: Steps in the Right Direction
  Economic and Political Weekly, Bombay, XXIII, 49, Dec. 3, 1988, pp. 2575-2577
Der Weg in die Krise: Amerikanisches Roulette und Internationales Finanzkasino
  Links, Offenbach, No. 214, Jan. 1988, pp. 11-13
La Ruleta Norteamericana y el Casino Globonomico
  Le Monde Diplomatique en Español, Mexico, IX, 107, Enero 1988, p. 30
The Crash of '87: Amerikanisches Roulette und das Globonomische Kasino
  International Zeitschrift für Internationale Politik, Wien, No. 1, 1988, pp. 19-22
Corso di Crash
  Marxismo Oggi: Revista Bimestrale di Cultura e Politica, Milano, II, No. 1,
    Jan. 1988, pp. 11-18
Un proyecto modesto
  El País, Madrid, Feb. 9, 1988, p. 46
Andre Gunder Frank's Lecture
  Socialist Theory and Praxis, Athens, No. 3, March 1988, pp. 18-19
Third World: Lots of Taxation Without Much Representation
  Minnesota Daily, Minneapolis, May 6, 1988, pp. 9-10
Politik in der Krise des Weltmarktes: Wie Konkurrenten Zusammenarbeiten
  Arbeitshefte Entwicklungspolitik des DGB-Bildungswerkes, Düsseldorf, No. 8,
    Januar 1988, 8 pp.
Gorbachev: Un pas dans la bonne direction
  Pourquoi? Paris, No. 238, Octubre 1988, pp. 18-25
Il Mondo di Gorbaciov
  Il Manifesto, Roma, XVIII, No. 288, Dec. 7, 1988, p. 3

Andre Gunder Frank vaticina una nueva recesion economica
El Periodico de Catalunya, Barcelona, June 17, 1988, p. 37
La "perestroika" todavia tiene que llegar a EEUU
El Periodico de Catalunya, Barcelona, June 19, 1988, p. 56
La pitjor epoca?
Setze/Cambio 16, Barcelona, No. 11, julio 4, 1988, pp. 14-15
Das Weltkarusell (with H. Hofbauer, O. Kreye, O. Rajewitsch, & U. Stacher)
MOZ Alternative Monatszeitung für Politik, Wirtschaft und Kultur, Wien, No. 11, Nov. 1988, pp. 40-45
Ten Theses on Social Movements (with M. Fuentes)
World Development, Washington/Oxford, v. XVII, 2, Feb. 1989, pp. 179-192
Próxima Recesión Estadouinense Causaría Crisis Mundial
Homines, Puerto Rico, XII, Nos. 1 & 2, Marzo 1988-Enero 1989, pp. 127-130
World Debt, the European Challenge, and 1992
Economic and Political Weekly, Bombay, XXIV, No. 17, April 29, 1989, pp. 914-916
Weltverschuldungskrise, Europäische Herausforderung, und 1992
Das Argument, Berlin, No. 177, v. 31, No. 5, Sept./Oct. 1989, pp. 759-766
Blocking the Black Debt Hole in the 1990s
Economic and Political Weekly, Bombay, v. XXIV, No. 42, Oct. 21, 1989, pp. 2362-2363
Rostra, Amsterdam, No. 164, Jan. 1990, pp. 34-35
History at the Margin: Canada in the European Age (Book Review)
Studies in Political Economy, Ottawa, No. 29, Summer 1989, pp. 163-169
Review of **The State of Development Economics**, G. Ranis and T. P. Schultz, eds. (Oxford, Blackwell 1988) in
European Journal of Political Economy, Amsterdam, No. 5, 1989, pp. 141-142
El Desafío Europeo entre el Este y el Oeste en 1992
La Gazeta de los Negocios, Madrid, I, 5 & 6, April 3 & 4, 1989, pp. 31, 35
The Development of Underdevelopment (1966)
Monthly Review, New York, v. 41, No. 2, June 1989, pp. 37-51
Dez Teses Acerca dos Movimentos Sociais (with M. Fuentes)
Lua Nova: Revista de Cultura e Politica, São Paulo, No. 17, June 1989, pp. 19-48
Gorbachev and the UN: A Kaleidoscopic Vision
Development Forum, United Nations Department of Public Information, New York, v. XVII, No. 4, July-Aug. 1989, p. 4
World Debt, the European Challenge, and 1992
ENDpapers Nineteen, Nottingham, Spring 1989, pp. 22-29
Il Bimestrale, Roma, No. 3, June 1989, pp. 66-71
MOZ: Alternative Monatszeitung für Politik, Wirtschaft und Kultur, Wien No. 9, Fortz. Nr. 45, Okt. 1989, pp. 31-34
El agujero negro de la deuda
La Gaceta de los Negocios, Madrid, v. 1, No. 110, Sept. 8, 1989, p. 31

Los Problemas Financieros del Tercer Mundo: Causas y Consequencias de la Crisis de la Deuda Mundial
   Página Abierta, Santiago, Chile, v. I, No. 1, Oct. 1989, pp. 910—Naar de Finlandisering van Europa
   Het Parool, Amsterdam, v. 49, Nr. 13731, Nov. 23, 1989, p. 9
Europa, desde Helsinki hacia la Finlandización
   El País, Madrid, Dec. 9, 1989, p. 6
Skuldkrisen och den europeiska utmanningen
   Haften for Kritiska Studier, Stockholm, v. 22, No. 4, 1989, pp. 4-13
Europe From Helsinki to Finlandisation
   Economic and Political Weekly, Bombay, XXV, 2, Jan. 13, 1990, pp. 90-91
East European Revolution of 1989: Lessons for Democratic Social Movements (and Socialists?)
Europa del Este: doce lecciones de los acontecimientos de 1990
   Economic and Political Weekly, Bombay, XXV, 4, Feb. 3, 1990, pp. 251-258
   Third World Quarterly, London, XII, 2, April 1990, pp. 36-52
   Das Argument, Berlin, No. 180, v. 32, No. 2, March/April 1990, pp. 191-203
   Leviatán, Madrid, II Epoca No. 39, primavera 1990, pp. 15-32
   Revista Internacional, Prag, No. 381, No. 5-6, May-June 1990, pp. 29-33
   Nueva Sociedad, Caracas No. 108 Julio-Agosto 1990, pp. 60-74
   Problems of Peace and Socialism, Prag (No. 381). No. 5, 1990, pp. 37-40 (in Russian; also in English and French editions)
Review of **Latin American Theories of Development and Underdevelopment** by C. Kay
   Development and Change, The Hague, v. 23, No. 3, July 1990, pp. 560-562
A Theoretical Introduction to 5,000 Years of World System History
   Review, Binghampton, USA, v. XIII, No. 2, Spring 1990, pp. 155-248
The Cumulation of Accumulation: Theses and Research Agenda for 5000 Years of World System History (with B. K. Gills)
   Dialectical Anthropology, New York/Amsterdam, v. 15, No. 1, July, pp. 19-42
Europa od Helsinkja do Finlandizacije
   Medunarodna Politika, Belgrad, v. XLI, No. 957, Feb. 6, 1990, pp. 9-11
El Agujero Negro de la Deuda
   El Gallo Ilustrado Suplemento Dominical de El Día, Mexico, April 8, 1990, pp. 5-6
Galoppierender Kapitalismus
   MOZ Monatszeitung für Politik, Wirtschaft und Kultur, Wien No. 52, May 1990, pp. 40-42
Otra mirada a la historia (en transición)
   El Día, Mexico, Suplemento Especial XXVIII Aniversario, Junio de 1990, pp. 3-6
Ningún fin a la historia! Historia sin fin?
   El Gallo Ilustrado 1464 Semanario de **El Día,** Mexico, 15 de julio de 1990, pp. 2-10

The Thirteenth-Century World System: A Review Essay
  Journal of World History, Hawaii, I, No. 2, 1990
De Quelles Transitions et de Quels Modes de Production s'agit-il dans le Système-
  Monde Réel? Commentaire sur l'Article de Wallerstein
  Sociologie et Societés, Montreal, v. XXII, No. 2, Oct. 1990
Economía política del conflicto Norte-Sur en el Pérsico
  El Gallo Ilustrado 1473 Semanario de El Día, Mexico, Sept. 16, 1990
On the Silk Road: An Academic Travelogue
  Economic and Political Weekly, Bombay, XXV, 46, Nov. 17, 1990, pp. 2536-
  2539
Some Ups and Downs on the Silk Road: An Academic Travelogue
  World History Bulletin, Philadelphia, PA, USA, VII, 3, Fall/Winter 1990-91,
  pp. 7-11
Korak za Najmanje Losu Politiku (Interview with M. Drazic)
  Borba, Belgrad, LXIX, Nos. 315-316, Nov. 10-11, 1990, pp. 1, 4-5
Otra Mirada a la Historia (en Transición)
  Punto Final, Santiago, XXV, No. 223, Octubre de 1990, pp. 22-23
No Escape From the Laws of World Economics
  European Labour Forum, Nottingham, No. 2, Autumn 1990, pp. 36-40
No End to History! History to No End?
  ENDpapers 21, Nottingham, No. 21, Autumn 1990, pp. 52-71
A Plea for World System History
  Journal of World History, Hawaii, II, 1, Spring 1991, pp. 1-28
  Cuadernos Americanos, Mexico, XXX, 4, Dec. 1991
Ökonomische Ironien in der Welt Politik
  Starnberger Forschungsberichte, Starnberg, Germany, No. 1, March 1991,
  pp. 19-42
Algunos Altibajos en la Ruta de la Seda
  El Gallo Ilustrado Semanario de **El Día,** Mexico, No. 1489, Jan. 6, 1991, pp. 1-5
Another Look at History (in Transition)
  IFDA Dossier, Geneva, No. 80, Jan.-March 1991, pp. 77-84
Transitional Ideological Modes: Feudalism, Capitalism, Socialism
  Critique of Anthropology, v. 11, No. 2, Summer 1991, pp. 171-88
Ironías de la Economía Mundial
  Punto Final, Santiago, XXV, No. 243, July 15, 1991, pp. 10-11
The Underdevelopment of Development
  Scandinavian Journal of Development Alternatives, Special Number, v. X,
  No. 3, Sept. 1991, pp. 5-72
Bibliography of Publications 1955-1990 (of A. G. Frank)
  Scandinavian Journal of Development Alternatives, Special Number, v. X,
  No. 3, Sept. 1991, pp. 75-131
Latin American Development Theories Revisited: A Participant Review Essay
  Scandinavian Journal of Development Alternatives, Special Number, v. X,
  No. 3, Sept. 1991, pp. 133-150

Nueva visita a las teorias latinoamericanas del desarrollo. Un ensayo de reseña participativo
Nueva Sociedad, Caracas, No. 113, mayo-junio 1991, pp. 67-78
Economic Ironies in World Politics
Economic and Political Weekly, Bombay, XXVI, 30, July 27, 1991, pp. 93-102
Economic Review, Colombo, Sept.-Oct. 1991, pp. 1-3, 41-49
Cuadernos del CENDES, Caracas, No. 15, 1991
No Escape From the Laws of World Economics
Review of African Political Economy, No. 50, 1991, pp. 21-32
A felhalmozas felhalmozadasa [The Cumulation of Accumulation] (with B. K. Gills)
Eszmelet, Budapest, Nos. 11-12, Sept. 1991
Demokraclaarusitas az antidemokratikus [Marketing Democracy in an Undemocratic Market]
Eszmelet, Budapest, Nos. 11-12, Sept. 1991
Third World War in the Gulf: A New World Order Political Economy
Notebooks for Study and Research, No. 14, Amsterdam/Paris, June 1991, pp. 5-34
ENDpapers 22, Nottingham, UK, Summer 1991, pp. 62-110
Economic Review, Colombo, v. 17, Nos. 4 & 5, July/Aug. 1991, pp. 17-31, 54-60, 68-73
Sekai, Tokyo, No. 560, Sept. 1991, pp. 68-82
Economía Política del Conflitto Nord-Sud
Marx Centuno, Milano, VII, No. 4, Feb. 1991, pp. 14-20
Holier Than Thou in the Gulf: A Curse on Both Your Houses
Journal für Entwicklungspolitik, Wien, v. VII, No. 1, Spring 1991, pp. 91-105
Une Guerre Très Peu Sainte
Revue d'Etudes Palestiniennes, Paris, No. 39, Spring 1991, pp. 45-64
Der Krieg der Scheinheiligen: Seid Verflucht Alle Beide
Blätter für Internationale Politik, Bonn, No. 3, March 1991, pp. 291-302
EMW-Information, Evangelisches Missionswerk, Hamburg, 92, Mai 1991, pp. 3-17
Waarom Golforlog?
't Kan Anders, Delft, No. 2, 1991, pp. 17-32 (also issued as a separate pamphlet)
Mas Sagrado que Vosotros en el Golfo: Una Maldición sobre las Casas de Ambos
El Gallo Ilustrado Suplemento de **El Día,** Mexico, Feb. 10, 1991, pp. 1-9
Dos Santurones en le Golfo Pérsico
Punto Final, Santiago de Chile, Feb. 11, 1991, pp. 14-18
Correo de los Andes, Mérida, Venezuela, Feb. 18 & Mar. 11, 1991
Paradoxes Géopolitiques-Economiques d'une Guerre
La Brèche, Lausanne, v. 21, No. 467, Mars 8, 1991, pp. 9-11
Politische Ökonomie des Golf Krieges
Das Argument, Berlin, v. 33, No. 186, March/April 1991, pp. 177-186
Ironias Económicas y Geopolíticas en el Golfo Pérsico
El Día Latinoamericano, Año 1, No. 45, April 1, 1991, pp. 12-14

EE. UU. en el Nuevo Orden Mundial
  Punto Final, Santiago de Chile, XXVI, No. 248, Sept. 23, 1991, pp. 14-15
The Five Thousand Year World System: An Interdisciplinary Introduction (with B. K. Gills)
  Humboldt Journal of Social Relations, Arcata, CA, v. 18, No. 1, Spring 1992, pp. 1-79
World System Cycles, Crises, and Hegemonial Shifts 1700 B.C. to A.D. 1700 (with B. K. Gills)
  Review, Binghamton, XV, 4, Fall 1992, pp. 621-698
The Centrality of Central Asia
  Studies in History, New Delhi, VIII, 1, Feb. 1992, pp. 43-97
  Bulletin of Concerned Asian Scholars, Boulder, USA, XXIV, No. 2, April-June 1992, pp. 50-74
Rejoinder [to Comments on the Centrality of Central Asia]
  Studies in History, New Delhi, VIII, 1, Feb. 1992, pp. 118-122
  Bulletin of Concerned Asian Scholars, Boulder, USA, v. XXIV, No. 2, April-June 1992, pp. 80-82
Fourteen Ninety-Two Once Again
  Political Geography Quarterly, London, v. 11, No. 4, July 1992, pp. 386-393
Transitional Ideological Modes: Feudalism, Capitalism, Socialism
  Oriens/BOCTOK, Moscow, No. 2, 1992 (in Russian)
Third World War: A Political Economy of the Gulf War and the New World Order
  Third World Quarterly, London, v. 13, No. 2, Spring 1992, pp. 267-282
Nothing New in the East: No New World Order
  Social Justice, San Francisco, v. 19, No. 1, Spring 1992, pp. 34-61
World Economic Crisis Once Again
  Economic and Political Weekly, Bombay, Feb. 29, 1992, pp. 437-438
  Economic Review, Colombo, v. 18, Nos. 1 & 2, April-May 1992, pp. 2-4
Economic Ironies in Europe: A World Economic Interpretation of Politics in East-West Europe
  International Social Science Journal, UNESCO, Paris, No. 131, Feb. 1992, pp. 41-56
  Revue Internationale des Sciences Sociales, UNESCO, Paris, No. 132, May 1992, pp. 279-297
  Revista Internacional de Ciencias Sociales, UNESCO, Paris, No. 132, May 1992, pp. 267-284
Latin American Development Theories Revisited: A Participant Review Essay
  European Journal of Development Research, v. 3, No. 2, Dec. 1991, pp. 146-159
  Latin American Perspectives, Riverside, CA, USA, Issue 73, v. 19, No. 2, Spring 1992, pp. 125-139
The U.S. Economy. A Review of Bernard Nossiter's **Fat Years and Lean: The American Economy Since Roosevelt**
  Z Magazine, Boston, v. 5, No. 1, Jan. 1992, pp. 63-66

Privatization: Sham Debate
   Economic and Political Weekly, Bombay, Feb. 22, 1992, p. 432
Soviet and East European "Socialism": What Went Wrong? And Who Is Right?
   Economic and Political Weekly, Bombay, XXVII, 46, Nov. 14, 1992, pp. 1471-2474
El Subdesarrollo del Desarrollo—Extracto
   El Gallo Ilustrado, 1544, Semanario de **El Día,** Mexico, April 5, 1992, pp. 1-7
No Se Puede Estar En Todo, Pero Yo Se Los Dije
   El Gallo Ilustrado, 1560, Semanario de **El Día,** Mexico, May 17, 1992, p. 20
Crisis Económica Mundial, Una Vez Más
   El Gallo Ilustrado, 1561, Semanario de **El Día,** Mexico, May 24, 1992, pp. 1-4
I Snova Mirovoi Krizis [The World Crisis Once Again]
   Problemi Teorii i Praktiki, Moscow, No. 3, 1992, pp. 60-62
McWorld: Divide o Impera? Ambas Cosas!
   El Gallo Ilustrado, 1570, Semanario de **El Día,** Mexico, July 26, 1992, pp. 1-4
Saludo y Mensaje
   Nueva Sociedad, Caracas, No. 120, Edicion XX Aniversario, July-Aug. 1992, pp. 178-179
1492 y América Latina al Margen de la Historia del Sistema Mundial
   El Gallo Ilustrado, 1583, Semanario de **El Día,** Mexico, Oct. 25, 1992, pp. 2-7
I Was Never Invited Back
   News from Ukraine, Kiev, Nov. 8, 1992, p. 3
Hitting Yourself While You're Down (in Russian)
   Delo, Novgorod, Nov. 28, 1992, p. 6
The World Is Round and Wavy: Demographic Cycles and Structural Analysis in the World System. A Review Essay of Jack A. Goldstone's
   Revolutions and Rebellions in the Early Modern World
   Contention, Indiana University Press, v. 2, No. 2, Winter 1993, pp. 107-125
Que salió mal y quién tiene la razón? Un debate sobre el socialismo soviético y euroriental
   El Gallo Ilustrado, Semanario de **El Día,** Mexico, No. 1596, Jan. 24, 1993, pp. 1-6
América Latina al margen del sistema mundial. Historia y presente.
   Nueva Sociedad, Caracas, No. 123, enero-feb. 1993, pp. 23-34
Ironías económicas en la política mundial
   Cuadernos del CENDES, Caracas, No. 15/16, Sept. 1990-April 1991, pp. 229-256 (published 1993)
Soviet and East European "Socialism": A Review of International Political Economy of What Went Wrong
   Economic Review, Colombo, Nos. 2 & 3, May/June 1992, pp. 28-39
Ten Theses on Social Movements (with M. Fuentes)
   Society and Nature, Colorado/London, 1, No. 3, 1993
1492 and Latin America at the Margin of World System History: East-West Hegemonial Shifts (992-1492-1992)
   Comparative Civilizations Review, Colorado/London, No. 28, Spring 1993, pp. 1-40

World System Economic Cycles and Hegemonial Shift to Europe 100 B.C. to A.D. 1500 (with B. K. Gills)
  Journal of European Economic History, Rome, XXII, 1, July 1993
Bronze Age World System Cycles [& Comments and Reply]
  Current Anthropology, v. 34, No. 4, Aug.-Oct. 1993, pp. 383-429
América Latina al Margen de la Historia del Sistema Mundial
  América por el Desarrollo, No. 0, 1993, pp. 26-34
The World System in Asia Before European Hegemony
  The Historian, v. 56. No. 4, Winter 1994, pp. 259-276
Inside Out or Outside in [The Exogeneity/Endogeneity Debate]
  Review, Binghamton, XVII, 1, Winter 1994, pp. 1-5
Soviet and East European "Socialism": A Review of International Political Economy of What Went Wrong
  Review of International Political Economy, I, No. 2, April 1994, pp. 113-157 [including discussion]
Confusion Worse Confounded: Through the Looking Glass of Matt Melko in Wonderland
  Comparative Civilizations Review, Colorado/London No. 30, Spring 1994, pp. 22-29
Is Real World Socialism Possible?
  Society and Nature, No. 6, Summer 1994, pp. 152-175
Nothing New in the East: No New World Order
  Iranian Journal of International Affairs, Teheran, IV, No. 3, 1994
Hegemony and Social Change [Forum]
  Mershon International Studies Review, The Ohio State University, No. 2, 1994
"Coping with Globalization"
  Economic and Political Weekly, June 18, 1994, pp. 1520-1521
"Mondiale Systeemverandering na de Koude Orolog (Review)"
  Internationale Spectator, v. 48, No. 10, Oct. 1994, pp. 519-520
"The Modern World System Under Asian Hegemony: The Silver Standard World Economy 1450-1750." With B. Gills. Department of Politics Discussion paper, University of Newcastle, England, 1994/1995
Review of **Islamic and European Expansion: The Forging of a Global Order.** ed. Michael Adas for the American Historical Association. **Journal of Asian Studies,** forthcoming
Review of **The Colonizer's Model of the World: Geographical Diffusionism and Eurocentric History,** J. M. Blaut. Annals of the American Association of Geographers, forthcoming
Review of **Historical Atlas of East Central Europe** by P. R. Magoscsi
  Political Geography Quarterly, forthcoming

Index

Abstract expressionism, in art of hegemony, 273 274
Abu-Lughod, J., 142, 228-229, 232, 239
Academic art, 271
Accumulation, capital. *See* Capital accumulation
Addo, Herb, 137, 143
Affirmative action, 332
Africa:
    bourgeoisie in, 202, 208, 209
    colonial assault on, 206-207
    compared to Asia and Latin America, 205
    debt burden of, 117, 118-119, 121
    development thought and, 143
    dissertation research on, 126
    economic destruction in, 162, 202-211
    elections in, 355
    exports and, 205, 206
    geostrategic factors and, 206, 208-209
    groups of, 203-204
    in Fourth World, 198, 205, 209
    intellectuals of, 79, 81, 83
    liberation movements in, 202-203, 207-209
    Marxism of, 60
    new world system elements and, 209-210
    nonaligned movement in, 204
    per capita income in, 18
    peripheral societies in, 80
    slave trade from, 158
    socialism in, 203, 204, 205
    solutions for, 81-83
    Wallerstein and, 130
    weaknesses of, 207-208
    women in, 47
    See also Sub-Saharan Africa
Africanization, 39
Akamatsu, Kaname, 173
Allen, Tim, 306
Allende, Salvador, 28, 30, 31-32, 297, 302
Alliance for Progress, 26, 317, 319, 354
Almeyda, Clodomiro, 28
Almond, G., 2
American hegemony, 260, 273-274. *See also* United States
Amin, Samir, 11, 30, 31, 42, 163, 282
Anthropology, 23, 85-98
    diffusionist views in, 86-87, 93
    elite strategies and, 298, 299
    evolutionist views in, 85-87
    functionalist views in, 87

405

linguistics and, 92-93, 96
Anti-heroic practices, of women, 349
Antisystemic movements, 281, 282. *See also*
    Social movements
Apathy of peasants, to development, 290-292
Arab world, 82, 209
Argentina, 148
Armah, Ayi Kwei, 137-138
Armaments, monopoly of, 211
Arndt, H. W., 18, 23
Arrighi, Giovanni, 282
Art deco, in art of hegemony, 273
Art history:
    hegemony/rivalry cycles of, 258-275
    stages of, 267
    transition periods of, 265-267
ASEAN (Association of Southeast Asian
    Nations), 186, 192
Aseniero, George, 175
Asia:
    compared to Africa, 205
    debt burden of, 7, 117, 118, 121
    economic destruction in, 162
    economic growth in, 169-173
    in world-system, 169-194
    Marxism of, 60
    peasant movements in, 294
    social movements in, 49
    See also East Asia; Southeast Asia; *and*
        names of specific countries
Asian Tigers. *See* Hong Kong; Singapore;
    South Korea; Taiwan
Association of Southeast Asian Nations
    (ASEAN), 186, 192
Athens, compared to Sparta, 228, 240(n3)
Australian aborigines, 93
Authoritarianism, in Southeast Asia, 181-182
Autonomy, and women's interests, 346-351

Bagu, Sergiu, 156
Bambirra, Vânia, 26, 156, 163
Banda, 208
Bandung project, 60, 79, 160, 179-180, 202
    results of, 204-205, 208
Barber, Bernard, 50-51
Baroque, in art of hegemony, 268-269
Belgian colony, in Africa, 207
Bergesen, Albert, 31, 317

Bernal, M., 43
Berry, Brian J. L., 102, 109-110
Biculturation, 94
Blomstrm, Magnus, 168
Bolivia, 159
Books, of Frank's works, 363-377
Booth, D., 4, 9
Bosnianization, 39, 51
Boulding, Kenneth, 22
Bourgeoisie, 64, 68-70, 202
    elite strategies and, 303
    in Africa, 202, 208, 209
    in Latin America, 148-149, 152-153,
        155-156, 159-160, 354
    role of, 59-60
    strategic groups and, 300
    voluntarism and, 283
Bowles, Chester, 289
Braudel, Fernand, 163, 239
Brazil, 25-28, 148, 152, 162-163
    coup d'état in, 159-160
    economic miracle in, 165
    Paraguayan War in, 158
    social movements and, 306
Brenner, R., 129
British hegemony, 261, 270-271
Brizola, Leonel, 25
Brookfield, Harold, 103, 110
Brown, Lawrence A., 109
Brzezinsky, Zbigniew, 300
Buttel, F., 4

Callaghan, James, 33
Camdessus, Michel, 113
Campos, Roberto, 25
Capital accumulation, 11, 32, 230
    as driving force, 41-42, 226, 229
    as ultimate determiner, 44
    ceaselessness of, 226
    comparisons of, in world-systems,
        250-252
    five thousand years of, 219
Capital flow, South to North, 34-35
Capitalism, 4, 90, 96
    African economic catastrophe and, 202-209
    alternative to, 8
    as lacking real basis, 44
    as obstacle to democracy, 78

as savagery, 74
changes needed in, 356-357
Columbus and, 130
contradictions of, 201-202
critiques of, 68-72, 73
delinking from, 61-63
peripheral formations of, 60-61
perniciousness of, 356
polarizing nature of, 58-59, 61-64
pre-capitalism and, 67-68
rational ethos and, 67
without capitalists, 202-203
See also World capitalism
Capitalists, charisma of, 301-304
Cárdenas, Lazaro, 149
Cardenism, 156, 157, 160
Cardoso, Fernando Henrique, 28, 29, 30, 323
Carter, Jimmy, 33, 161, 162
Casablanca Group, 203-204
Casanova, Pablo Gonzalez, 29, 30
Castro, Fidel, 318
Catholic Church, 49, 296-297, 323-324.
    See also Liberation theology
Ceaseless accumulation, 226
Ceaucescu, Nicolae, 38
Center periphery structure, 10, 12, 44,
    231-233, 354
    comparisons of, in world-systems, 252-255
    erosion of, 210
Central Intelligence Agency (CIA), 295
Central world-system, 245, 247, 248
Centrism, in world history, 236
CEPAL. See Comision Economica para
    América Latina
Change, in world-system, 354, 355-359
Charisma, in social movements, 286, 291,
    301-304. See also Leadership
Chase-Dunn, Christopher, 239
Chaudhuri, K. N., 227
Chiang Kai-shek, 284
Chicago school:
    of economists, 22-23, 33
    of world development theorists, 224-225,
    279
Chiefdom systems, 249
Chilcote, Ronald, 168
Chile, 148
    dependency theory and, 30-33
    social movements in, 292, 297-298

China, 161, 229
    social movements in, 280, 283-286
China, Greater, 190-191
China, People's Republic of, 165, 170
    in world-economy, 189-191
China, Republic of. See Taiwan
Chonchol, Jacques, 24
Christianity, and linear world history, 219-220
Chun Doo Hwan, 182
CIA (Central Intelligence Agency), 295
Cities, 102, 229, 239, 251
Civilization, global, 167
Civilizations:
    barbarism and, 147-148, 154
    world history and, 220-223, 240
Classification, in geography, 100-101
Clinton, Bill, 172
Cockcroft, Jim, 29
Cold war, 208-209
Cold war order (CWO), 127, 133, 134
Collectivism, of global civilization, 167
Colombia, 148
Colonialism, and neocolonialism, 208
Colonization, models of, 206-207
Columbus, Christopher, 51, 130, 141
Comision Economica para América Latina
    (CEPAL), 25, 26, 30, 115, 148,
    150-152, 154, 156
Command economy, 227
Communication:
    control and, 106-107, 108-109, 111-112
    humanist program for, 212
    in management approach, 303-304
    mapping of, 103-104
    monopoly of, 211
    of culture, 105-106
Communication nets, 222-223, 240
Communism, 175, 203, 285
    in Latin America, 150, 155, 354
Community development, 288-295
Conceptual art, 274-275
Conservative liberalization, 161
Continuity thesis, 11-12
    cosmopolitan humanocentrism and,
    236-238
    historical materialism and, 225-231
    structuralism and, 231-236
Core-periphery structure.
    See Center-periphery structure

Core powers, hegemonic, rise and fall of, 249-250
Core-wide empire, 249-250
Corporations, as strategic groups, 298, 300
Corridors, of Eurasian economy, 229
Coser, Lewis, 305
Cosmopolitan humanocentrism, 236-238
Costa Rica, 312-313, 335(n1)
Counterstrategies, elite. *See* Elites; Elite strategies
Creative pessimism, 137, 138-139, 143
Crisis management, 19, 80-81
Critical thinking, 136
Cuba, 24-25, 159
Cultural colonialism, 110
Cultural creolization, 94-95
Cultural ecology, 89
Cultural hegemony, 263
Cultural lag, and art of hegemony, 266
Cultural portfolios, 95
Cultural revolution, in China, 161, 285
Cultural signifiers, 92, 97
Cultural values, 78
Culture, 85-86, 93-96
  as architectural entity, 89
  as learning, 105
  complexity of, 131-132
  cycles of, 258
  diversity of, 219, 220-221, 334, 335
  geography and, 99-112
  grand, 131-132, 136
  homogenization of, 211
  humanist program for, 212
  identities in, 95
  indigenous, 326-327, 333-335
  in world-system, 259
  politics linked with, 71
  questions about, 134
  See also Anthropology; Art history; Civilizations
Cumulation of accumulation, 229
CWO (Cold war order), 127, 133, 134
Cycles, xii, 40, 42-43
  calibration of, 238-239
  causality of, 239
  of art history, 258-275
  of center-periphery complexes, 232-233
  of evolutionary change, 356
  of hegemony/rivalry, 258-275

  of international trade, 230
  of Latin American economics, 157
  of social movements, 282, 307
  of transitions, 245-246
  of transportation, 104
  of world history, 219-220
  world systemic, 230, 238-239
  See also Continuity thesis; Kondratieff phases

Dag Hammarskjöld Foundation, 47
Debt crisis, 6-8
  creditors' view of, 113-114
  debtors' view of, 114-116
  dependence and, 34-35
  resource transfer and, 120-122
  statistics of, 116-122
  See also Economic crises
Debt service payments, 35, 114, 117-120, 122, 164
Debt service ratio, 117, 119
Defoe, Daniel, 315
de la Fuente, Julio, 94
Delinking, 128, 354
  democratization and, 78
  from world capitalist system, 61-63, 64-65, 210
  from worldwide development, 329, 332
  impossibility of, 45, 139
  involuntary, 45-46
Deloria, V., Jr., 326
Democracy, and humanist program, 214
Democratization, 4, 78, 82
Demographic transition, 109
Denationalization, 184
Deng Xiaoping, 285
Dependency theory, 2-3, 57, 58-61
  anthropology and, 90
  critical historical approach and, 157
  criticisms of, 3, 161-162, 163
  death of, 32, 33
  development of, 26, 27, 28, 29-32
  disappointment with, 138
  power elites and, 298
  radical politics of, 354
  refuted in East Asia, 170-171
Dependentistas, 2, 5, 287, 293, 354
De Saussure, Ferdinand, 92

de Soto, Hernando, 305
Developing, real meaning of, 353
Development:
    as acquisition of knowledge, 166
    as domination of nature, 326
    as growth, 21, 26, 35, 142, 143, 148
    as liberating process, 78, 201
    as progressive social design, 78
    as radical reform, 284-290
    as technological process, 139
    as vague ideological concept, 204
    as Westernization, 140
    capitalist expansion and, 73
    central premise for, 350
    conservative version of, 354
    continuity thesis and, 225-240
    crises and, 6-9, 19
    criteria of, 204-205
    criticisms of, 74-79
    defined by elites, 48
    development of, 20-22
    homogeneity of, 314, 328, 335, 343
    inadequate models of, 46
    industrialization as key element of, 148
    questions about, 125-126
    radical version of, 354
    socialist, 353
    sustainable, 135
    theories of, 1-6, 8-9
    women's interests and, 349-351
Developmentalism:
    methodology for study of, 126-128,
        131-132
    neo-radical perspectives of, 125, 133-138,
        143
    questions about, 125-126
Developmentalist authoritarianism, 181-182
Development geography, 102-103
Development of underdevelopment, xii, 27,
        28, 140, 178
    coining of, 11, 17
    debt crisis and, 35
    sloganized by establishment, 32
    See also Underdevelopment of develop-
        ment
Development problématique, 130
Deviants, 314, 325-327. See also Political
        deviants
Dhanagare, D., 280

Diakonoff, I. M., 251
Dialectical motions, of history, 133, 134,
        135-136
Diaz, Porfirio, 288
Diffusionists, 127, 128
    in anthropology, 86-87, 93
Disarmament, in humanist program, 212
Diversity:
    of culture, 219, 220-221, 334, 335
    of human society, 218-219, 220-221
    of indigenous peoples, 326
    of nature, 334-335
    of Third World, 80
    of women's interests, 343-351
Dos Santos, Theotonio, 26, 32
Dualisms, 26-27, 46, 142, 319
Dualists, 127, 128

East Asia:
    compared with Eastern Europe, 37, 38
    dependency theory refuted by, 170-171
    economic growth of, 169-173
    export-led growth in, 33-34
    industrialization of, 173-175
    in world-system, 173-189
    peripheral societies in, 80
    protectionist responses to, 172
    transformations in, 176-178
    World Bank analysis of, 172-173
    See also Southeast Asia and names of
        specific countries
Eastern Europe:
    compared with East Asia, 37, 38
    debt burden of, 8
    economic crises in, 37-38
Echevarría Álvarez, Luis, 160
ECLA. See United Nations Economic
        Commission for Latin America
Ecology movement, 166.
        See also Environment; Nature
Economic crises, 49, 171, 183
    nineteenth century, 151
    twentieth century, 34-40, 169, 184-185
    See also Debt crisis
Economic regulations, of humanist program,
        212
Economics:
    ancient, need for study of, 239-240

delinked from politics, 128
macro- and micro, 20-21
Economic self-interest, 358
Economy of pillage, 207
Ecuador, 159
Edwards, Chris, 35
EEC (European Economic Community), 208
Egalitarianism, compared to individual
    diversity, 167
Eggers, Melvin, xiii
Egyptian cities, 229
Ekholm, Kasja, 245, 248
Elites:
    as definers of development, 48
    in Third World, 137-138
Elite strategies, and social movements,
    295-308
El Salvador, peasant movements in, 290
Emancipatory processes, 351
Empires, rise and fall of, 248-250
Engels, Friedrich, 73
Entitlement theory, 322
Environment, 48, 78, 82, 166
    as index of underdevelopment, 107
    devastation of, 10, 75
    developmental costs and, 19
    See also Nature
Equalities:
    anthropology = ideology, 299
    applied anthropology = politics, 299
    centers = industrial regions, 210
    democracy = free market, 237
    development = Westernization via in-
        dustrialization, 140
    growth = development, 21, 26, 35
    industrial growth = development, 142
    peripheries = nonindustrial regions, 210
    theory = history, 129
    trialectical thinking = critical thinking, 136
Era of Bandung, 179
Esteva, Gustavo, 306
Ethics, 324-325
Ethnology. See Anthropology; Culture
Eurasiacentrism, 247
Eurasian world economy, 227, 228, 231, 233-
    235
    corridors of, 229
    integration of, 238
Eurocentrism:

alternative to, 41
closedness of, 143
of developmentalism, 125, 130, 132-133
rejection of, 236, 334
undermining of, xiii
Europe, Eastern. See Eastern Europe
European Economic Community (EEC), 208
European models, of world history, 219-220
Evans, P., 4, 5
Evers, Hans-Dieter, 282
Evolutionists, in anthropology, 85-87
Exploitation, 12, 280, 291-292
Exports, 150-153, 205-206
    growth led by, 33-34

Fairbank, John King, 40
Faletto, E., 29
Fascism, 70, 133, 160
Feminist movement, 48, 65-66, 74, 78, 307.
    See also Gender; Women
Feminist perspective, 343-344. See also
    Gender; Women
Feudalism, 36, 44, 59, 245
    as underdeveloped system, 127-128
    incorrect views of, 227, 317
    in Latin American analyses, 150, 155-156
Fisher, Irving, 119-120
Five thousand years, of world system(s).
    See World system(s); World-system(s)
Forbes, D. K., 110
Foreign debt statistics, 116-122
Foreign exchange, 119-120, 152
Formalism, in art of hegemony, 271
Formal-tradition perspective, of women's
    movement, 343-344
Foster-Carter, A., 26
Fourth World, 80, 198, 205, 209, 213
Four tigers. See Hong Kong; Singapore;
    South Korea; Taiwan
Frank, Andre Gunder:
    as teacher, 124-125, 129, 143
    at CEPAL/ECLA, 279-280
    at University of Chicago, 22-23
    at University of Michigan, 22
    autobiographical essay by, 17-52
    biographical sketch of, xii-xv
    children of, 24, 35-36
    creative pessimism and, 138-139, 143

degradation of, 317-321
deviant, viewed as a, 315-321
expanded ideas of, 257, 330
humor of, 329
in Germany, 22, 35
in Latin America, iv, 24-35
letter of July 1, 1964, 27, 316-318
names of, 27
reversals of, 138-143
United States, barred from, 27
wife of, xii, xiii, xiv. *See also* Fuentes,
    Marta
Frank, Andre Gunder, words of:
compared with mainstream
    interpretations, 320
in autobiographical essay, 17-52
on Benjamin Higgins, 329
on dominant forces, 307-308
on dual societies, 316-317
on history, 129
on liberal positivism, 317
on policymakers, 328
on post 1500 world system, 336(n5)
on social movements, 65, 330-333,
    337(n6)
on transideological partnerships, 195
on underdevelopment analysis, 316
on whole dynamic of world development,
    225
on world-economy cycles, 182-183
reversal analysis and, 139-142
See also Development of underdevelop-
    ment; Underdevelopment of development
Frank, Andre Gunder, works of:
bibliography of, 360-401
in autobiographical essay, 17-54
in biographical sketch, xii-xiv
Frank, Paulo, 35-36
Franzylbert, Fernando, 164
Freedom:
false discourse of, 357
true implementation of, 358
Free markets, 33, 237, 355, 358-359
Freire, Gilberto, 148
French structuralism, 92
Friedman, Jonathan, 245, 248
Friedman, Milton, 22, 33, 317
Fuentes, Marta, xiii, 24, 57, 326
death of, xii, xiv, 18

on social movements, 306-308, 330-333
Fukuyama, Francis, 8, 133
Functionalists, in anthropology, 87
Furtado, Celso, 25, 151, 156
Future world-system, strategies for, 359

Galbraith, John Kenneth, 70, 74
Galjart, Benno, 280
Galtung, Johan, 127-128, 132
Gandhi, Indira, 192
Gandhi, Mahatma, 192
Gandhi, Rajiv, 192
Garcia, Pio, 32
GATT (General Agreement on Tariffs and
    Trade), 82, 212
GDP (gross domestic product), 114, 116-117,
    119-122, 190
Gedicks, Al, 299
Gender:
polarization of, 39
subordination of, 345-346
See also Feminist movement; Feminist
    perspective; Women
Geneen, Harold, 302, 303
General Agreement on Tariffs and Trade
    (GATT), 82, 212
Geographical connectedness, 101
Geography:
classification and measurement in, 100-
    101
culture and, 99-112
maps and, 100-101, 103-104, 106-107
of communication, 103-107, 108-109, 111-
    112
of development, 102-103
of foreign presence, 107, 108-109
physical, 101
politics and, 105-106, 111-112
research in, 109-112
social, 102-103
Geopolitical issues, xiii
Geostrategic factors, and Africa, 206, 208-209
Germany, unification of, 8, 38
Gerschenkron, A., 5
El Ghonemy, Riad, 280
Giddens, A., 351
Gills, Barry K.:
on capital accumulation, 11

on world history, 219, 220, 221, 222, 223
on world system, 41-44, 247
on world-system, 244-245
Gilpin, Robert, 232
Ginsburg, Norton S., 102
Global anthropology. *See* Anthropology
Global civilization, 167.
    See also Civilizations
Global economy. *See* World economy;
    World-economy
Globalization, humanist program for, 212-214
Global law of value, 61
Gorbachev, Mikhail, 40-41, 45, 51, 63, 319
Gordon, Lincoln, 25
Gould, Peter, 102
Grammatological systems, 92-93, 97
Grand culture, 131-132, 136
Greater China, 190-191
Gross domestic product (GDP), 114, 116-
    117, 119-122, 190
Group of the Seven Industrialized Countries
    (G7), 113-114
Growth, as development, 21, 26, 35, 142,
    143, 148
G7 countries, 113-114
Guevera, Che, 295, 298
Gutierrez, Gonzalo, 30
Gutierrez, Gustavo, 323, 324

Hagen, Everett, 23
Haggard, S., 9
Hall, T., 239, 246, 248
Hannerz, Ulf, 94
Hapsburg hegemony, 262, 264
Harnecker, Marta, 32
Haya de la Torre, V. R., 149
Hegemony:
    definition of, 231
    transitions of, 230-233, 235, 249-250,
    265-267
Hegemony/rivalry competition, 40, 42
Hegemony/rivalry cycles, and art history,
    258-275
Herder, Johann Gottfried von, 220, 221
Hettne, Bjorn, 168
Hierarchy formations, in world-systems,
    254-255
Higgins, Benjamin, 17, 23, 321, 329

Hirschman, Albert, 23
Historical materialism, 225-231
Historical reconceptualization, 10-13
Historiography, 237
History, 91, 195, 255
    as theory, 129
    as unfoldings of cultures, 132
    dialectical steps of, 133-136
    trialectics of, 135-136
    See also World history
Hodgson, M., 224-225
Homogeneous development, 314, 328, 335,
    343
Hong Kong, 178
    exports and, 183
    growth of, 7, 170, 186-187
    in Greater China, 190-191
Hoselitz, Bert, 22, 23, 318
Hout, W., 168
Humanist program, for globalization, 212-214
Humanocentrism, xiii, 41, 236-238, 334
Human rights policies, of United States, 161,
    162-163
Humor, 328, 329
Hunt, D., 26
Huntington, S., 2, 305, 306
Huxley, Aldous, 232
Hymes, D., 299
Hyphen, in terminology, 42, 224, 225, 233,
    235, 255(n1)

Identities, multiple, of women, 346-347
Identity, and culture, 95, 97-98
Identity politics, 263
IMF. *See* International Monetary Fund
Immediate strategy, for world-system
    change, 357
Imports, growth led by, 37
Import substitution, 151-152, 158-159, 201,
    207
Incarceration rates, 336(n4)
Income:
    negative distribution of, 164-165
    per capita, 18, 122
    rising, 186
India, 80, 117
    community development in, 288-289, 293
    in world-economy, 192-194

Indigenous peoples, 150, 280, 288
    demise, prediction of, 334
    diversity of, 326
    humor of, 328
    justice and, 325-329, 333-335
    resistance of, 325-328
Indigenous solutions, for underdevelopment,
    110-111
Individuals, in global civilization, 167
Indonesia, 7, 179, 180, 182, 192
    growth of, 170
    in Greater China, 191
Industrialization:
    as development, 142, 143, 148
    as Westernization, 140
    important substitution and, 152
    national liberation and, 199-201
Inflation, in Latin America, 152
Injustice. *See* Justice
Innovative entrepreneur, 150
Institutional realism, in art of hegemony, 272
Intellectuals, 74, 79, 81, 83
    in Latin America, 150, 156
Interaction spheres, of culture, 87
Internal markets, and industrialization, 199-
    201
International capital. *See* World capitalism;
    World-capitalism
International Monetary Fund (IMF), 161,
    192, 300, 304
    debt crisis and, 113-116, 118
    removal of, 82, 212
    role of, 6-8
International relations field, limitations of,
    126, 127
Islamic fundamentalism, 65

Japan, 7, 185-188
    growth of, 170
    industrialization of, 173-175
    postwar changes in, 176-177
    social movements in, 286
    U.S. trade imbalances with, 184-185
Jenkins, Rhys, 35
Jihad, 50-51
John, J., 280
Johnson, Dale, 29
Justice, 312-314, 318, 321-325

indigenous peoples and, 325-329, 333-335

Kampuchea, 139
Kasavubu, Joseph, 203
Kaufman, R., 9
Kay, Cristóbal, 168
Kennedy, John F., 319
Kenyatta, Jomo, 208
Keynes, John M., 20, 119-120
Keynesians, 18, 20, 22, 110, 274, 354
Khomeini, Ayatollah, 322
Khrushchev, Nikita, 354
Kirkpatrick, Jeanne, 39
Kohl, Helmut, 161
Kondratieff phases, 20, 32, 35, 42, 251, 282,
    354
Korea, 173-175. *See also* South Korea
Kubitscheck, J., 156
Kuhn, Thomas S., 26

Labor movement, changes in, 48-49, 96
Land reforms, 24, 34, 285-288
Language:
    diversity of, 218, 220
    in world history, 217-219, 220
    See also Linguistics; Terminology
Latifundios, 149, 152, 153, 199
Latin America, 147-167
    bourgeoisie in, 148-149, 152-153,
        155-156, 159-160, 354
    Cardenism in, 156, 157, 160
    civilization/barbarism and, 147-148, 154
    communism in, 150, 155, 354
    compared to Africa, 205
    coups d'tat in, 159-160, 163
    debt burden of, 7, 115-116, 118-119, 121
    economic crises in, 151, 158, 162
    economic restructuring and, 158-162, 164-
        166
    exports from, 150-153
    expropriation from, 156, 164-165
    feudalism models for, 150, 155-156
    import substitution in, 151-152, 158-159
    indigenous peoples of, 150, 280, 288
    intellectuals of, 150, 156
    international capital and, 152-160, 163-
        165

latifundios in, 149, 152, 153, 199
liberation theology in, 49, 323-324
oil industry in, 153-154
per capita income in, 18
peripheral societies in, 80
political will of, 350
progress in, 147-148
social movements in, 295-298, 351
women's interests and, 342-351
See also names of specific countries
Latin American Economic System (SELA), 160
Latinamericanization, 39
Law:
cultural diversity and, 334
in indigenous culture, 333
of value, 61
Leadership:
in social movements, 281, 286, 287, 291-292, 295-296
in strategic groups, 300-304
Lebanonization, 39, 51
Lee Kuan Yew, 180, 193
Lenin, Vladimir, I., 72
Lerner, David, 23
Lernoux, P., 297
Levantine cities, 229
Lévi-Strauss, Claude, 92, 97
Liberal democracy, 134, 149
Liberation:
through development, 78
through socialism, 64-66
Liberation anthropology, 298
Liberation movements, national. *See* National liberation movements
Liberation theology, 30, 49, 296-297, 298, 323-324
Lindblom, Bob, 23
Linguistics, and anthropology, 92-93, 97. *See also* Language
Long March, 284
Long-run strategy, for world-system change, 359
Loudon, John, 300
Lumumba, Patrice, 203

Maastricht process, 51
Mabogunje, Akin, 103, 110

Macroeconomics, 20-21
Malaysia, 7, 170, 180, 182, 188, 191
Malinowski, Bronislaw, 93
Mamak, Alex, 299
Management, and elite strategies, 302-303, 304
Manifesto realism, in art of hegemony, 272-273
Mannerism, in art of hegemony, 267-268, 274-275
Mannheim, B., 299
Maoism, 60-64
Mao Ze-dong, 283, 284-285, 287, 291
Maps, 100-101, 103-104, 106-107
Marcos, Ferdinand, 180, 182
Marglin, S. A., 302
Marini, Ruy Mauro, 26, 29, 32, 157, 163
Marx, Karl, 3, 18, 68, 73, 133, 283
Marxism, 18, 77, 150, 161, 246
art of hegemony and, 271
capitalism and, 4, 11, 58-59, 68-72, 245
ceaseless accumulation and, 226
cultural ecology and, 89
incompleteness of, 69
nature and, 10
universalist vision of, 66
world system and, 219
See also Neo-Marxism
Materialism, historical, 225-231
Mayfield, Robert C., 102
McClelland, David, 2, 23
McNamara, Robert, 300, 303
McNeill, William H., 224-225, 237, 240
McWorld, 50-52, 329
Mead, Margaret, 23-24
Measurement, in geography, 100-101
Media, monopoly of, 211. *See also* Communication
Medici, Emílio G., 162
Menshikov, Stanislaw, 302
Mercantilism, and dependency theory, 60, 61
Mesopotamia, world-system in, 244-245, 247
Mesopotamian cities, 229
Mexican Revolution, 149, 157
Mexico, 28-30, 148
anthropological study of, 88
debt burden of, 114, 119
indigenous peoples of, 280, 288
pocho culture of, 94

social movements in, 287-288
Microeconomics, 20-21
Middle-class movements, 296
Middle East, geostrategic factors of, 209
Middle strategy, for world-system change,
    357-358
Mies, M., 307, 331
Migration, from rural to urban areas, 162
Mills, C. Wright, 299, 302
Minimalism, in art of hegemony, 273-274
Minorities, 39, 47
Mobutu Sese Seko, 203, 208, 209
Modelski, G., 239
Modernization theory, 1-3, 4, 5, 195(n4),
    202, 289
    development of, 21
    dualism and, 46
    limitations of, 2-3, 9-10
    national liberation and, 199
    polarization and, 77
    social movements and, 293
    variants of, 90-91
Modes of production, 4, 11, 44
    anthropology and, 96
    art history and, 258
    economic alternatives and, 148
    geography and, 105
    in Athens, 228
    state and private roles in, 239
    transformations of, 245-246
Moi, Daniel Arap, 208
Momsen, Janet Henshall, 109
Monopolies, five, 210-211, 212
Monoproduction, 148
Monrovia Group, 203-204
Moore, B., 5
Mouffe, C., 345
Mouzelis, N., 4
Movements, social. See Social movements
Muluba, 203
Musgrave, Richard, 22
Muslim world, 49
Myrdal, Gunnar, 18, 47

Nader, Laura, 299
Nash, June, 299
National bourgeois project, 64
National liberation movements, 202-203,
    207-209

as criterion for development, 204-205
    industrialization and, 199-201
Natural resources:
    access to, 206, 211, 212
    dominant consumption of, 350
Nature, 10, 206
    control over, 68, 326, 334
    diversity of, 334-335
    See also Environment
Nederveen Pieterse, J., 350
Nehru, Jawaharlal, 192
Neoclassicism, 18, 270-271
Neocolonialism, in Africa, 208
Neoliberalism, 8, 162
Neo-Marxism, 4, 5, 75-76, 77.
    See also Marxism
Neo-radical Third World perspectives, 125,
    133-138, 143
Neorealism, in art of hegemony, 275
Neo-Weberian concepts, 5
Neutral realism, in art of hegemony, 272
Newly industrialized countries (NICs),
    174-175, 178, 186-189, 194
New world orders, 134, 138
NICs. See Newly industrialized countries
Nietzsche, Friedrich W., 133
Nixon, Richard M., 354
Nkrumah, Kwame, 24
Nonaligned nations, 160, 204
North American Indians, 93, 94, 330, 337(n8)

O'Donnell, G., 9
OECD (Organization for Economic Coopera-
    tion and Development), 115, 116
Oil industry, in Latin America, 153-154
Oman, C. P., 168
OPEC (Organization of Petroleum Exporting
    Countries), 160
Operatives, compared to intelligentsia, 74
Optimism, 134, 137, 354, 355-356
Organization for Economic Cooperation and
    Development (OECD), 115, 116
Organization of Petroleum Exporting
    Countries (OPEC), 160

Packard, Vance, 303
Pan-Africanism, 82
Pan-Arabism, 82

Paraguayan War, 158
Parsons, T., 2
Participatory action research, 290-292
Participatory democracy, 149
Peace movement, changes in, 48
Peasant movements, 290-295. *See also* Social movements
Peltier, Leonard, 316
People's movements. *See* Peasant movements; Social movements
People's Republic of China. *See* China, People's Republic of
Peres, Andrés, 160
Perestroika, 63, 319
Periodical articles, by Frank, 377-401
Peripheral countries:
    as debtors, 115-122
    as modern Third World, 205
Peripheral regions, 231-233, 252-255, 354. *See also* Africa; Asia; Latin America
Periphery-center structure. *See* Center-periphery structure
Perloff, Harvey, 22, 324
Perón, Juan D., 159
Peru, 149, 162
Peruvian Revolution, 162
Pessimism, 46, 134, 354, 355-356
    creative, 137, 138-139, 143
Peters, T. J., 302-303, 304
Petras, J., 305
Petroleum industry, in Latin America, 53-154
Philippines, 180-182, 188, 191
Philosophy, and justice, 323, 325
Phoenician cities, 251
Physical geographers, 101
Pinochet, Augusto, 33
Planetary civilization, 167
PMNs (Political/military interaction networks), 248, 252
Point Four, of the United States, 353, 354
Poland, 19, 39
Polanyi, K., 5
Polarization:
    capitalism and, 58-59, 61-64
    in economic crisis, 39, 51
    modernization and, 77
Political deviants, 314-321, 325-327
Political economy, 4, 5, 50, 193

anthropology and, 91, 97
as perennial philosophy, 232
Athens/Sparta and, 228, 240(n3)
cosmopolitan praxis and, 238
delinking and, 128
Political/military interaction networks (PMNs), 248, 252
Political strategy, for changing the world-system, 356-359
Politics:
    linked with culture, 71
    of communication, 105-106, 111-112
    of national liberation, 199
    of world political system, 212-214
    women's interests and, 347-351
Pool, Ithiel de Sola, 23
Popular perspective, of women's movement, 343-344
Positivism, 147
Postmodernism, 9, 69-70, 77
Powell, G., 2
Power elite. *See* Elites; Elite strategies
Prado Junior, Caio, 156
Prebisch, Raúl, 30, 47, 150, 160, 164, 293, 354
Precapitalism, 67-68, 153, 155
Preston, Lewis, 113
Private capital, role of, 227-228, 230
Privatization, 39, 119
Production, modes of. *See* Modes of production
Productivity, total, 23
Progress:
    as surrogate for God, 68
    Latin American middle class and, 147-148
Proliferation, of armaments, 211
Protectionism, 172, 192
Puerto Rico, 88, 89
Pye, D., 2

Quijano, Anibal, 24, 29-30

Radical reforms, social movements for, 284-290
Radical Third World perspectives, 132-133, 135, 142-143
Rao, P. V. Narasimha, 192, 193

Reagan, Ronald, 161, 162
Reaganomics, 33
Real developing countries, 80
Realism, in art of hegemony, 271-273
Recession, in United States, 36-37
Redfield, Robert, 88
Reich, Robert, 50
Religion:
    justice and, 323-324
    social movements and, 65, 288, 291, 306
    See also Liberation theology
Renaissance, and art of hegemony, 264-265
Renamo, 209
Research-through-action, 290
Rhee, Syngman, 287
Rhodes, William, 114, 115
Ribeiro, Darcy, 164
Rivalry/hegemony competition, 40, 42
Rivalry/hegemony cycles, and art history,
    258-275
Robinson, W. I., 306
Rockefeller, David, 300
Rococo, in art of hegemony, 269-270
Romanticism, in art of hegemony, 270-271
Rostow, W. W., 2, 23, 26, 289
Rostowians, 110
Rural economies, destruction of, 162
Rushdie, Salman, 315
Russian Revolution, 70

Sachs, Jeffrey, 355
Sacred society, 337(n7)
Sahlins, M. D., 92
Santos, Milton, 103
Sao Paolo Forum, 306
Saussurean linguistics, 92
Savimbi, Jonas, 209
Schiller, Herbert, 303
Schneider, Jane, 252
Schultz, T. W., 23
Schumpeter, Joseph A., 150
Schuurman, F. J., 9
SELA (Latin American Economic System),
    160
Self-interest, economic, 358
Shah of Iran, 322
Shared hegemony, 232
Shiva, V., 307

Signifiers, cultural, 92, 97
Simonsen, Roberto, 151, 156
Singapore, 165, 178, 180, 191, 193
    exports and, 7, 183
    growth of, 7, 170, 186-187
Singh, Manmohan, 193
Sklair, L., 4
Slave trade, 158
Smith, Adam, 18, 270
So, A. Y., 168
Social change, 23-24
Social development, equity of, 141
Social geography, 102-103
Socialism, 62-64, 203, 204, 353
    as criterion for development, 205
    as lacking real basis, 44
    economic crisis and, 37-38
    humanist globalization and, 212
    modernization theories and, 90
    Third World movement toward, 160
Social movements, 12, 72, 110, 279-280
    by middle class, 331
    changes in, 48-50
    community development and, 288-295
    competition among, 295, 331
    cycles of, 282, 307
    elite counterstrategies and, 295-308
    emergence of, 293-294
    for radical reform, 284-290
    future of, 304-308
    in Latin America, 295-298, 351
    in world system, 281
    leadership in, 281, 286, 291-292, 295-296,
        300-304
    middle-class, 296
    of previous centuries, 281-284
    progressiveness of, 65-66
    research agenda for, 330-333
    voluntarism in. See Voluntarism
Social realism, in art of hegemony, 273
Social sciences:
    crisis in, and elite strategies, 298-299
    limitations of, 126
    nature of, 5-6, 67
    study of deviants by, 314
    terminology in, 218
Social thought, 67, 72-74
Sociology of liberation, 298
South Africa, elections in, 355

Southeast Asia:
  as peripheral region, 178-182
  authoritarianism in, 181-182
  Bandung project and, 179-180
  growth of, 170
  new NICs of, 187-189
  peripheral societies in, 80
  transnationalization in, 179-182
  See also names of specific countries
South Korea, 165
  as NIC, 174-175, 177-178
  exports and, 7, 183
  growth of, 7, 170, 186-187
  social movements in, 287
  See also Korea
Sovietism, 203
Soviet Union:
  as planning model, 150
  collapse of, 162, 245
  debt burden of, 8
  economic crisis in, 38
  Frank's dissertation on, xiv, 23
  Marxism in, 70, 71, 76
  perestroika in, 63, 319
  socialism in, 62, 63, 353-354
  strategic African positions and, 208
Sparta, compared to Athens, 228, 240(n3)
Spatial factors, of geography, 104-106
Spatial solutions, for underdevelopment, 110
Spengler, Oswald, 220, 221
Spiritual awareness, in social movements, 288, 291
Stages, of art history cycle, 267
State-based systems, 249, 251, 253-254
Stavenhagen, Rodolfo, 27
Stephens, J., 4, 5
Steward, Julian, 88, 89
Strategic groups, 282-283, 297-300, 308
Strategies, for changing the world-system, 356-359
Structuralism, of world historical development, 231-236
Sub-Saharan Africa, 7, 46, 208. *See also* Africa
Suharto, 179, 180, 182
Sukarno, 179
Summers, Lawrence, 116
Sunkel, Oswaldo, 164
Super-accumulation, 230
Surplus, transfer of, 34, 234

Survival strategies, 140
Sustainable development, 135
Systems, terminology of, 44
Systems analysis, world. *See* World system theory; World-system theory

Taiwan, 165
  as NIC, 174-175, 177-178
  exports and, 7, 183
  growth of, 7, 170, 186-187
  industrialization of, 173-175
  in Greater China, 191
  social movements in, 286-287
Taylor, Lance, 173
Technology:
  for rational use of tropics, 166
  monopoly of centers of, 210
Teggart, Frederick J., 225-226, 234
Terminology:
  of deviance, 314, 325
  of diversity, 326
  of systems, 44
  of world history, 217-219
  of world system theory, 234-235
  See also Hyphen
Thailand, 170, 180, 182, 188, 191
Thatcher, Margaret, 161, 162
Thatcherism, 33
Theology of liberation. *See* Liberation theology
"Theory equals history," 129
Third World:
  debt burden of, 113-122
  differentiation of, 7
  diversity of, 80
  elites in, 137-138
  environmental contamination of, 107
  exploitation of, 131, 138, 140
  foreign presence in, 108-109
  intellectuals of, 74, 79, 81
  in world system, 166-167
  marginalized Fourth World and, 198, 205, 209
  migration to urban areas of, 162
  movement toward socialism, 160
  postmodernist view of, 77
  radical perspectives of, 125, 130, 132-138, 142
  solutions for, 81-83

structural adjustment in, 213
  See also Africa; Asia; Latin America; and
    names of specific countries
Third World radicalism. See Neo-radical
  Third World perspectives; Radical
  Third World perspectives
Thompson, W. R., 239
Thurow, Lester C., 169
Tilly, Charles, 129, 130, 131
TINA (there is no alternative) syndrome,
  8, 82
Tokens, of communication, 105
Torres, Camilo, 295-296
Total productivity, 23
Touré, Sekou, 24
Toynbee, Arnold, 220, 221
Trade balance, 184-186. See also Exports;
    Imports; Import substitution
Transideological partnerships, 195
Transitions:
  demographic, 109
  in art of hegemony, 265-267
  in world historical development, 230-231
  in world-system, 356-357
Transnationalization, 179-182, 184
Transportation routes, 103-104
Trialectical thinking, 135-136
Tributary societies, 67
Trilateral Commission, 161, 300, 304-305
Trotsky, Leon, 64, 66
Truman, Harry, 289, 353
Tshombe, Moise Kapenda, 203

Ukraine, Frank's dissertation on, xiv, 23
UNCTAD (United Nations Conference on
    Trade and Development), 160
Underdevelopment:
  as capitalist expansion, 59
  as poverty, 107
  communication and, 111-112
  feudalism and, 127-128
  geography of, 106-107, 108-109, 110, 111
  solutions for, 110-111, 356-359
  theories of, 1-6
Underdevelopment of development, coining
    of, xi, 17. See also Development of un-
    derdevelopment
Unemployment, 122
United Nations, 82, 280, 293

United Nations Conference on Trade and
    Development (UNCTAD), 160
United Nations Economic Commission for
    Latin America (ECLA), 25, 26, 30,
    115, 148, 150-152, 154, 156
  core/periphery concept and, 354
  dependency theory and, 161, 164
  Frank at, 279-280
United States:
  aid to South Korea and Taiwan by, 177
  as center of world capitalist system, 175
  Central Intelligence Agency, 295
  development as objective of, 353-354
  Frank barred and degraded by, 27, 317-321
  hegemony of, 21, 158, 353-354
  human rights policies of, 161, 162-163
  incarceration rates in, 336(n4)
  monopoly of armaments by, 211
  protectionism by, 172
  recession in, 36-37
  strategic African positions and, 208-209
  trade imbalances of, 184-185
University of Chicago, 22-23. See also
    Chicago school
University of Michigan, 22
U.S.S.R. See Soviet Union
Utopistics, for world-system change, 359

Value, law of, and polarization, 61
Vandergeest, P., 4
Van der Pijl, K., 300
Vargas, Getúlio, 159
Venezuela, 154, 159, 160
Vico, Giambattista, 220, 221
Vietnam, 188, 295-298, 302-303
Vitale, Luis, 156
Voluntarism, 281-283, 285, 300
  management approaches and, 302, 303
  peasant apathy and, 290
Vuscovic, Pedro, 30

Wallerstein, Immanuel, 163
  Africa and, 130
  capitalist world system and, xii
  on ceaseless accumulation, 226
  on differentiae specificae of world-sys-
    tem, 41-42, 226, 245
  on social movements, 281

on social sciences, 5-6
on trade, 233
on world-empire, 249
Waterman, P., 351
Waterman, R. H., 302-303
Weber, Max, 67, 71, 301-302
Weberian concepts, and comparative political
  economy, 4-5
Westernization via industrialization, 140
Wheeler, Mortimer, 225, 234
White, Gilbert F., 102
Wignaraja, G., 168
Wilkinson, David, 245, 249
Wolf, Eric R., 5, 31, 130-131, 164, 285, 299
Wolfflin, H., 260
Women:
  autonomy and, 346-351
  emancipatory processes and, 351
  failures of development and, 349-351
  geographical studies of, 109
  interests of, 342-351
  productive work of, 47
  social movements of, 48, 78, 285, 288,
    291, 307, 331-332
  See also Feminist movement
Words, in world history, 217-219. See also
    Language; Terminology
World Bank, 161, 300
  analyses of East Asia by, 172-173
  debt crisis and, 113-118, 121-122
  interpretations of success by, 200
  removal of, 82, 212
  role of, 6-8
  South Korean and Taiwan defiance of, 178
World capitalism, 58-66
  Africa and, 200-213
  Asia and, 175-195
  Latin America and, 157-167
  See also Capitalism
World-capitalism, 129
World economy:
  centers of, 171-172, 175
  crises in, 169, 171
  monetary flow and, 210-211
  restructured, 158-162, 164-166, 183-184
  socialism and, 37-38
  trade as sufficient for existence of, 233-234
World-economy:
  changes needed in, 356-357

China in, 189-191
India in, 192-194
transideological partnerships in, 195
World-empires, 249-250
World history, xii, 41-50
  Chicago school of, 224-225
  civilizations and, 220-223
  cosmopolitan humanocentrism of, 236-238
  cosmopolitan praxis and, 238
  historical materialism of, 225-231
  language of, 217-219
  models of, 219-220
  reconceptualization of, 10-13
  structuralism of, 231-236
  transitions in, 230-231
World political system, 212-214
WORLD SYSTEM, 41
World systemic cycles, 230, 238-239
World system(s):
  capital accumulation and, 226, 229
  civilizations and, 221-223, 240
  communication nets of, 222-223
  evolution of, 40, 45
  five thousand years of, 11, 40-44, 164,
    219, 225, 276(n2), 336(n5)
  hegemony of, 231-232, 235
  humanist program for, 212-214
  monopolies and, 210-211
  new elements of, 209-210
  social movements in, 281
  Third World in, 166-167
  world-system and, 141
World-system(s), 169-194
  art style and, 265-267
  capital accumulation and, 41-42, 250-252
  centers of, 188-189
  central, 245, 247, 248
  change strategy for, 356-359
  civilizations and, 221
  core/periphery relations in, 252-255
  culture in, 131-132
  current, failures of, 355
  evolution of, 255
  five thousand years of, 141-142, 244-245,
    248
  Frank's reversals and, 138-143
  hegemons and empires in, 249-250
  hegemony/rivalry cycles in, 258-275
  in Northern California, 247

methodology for study of, 141
overloading of, 357-359
radical views of, 132-138
world system and, 141
World system theory:
dichotomies rejected by, 236, 240
global civilization in, 167
Marxism and, 219
minimalist sense of, 235, 238
misconceptions of, 233-236
need for, 10-13, 163-164

pillars of, 41-44
research agenda for, 238-239
single system fallacy and, 234
structuralism of, 231-233
trade, as basis of definition, 234
World-system theory, 173, 195, 225, 235
methodology of, 129-131, 246-248

Zapata, Emiliano, 287-288, 291
Zelinsky, Wilbur, 109

Robert Denemark, Sing Chew, and Gunder Frank, Irvine, California, April 1994.
Photograph by Albert Bergesen.

About the Editors

Sing C. Chew is Professor of Sociology at Humboldt State University and Editor of the *Humboldt Journal of Social Relations*. Prior to his current appointment, he was Associate Director, Office of the Vice-President, at the International Development Research Center (IDRC). He is the author of *Logs for Capital: The Timber Industry and Capitalist Enterprise in the 19th Century*. His main research interest focuses on world accumulation, deforestation, and its consequences over five thousand years of world history. Completion of the first phase of this research will be published in the forthcoming book *World Ecological Degradation: The World System of 25,000 B.C. to A.D. 1990*. He lives in Arcata, California, among the ancient redwood forests of the Pacific Northwest.

Robert A. Denemark is Associate Professor of Political Science and International Relations at the University of Delaware, Past President of the International Political Economy Section of the International Studies Association, and coordinator of its World Historical System Subsection. His work has appeared in *International Studies Quarterly, Review of International Political Economy, Review,* and other journals and edited volumes. He is co-editor of the *International Political Economy Yearbook*. His research interests center on the political economy of violence and the dynamic effects of trade in world system history. He lives in Newark, Delaware, among the carcinogens of the industrial and postindustrial eras.

About the Contributors

Professor Herb Addo
Institute of International Relations
University of West Indies
St. Augustine
Republic of Trinidad and Tobago

Dr. Samir Amin
Forum du Tiers Monde
B. P. 3509
Dakar
Senegal

Dr. George Aseniero
Dapitan City, ZN 7101
Philippines

Professor Albert Bergesen
Department of Sociology
University of Arizona
Tucson, Arizona 85721

Professor Christopher Chase-Dunn
Department of Sociology
Johns Hopkins University
Baltimore, Maryland 21218

Professor Sing C. Chew
Department of Sociology
Humboldt State University
Arcata, California 95521

Professor Robert A. Denemark
Department of Political Science
University of Delaware
Newark, Delaware 19716

Professor Theotonio Dos Santos
Av. Epitacio Pessoa 2566 Bloco A, Apto. 502
Lagoa 22471 Rio de Janeiro, RJ
Brazil

Professor Andre Gunder Frank
96 Asquith Avenue
Toronto, Ontario
Canada M4W 1J8

Professor Barry K. Gills
Department of Politics
University of Newcastle Upon Tyne
Newcastle Upon Tyne
England NE1 7RU

Professor Gerrit Huizer
Third World Center
Katholieke Universiteit Nijmegen
Postbus 9108
6500 HK Nijmegen
Netherlands

Dr. Otto Kreye
Starnberger Institut
Postfach 1666
82319 Starnberg
Germany

Professor Pat Lauderdale
School of Justice Studies
Arizona State University
Tempe, Arizona 85287

Professor William H. McNeill
P.O. Box 45
Colebrook, Connecticut 06021

Dr. Virginia Vargas
Centro Flora Tristan
Parque Hernan Velarde #42
Lima 1
Peru

Professor Philip L. Wagner
995 Auberneau Crescent
West Vancouver, British Columbia
Canada V7T 1T4

Professor Immanuel Wallerstein
Fernand Braudel Center
State University of New York at Binghamton
P.O. Box 6000
Binghamton, New York 13902-6000

Professor Eric R. Wolf
4 Blueberry Hill Road
Irvington, New York 10533-1402

Praise for this volume . . .

"Written by activists and researchers who are at the cutting edge of the field, this volume discusses a variety of fascinating topics, including comparing world systems, global anthropology, economic catastrophe in Africa, the art of hegemony, social movements, and underdevelopment and its remedies. In addition—with a complete bibliography of publications of Andre Gunder Frank and his autobiographical historical account —this volume is an invaluable tool to understanding Frank's complex intellectual development, from his study of human capital at the University of Chicago, his revolutionary dependency analysis of Latin America and exploration of world economic crisis, to his recent investigations of five thousand years of old world system history."

—Alvin Y. So, *Professor and Graduate Chair*
University of Hawaii, Manoa

"The idea that modern underdevelopment is a product of development rather than of leftover traditionalism is a central and useful contribution in modern social science. Andre Gunder Frank was a central figure in its creation and elaboration. Sing C. Chew's book . . . gives a very clear vision of how this idea has evolved, changed, and expanded. . . . Intellectual contributions . . . are clearly depicted . . . in this comprehensive book, which is an extremely useful portrayal, not only of Gunder Frank's varied and changing ideas, but of the whole line of thought."

—John W. Meyer, *Professor of Sociology, Stanford University*

ISBN 0-8039-7260-1 hardcover / ISBN 0-8039-7261-X paperback

ISBN 0-8039-7261-X

90000

9 780803 972612

SAGE Publications
International Educational and Professional Publisher
Thousand Oaks London New Delhi